PICTURE HISTORY OF WORLD ART
II

PICTURE HISTORY

Volume II

VALENTIN DENIS AND T. E. DE VRIES

Editors

OF WORLD ART

Renaissance to Modern Art
Oriental and Primitive Art

HARRY N. ABRAMS, INC., *Publishers*

NEW YORK

Library of Congress Catalog Card Number: 65–26642

Printed and bound in the Netherlands.

CONTENTS

RENAISSANCE

GENERAL INTRODUCTION: POLITICAL AND SOCIAL LIFE   The fall of Constantinople to the Turks in 1453 marked the end of the Byzantine Empire. In the West the sovereignty of the Holy Roman Emperor was limited to the Germanic regions. There began a long struggle between the Hapsburgs and the kings of France, in which the morality of both sides conformed to the unscrupulous self-interest recommended by Machiavelli (*Il principe*, 1513). In the sixteenth century two new great powers arose, Spain and England, one bone of contention between these powers being the former Burgundian Low Countries. But the voyages of distant discovery by Christopher Columbus, Vasco da Gama, Ferdinand Magellan, and many others gave rise to much greater contentions. The important seaports of the world were no longer on the Mediterranean (as Alexandria, Venice, Genoa, and Marseilles were), but on the Atlantic: Lisbon, Cadiz, Bordeaux, Rouen, and above all Antwerp, and later London and Amsterdam as well.

A relentless struggle arose for mastery of the seas. From the outset, but especially after Philip II had seized Portugal and the Portuguese colonies in 1580, England and the Netherlands rejected the Iberian legal concept of the *mare clausum*, a principle according to which only Spanish and Portuguese ships could use the sea routes they had discovered. The Spanish Armada was defeated (1588), Turkish sea power had been annihilated by Spain and Venice at Lepanto (1571). Absolute monarchy triumphed in many countries. Louis XII, François I, and Henri II reigned in France increasingly free from the influence of the clergy (Concordat of 1516), the people (a powerless States-General), and the nobility (the king had a large professional army). Civil war between Huguenots and Catholics slowed the course of French affairs in the second half of the sixteenth century. The absolutism of the Tudors in Great Britain was never complete; the power of the nobility was broken by Henry VII and that of the clergy by Henry VIII, but Elizabeth I always had to reckon with Parliament during her brilliant reign. On the other hand, the Spanish Cortes went into a long eclipse, which lasted till the nineteenth century; Philip II acted entirely at will. Political absolutism was encouraged by the study of Roman law.

The ever-expanding trade with the colonies (chiefly in precious metals and spices) gave rise to large-scale mercantilism. Thenceforth national economy took the place of local small trading: governments set up manufactures within their own countries and customs barriers at their borders. And a new social class arose, the bankers. Important family names occur in Germany (Hochstädter, Welser, and above all Fugger), in Czechoslovakia (Turzo), in France (Angot), and, more than anywhere else, in Italy, including Rome (Altoviti), Siena (Chigi, della Rovere), and Florence (Pazzi, Strozzi, and above all Medici). In order to increase their enormous profits, they soon turned from trade in goods to the money trade (gold and silver); they already used international bills of exchange and market reports. The clergy and the nobility, the former landowners, gradually lost four-fifths of their income. The minor nobility saw their only chance of survival in merging with the rising bourgeoisie, who alone had the means to buy land. This social displacement was everywhere furthered by the monarchs, by their sale of high office, titles of honor, and patents of nobility, especially because, in their perpetual shortage of funds, they had to make large loans. During his election campaign for the imperial throne, Charles V borrowed 310,000 gulden from Jacob Fugger. This made capitalist domination and political leadership inseparable. Lorenzo the Magnificent ruled as a despot in Florence, as a result of his family's accumulation of wealth. The common people did not share in this golden shower. The condition of the peasants was still wretched. The rising industries used more and more wage workers, who soon formed a worker proletariat that kept making demands (shorter hours, better pay, and abolition of payment in kind) but actually gained few of them. All in all, the life of the average man was certainly not bettered; on the contrary. Eventually an outlet for some was emigration to America. Most of the positive aspects of the Renaissance (science, art, fashion) were restricted to a small elite, gradually enlarged by the rising middle class.

PHILOSOPHY, RELIGION, AND SCIENCE   Philosophy is one of the few areas in which the Renaissance did not produce an outstanding figure, and hence registered no pathfinding breakthroughs. It was more a time of action than of thought. Two tendencies can be distinguished. One strove merely to continue to build on the Christian tradition, especially in Portugal and Spain (universities of Coimbra and Salamanca). The last glow of scholasticism came with Francisco de Suarez, about 1600. His eclectic method tried to adapt the great medieval syntheses (Thomas Aquinas, William of Occam, and Duns Scotus) to the most important concerns of his contemporaries. Without achieving a complete theory of his own, Suarez helped in the transition from medieval to modern thought, defending the "divine right of the people" against royal absolutism (James I wrote *Triplex cuneus*, defending the oath of allegiance, in 1606). Francisco de Victoria courageously raised the colonial question (*Relectio de Indis*, 1557). Parallel with the "rebirth" of pre-Christian letters and fine arts, the other philosophical current of the Renaissance was an interest (in Italy) in the great thinkers of antiquity. The theories were too divergent, however, to reach any positive result. Platonism had already been practised by Cardinal Nicholas Cusanus (*De docta ignorantia*, 1440). Marsilio Ficino strove to achieve a reconciliation between the doctrine of Plato and Christian Revelation (*Theologia platonica*, 1482). Out of this grew the Christian Humanism of Erasmus and Justus Lipsius.

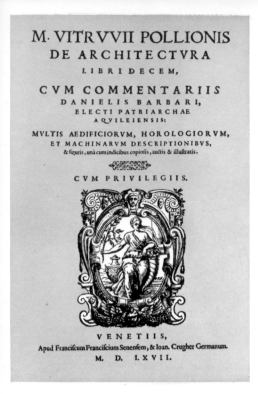

The repercussions in art are abundantly plain. The Academy of Ficino, supported by the Medicis, had a profound influence on Florentine artists (Botticelli, Michelangelo), and Raphael did not hesitate to paint *The School of Athens* (1510–11) to complement *The Dispute of the Holy Sacrement*. Averroism, on the other hand, defended fatalism and the mortality of the soul. Pietro Pomponazzi (*De immortalitate animae*, 1516) was able to assert these doctrines freely at Padua, despite their danger to the faith, because the university there was protected from the Inquisition by the Venetian Senate. Skepticism contested the possibility of consecutive truths, in connection with the sensational discoveries of science (Montaigne, *Essais*, 1580). The mode of thought in Thomas More's rational system of government (*Utopia*, 1516) led in Machiavelli to the denial of all moral obligations: when the interest of the state is concerned, every means is good, since the goal alone counts. It should be noted that all these tendencies were directed against outworn Christian Scholasticism.

The Roman Catholic Church might have more successfully opposed the pagan influence of classical antiquity, if internal dissensions had not been a much greater danger to it. It is true that shameless abuses had given rise to these schisms: financial manipulation, delegation of pastoral duties, nepotism, and simony. All this had for a long time shown the need of reformation. Yet, the ecumenical councils, down to and including the Lateran Council (1512–17), had emphasized mainly the supremacy of Rome. Local efforts at reform (St. Vincent Ferrer, St. Bernardino of Siena) could not prevent the Reformation. The coercive power of the pope was rejected by Martin Luther, John Calvin, and Henry VIII. Like other great minds of the Renaissance, Luther and Calvin went back to ancient sources, but this time to early Christianity. Soon the supporters of these (and other) reformers came to be called Protestants; the name was first given in 1529 to the German princes who, at the Diet of Speyer, "protested" in favor of Luther.

All Protestants were united in their rejection of the Papacy, but their individualism led to the proliferation of sects. The end result was the destruction of Europe's spiritual unity. The situation became worse when the Reformation received political application, in the formula *cuius regio, eius religio* (of whom the region, the same religion). Either a religious minority was despotically suppressed or frightful religious wars and destructive iconoclasm were unchained.

During the Renaissance, printing was the newest and most important propaganda means. 1. Vitruvius, De architectura, a Roman work of the first century, was first printed about 1486, and well-known editions include those of 1511 by Fra Giocondo and 1567 by Daniele Barbaro (title page shown here, with woodcuts by Andrea Palladio). 2. In 1534 Martin Luther published his German Bible. 3. The Counter Reformation also made full use of printing, which reached its high point at Antwerp in the works printed by Christophe Plantin (Antiphonarium, 1573). 4. In 1444 Michelozzo began the Palazzo Medici (later Riccardi) in Florence. Majestic dimensions,

6

7

regular division of the surfaces, many windows, graduated rustication, and marked horizontal emphasis. 5. Even more refined in line and balanced in proportion is the Cancelleria in Rome, 1483–1511; the authorship of the building has never been established. 6. In contrast to the detailed work and vertical emphasis of the Gothic, Brunelleschi's San Lorenzo, Florence, 1421, is all simplicity and balance. 7. In Sant'Andrea, Mantua, 1472, Leone Battista Alberti designed the prototype for church interiors of the later Baroque. 8. In 1446 Alberti rebuilt San Francesco, Rimini. The façade's classical purity of style is derived from the Roman triumphal arch. 9. Ancient Rome is also the inspiration of Bramante's classic and graceful Tempietto, 1502, in the cloisters of San Pietro in Montorio, Rome. The dome of this little temple is already a first sketch for the grand dome of St. Peter's. (The heavy lantern is not by Bramante.) 10. Except for subsequent contributions by Michelangelo (central window over entrance, and heavy cornice), the façade of the Palazzo Farnese in Rome, 1514–34, is the work of Antonio da Sangallo the Younger. 11. The Piazza del Campidoglio, 1536, is one of Michelangelo's finest creations. The Museo Capitolino (left) and the Palazzo dei Conservatori (right) have open galleries; at back, the Palazzo Senatorio (engraving by E. Dupérac, 1569).

8

9

0

11

12

13

1

In the end, the Roman Catholic Church lost most of Northern Europe. The Council of Trent (1545–63) could not remedy that. Yet, the Counter Reformation produced an earnest improvement within the Roman Catholic Church, even before the council: along with powerful bishops (Thomas of Villanova at Valencia and Charles Borromeo at Milan), she had many sainted founders of monasteries and orders (Jeanne de Valois, Angela Merici, Ignatius of Loyola, and Philip Neri). Missionary work was carried on with ardor (Francis Xavier, Turibius, and Francis of Solano).

The sudden growth of science is one of the most characteristic features of the Renaissance period. With or without aggressive intentions, the scientific emancipation was an attack against speculative Scholasticism and traditional philosophy, and at the same time against the accepted "truths" of faith and the authoritarian attitude of the clergy. In particular, the experimental results were so spectacular and so inspiring that the scientists, if they did not reject the idea of God, subordinated it. The study of mechanics made enormous progress, thanks to Simon Stevin (*Statica*, 1586), who also helped in the progress of mathematics (*Wisconstighe Ghedachtenissen*, about 1605); his *Tafelen van Interest* are the first interest tables published (1582).

Mathematics made giant steps forward with Ludolf van Ceulen (*Van den Circkel*, 1596) and John Napier, the inventor of logarithms (*Mirifici logarithmorum canonis descriptio*, 1614). Thanks to the expansion of navigation (compass, and log for measuring the ship's speed, 1577), geographers and cartographers soon came to the fore, especially in the southern Low Countries (University of Louvain). In 1529 Gemma Frisius published an improved edition of Peter Apianus' *Cosmographicus liber*. Much more important is the map of the world by Gerard Mercator, *Orbis terrae descriptio ad usum navigan-*

tium (1569). His great fame, however, is due mainly to his copperplate *Atlas* (1595). Compared to this homogeneous book of maps, the *Theatrum orbis terrarum* (1570) of Abraham Ortelius was only a loose collection. The capitalist idea of colonization also promoted mining and metallurgy (Georgius Agricola, *De re metallica*, 1556). Imports of exotic plants led to medical interest in botany. In the publications of Rembert Dodoens (*Cruydenboeck*, 1554) and Karel van Sluys (*Rarium plantarum historia*) the many illustrations include one of the then recently introduced potatoes. The revelation of human anatomy by Andreas Vesalius (*De humani corporis fabrica*, 1543) brought about a revolution in therapy; Titian and Michelangelo followed his demonstrations at Padua, about 1540. Engineers (such as Leonardo da Vinci) were in charge of naval architecture, city planning, military fortification, and artillery. But the most revolutionary conquest of science took place in astronomy. As early as 1494 Nicolaus Copernicus established two basic principles: the motion of the earth and hence the entire theory of the solar system. Because of fear of the Inquisition publication was delayed until 1543 (*De revolutionibus orbium celestium*, with dedication to Pope Paul III), and even as late as 1616 came the embarrassing condemnation of Galileo Galilei. In the meantime a heliocentric theory had been established by Tycho Brahe. Even the calendar was reformed by Gregory XIII (1582). Although less startling, the achievements of the social sciences were also very important.

The history of art flourished in two directions: the biographical *Lives of the Painters, Sculptors, and Architects* of Giorgio Vasari, 1550 and 1564, and *Het Schilderboek* of Carel van Mander (1604) and the iconographical (Johannes Molanus, *Picturis et imaginibus sacris*, 1570, and Cesare Ripa, *Iconologia*, 1593). Many stimulating archaeological discoveries were made: the *Apollo Belvedere* in 1480, the

15

16

1

8

19

1579, Vicenza, completed by Vincenzo Scamozzi, the oldest remaining enclosed theater building. This view shows the illusionistic perspective of the permanent architectural stage-set. 16. The striking feature of Palladio's Loggia del Capitano, 1572, in Vicenza, is his bold use of the colossal order. 17. In 1550 Pirro Ligorio built the Villa d'Este, Tivoli, and designed its splendid garden (including this Organ Fountain). 18 Château of Chambord, begun by François I in 1519 as an early French adaptation of Italian Renaissance. 19. The François I wing of the château at Blois (1515–25) has a spiral staircase,

12. The garden front of the Villa Medici, by Annibale Lippi, 1544, is typical of Roman Mannerism of the mid-sixteenth century : not grand, but original and graceful. 13. Important for the future is the Mannerist trend of Jacopo Sansovino in Venice. On the Library, 1536, he contrasts the enriched friezes of the two classic orders. 14. Michelangelo made the design (1557) for the dome of St. Peter's, Rome, later executed by Giacomo della Porta who placed the cupola on the existing drum. 15. The great architect of the late Renaissance in the region of Venice was Andrea Palladio. This is the stage of his Teatro Olimpico,

20

21

Laocoön in 1506, and the catacombs. Roman law was revived (Jacques Cujas) by the assiduous study of the ancient written sources, and classical philology made great strides (Justus Lipsius, *Tacitus*, 1574). Even the fame of the greatest of the humanists, Erasmus of Rotterdam, rested originally on his edition of *Adagia* (1500, enlarged 1508), a collection of short sayings from classical authors. Humanism was interested in all the achievements of the human spirit. But Christian humanism hoped to reconcile pagan antiquity (*humaniora*) and faith (*theologia*). Erasmus recommended the comparative study of the Hebrew, Greek, and Latin versions of the Bible (Louvain, Collegium Trilingue, 1517), followed in this by Guillaume Budé (Paris, Collège de France, 1530).

Without printing, the rapid spread of all the sciences would have been inconceivable. Gutenberg in Germany, in the mid-fifteenth century, was followed in Italy by Aldus Manutius, in France by Claude Garamond, in England by William Caxton, in Holland by Jacob Bellaert, and others, and in the south Netherlands by Thierry Martens. The high point was reached in Antwerp, where the celebrated *Biblia regia* of Christophe Plantin (1568–72) is only one of his fifteen hundred publications. Certain libraries became unprecedentedly large (Vienna, nine thousand volumes) and were made accessible to all scholars (Oxford, Bodleian Library, 1602). It was no accident, therefore, that the use of eyeglasses increased greatly. The spectacle makers of Nuremberg were already famous in 1482.

22

23

simpler than one at Chambord, and partly open to the outdoors ; both have rich Renaissance decoration. 20. Philibert Delorme was the architect of the château at Anet ; the basic plan of the chapel, shown here, is in the form of a Greek cross. 21. In 1546 Pierre Lescot began erection of the new Palais du Louvre in Paris, with the southwestern corner of the Square Court ; emphasis is on sculptured decoration, by Jean Goujon. 22. Town hall of Antwerp, 1561, by Cornelis Floris, the outstanding Renaissance building of Flanders. 23. Town hall of Franeker, 1591, probably the most important example in the Netherlands.

24. Palace of Emperor Charles adjoining the Alhambra at Granada, 1526, by Pedro Machuca, is perhaps the first case of a sound application of the Italian Renaissance in Spain. 25. Juan Bautista de Toledo's design for the Escorial, near Madrid, was brilliantly executed by Juan de Herrera, 1563–84. 26. To appreciate the daring of Herrera's desornamentado, or classical bareness, we need only look at the façade of the University of Salamanca, about 1500, an ideal model of the Plateresque style: Late Gothic in spirit, but with decorative motifs from both Moorish and Italian Renaissance sources. 27. In 1572 Jacob Wolff built the town hall of Rothenburg, Bavaria. The Italian borrowings (steps forming a terrace, spiral staircase) do not completely mask the Flemish influence nor the typical German tradition. 28–30. English architects built chiefly palatial houses. The Renaissance was only slowly understood here, so that Late Gothic continued in vigor down to about 1600. 28. Longleat House, near Bath, built for John Thynne, 1567–80. 29. After 1600 the Italian style was better assimilated, thanks to Inigo Jones, who introduced Palladianism into England, as in the Queen's House, Greenwich. 30. Hardwick Hall, architect unknown, near Mansfield, 1590–97.

Page 13. Andrea della Robbia, Virgin Adoring the Child, enameled terracotta, typical of the Renaissance in the striving for a joyous and completely external beauty of form.

15

31. Sculptured Renaissance motifs on the façade of the Certosa, Pavia, 1491, by G. Solari, G. A. Amadeo, and others. 32. As early as 1425, Lorenzo Ghiberti began this master-piece of Renaissance sculpture, the pair of bronze doors, called Gates of Paradise, for the Florence Baptistery. 33. Bronze equestrian statue by Donatello of Erasmo de' Narni, called Gattamelata, 1453, in Padua. 34. Adam and Eve, on the main portal of San Petronio, Bologna, sculpture in relief by Jacopo della Quercia, about 1430. 35. Verrocchio's bronze equestrian statue of Bartolommeo Colleoni, 1481–88, in Venice.

Page 14. Lorenzo Lotto, Portrait of a Young Man (about 1505): a personal style of great sobriety, psychological depth, and unusual colors in a fine example from the early period of this talented Venetian.

36. In this marble portrait bust of Diotisalvi Neroni, 1464, Mino da Fiesole arrived at a singular compromise between the Roman costume and contemporary realism. 37. Antonio Pisanello's bronze medal with the bust of Duchess Cecilia Gonzaga marks a high point in the history of numismatics and is a typical example of the Florentine Early Renaissance. 38. Wall tomb of Carlo Marsuppini in Santa Croce, Florence, by Desiderio da Settignano, about 1454. 39. Mannerism appears in the work of Leone Leoni, the Lombard bronze sculptor. 40. The Pietà, begun about 1546 by Michelangelo, in the Duomo at Florence. It can be regarded as one of the best examples of the Christian intensity of his late work.

36

37

LITERATURE AND DRAMA A striking purification of the Latin language was due to the "revival" of classical learning. In verse and prose the early humanists, Petrarch and Boccaccio, were already returning to pre-Christian culture. On the other hand, the vernacular began to be appreciated for the first time in many countries; in 1549, for example, Joachim du Bellay published his *Défense de la langue française*. There was a revulsion against most of the literary forms of the Middle Ages (rondeau, ballade, virelay, mystery and morality plays), and a borrowing of new forms from the classics (elegy, epigram, heroic, pastoral, and satirical poetry, tragedy, and comedy). Petrarch started the vogue for the sonnet sequence. In Italy, too, the language of the people had reached early fruition in Dante, and was used in love lyrics by Lorenzo de' Medici, in drama by Angelo Poliziano (*Favola d'Orfeo*, 1471), and in pastorals by Jacopo Sannazzaro (*Arcadia*, 1481). During the Cinquecento it triumphed in the chivalric epic (Ludovico Ariosto, *Orlando furioso*, 1516, and Torquato Tasso, *Gerusalemme liberata*, 1581), in satire with Pietro Aretino, and in the prose novel with Luigi da Porto (*Giulietta e Romeo*). Michelangelo wrote bitter passionate poetry. For many years classic principles of drama were followed (Giangiorgio Trissino), but about 1550 the brilliant career of the *commedia dell'arte* began, in which a spontaneous performance is worked out on a fixed pattern. This sort of comedy employed stereotyped characters (with masks), and was adopted in France (*comédie italienne*). Pastoral poetry led to the opera: Ottavio Rinuccini's *Dafne* (1594), *Euridice*, and *Arianna* were set to music by Caccini and Peri, and later by Monteverdi.

Although Jean Molinet, Jean Lemaire de Belges, and other rhetoricians felt that they had to cram the French language with Latinisms in order to be fashionable, fortunately this was not done by the Pléiade, a group of poets which included Pierre de Ronsard and Joachim du Bellay. Their forerunners were Clément Marot (*Psautier huguenot*) and the Lyons group (Maurice de Scève). Metric verse on the classical model was the ideal of Jean-Antoine de Baïf. The most important writers in prose are the very original François Rabelais (*Pantagruel*, 1532–52) and Michel de Montaigne (*Essais*, 1580), more

38

40

39

41. *The Mannerism of Giambologna (Giovanni da Bologna) is expressed in his masterpiece, Flying Mercury, bronze, about 1565. 42. Initially the Renaissance did not completely dominate the Late Gothic style in the work of such French sculptors as Michel Colombe. This is clear in his relief St. George and the Dragon, 1508. 43. Few statues show as clearly as does the Diana of Anet, about 1552, that the Mannerist Italians at Fontainebleau drew able, classically inclined followers. The statue, formerly attributed to Jean Goujon, may be by Germain Pilon.*

41

42

under the influence of Plutarch and Seneca. Medieval forms of drama lasted till about 1550 (*jeux de mystère, moralités, soties*). At the same time, Latin and even Greek tragedies were played, for the most part in French. In 1551 Théodore de Bèze wrote the first religious tragedy (*Abraham sacrifiant*) and in 1552 Etienne Jodelle the first tragedy in classical style (*Cléopâtre captive*). The comedies are mere adaptation of Italian plays; e.g., Pierre de Larivey's *Les esprits* follows Lorenzino de' Medici's *Aridosio* closely.

The English language came to its full flower in the Elizabethan age, with the poetry of Edmund Spenser, the prose of Francis Bacon, and the plays of William Shakespeare.

MUSIC AND DANCE   In the sixteenth century the old art of polyphony, chiefly religious and vocal, came to perfection, while at the same time secular music matured greatly, in new genres, sometimes with instruments or for them alone. Gradually the texture of polyphony was simplified; in the course of time the highest voice became dominant. This led to the development of the homophonic style, in which the lower voices could be said to form sequences of chords. Out of contrapuntal homophony came harmonic homophony, which produced the monodic style of the Baroque age (with figured bass).

The preference for tenor masses gave way to the parodic form, settings of an already existing religious (and in the course of time, preferably a secular) polyphonic work. During the sixteenth century the Flemish composers were outstanding: Jacob Obrecht, Josquin des Prés, Filippus de Monte, Orlando Lasso, and Adriaan Willaert. Willaert founded the Venetian school, with its strong chromaticism and separate double choirs. Palestrina's compositions were entirely in the spirit of the Council of Trent: intelligible text and religiously expressive music (*Missa Papae Marcelli*). The Protestants set the Psalms vigorously in several voices: Claude Goudimel and Claude Lejeune in France (*Psautier huguenot*), Hans Leo Hassler in Germany. The innumerable *geistliche Lieder* of Johann Eccard and Michael Praetorius (also a musical theorist) were greatly admired.

Every human feeling found expression in secular songs, with the theme of love by far the foremost. In Josquin des Prés, Claudin de Sermisy, and Clément Jannequin (*Bataille de Marignan*, 1515) the gay French chanson remained true to polyphony, but after 1550 Lasso, Claude Lejeune, and Guillaume Costeley (*Allons, gay, bergères*) preferred homophony. The Italian madrigal, usually joyous (Lasso, Luca Marenzio), became dramatic after 1600 (Monteverdi); it was shortly replaced by opera. German song was generally melancholy: Lasso, Hendrik Isaac, Ludwig Senfl, and Hans Leo Hassler (*G'müt ist mir verwirret*).

The importance of instruments is evident in the publication of treatises on instruments by Sebastian Virdung (1511) and Martin Agricola (1529), and even more so from the already considerable repertory for all kinds of instruments. The beginnings were modest: the *canzoni* for organ, lute, and guitar were but transcriptions of vocal works. But soon compositions were written specially for the lute (Luis Milan, 1535, and Hans Neusiedler), organ (*ricercari*, fugues, and toccatas by Andrea and Giovanni Gabrieli), and virginal (William Byrd). Dance music was everywhere (*allemande, tordion, pavane, gaillarde*) and flourished especially at the French court (Pierre Attaignant, 1555), usually performed by viols; once Henry II had at his service the group of viol players under Baltazzarini da Belgioioso. Out of the dance suite there later (after 1600) came the sonata.

43

44

45

4

SPIRIT AND NATURE OF THE STYLE   Vasari's *Lives* already uses the word *rinascità*. In fact the period was initially, but certainly not exclusively, a rebirth of the culture of antiquity (humanism, architecture). Out of this there naturally came two divergent trends, according to whether Roman realism or Greco-Roman idealizing was followed. The Renaissance always fluctuated between these two poles. By and large, the course of development was from realism to stylization. The principal centers and patrons in Italy were successively Florence (the Medici), Rome (Popes Julius II and Leo X), and Venice (the doges).

In view of the brilliant conquests by human reason on the scientific level, *ratio* could not but enter into art. For many artists the highest ideal was the representation of space and volume. Because of this view of depth and its logical consequences, art was subordinated to nature (e.g., landscape). This led to the central importance of perspective, and the cooperation of scientists and other men of learning in solving the problems thus posed. It is no wonder, therefore, that art sometimes seems cerebral (Paolo Uccello, Andrea Mantegna). For Leone Battista Alberti, the artist is first and foremost a technician, an engineer.

Even more than a return to antiquity, even more than a mastery of the world in depth, the Renaissance is a glorification of man. Individualism, pride, and riches were a breeding ground for the portrait. Caricature (Pieter Bruegel) and even naturalistic ugliness (Domenico Ghirlandaio and Quentin Metsys) were also inevitable. Still, the nude figure was and remained the center of interest; although it was idealized after the fashion of antiquity, the science of anatomy made ever greater demands in this domain.

There was a multiplication of subjects (mythological, allegorical, and purely secular), but subject matter was relatively incidental to beauty of form, defined with balance and elegance, clarity and harmony. In fact, the outer form came to be of more importance than the content. By the mid-sixteenth century, this reversal of customary notions was felt to be a serious danger to religious art (Council of Trent). A great master like Michelangelo found the solution, however: fidelity to the religious spirit and devotion to the forms of classical antiquity, forms that had never been surpassed before him. Therewith he said farewell to the sunny, carefree joy that the work of his contemporaries typified.

44. Despite the extreme realism with which the corpse of Prince René de Châlon is represented, 1544, Ligier Richier here achieved an enduring work. 45. Of the extensive work of Jacques Dubroeucq, only a small amount is left, including this Annunciation, 1535–49. Cornelis Floris was the greatest name in Renaissance sculpture, as in architecture, in the southern Netherlands: choir gallery in the cathedral, Tournai, Belgium, 1573. 47, 48. Both German and foreign sculptors and many skilled metal-founders were called on for the cenotaph of Emperor Maximilian I in the Hofkirche, Innsbruck, 1502–83. The heroic bronze figure of King Arthur (Fig. 47) and that of Theodoric were designed in 1512 by Peter Vischer the Elder and set up after 1550. On the sarcophagus, Alexander Colyn of Malines carved reliefs of events in the emperor's life (Fig. 48). 49. Choir stall, St. Gertrudis, Louvain, by

47

48

50

51

2

Mathijs de Wayer, 1543, shows the Late Gothic still predominant. 50. The Hercules Fountain in Augsburg by Adriaan de Vries, 1596, shows how the graceful, restless Mannerist style persisted. 51. Choir stall in the Great Church, Dordrecht, by Jan Aertz van Terwen, 1538, where a full-blown Renaissance style appears (in contrast to the earlier, still Gothic, example of Fig. 49). 52. St. John the Baptist, relief from Alonso Berruguete's choir stalls in the cathedral, Toledo, 1539, is Mannerist and anticlassical. Wood carving had a splendid flowering in Spain. 53. The very moving pathos of Juan de Juni's Mourning over Christ at Segovia, 1571, belongs rather to the Baroque.

53

54

55

56

54–56. Renaissance sculpture began brilliantly in England because of the presence of Italian masters. In particular, Pietro Torrigiano did his best work there, such as the marble portrait bust of Henry VII, 1512 (Fig. 54). Two examples of different trends after 1600 are the stiff monument to Shakespeare (Fig. 55) in Holy Trinity, Stratford-on-Avon, by Gerard and Nicholas Johnson, and the elegant Elizabeth I (Fig. 56), by Nicholas Stone, in the London Guildhall.

ARCHITECTURE The rediscovery in 1414 of a copy of Vitruvius's *De architectura*, written in the first century A.D., led to the composition of similar technical treatises: Leone Battista Alberti (*De re aedificatoria*, 1452), Serlio, Vignola, and Palladio (1570) in Italy, Philibert Delorme and Jacques Androuet Ducerceau in France. Like Vitruvius, Fra Luca Pacioli (*De divina proportione*) and Albrecht Dürer stress the importance of correct proportions in artistic production outside of architecture. Brunelleschi was an outstanding pathfinder who gave new life to the conceptions of the dome (in Florence, Duomo, design for Sta. Maria degli Angeli), the Corinthian order, the coffered ceiling, and the central plan. Alberti borrowed from antiquity the triumphal arch and the superimposing of the three classical orders. He designed church plans both in the form of a Greek cross and in that of a Latin cross with side chapels instead of side aisles. Palace architecture, demonstrated in Florence by the Palazzo Medici (1444, later called Palazzo Riccardi), assumed a less massive aspect in Rome (Cancelleria, 1485) and Venice (Palazzo Vendramin-Calergi). The Palazzo Farnese in Rome (Antonio da Sangallo the Younger, 1534, and Michelangelo, 1548) soon ranked as a model. Although Renaissance city planning had already been inaugurated before 1500, by Bernardo Rossellino at Pienza and Bramante at Vigevano and others, the first major achievements date from the Cinquecento in Rome, thanks to Michelangelo's Capitoline Hill and especially to Domenico Fontana (radical renovation of the city, 1585–90). The architectural summit of the Renaissance was the Basilica of St. Peter, and the Vatican Palace, by Bramante, Michelangelo, and others. In the north of Italy, two great Renaissance architects were Jacopo Sansovino and Andrea Palladio.

Sooner or later, Italian Renaissance architecture was adopted and adapted in other countries (although without the open terraces and loggias of a hot climate). In France around 1530 decoration became as luxuriant as during the Late Gothic period, but the elements are often borrowed from north Italian monuments such as the façade of the Certosa of Pavia. As soon as Italian architects came to work on the scene, greater purity of style resulted (Serlio at Ancy-le-Franc, 1546). The French masters followed classical models in their own way, especially Pierre Lescot (Louvre) and Philibert Delorme (Anet).

The success of Renaissance motifs was great in Flanders. In 1539 Pieter Coecke van Aelst made a Dutch translation of Vitruvius and in 1561–65 Cornelis Floris built the harmonious town hall of Antwerp.

The Plateresque style in Spain was a fusion of Late Gothic forms, Mudejar ornament, and Italian Renaissance detail (Salamanca, façade of the university). In 1526 Machuca began a palace of classical sobriety for Emperor Charles V at Granada. Under Philip II, Juan de Herrera attained an unusual degree of severity in the palace of the Escorial. In the Protestant countries, the Renaissance came late and was applied at first in details, as on Hardwick Hall (begun 1590) in England and on Rothenburg Town Hall (begun 1571) in Germany.

SCULPTURE The Italians took over from antiquity their love of marble and bronze. Easier to work but much more brittle is polychrome glazed terracotta (Luca della Robbia). Ghiberti surpassed all rivals with his gilded bronze "Gates of Paradise" for the Baptistery, Florence (1425), with skillful treatment of the basic classical prin-

57. The Tribute Money, one of Masaccio's frescoes in the Brancacci Chapel in Santa Maria del Carmine, Florence, 1425–28, is marked by plasticity of figures, heroic conception of biblical scenes, and apparent illumination of the picture by the light that enters the chapel itself. 58. For Filippo Lippi, the purpose was different. Everything aims at the joy of life of pagan humanism. Hence the bright colors and seductive clothing in Salome's Dance, 1456–66, in the Duomo, Prato. 59. Ghirlandaio's portrait of Giovanna Tornabuoni, 1488, still has traces of piety and yet this woman is more proud than prayerful. 60. Botticelli painted many mythological and allegorical paintings, such as the Spring, 1478.

58

59

ciples (balanced composition and lifelike human figures), successful effects of depth, splendor, and daring technique. A distant fore-runner of Michelangelo was Jacopo della Quercia. Donatello's nude figure of *David* (1430–32) and his equestrian statue of Gattamelata show a determined return to Roman sculpture, while his dancing *putti* are echoes of the joy of the Renaissance. Also typical of the Quattrocento are bronze medals (Pisanello) and sumptuous marble wall tombs (Desiderio da Settignano). The mightiest sculptor of all dominated the High Renaissance: Michelangelo. He took over idealization of the human body from classical times. The genius of his personality gave each figure gigantic proportions, of the body or of the spirit. His unbounded imagination (tomb for Julius II) was often thwarted by circumstances. Perhaps under the continuing in-fluence of Savonarola, sorrow finally became his highest theme, as in his late versions of the *Pietà*. After him, Mannerism was charac-

60

67

6

67. *From 1508 to 1520 Raphael decorated four rooms in the Vatican for Pope Julius II, one scene being* The School of Athens, *perhaps the highest expression of the classical Renaissance. 68. Jupiter and Io by Correggio, about 1532. Both in mythological and Bible scenes, Correggio's manner was theatrical. 69. La Belle Jardinière, 1507, Raphael's first step toward academicism. 70. Madonna with Bowl, 1530, by Correggio. 71. Madonna with the Long Neck, 1534, by Parmigianino.*

Page 25. *Hieronymus Bosch,* Temptation of St. Anthony, *one of his last works, with no religious feeling, but the influence of medieval folk tales, erotically intended eccentricities, caricature, landscape, and very individual coloring.*

69

70

71

72

73

74

Page 26. G. A. Amadeo, Cappella Colleoni, Bergamo, 1476; profusely decorated, like the façade for the Certosa at Pavia (Fig. 31).

75

76

72. For Giorgione the subject was apparently meaningless or at least hidden to us now, as in the mysterious Tempest, about 1505. 73. The splendid Doge Leonardo Loredano, after 1501, by Giovanni Bellini, is really modeled by the light. 74. In Madonna with Members of the Pesaro Family, 1526, Titian completely reworked the religious compositions of his predecessors; using a diagonal main line, he introduced human sensibility, poignancy, and tension. 75. Tintoretto's decoration of the Scuola di San Rocco in Venice may be regarded as the last important cycle in the religious domain. This large canvas is Christ Before Pilate, 1566–67. 76. Pope Paul III and His Grandsons, 1545, by Titian, one of the best portraitists of all times. 77. It is usually fruitless to seek religious attitudes in Veronese. Christ in the House of Levi, 1573, is remarkable in conception and format. The shimmering color is amazing.

77

78. Italian artists, Giovanni Battista Rosso (or Rosso Fiorentino) and Francesco Primaticcio, set the pace in the School of Fontainebleau. For the most part the names of their French disciples are unknown, although those disciples left some masterworks, such as this Sabina Poppaea, about 1555. 79. In portraiture, Italian and Flemish influences were fused; Jean Clouet, François I, about 1525–30. 80. François Clouet's portrait Elizabeth of Austria is a precious document for costume. 81. Sketch for a portrait of Mary Stuart, about 1560, by François Clouet.

78

especially in female nudes with slim forms, a play of light and shadow, and a sensuous joy of life. The color was incidental, even in the best of the French portraitists, who still felt the Flemish influence (Jean and François Clouet). Pencil drawing was their most expressive medium. Immediately after Metsys, the numerous Italianizers ("Romanists") triumphed in Flanders (Jan Gossaert). Antonio Moro was an outstanding portraitist. But the Flemish nature came into its own in the folk pictures of a genius, Pieter Bruegel the Elder. He regarded the subject proper as incidental; the landscape and, still more, the common man got his full attention. The problem of light urged him on to a preimpressionistic stipple technique. The art of Hieronymus Bosch, his northern predecessor, shows eccentricities based on humanity, but Bosch's renewal of landscape had certain consequences in later art. The other Dutch painters were mostly Romanists (Jan van Scorel, Maarten van Heemskerck, and the very individual Lucas van Leyden). This was also the case in Spain (Luis de Vargas), where Moro had an able disciple (Alonso Sanchez Coello). Extremely effective are the visionary abstractions and elongated figures of El Greco. The most Italianizing German of the age was the sometimes erotic Lucas Cranach the Elder. Albrecht Altdorfer played a large part in the rise of magnificently conceived landscape. With Hans Holbein the Younger, portraiture rose to great heights.

Albrecht Dürer was much interested in graphic art (wood and copper engravings). His extensive work indicates the variety of the problems, anxieties, and achievements of humanism and the Renaissance. He powerfully reworked the many influences of Italy (*Melancolia*, 1514). In Italy, before 1500, Antonio Pollaiuolo was a great innovator in the field of copperplate engraving. The success of graphic art was great in every country, indeed, but especially so where, for religious or other reasons, painting was of minor importance. This is the case in Holland (Jan Swart, Dirck Coornhert, Hen-

he was a forerunner of the Baroque, along with his important contemporaries in Venice. Giorgione devoted much attention to depicting the atmosphere in landscape. Titian endowed every subject with a magnificence hitherto unknown, including his portraits, although portraiture had had remarkable practitioners before him (Ghirlandaio, Giovanni Bellini, Raphael); he created the type of the Venetian woman, both gorgeously dressed and in the nude. The composition of his large canvases is often based on diagonal lines, as in Tintoretto. Tintoretto definitively established chiaroscuro, and gave the common man an important role. In the sunny work of Paolo Veronese the glittering festivals of Venice are shown, even in his majestic scenes from the Bible.

Helped by Primaticcio and Rosso, the school of Fontainebleau continued in France the Mannerist trend of Correggio and Parmigianino,

79

80

81

drick Goltzius, and in particular the very able Lucas van Leyden), and even more so in Germany, where the name of the graphic artists is legion (the chief figures, after Dürer, are Albrecht Pfister, Hans Burgkmair, Hans Sebald Beham, and Altdorfer). In addition to original prints, many artists engraved copies of paintings and other works of art; thus, the graphic arts were the most powerful means of propaganda for the Renaissance throughout Europe.

DECORATION, FURNITURE, AND MINOR ARTS Renaissance interiors show constantly increasing comfort and luxury, along with greater beauty of form and technical ability. At the outset Florence set the tone. Mosaic and majolica tiles (sometimes with figures) were used for floors. Both beamed and coffered ceilings were polychromed and gilt. Frescoes and tapestries adorned the walls. Small rooms had wainscoting all around, with intarsia (wood-inlay) panels.

Bruegel the Elder, the most important Flemish master of the sixteenth century. He loved the peasants' labor and days of festival. Bruegel took only the monumentality from the Renaissance style then in fashion.

82. With Quentin Metsys the genre picture made its appearance in Flanders; Banker and His Wife, 1514. 83. The best of Metsys' work are a few excellent portraits, such as Petrus Aegidius, 1517. 84. The high point of the art of the portrait in the Low Countries was reached by Antonio Moro (Anthonis Mor), as in his Alexander Farnese, 1557. 85, 86. Return of the Herd, 1565, and Wedding Feast, about 1568, by Pieter

87

88

87. In Hieronymus Bosch, human folly was the occasion
for bitter mockery. His Hay Wagon jeered at greed for
money and power. 88. Lucas van Leyden excelled in
many aspects, including color, but perhaps his Self-
portrait, about 1511, is his greatest achievement.
89. Family Portrait, by Maarten van Heemskerck,
before 1532. Most painters in the Netherlands were
Romanists. 90. The Mannerist imitation of Michelangelo appears mainly in Bible scenes, such as The
Good Samaritan of Jan van Scorel (1537). 91. The
portrait of Elizabeth of Valois, 1564, shows that
Alonso Sanchez Coello was a dutiful student of A.
Moro and appreciated the Flemish coloring, but that,
because of his exclusive Mannerism, he achieved no
depth. In Spain two trends can be distinguished, the
rich documentary art of portraiture and an unlimited
imitation of the Italian Renaissance.

91

92

After the brightly colored furniture of the Quattrocento, people turned to unpainted walnut and, in the north, oak, now decorated only with carving. Columns and pilasters, grotesques and cartouches, betrayed the influence of architecture. After 1550 there appear herms, ordinary human figures, and medallions with heads.

In due time seats were upholstered in leather or fabric: chairs, folding or ordinary, benches, and even stools. There were small utility tables on columns or balusters and, as luxury pieces, tables on pedestals. Four-poster beds had heavy or light curtains, depending on the climate; the same was true of the widely used alcove bed. The Italian bridal chest (*cassone*) was decorated with painted or inlay work, and after 1500 with reliefs. Chests and dressers were in use north of the Alps especially.

The arts and crafts flourished in every respect. The trade of the goldsmith was fostered by skillful artists (Benvenuto Cellini, the Jamnitzers, Dürer). Both Italian (Faenza) and French majolica works had enormous success. The first bookbindings stamped in gold were made before 1500 for Matthias Corvinus, king of Hungary. His best-known successor as patron was the French bibliophile Thomas Mahieu. The ornaments of the Parisian bindings (*semé, entrelacs, à la*

5

92. Luis de Vargas was so dazzled by the anatomical models of Michelangelo that his retable, Adam and Eve in Adoration of Our Lady, 1561, was given the nickname of "La Gamba" (The Leg). 93. In Spain El Greco developed his individualistic Mannerism after having been trained in Venice and Rome. His visionary art, e.g., the Annunciation, is marked by emotional composition and cold colors. 94. The Two Ambassadors, 1533, is an instance of the effective portrait art of Hans Holbein the Younger.

95. Venus and Cupid, about 1525, by Lucas Cranach the Elder. The artistic value is often overshadowed by the erotic aspects. 96. Painting in England during the sixteenth century was mainly by foreigners. The Fleming Marcus Gheeraerts the Younger's portraits, such as Queen Elizabeth, seldom have any value beyond the historical. 97. Albrecht Altdorfer's Alexander's Victory over Darius, 1529. His huge landscape, with its fabulous lighting, can already be regarded as a distant forerunner of German Romanticism.

98

fanfare) were adopted everywhere. Precious ceremonial weapons were produced in many workshops in Italy, Spain, and Germany. Brussels was the foremost center in Europe for the art of tapestry (Bernard van Orley), from foreign cartoons as well (Raphael). Elsewhere, most weaving mills were set up by Flemings. For silk, first Venice and then Lyons were important. Flemish and Italian lace was preferred in every country; books of patterns spread the Renaissance motifs.

COSTUME Never before had the word 'fashion' been so applicable as in this age of pomp and extreme individualism. In order to exhibit personality, wealth, and status, people were ready to spend fortunes on garments. Hence the popularity of the most expensive materials: silk, damask, velvet, lace, fur, gold and silver brocade. In addition there were gems, pearls, and innumerable furbelows. At one time Emperor Charles V owed his tailor 31,400 pounds! The first fashion books appeared in Italy (Eneas Vico), Flanders (Abraham Bruyn), and France (Jean Boissard); a synthesis was made by Cesare Vecelio

99

10

101

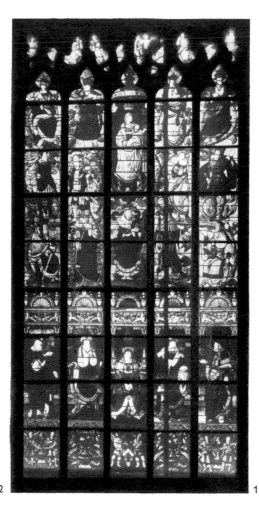

98. *Battle of Ten Naked Men, 1470, engraving by Antonio del Pollaiuolo.* 99. *The great transition in Dürer's art, from Late Gothic to Renaissance, came about in his woodcuts of the Apocalypse, e.g., The Opening of the Fifth and Sixth Seal.* 100. *Maximilian I, 1520, copperplate engraving by Lucas van Leyden.* 101. *Léonard Limousin was the leading artist in enamel.* 102. *Despite some Renaissance decorative motifs, the style of Aerdt Nortkens' stained glass is still Late Gothic; Tree of Jesse, 1506, in St. Godard, Rouen.* 103. *Window with Charles V and Isabella of Portugal, in St. Michael's Cathedral, Brussels, 1537, by Bernard van Orley.* 104. *Polychrome plate by Bernard Palissy (d. 1589), the great French potter.* 105. *About 1520 the Casa Pirota, a workshop at Faenza, made it fashionable to use white and dark-blue glazes on a lavender-blue enamel foundation.*

102

103

104

105

106

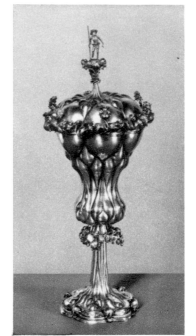

108

109

107

110

(Venice, 1590). The result was that costume was internationalized; this phenomenon roused Rabelais to indignation. At first, Charles V gave Germany a leading position. Up to about 1550 a massive, imposing silhouette was aimed at for both men and women. Only older men and scholars remained true to the long gown; young men chose the short doublet with puff sleeves and a wide collar. The head looked squarish, with the flat cap and the short beard cut horizontally across. The shoes were broad-toed and clumsy-looking. After the fashion of the Swiss and Dutch landsknechts, every garment had slashing, including women's clothing. Women sometimes wore berets, but usually a white cap with fine lappets. The turned-back oversleeves further burdened the silhouette.

106. The direct influence of major painting on the art of tapestry is striking. Although Flemish weavers set up ateliers abroad as well, Brussels remained the most important center. Bernard van Orley made the cartoons for the famous series of Maximilian's Hunts. 107. Dürer supplied sketches for ornamental goblets. There was a great flowering of the art of the silver- and goldsmith. 108. Bossed goblet, dating from about 1500, probably derived from a design by Dürer (see Fig. 107). 109. Renaissance architecture

visibly influenced the monumental monstrance by Juan de Arfe, at Seville, 1580–87. 110. The drinking horn of the Amsterdam Guild of Arquebusiers, 1547, is a ceremonial piece, notable for the handsome foot in precious metal. 111. The French bibliophile Thomas Mahieu, secretary to Catherine de Médicis, was a patron of luxury bookbinding in Paris,

111

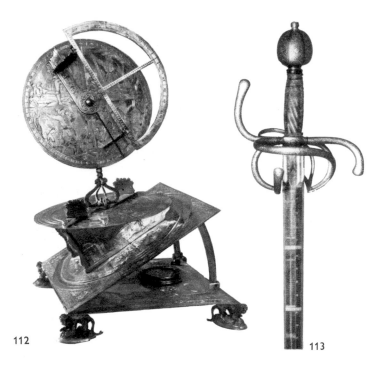

112

113

115

In the second half of the sixteenth century a taller appearance was the aim, but the general effect remained massive. Spain launched the new fashion, affected by Philip II's strict ideas, at least in the main outlines. Instead of the square décolletage, the neckline was very high. The edge of the shirt formed a stiff pleated collar, the forerunner of the seventeenth-century millstone ruff (*fraise*). Padding and whalebone gave the close-fitting doublet the ideal figure of a man. It hung like a skirt over the short puffed breeches. The higher hat had a fine feather. Women wore a tight, pointed bodice over a bell-shaped skirt, all but unpleated. The similar German and Netherlands *vlieger* had no waist at all. The French dressmakers preferred handsome colors to the uniform Spanish black. At the time of Henry III they created the pointed doublet for men and the billowing skirt (with a farthingale) for women. This was the beginning of the fashion of the Baroque age.

116

117

114

1550–75. 112. Astronomical instrument by Johann Richter, 1568. 113. Beautiful and precious arms and armor were produced in every country. Calendar sword of Charles V, with a calendar and zodiacal signs etched on its blade, forged in 1530 by Ambrosius Gemlich of Munich. 114. In 1490–96 Vittore Carpaccio painted The Legend of St. Ursula in Venice. The furnishings in this detail of her Vision are exceptionally elegant and sober. The high headboard and low footboard of the bed are connected by a fine canopy on very high posts; a holy picture, a statue over the door, a pair of vases, small chairs,

and other furniture can be seen. 115. The Studiolo of Duke Federigo da Montefeltro in the Ducal Palace at Urbino is a richly decorated room. The intarsia of the wainscoting is after drawings by Botticelli and others. 116. This page from a sketchbook by Pisanello has two studies for costumes, indicating that about 1450 Florence was a fashion center. 117. The Ditchley Portrait, by an unknown artist, shows Queen Elizabeth in 1592. The tight bodice contrasts with the billowing skirt; the vertical is accentuated by the high shoulders and the standing lace collar.

118

119

120

118. *Florentine cassapanca, 1500–50. Here the decoration is very restrained. These chest seats generally have high backs and armrests.* 119. *Classic draw-leaf table, Netherlands, about 1600; because of its nine Tuscan columns, it is also called a column table.* 120. *The dresser is often small in size, but richly carved.* 121. *Flemish oak cupboard, about 1550.* 122. *In contrast to the delicate canopy bed Carpaccio gave St. Ursula, this English walnut four-poster is heavy in structure and decoration. The Baroque is close at hand.*

121

122

SEVENTEENTH CENTURY

GENERAL INTRODUCTION   The seventeenth century in Europe is a time of great diversity. Sharp political, social, and cultural divergences exist among the most important nations, and within each nation, far-reaching differences appear between different periods of the century. Neither in society, politics, or culture can a description be given that is applicable to all of Europe; each country has a pattern of its own, with its own extremes. Moreover, religious boundaries, which were particularly sharp in the seventeenth century, cut across Europe. The sixteenth century had seen the opening of a new world, with an expanding horizon; Spaniards, Portuguese, British, Netherlanders, and French sailed to far seas and new shores. Other seafaring nations and cities (Venice and Genoa) lost power and importance, although without losing ground culturally—indeed, the seventeenth century was a time of cultural abundance for Italy. Economic prosperity fell to the share of the seafaring lands of Western Europe.

In *France* the conversion of Henri IV (1553–1610) to Catholicism meant the end of the Wars of Religion (1593). In 1598 he proclaimed the Edict of Nantes, which gave the Huguenots a certain amount of freedom and support. After his death, his widow Marie de Medici was regent for her minor son, Louis XIII (1601–43). He was declared of age in 1614 and summoned the Estates-General in order to counteract the prevailing discontent, but the influence of the young king was too small to be effective. In 1624 Cardinal Richelieu took the helm, ruling sternly and establishing royal absolutism. One of his objectives was to combat the power of the Hapsburgs, and in a short time he made France the leading power in Europe. In 1642, he was followed by an Italian, Cardinal Mazarin, who virtually ruled until 1661. He had to reckon with the Fronde, an uprising by the nobility and the Parlement (1648–53). From 1643 to his death, Mazarin held the regency with the queen mother, Anne of Austria; when he died, Louis XIV took over the rule for himself.

For the *Low Countries*, both the north (Holland) and the south (now Belgium), the seventeenth century was agitated. The separation of the two became a fact with the Union of Utrecht, in which (1579) the southern provinces made peace with the Spanish general, Alessandro Farnese. After the fall of Antwerp in 1585, the river Scheldt was closed to traffic; this was the death blow to the prosperity of the city. By 1600 the center of trade and navigation had shifted to Holland. Philip II appointed his daughter Isabella and her husband Albert of Austria rulers of the Netherlands in 1598, with the task of bringing the northern Netherlands under their rule. The Twelve-Year Truce (1609–21) brought a breathing space in the war against the northern provinces. When Albert died without issue in 1621, the south came under Spanish rule again, with Isabella as governor. 's Hertogenbosch was captured from the Spanish in 1629 and Maastricht in 1632. Isabella died the following year and was succeeded by the Cardinal Infante Ferdinand, brother of Philip IV. A turbulent time of battles ensued. The Treaty of Münster (1648) ended the Eighty Years' War; the Scheldt estuary was permanently controlled by the Dutch, and North Brabant and Zeeland were surrendered to the Dutch Republic. Only the fact that the United Provinces (as the independent Netherlands was called) together with England, fought the French on the territory of the Spanish Netherlands saved them from complete annexation by France. Culture flourished despite all this due to the Counter Reformation, which reigned supreme in the southern Netherlands, not only as a spiritual movement, but in art as well. In Holland economic prosperity soared. By 1600 her trading ships were going to India. The Dutch East India Company (1602) soon drove all competing nations from the trade routes and laid the basis for the later colonial empire. Jan Pietersz. Coen, Governor-General (1614–29) at Batavia, the Dutch capital in Java, extended the power of the company over the entire Indonesian Archipelago and far beyond. The Dutch West India Company, founded in 1621, made settlements on the coasts of North and South America, and on the west coast of Africa. As navigation was entirely in the hands of Dutch cities, Amsterdam in particular, wealth naturally concentrated there and had a great attractive force for artists, intellectuals, and craftsmen of all kinds; they found opportunities in Amsterdam and in other cities of Holland that were lacking in their native towns. Among them were a great number of south Netherlanders: the scholar Daniel Heinsius, the architect Lieven de Key, the painter Frans Hals, the sculptors Artus Quellinus and Rombout Verhulst. The greatest printers of Holland, Plantin and the Elzeviers, also came to Amsterdam from elsewhere.

The Dutch golden age, which began about 1600, ends with the French invasion in the disastrous year of 1672, after which the power and prosperity of Holland, if they did not end, at least leveled off or began to diminish. The national culture lost ground to foreign fashions and conceptions. The power-and-patch days began: for Holland, the eighteenth century began with the accession of Stadtholder William III in 1672. Still, the last quarter of the seventeenth century is an interesting period of cultural history, in that Dutch art and culture, without losing their own value, were enriched by contributions from without.

For *Germany*, the seventeenth century marked a low point, after the tragedy of the Thirty Years' War (1618–48) in its first half. It was essentially a religious war, which split the country into an uncounted number of small states, while the Emperor's power all but disappeared. Naturally, the country's economy went through a desperate crisis. In the second half of the century, French expansion was felt in the form of the league of the Rhine (1658) and the loss of Strasbourg and Franche-Comté (1681). Meanwhile, the two powerful states of Prussia and Austria contested for power. As a result of

all this, Germany, at the time when most other countries were expanding their colonial possessions, was shut out of the competition by its political and economic helplessness. The fragmentation into innumerable petty states, each with its court, impeded the development of society and promoted the growth of large landed estates. All in all, it was well into the eighteenth century before Germany played any important part in European civilization.

For *Spain* too, the seventeenth century was far from glorious in politics and economics. If we say that the kings who followed each other (Philip III, Philip IV, Carlos II) were unimportant, we are flattering. The country's power fell catastrophically; it lost Holland, Portugal, Sardinia, Roussillon, Artois, and Luxembourg, and Jamaica overseas. There was constant unrest in Spain as well as in Sicily and Naples. Despite decay and political disaster, however, the seventeenth century in culture was Spain's *siglo de oro*, her golden age.

In *England*, James I reigned for the first quarter of the century (1603–25), including Scotland and Ireland in his dominion. Under his reign the basis was laid (not least by the reckless extravagance of the court) for the civil war that broke out (1642) under his son and successor Charles I (1625–49), essentially a religious war, like the Thirty Years' War in Germany. The strict Calvinist Puritans under Oliver Cromwell (1599–1658) came out the victors, and the king died on the scaffold. Neither the subsequent uprisings and wars (with Ireland, Holland, Spain, and France) nor the mentality of the Puritans produced a favorable climate for art; but on the other hand, a series of victories consolidated the power of England abroad and its internal unity. After Cromwell's death the Protectorate came to an end and the Stuarts returned (Charles II, 1660–85). Charles' brother James II was converted to Catholicism at his second marriage, to Maria of Modena. The Protestant party, fearing Catholic persecution, called for help on the king's son-in-law, William III of Orange, who reigned jointly with his queen, Mary II (1689–94). They were followed

1. Paris, Place des Vosges, designed 1603 as the Place Royale. 2. Balleroy, Calvados: this château, built about 1625–36, is a good example of Louis XIII architecture. 3. Paris, the Jesuit church of St. Paul–St. Louis, 1627, a French interpretation of the Baroque.

4. Blois, wing for Gaston d'Orléans, 1636, by François Mansart. The clear symmetry is typically French, as is the use of high roof forms. The staircase of the previous century, built for François I, is visible on the right.

by Queen Anne. In England too the eighteenth century was more generous to art than the seventeenth.

Denmark flourished under Christian IV (1588–1648), but this king was unsuccessful in his wars. Frederick III, his successor, was forced by the Swedes to sign the humiliating Treaty of Roskilde (1658). He called the Dutch Republic in to help him, and recovered some of what he had lost. In the field of art too the Dutch were predominant in seventeenth-century Denmark.

The seventeenth century was no time of peace and equilibrium in *Sweden* either. King Gustavus Adolphus (1611–32) was a warlike figure who aimed at hegemony over the Baltic. His successor, Queen Christina, left the government to Chancellor Oxenstierna, and abdicated after being converted to Catholicism. Under Charles X the kingdom became a great power. Despite the wars, the successive kings and regents brought the country to prosperity, gratefully employing the aid of Dutch specialists and financiers. Dutch cultural influence was also great.

In *Russia* the dynasty of Rurik died out at the end of the sixteenth century. Great troubles fell on the country, and the Poles took advantage of the difficulties to penetrate all the way to Moscow. The tide turned after Michael Romanoff became Tsar (1613–45). Especially under his successor, Alexis (1645–76), Russia became a great power. The first contacts were made with the West, and in 1649 a code of law was introduced that remained in force until late in the nineteenth century. After Alexis's death, his sons Ivan V, Fyodor III, and Peter ruled successively. Peter, surnamed the Great, was tsar 1689–1725; he turned Russia entirely toward the West, thereby laying the groundwork for her later power in Europe.

Poland entered upon a period of political decline in the seventeenth century, from which she could not be saved even by the great king John III Sobieski (1674–96), who freed Europe from the Turkish peril.

5. *Augsburg, the Rathaus, 1615–20, by Elias Holl, continuance of the Renaissance traditions. 6. The façade of the evangelical church in Bückeburg, Germany, shows that the Lutheran community gave more leeway to the Baroque than the Calvinists did. 7. Danzig, Arsenal, 1602, by Antonie* *van Opbergen, in the style related to the ornament patternbooks of the Netherlands, especially those of Hans Vredeman de Vries. 8. Salzburg, cathedral, 1611–28, by the Italian Santino Solari. 9. Vienna, Hofburg, the so-called Leopoldinische Trakt, 1660–82, by Lucchesi and Carlone.*

19. Mons, Belgium, belfry, 1662, by Jules Ledoux. 20. Brussels, Grote Markt, guild house of the bakers, known as the "King of Spain," 1697, attributed to Jan Cosijn. 21. Louvain, façade of the church of St. Michael, 1650–66, by Willem Hesius, one of the richest productions of the Flemish Counter Reformation.

In *England* Shakespeare's most fruitful years fall within the seventeenth century. Francis Bacon was a philosopher, jurist, and essayist. An influential poet was John Donne. John Milton, author of the epic *Paradise Lost*, is one of the greatest of writers.

Polish literature went through a Baroque phase, with historical epics (Waclaw Potocki) and didactic works (Andrzej M. Fredro). Also of importance is the lyric poet Wespazjan Kochowski (1633–1700).

MUSIC AND DANCE Seventeenth-century music was strongly under the influence of Italy, where accompanied monody had great success. In that century the opera, originally a product of the effort to revive classical drama, came to develop in a totally different way. Bel canto was developed, in which the music, and in particular the arias, became most important. Venice and Naples were centers influencing all Europe. Oratorio flourished, and was guided by the German H. Schütz in a direction that reached its high point in the work of J. S. Bach. Catholic church music too came under the influence of the monodic style, but still more of what was called the *concertante* style, in which two or more groups "compete" against each other. This style was developed furthest in purely instrumental music, and the concerto grosso and the solo concerto were the result, forms that were much employed by composers around 1700. The Baroque manifests itself in the feeling for the dramatic, for pomp

22. Antwerp, St. Carlo Borromeo, 1615–21, built by the Jesuits Pieter Huyssens and François Aiguillon. 23. Interior of St. Paul's Cathedral, London, 1675–1710, the masterpiece of Christopher Wren. 24. Hillerød, Denmark, Frederiksborg Castle, 1602–25, built by members of the Steenwinckel family, Dutch architects.

25. Stockholm, Riddarhuset, 1663, designed by Justus Vingboons and completed by Jean de la Vallée. 26. Moscow, Kremlin, Church of the Twelve Apostles, 1656, built in the archaizing style championed by Patriarch Nikon. 27. Ostankino, near Moscow, Church of the Trinity, 1668; the details show the influence of Western Baroque.

and mobility, for light and shadow, achieved by alternation of groups of players or singers, or of registers (organ and harpsichord music). Organ music flourished with Girolamo Frescobaldi (1583–1643) and Jan Pietersz. Sweelinck (1562–1621). A typical product of the time is also chamber music (e.g., Corelli), out of which came the "gallant style" (François Couperin).

STYLE AND CONCEPTION OF STYLE   It is difficult to define one generally prevailing style in the seventeenth century. Some common traits prove to be external in nature when more closely examined. The Baroque develops in its greatest purity in Italy, especially in Rome; its apparent arbitrariness actually obeys strict rules, developed out of the objectives of the Renaissance. In countries into which this style was imported by Italians (south Germany, Austria, Poland) we recognize it, but, as soon as its outer forms and means of decoration are taken over by native architects, the nature of the style changes, and the starting point is no longer the Italian conception of space, and vision of harmony and clarity. In other places, e.g., in the southern Netherlands, the spatial construction and methods of the Gothic were reinterpreted with Baroque ornaments. France, after a

28

29

brief hesitation at the beginning of the century, abandoned the Baroque resolutely and adhered to Classicism. The situation in England is little different. By and large it can be said that most of Western Europe accepted the Baroque only conditionally, and that it was taken over, although with regional interpretations, by the central and southern portions of the continent and exported via Spain and Portugal to America. As for the visual arts, Italy, followed by the Low Countries, is the center of radiation and influence. In this domain we can speak of an international Baroque movement that develops, even in the north Netherlands, parallel to the realistic trend. The Flemish Baroque of Rubens and Van Dyck had greater influence abroad than the Dutch realism, especially in England and France.

ARCHITECTURE Several tendencies must be distinguished in *French* architecture of the early seventeenth century. One continues the indigenous traditions and makes use of the color contrast between brick and stone, the latter being used to frame the windows and mark the corners of the structure. Clarity and symmetry are the aims. No other national architecture obeys rules so strictly as does the French. It could not but be driven into the arms of Classicism. At first, however, and especially in religious architecture, a moderate Baroque was practiced. This is largely due to Jesuit influence. A typi-

30 31

28. Cardinal Richelieu, by Jean Warin, before 1642, modeled from life. 29. Paris, galleried rood screen in the church of St. Etienne-du-Mont, 1525–35, balustrades possibly by Philibert Delorme before 1545, and completed at the beginning of the seventeenth century, to which period the monumental doorways to the aisles belong. 30. Berlin, The Great Elector, 1698, equestrian statue by Andreas Schlüter, German work comparable to that of the Italians. 31. St. Bruno, by Juan Montañez, first half of the seventeenth century, polychrome wood. 32. St. Francis, by Pedro de Mena,

33

after 1663, polychrome wood. 33. Delft, Nieuwe Kerk, Tomb of William the Silent, begun in 1614 by Hendrick de Keyser, completed in 1622 by his son Pieter; bronze and marble. 34. Madonna, by Jean Delcour, 1691, bronze. Delcour was more influenced by Bernini than any other Dutch sculptor. 35. God the Father, by Artus Quellinus the Younger, 1682, in the church of St. Salvator, Bruges, marble. 36. Tomb of Bishop A. Triest, by Jérôme Duquesnoy, in the church of St. Bavo, Ghent, completed in 1654 by François Duquesnoy.

32

34

37. Charles de Gonzaga, Duke of Rethel, medal by G. Dupré.

35 **36** **37**

cal French style arises, of which one of the chief elements borrowed from the Italian Baroque is the dome. Jacques Lemercier designed one as early as 1635 for the church of the Sorbonne; soon after comes François Mansart's church of the Val-de-Grâce in Paris. Italian influence can be traced in various church façades, notably in the two just named. The façades of St. Gervais (1616–21) and the Jesuit church of St. Paul–St. Louis (1627) are reminiscent of the Baroque via Flanders, but this element is very moderate in all the cases mentioned, and shows a classicist tone. These conceptions of style prevail too in the rural châteaux and in the private palaces (hôtels) in Paris and elsewhere. Thus, the wing of the château at Blois built for Gaston d'Orléans by Mansart in 1636, has the three-part division in height and the double columns and pilasters, but adds the typically French high roof. The symmetry too is French: a broad front with a central pavilion providing the main entrance, and two wings coming forward at right angles to form a forecourt. This is the basic plan of the hôtels, and in expanded form it reaches its high point at Versailles. The Palais du Luxembourg (1615 on) in Paris has some details that recall Florentine models, but it remains true to the French type in its ground plan.

The architecture of the *southern Netherlands* in the seventeenth century adheres completely to the international Baroque movement. It takes much from abroad, especially from Italy, but is able to put much of its own spirit into the artistic product. The difference is defined in the first place by the northerner's entirely different conception of mass and space, essentially at variance with the Italian way of seeing things. The climatic difference plays a large part, as well. At the same time, a large part of the Gothic tradition remained alive in Flanders.

The architecture of the Flemish Baroque begins at the time of the Twelve-Year Truce. In 1609 the first stone was laid for the octagonal domed church at Scherpenheuvel, designed by Wenzel Coberger of Antwerp. The Jesuit order gave the impulse to this architecture and provided some of its principal architects. The outstanding figure, Pieter Huyssens, a lay brother of the order, built churches at Antwerp, Bruges, and Namur. Another Jesuit, Willem Hesius, designed St. Michael's in Louvain, with its exuberant façade.

Three directions are discernible in *Dutch* architecture of the seventeenth century: the continuation of the Late Renaissance, the Baroque, and Classicism. Lieven de Key belongs to the first trend, along with Hendrick de Keyser (e.g., in Amsterdam, the Westerkerk and the Zuiderkerk with their towers, and the Exchange, now pulled down), and his son (East India House, Amsterdam). The Baroque, most prominent in Friesland and Groningen, produced tombs and architectural details rather than large structures.

Meanwhile Dutch architecture was going through a basic change. The last reminiscences of the medieval tradition — tall gables and emphasis on the vertical at the expense of the horizontal—disappeared, making way for the principles of Classicism. At first the French influence was predominant. About 1630 Dutch Classicism took on its own form, e.g., in the Mauritshuis at the Hague. Jacob van Campen had a part in this building; he was the great promoter of the new style. The architecture of Dutch Classicism is marked by a stiff dignity and preference for the colossal order of pilasters on the façades. Special mention should be made of Protestant church architecture. It was inspired by Gothic conceptions of space, but it also created central spaces of its own, closer to the Italian Renaissance than to the Baroque.

German architecture of the seventeenth century likewise belongs, at the outset, to the late flowering of the sixteenth-century Renaissance, until by 1620 the start of the Thirty Years' War put an end to building; the second half of the century is still crushed by the aftermath of that great conflict. It was only in the eighteenth century that the Baroque got its chance in Germany. But in the short time between 1602 and 1618, the German Renaissance may be said to have taken shape. Only then did the architects realize the specific value of an enclosed plan, of the symmetrical arrangement of accents, of the organic connection of decorative volumes and forms. All sorts of foreign influences are felt; thus, the Danzig Zeughaus (1602) is inconceivable without the Dutch influence that was felt throughout northern Germany.

Catholic church architecture was so much under Italian influence that it was often entrusted to Italian architects. A typical case is Salzburg Cathedral (1611–28); Vincenzo Scamozzi made a first project

38

38. Terpsichore, by Eustache Le Sueur, about 1652. Le Sueur painted both religious and mythological subjects, showing his admiration of Raphael. 39. Peasants at Dinner, by Louis Le Nain, 1642; genre painting with an accent of its own that is typically French. 40. Funeral of Phocion, by Nicolas Poussin, 1648; perfect figures in a heroic landscape, with a reserved and rational beauty. 41. Louis XIII Being Crowned by Victory, by Philippe de Champaigne, painted after the French victory at La Rochelle in 1628. 42. Hagar and Ishmael Renounced by Abraham, 1668, by Claude Lorrain. Huge vista, broad landscape.

39

40

41

42

43. Tobias and the Angel, by Adam Elsheimer, 1608.

43

that was followed by a more modest one by Santino Solari. We find the same phenomena at Munich, Würzburg, and other important centers. Frenchmen and Netherlanders were also active, especially at the courts of the princes; this invasion is not only a passing fashion but also a proof of the anemia of the local culture. It was again an Italian, Andrea Spezza, who built the Waldstein Palace in Prague for Wallenstein (1621–28); Lucchesi and Carlone built the Leopoldinische Trakt of the Vienna Hofburg (1660–82) and Francesco Caratti the Czernin Palace in Prague (1670–82). Here, and in almost all the Viennese palaces of this period, we see the colossal order used above a rusticated ground floor. In church architecture Westphalia and the Rhineland remain true to the Late Gothic tradition until far into the seventeenth century, apart from some Baroque influences from the southern Netherlands.

Seventeenth-century *Spanish* architecture was to a great extent in a phase of transition from the great age of Herrera to the Churriguerresque style of the end of the century. Spain borrowed heavily from Italy at that time, and the court architect was an Italian, G. B. Crescenzi (1577–1660), with great influence; he gave Baroque decoration to much of the interior of the Escorial, e.g., the Royal Pantheon. Juan Martinez did the same with Gothic churches in Seville. From 1626 on the Jesuits Sanchez and Bautista built the church of San Francisco Javier in Madrid (rededicated as San Isidro el Real in 1767); they remained true to the type of the church of the Gesù in Rome, but handled the Baroque trappings with great freedom. Toward the end of the century Italian, Spanish, and Moorish influences mingle with decorative forms that seem to be influenced by India and America. As in Spanish sculpture, the various techniques fuse, with no logic but with amazing wealth of detail and movement. This style gets its name from José Churriguerra of Salamanca (1650–1723). It is a form of Spanish rococo, actually a part of the cultural history of the eighteenth century.

In *Portugal* the Spanish domination (1580–1640) brought with it the Spanish style, especially in reredos architecture. Thus, the high altar of the cathedral of Miranda do Douro (1610–40) was made in Valladolid. It was only at the end of the seventeenth century that Portuguese style took on a character of its own: spiral columns with rich ornamentation are combined with concentric arches.

In *England* Inigo Jones was a pioneer, abandoning the Tudor style and going over to a Palladian Classicism. His chief work is the Banqueting House in Whitehall. Still greater was the influence of Christopher Wren, the mathematician, astronomer, and architect. His great opportunity came after the London Fire in 1666, when he directed the reconstruction, including the rebuilding of 53 churches. His masterpiece is St. Paul's Cathedral. The ground plan, in the form of a cross with nave and side aisles, has a length reminiscent of the traditional design of English Gothic cathedrals. Crowning it is a magnificent dome. In general, his style too is closer to Palladio and Classicism than to the Baroque.

In *Scandinavia* seventeenth-century architecture was largely imported, the Netherlands playing a leading role. At the end of the sixteenth century the Netherlands Renaissance was transplanted to Denmark by Antonie van Opbergen (first phase of the castle of Kronborg at Elsinore, 1577). Members of the Steenwinckel family worked in various capacities for Christian IV (Frederiksborg, near Hillerød, 1602–25; Rosenborg, Copenhagen); their architecture was permeated

44

44. The Infante Philip Prosper, by Diego Velázquez, about 1659. 45. The Surrender of Breda, by Diego Velázquez, about 1635. Velázquez is as marvelous in his historical scenes as in his portraits.

46. Portrait of Carlos II, King of Spain, 1665–1700, by Claudio Coello. 47. Children Playing Dice, about 1660–80, by Bartolomé Esteban Murillo. The Spanish master's caressing light transposes the beggar children into a poem of human sympathy.

45

46

47

53

Vasconcelos was active (San Francisco, 1669–74). Argentine architecture is much more sober than that of the northern regions. In Portuguese Brazil the great flowering did not come until the eighteenth century, after rich new diamond and gold mines had been discovered. But even in the seventeenth century there was already an important phase, the *igrea toda de ouro*, with the entire interior of the church covered with gilded carving; the oldest example is the Jesuit church of San Salvador, now Bahía (1665–70).

SCULPTURE   During the period from 1600 to 1660 *French* sculpture went from naturalism to a classicizing taste, with a marked preference for bronze. But the Netherlanders continued to set the tone to a great extent with their realism, although in diminished measure; e.g., Gerard van Opstal of Brussels, whom Richelieu called to Paris, and Jean Warin of Liège, one of the best medalists of his time. Classicism is evident from the outset. We see it grow in the work of

the French sculptors Gilles Guérin, whose groups later adorned the park at Versailles, Jacques Sarazin, François Anguier, and his brother Michel, whose most important work comes in the age of Louis XIV; but we also see a coldness creep in.

53. View of Delft, by Jan Vermeer; one of the most beautiful views in all Dutch art. Probably early in his brief career. 54. Mill at Wijk near Duurstede, by Jacob Ruisdael. Dutch landscape always includes water, and light from the high clouds. 55. Bowling, by Jan Steen, about 1652. Here Steen shows himself to be as great a master

of landscapes as he is of the figure. 56. Sunny River, by Albert Cuyp; in Cuyp's landscapes, the light is the protagonist.

Page 51. Detail of Officers and Sergeants of the Company of St. Joris, by Frans Hals. Traditionally dated 1639.

55

56

and in the Vierschaar) and Rombout Verhulst (the tomb of De Ruyter in the Nieuwe Kerk, Amsterdam).

Not until the end of the century did *Germany* have a sculptor of great importance, Andreas Schlüter (1664–1718). His equestrian statue of the Great Elector in Berlin has a bearing that places it in the line of the great Italians.

Spanish sculptors of the seventeenth century raised their quest for reproduction of the reality into what is called *verismo*, sometimes approaching the fanatical in the intensity of the faces. The expression of movement in space remains limited, however. The subjects are almost exclusively religious. Some important figures are Gregorio Fernandez, who worked in Valladolid, Juan Montañez, Alonso Cano, a universal artist who was also an architect and a painter, and Pedro de Mena, a pupil of Cano. In particular, the Spanish sculptors used naturalistic polychromy in attempting to come as close as possible to nature.

Sculpture in Mexico can be regarded as a branch of Spanish sculpture, and was under the direct influence of the masters in Granada and Seville. Stucco decoration also flourished (chapel of the Rosary in Santo Domingo in Puebla, and Santo Domingo in Oaxaca). The altar screens aimed at harmony and balance in the proportions at the outset, but toward the middle of the century the influence of Bernini led to ever greater movement. The choir stalls are also important.

PAINTING   In *France* in the beginning of the seventeenth century the tone was set by the second school of Fontainebleau. The painters there are no longer Italians, but Frenchmen and Flemings, all of whom had undergone the direct or indirect influence of Italy. Only slight traces of their work remain.

The talent of Simon Vouet, who returned from Italy in 1627, overshadowed the painters that were still working in the old manner. His color, influenced by the Venetians, and his skill in composition reconcile us to his weakness in draftsmanship. His pupil Eustache Le Sueur is a much greater talent, perhaps one of the last painters of

The *Flemings* named above were not the only ones to seek their fortunes abroad. François Duquesnoy made a name for himself in Italy, partly as a collaborator of Bernini. Jean Delcour of Liège remained at home, but was greatly under Bernini's influence. Lucas Fayd'herbe, also an architect, was one of the outstanding sculptors of the time. *Holland* too had its architect-sculptor, Hendrick de Keyser, whose sculptures on the tomb of William the Silent in Delft are among the best productions of Dutch sculpture. Later the commissions went almost entirely to south Netherlanders, such as Artus Quellinus (sculptures on the pediment of the Amsterdam City Hall

Page 52. Sketch by Peter Paul Rubens for his altarpiece in the Church of the Augustinians at Antwerp, painted as a model for the person who gave the commission. Around the enthroned Madonna and Child a host of saints.

57. Still Life, by Willem Claesz. Heda, 1634. 58. The Shepherd Boy, by Karel Dujardin; typical work of a Dutch Italianizer. 59. The Cellar Room, by Pieter de Hooch, about 1658; atmosphere and light.

true religious art that France produced. But French painting of this period is best known for two very great masters who worked mainly in Italy: Nicolas Poussin (1594–1665) and Claude Lorrain (1600–82). Poussin is the painter of the perfect figure in the majestic, heroic landscape of a typically French restrained and rational beauty. Claude Lorrain, on the other hand, observes the phenomena of light in nature and sets them down in large, rhythmically structured landscapes and port scenes, transposed to a poetical sphere that has the abstractness of a dream.

It is not surprising that we meet with south Netherlanders in the field of portraiture. Frans Pourbus the Younger regenerated French portraiture by grafting on to it Dutch realism and Italian *grandezza*. Philippe de Champaigne, born in Brussels (1602–74), continued the process; his portraits breathe an earnest, rather melancholy spirituality. The brothers Le Nain, Antoine, Louis, and Mathieu, are the portrayers of the life of French bourgeoisie and peasantry, in a way that raises their work far above what we usually call genre painting.

Engraving and etching flourished along with painting. The period of Henri IV already had some interesting masters: Thomas de Leu and Léonard Gauthier. The many prints of Abraham Bosse give us a picture of the life of his time. But undoubtedly the greatest of all, and one of the outstanding graphic artists of all time, was Jacques Callot (1594–1635). With incomparably telling drawing he charac-

terizes his figures: Italian dancers, grotesque hunchbacks, beggars in rags, soldiers in the field, always spirited and sometimes tragic.

In the *Flemish Netherlands* (now Belgium), the seventeenth century was a period of high achievement, headed by the name of Peter Paul Rubens (1577–1640). He was a genius, many-sided and of great vision, who painted not only large altarpieces and historical scenes but also portraits, hunting scenes, and landscapes; and he managed, along with the production of an enormous body of work, to perform diplomatic and government functions as well. His pupil Anthony van Dyck (1599–1641) became an international portrait artist, who painted at the English court from 1632 on. The third in the series of the very great is Jacob Jordaens (1593–1678), in whom realism appears at its strongest. After them come a number of lesser masters, who expressed the life of the people sometimes in dramatic form. The most attractive is certainly Adriaen Brouwer, the observer of the rough life of the slums and taverns. David Teniers the Younger is more idyllic. Jan Bruegel painted delicate, almost decorative landscapes, which he let others fill in with figures.

In *Holland*, too, painting reached hitherto unknown heights, especially in Amsterdam, but in other cities as well—Haarlem, Leyden, Delft, and Utrecht. Rembrandt Harmensz. van Rijn (1606–69), the greatest of all, was close to the Baroque at first, but in his later work reached solitary heights. Frans Hals (about 1580–1666) of Haarlem, born in Antwerp, became Holland's greatest painter of portraits. Jan Vermeer of Delft (1632–75) created city views and interiors with figures, clear and yet mysterious. The number of landscape painters is almost endless. We mention only Jan van Goyen, Salomon van Ruysdael, his nephew Jacob van Ruisdael, Hercules Seghers, Philip Koninck, and Albert Cuyp. Another group, known collectively as the Bentvueghels, went to Italy in search of new impressions. Still life painters included Willem Claesz. Heda, Jan Davidsz. de Heem, Abraham van Beyeren, and Willem Kalff. In genre painting Jan Steen has a place apart, as does Pieter de Hooch in interior scenes. Seascapes and naval battles are typically Dutch genres, in which the Van de Velde family of painters, among others, excelled. Group portraits of civic guards and corporate bodies, a genre that had already been practiced by Frans Hals and Rembrandt, found a virtuoso in Bartholomeus van der Helst. The Utrecht school of painters was more internationally oriented than that of the other cities. At the end of the century the international Classical-Baroque style became dominant in Holland too, as it was elsewhere.

Not much need be said of seventeenth-century *German* painting. The only important figure is Adam Elsheimer (1576–1610), whose landscapes show a remarkable harmony between figures and surroundings. His influence on Rembrandt is unmistakable.

Three great figures dominate the golden age of *Spanish* painting: Domenico Theotocopouli, called El Greco (1548–1625), Diego Velázquez (1599–1660), and Bartolomé Esteban Murillo (1618–82). El Greco was born on Crete and his career took him from painting icons in his native country, through Venice and Naples, to Spain. This hybrid training is reflected in his highly personal work. The ascetic stylization of the icon figures is coupled with the shimmering light and impressionistic technique of the Venetians.

Velázquez, on the other hand, was a court painter, a typical Baroque artist, a Bernini of painting. He is a luminist, colorist, and impressionist, all at once. His portraits, especially those of the royal family and their surroundings, are incomparable. He is equally great and remarkable in his historical pieces, such as the *Surrender of Breda* (*Las Lanzas*).

Finally, Murillo could be called the Spanish Raphael: as compared to Velázquez the realist, he is the great idealist. He should not be regarded as merely the creator of Madonnas without number, but also as the painter of beggars, and especially beggar children.

Jusepe de Ribera belongs rather to the history of Italian art. Francisco de Zurbarán is a powerful realist in his many religious paintings.

For painting and sculpture, seventeenth-century England relied much but not entirely on foreigners, especially from the Netherlands and France. Portraits particularly were in demand, and in this domain Anthony van Dyck was preeminent. Peter Lely, another Netherlands portraitist, had a meritorious disciple in John Hayls.

In *Scandinavia* too the active painters were mainly Netherlanders: Jacob van Doordt, Peter Isaacsz., Werner van de Valckert, and Abraham Wuchters worked in Denmark; Govert Camphuysen, Martinus Mytens, and others in Sweden.

In *Russia* religious painting during the seventeenth century was on the defensive against the Catholic and Lutheran influences from the West. It became an official enterprise. The central workshops for icon painters in the Kremlin, under the direction of the church authorities, prescribed the fixed iconographic types. In addition to this there also appear, especially in fresco painting, stories from the church history of the Russian people. At the same time, northeastern Russia saw the flowering of the so-called Stroganov school, the core of which consisted of dated and signed icons of the sixteenth and early seventeenth centuries, small in format and refined in workmanship, with bright colors and copious gilding. After the Polish War icon painters of the Stroganov school were called to Moscow; a fusion took place with the Moscow school, the most prominent exponent being Prokopi Khirin (in Moscow, 1620–42). Since the river Dvina down from Archangel provided the entry for foreign merchants coming to Moscow, Western influences had there their greatest effect. This is the reason why we now begin to see a certain spatial effect occasionally in Muscovite icons as well, with landscape backgrounds and more lifelike expressions for the heads. Less strong but unmistakable is the effect of Chinese painting of the Sung dynasty.

Simon Ushakov (1626–86), a versatile artist, was also outstanding as a painter. His work shows the influence of Flemish and Dutch Renaissance art. By the beginning of the reign of Tsar Alexis (1645–76), the Russian Middle Ages may be said to have come to an end. After 1667 the influence of the more liberally educated Ukrainian clergy increased, and this led to Western and Latin infiltration. Another sign of the times was that portrait painters got their first

60. Landscape with Cattle, by Paul Potter, 1653; Potter is a painter not only of cattle but also, and especially, of nature and light. 61. Philip Koninck is the painter of wide vistas, as in this river landscape, 1654. 62. Still Water, by Willem van de Velde the Younger. 63. Peasant Quartet, by Adriaen Brouwer, about 1625.

63

64

6

66

64. The Lion Hunt, by Peter Paul Rubens, about 1617. This canvas, full of movement and violence, shows how different Flemish Baroque was from Dutch realism. 65. Hélène Fourment in Bridal Costume, by Rubens, about 1630. 66. Return from the Fields, by Rubens, a painter of universal genius.

chances and that foreign artists taught Russian pupils. Further, the Bible prints of N. J. Visscher, among others, served as models for local painters and, especially at Yaroslavl, even for frescoes. Nonetheless, the execution remained typically Russian, with a distant echo of Byzantium. Only in the eighteenth century did painting surrender unconditionally to the West.

Also in *Poland* the influence of Netherlands painters was dominant, among others, Peter Danckerts, Anthony Waterloo, and Abraham van Westervelt. The Polish brothers Bogdan Theodor Lubieniecki and Christoph Lubieniecki studied in Amsterdam in the atelier of Gerard (de) Lairesse.

Painting in *Latin America* was largely religious folk art, harsh in color and naïve in style, modeled on engravings from Antwerp, Augsburg, Rome, and Paris. Even if one includes the portraits, it is handiwork more than art. Here and there, however, and especially in Mexico, artists were able to follow the European trends. Baroque painting in Mexico, properly so called, was influenced by Rubens and Zurbarán (José Juarez, about 1615–about 1667); the influence of Murillo was added later. In Cuzco and Lima too, which were less important centers for painting than Mexico, the influence of Flemish prints was very strong. Mestizo culture, a mixture of naïve folk art and European influences, flourished mostly in Cuzco.

MINOR ARTS AND FURNITURE   Pictures of seventeenth-century *French* interiors, e.g., in prints by Abraham Bosse, show only a limited number of pieces of furniture, and they are of only a few kinds. For the most part, the simpler pieces were lost and only the more expensive survived, so that the picture we now have of French furniture production (and this applies to that of other countries as well) is somewhat distorted. Tables occur rarely; and when they were covered with a cloth coming down to the floor,

68

67. The Children of Charles I of England, by Anthony van Dyck, 1635. 68. The Sculptor Colijn van Nole, by Anthony van Dyck, about 1630. 69. The Mourning over Christ, by Anthony van Dyck. Van Dyck is primarily a great portrait painter; his religious works are not always free from sentimentality. 70. As the Old People Sang, so the Young People Piped, by Jacob Jordaens, 1646. What moves us in the art of Jordaens is its realism. 71. The Gamblers, by David Teniers the Younger (1610–90). Teniers gives a somewhat romantic view of the life of country people.

they must often have consisted of boards on trestles. Some have legs in the form of heavy balusters or columns; others are on X-shaped supports, wide apart at top and bottom. The chairs are stiff and square, with the backs often rectangular and the feet connected by rungs; seats and backs were upholstered. The rungs and feet were turned; the arms were sometimes curved, ending in volutes. Tapestry, velvet, damask, and gold-stamped leather were used for the upholstery. As time went on, chairs and armchairs were more and more richly decorated. The bedstead was among the most important pieces of furniture in the seventeenth-century interior. The barely visible woodwork was usually decorated simply, but very costly materials were used for the draperies. Of the furniture for storage purposes, the cabinet is the most luxurious. It is a broad chest on a tablelike bottom. The front may come down, or have doors; the complicated interior is decorated with incrustation, sculpture, or incised metal. Rich decoration adorned the outside of the cabinet when closed; mythological subjects were favorite motifs.

Many Netherlanders were among the makers of these cabinets, as

70

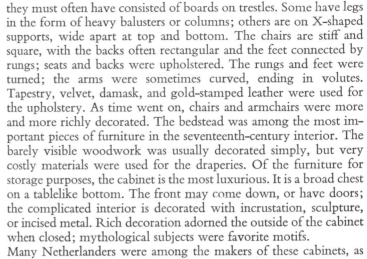

69

71

well as Frenchmen who learned their trade in the Netherlands. Tortoise shell, mother-of-pearl, ivory, and other costly materials were used to brighten the somber tone of the ebony of which the cabinets were often made. Cabinets of the same sort were also made in Germany, Spain, and Portugal. In structure and architectural motifs, the chests continued the conceptions of the previous period. They are more sturdy than decorative; the carved ornament is usually far from refined. The doors often have geometrical ornaments formed by moldings, and faceted knobs. The big clothing chests become less important and gradually disappear from the living rooms. Wall tapestries had always been prominent in France. At first they were woven almost exclusively in Flanders, but under Henri IV French industry began to come to the fore, although it was still directed by Flemings and men from Brabant. Cartoons by Rubens and Vouet, among others, were used for the work. However, the high point came under Louis XIV. Wall hangings were also executed in embroidery. Lace, which was required by the fashion, was made in northern France, and especially in Alençon, competing with the costly Flemish and Venetian varieties. Lyons was the great center of silk weaving. Relatively little work in precious metals has come down to us, but what we have, such as a golden jewel box in the Louvre, bears witness to great mastery of the art. Cutlery of this period is also relatively rare.

Jewels had an overabundance of gems and pearls, with relatively modest settings. Valuable watches were made in all sorts of shapes, especially at Blois.

Majolica was produced at Nevers; at first the Italian tradition was preserved, but later Persian and Chinese models were also followed. Nevers in turn influenced Rouen. In the course of the seventeenth century, Rouen tiles were supplanted by those from Delft.

The furniture of the *southern Netherlands* was at first entirely under the influence of Hans Vredeman de Vries (1527–1604). His *Différents Pourtraicts de Menuiserie* (or *Various Designs for Furniture*, 1588) broke with the old Gothic tradition that was still current, and gave a new direction to the art of furniture, not only in the Netherlands but also in distant countries. Its chairs and tables are closely related to French models. Typical for this period are the two-storied buffets, with the upper chest shallower than the bottom. They are richly decorated with caryatids, herms, lions' heads, and cornices. The clothing chest also disappears and is replaced by the chest of drawers.

Alongside the simple chairs with square or rectangular backs, such as we find in France, the Netherlands also had a more ornamental type under Spanish influence with a high back, much carving, and richly decorated front rung.

Clocks slowly ceased to be objects of luxury and became a part of the middle-class household; this change was to a great extent due to the invention of the pendulum clock by Christiaan Huygens in 1647.

A noteworthy phenomenon is the steadily increased production of silverware; the forms are luxuriantly Baroque, in contrast to the prevailing classicistic taste.

Glassware remained close to Venetian models; ceramics too paid initial tribute to Italy but gradually acquired its own character; this was especially true in the more important centers, such as Delft and Makkum, where the predominant influence was imitation of the Chinese. The products consist of ware for use and ornament, and wall tiles. The tone is set by the blue figures on a background of white tin glaze, but polychrome work also is found. The white undecorated Delft attains great beauty.

German furniture follows the international taste with respect to the form of chairs, although they are even heavier and more ornate. The same is true of storage pieces, whose decoration is less elegant and

73

72. The Fishmonger's Shop, by Frans Snijders (1576–1657); even in still lifes the Baroque is dynamic and superabundant.

74

73. Portrait of Nell Gwyn, attributed to Peter Lely (1618–80). 74. Portrait of a Danish Nobleman, by Abraham Wuchters (about 1610–83). 75. Icon of the Stroganov school, John the Baptist in the Wilderness, seventeenth century.

75

the form cruder than in neighboring countries. Ivory carving, in finely worked reliefs and small figurines, flourished in seventeenth-century Germany. Work in the precious metals, for which Augsburg was the main center, could not keep the high level it had reached in the previous period; here, too, gems and pearls supplanted fine metalwork. The silverware was more conspicuous for size than for beauty. Tin was employed as a cheap substitute for silver; work in tin attained a new high point, without producing great works of art. The glass industry flourished in Bohemia. Glass grinding was often practiced, and exports were greatly stimulated after the alchemist Kunkel (born 1630) had discovered the so-called ruby glass.

Starting in *Spain*, the use of cordovan leather for covering chairs and as wall decoration spread to other countries. Spanish chairs are noteworthy for their ornamented front rungs and backs, which are often shield-shaped, or consist of two superposed arcades of balusters. *English* furniture of the seventeenth century is divided into the "age of oak" (Tudor, Stuart, and Jacobean, to 1649) and the "age of walnut," which includes the reign of William and Mary (1689–94). The furniture of the first period is heavy rustic Late Renaissance; the William and Mary style, thanks to the influence of Daniel Marot, is hard to distinguish from the Dutch version of the Louis XIV style.

COSTUME The Spanish influence that dominated the beginning of the seventeenth century gradually faded, although black for clothing persisted for a long time in the court circles of the regents of the Netherlands. Spanish fashions naturally prevailed in the southern regions. In France a more dashing fashion had come in much earlier, in which the ruff was replaced by a flat-lying collar of lace or linen. Gold and silver braid were used profusely, and the unnatural padding of doublets and breeches was given up. A broad-brimmed felt hat was worn with an ostrich feather.

In women's fashion, the figure had recovered some of its naturalness when the farthingale became more reasonable in size. The décolletage was bordered by lace collars standing out wide or lying flat on shoulders and back. Costliness and luxury, especially among the nobility, went so far that in 1638 a royal edict tried to curb them, without much success. There were remarkable extremes in male costume, such as the *rhingrave* or petticoat-breeches—short breeches almost like a skirt, with legs two yards in circumference—combined with a doublet very short and very tight; boots with wide, loose folded tops or shoes with laces standing out; stockings with loops of ribbons hanging from them, and much linen and lace. Obviously, this called for long curling hair and plumed hats. The French style was adopted in much of Europe, even after 1660, when the soldier's jerkin, the *justaucorps*, came into fashion and the government of Louis XIV strove for more dignity, as the result of which much of the extravagance disappeared. The high, curled full wig came into use, while women wore trains and, on top of their high headdresses, the *fontange*, a kind of tall cap with a lace barbe hanging down the side of the face and over the breast.

76

77

Ifrael ex. Cum Priuil. Reg.

76. *Portrait of Henri IV of France,
by Léonard Gauthier, engraving.* 77. *La
Galerie du Palais, engraving by
Abraham Bosse, d. 1676 ; ladies and
gentlemen in the costumes of the time,
buying books, knicknacks, and lace in
a shop at the Palais-Royal in Paris.*

78. *Execution of Evildoers in a Camp
in the Field, by Jacques Callot
(1594–1635), etching.* 79. *Landscape
by Hercules Seghers (1590–1638), a
great artist fascinated with experiment
in etching techniques.*

80

81

82

80. Louis XIII armchair. The wooden parts are soberly decorated with turning and carving ; the square seat and rectangular back are upholstered. 81. Château de Fontainebleau, Salon Louis XIII. 82. Château de Cheverny, Chambre du Roi, about 1633–40. Characteristic of the Louis XIII period are the heavy ornament, the solid forms, and the emphasis on horizontal lines.

83

83. Moses Saved from the Waters, tapestry made in the Ateliers du Louvre after a cartoon by Simon Vouet. 84. Bowl of a silver goblet with the Judgment of Paris, by Paulus van Vianen, 1607. 85. Tapestry made in Brussels, about 1650, representing the months of January and February.

84

85

ITALIAN BAROQUE

GENERAL INTRODUCTION, POLITICAL LIFE Many great periods of civilization, in the course of their development, come to a playful final phase, dynamic and rich in form and color, that can be referred to as "baroque." It is a long afterbloom, an autumnal phenomenon, as reaction to the short summer of the 'classical' phase, which in turn arises out of less polished style of the "primitive" beginnings. In the primitive stage man outlines a new logic in thinking and form; he attains and possesses it during the brief classical period, whose balanced clarity cannot arrest him for long; then he consciously violates the harmony he has attained and goes over into a game of wit. He bends what was straight into curves; movement replaces repose; clarity and simplicity go over into complexity, multiplicity, and a turbid uncertainty in which shimmering spots wipe out the clear outline. The half-articulated word can sometimes evoke deeper emotion than the harmonious verse; the murmuring chorus drowns the monologue of the soloist. Only the virtuoso is the great artist, and all artists become virtuosos. The sensuous is primary; the rational is excluded as far as possible. Art is no longer a play of equilibrium, measure, and harmony, but one of effect, fantasy, movement—and excess.

The religious Baroque of the seventeenth century in Italy cannot be thought of apart from the Counter Reformation, and it is also, perhaps with too much emphasis, linked with the activity of the Jesuits. The Catholic Church accepted the Baroque all the more readily because the humanistic Renaissance, the culture of the classical period, had taken on a bad odor on account of its rationalism, pagan attitudes, and political associations. The Church threw into the scales of the balance the full weight of the emotion that the Baroque supplied, and this may well be what gave the victory in Italy and elsewhere. It is a notable fact that the founder of the Jesuit order, the Spaniard Ignatius of Loyola, was quite the opposite of a man of emotion, but his successors knew very well how to make the most of the possibilities inherent in emotional values. His Roman counterpart, Filippo Neri, was from the outset a typical representative of the Baroque mentality. But his influence was limited in place and time, while the influence of Ignatius's foundation became world-wide, perhaps just because it was less tied to a definite style of living, thinking, and imagery.

Politically, the period of the Baroque was a low point in Italy. Naples and Milan became Spanish possessions in 1559, marking the beginning of a long Spanish domination of a large part of the country. By the Treaty of Utrecht, 1713, Milan, Naples, and Sardinia went to Austria and the Duke of Savoy became King of Sicily, which he had to exchange for Sardinia in 1720. Thereafter, the successions of the duchies of Parma and Piacenza and the Grand Duchy of Tuscany became grounds for dispute. In 1738 the Infante Don Carlos, son of King Philip V of Spain and Elizabeth Farnese, ceded these regions to Francis of Lorraine in exchange for the Two Sicilies, but ten years later his younger brother Philip got them back, while Tortona and Novara went to Sardinia. In the midst of all this, the Papal States were an area of relative calm. In the seventeenth century Rome was the cultural leader, but was replaced in the role by Venice during the eighteenth century; the political power of the Serenissima had been broken, but Venice lived off her enormous wealth and old renown.

1-3. Three churches in Rome. The evolution of the Baroque church façade is readily seen: from calm, independent surfaces to concentrated dynamic movement, also at the street level. The pilasters are paired and the central axis receives special emphasis. 1. Santo Spirito in Sassia, façade (1585) probably from design of 1540 by Antonio da Sangallo the Younger. 2. Church of the Gesù (1573–75) by Vignola, Giacomo della Porta, and others. 3. Sant' Ignazio, 1645, by Orazio Grassi.

Page 65. Caravaggio, The Calling of St. Matthew, about 1597, Contarelli Chapel, San Luigi dei Francesi, Rome.

1

2

3

4

5

6

4–6. Three other churches in Rome, of the second divergent type of Baroque façade, undergoing the same sort of development as the first; the stronger effects of light and shadow are striking. 4. San Luigi dei Francesi, 1589, façade by Giacomo della Porta. 5. San Gregorio Magno, façade and atrium by G. B. Soria, 1633. 6. Santa Maria in Via Lata, façade by Pietro da Cortona, 1660.

PHILOSOPHY After what we have said concerning the nature and attitude of the Baroque, it is not surprising that philosophy was not its strong point. It is almost symbolic that one of the first acts of the seventeenth century was the execution in Rome of the eccentric genius, Giordano Bruno (February 17, 1600). His conception of natural philosophy was far in advance of his time, and influenced Goethe, Schelling, and Hegel. Galileo Galilei, too, saw far, but the inquisitors forced him to abjure his discoveries. His four closest disciples, Castelli, Cavalieri, Torricelli, and Viviani, known as the "four evangelists of science," founded the Accademia del Cimento (cimento = experiment) in Florence in 1657, which was the first in Europe to make meteorological observations, but it too was broken up by the Holy Inquisition after ten years. With all this activity, Scholasticism and Aristotle were put completely into the background. Rhetoric took the place of philosophy.

LITERATURE AND DRAMA Something of the same sort occurred in literature. Italy had many great artists in every field in the seventeenth century, but not a single great writer or poet. The literary men of this period, especially G. B. Marini, hid their poverty of spirit behind a mass of rhetoric and endless artificial verses. The only one who managed to rise above the fashion in some degree was Alessandro Tassoni, the satirist. As a reaction against the spirit of

previous generations, a society of lovers of poetry was formed in Rome in 1690, which called itself Arcadia; but although it wanted to devote itself to the simple and natural, its puerile pastorals were even more artificial than those of Marini and his epigones. The only man in the early eighteenth century who can be called a poet was Pietro Metastasio (1698–1782), but his fame too was short-lived. It was not until Carlo Goldoni (1707–93), the Venetian dramatist, that life came to literature, with a realism that still speaks to us. His art of the theater had forerunners in the popular commedia dell' arte, an old form of mime and improvisation that influenced the stage far beyond Italy, in particular the work of Molière.

MUSIC Along with plays, what were called melodramas were performed, presaging the opera with their music, singing, and ballet. The first major operas were those of Claudio Monteverdi (1567–1643). Religious oratorios, choral works with solo numbers, were also widespread; the best-known patron of this art form was Filippo Neri. Orchestral music took on definitive form; such concepts as the sonata, concerto grosso, concertino, etc., date from this period. Girolamo Frescobaldi (1583–1643) won fame as the organist of St. Peter's in Rome. Italy's greatest composer of the late seventeenth century was Alessandro Scarlatti (1659–1725); his son Domenico is best known for his harpsichord music. Pergolesi (1710–36) lived on in his *Stabat Mater* and in his comic opera, *La Serva Padrona*. In the field of chamber music we have such names as Arcangelo Corelli, Giuseppe Torelli, and Antonio Vivaldi (late seventeenth and early eighteenth centuries).

Page 66. G. V. Vanvitelli (1700–1773), View of the Tiber in Rome.

7

8

9

7–9. Three Late Baroque church façades in Rome, showing the development in the last phase. The front surface is curved and the ornaments lose their architectonic stiffness; the Rococo style will be the next step. 7. Santa Susanna, façade by Carlo Maderno, 1603. 8. San Marcello, façade by Carlo Fontana, 1683. 9. Santa Maria Maddalena, 1735, by Giuseppe Sardi.

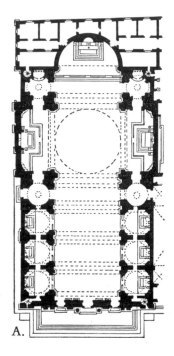

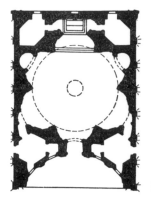

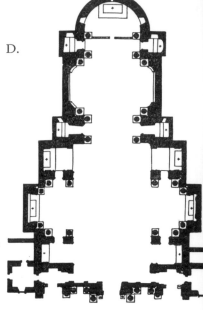

D.

A. The Gesù. The striving toward spatial unity shows clearly in replacing the side aisles by chapels opening on the nave and forming a part of its space. The ensemble is concentrated toward the domed space, where all the elements are bound together (see Fig. 10).
B. Sant' Andrea al Quirinale. The plan has the form of a transverse oval, surrounded by chapels.

B.

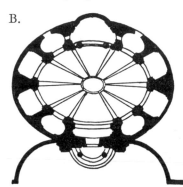

C.

C. Sant' Ivo della Sapienza. A circular plan based on the star-hexagon formed by two interlocking triangles.
D. Santa Maria in Campitelli, by Rainaldi, 1657. The form of this plan is a variant of that of the Gesù. By broadening and deepening the middle chapels of the nave, the spatial unity is even more complete. The many

freestanding columns and the narrowing of the domed space give rise to a rich perspective effect.

A.

ARCHITECTURE Rome was unquestionably the most important center of Italian Baroque, but various regions of southern Italy (Naples, Lecce) and Sicily (Noto, Palermo, Syracuse, Catania) were also important, since the art of the Spanish rulers combined with Italian elements to produce a special character. In the north, Turin and Venice are most significant. Florence and Bologna are less important for Baroque art, although Bologna played a large part in Baroque painting.

The major Baroque art is architecture and, not surprisingly, this reached its high point in Rome. For one thing, that city became the center of the Counter Reformation; for another, the ostentation and megalomania of the new style were quite in line with the Roman taste. Another important factor favoring the arts was the notorious nepotism of the seventeenth century; the wealth of relatives favored by the Popes was manifested in the building and decoration of great palaces and numbers of churches. Michelangelo (1475–1564) may in many respects be regarded as a forerunner and prophet of the Baroque, in that he breaks through the equilibrium of the Renaissance toward a freedom from classic forms that recurs in the work of the seventeenth-century masters. This freedom can be clearly seen in the Palazzo Farnese, designed by Antonio da Sangallo in 1534 and completed by the great Florentine in 1548; details of the upper story that he added are in many ways preludes to the Baroque. By comparison, the palace of the Lateran, which is forty years later (by Domenico Fontana, 1586), seems old-fashioned. Michelangelo's most "Baroque" creation, however, is his entrance hall to the Biblioteca Laurenziana in Florence, begun as early as 1524–34: volutes, curved staircase, coupled and engaged columns, broken and segmental pediments, all these are elements that were to be hallmarks of the seventeenth-century Baroque. The mighty grip with which he brought the relatively additive plan of Bramante's St. Peter's into a great unity conveys the spirit of the coming age.

Before the church of the Gesù, whose importance is sometimes ex-

aggerated, introduced the Baroque proper, church façades had already been built in Rome that mark a first phase of the new style: Antonio da Sangallo's Santo Spirito in Sassia (façade probably designed by him c. 1540, though executed later) and Guido de' Guidetti's façade for Santa Caterina dei Funari (1563). The role of Domenico Fontana is rather that of a harbinger than a creator of immortal works. Pope Sixtus V entrusted him with the plan for the great enlargement of Rome, beginning with the linking of the most important basilicas by straight streets that form the pattern on which the city was later organized. Fontana did not see the buildings as separate entities; he conceived of them in their relationship to the city plan and gave them a function within it. He was more a technician and engineer than an architect. The difficult technical task of erecting the heavy obelisk in St. Peter's Square could be entrusted to no one else (1586).

Giacomo Barozzi, called Vignola (1507–73), owes his fame to the church of the Gesù, begun by him and finished by Giacomo della Porta, who departed considerably from Vignola's design for the façade. The interior became the model for Baroque church construction in Italy and far afield: a broad nave, with the side aisles replaced by three chapels on each side opening on the nave (a pattern reminiscent of the Basilica of Maxentius near the Forum); a broad, light dome over the crossing; and a choir, with chapels between the arms of the cross, thus related with the plan of St. Peter's. The broad nave and the open space of the dome flow into each other, creating the unity of space that is typical of the Baroque, and at the same time the side chapels are tied in with the nave. The façade by Giacomo della Porta, possibly completed by Tristacci and De Rosis, is certainly no improvement over the sketch of Vignola, which has been preserved; this sketch continued the trend of Santo Spirito in Sassia and Santa Caterina dei Funari, and, if it had been carried out, would have made the Gesù the first genuinely Baroque church façade in Rome. All the Baroque elements in the existing façade, which is heavier than Vi-

gnola's, are already to be found in his design: rhythmic pairing of columns and pilasters, the projection of the central portions and consequent special emphasis on them, the playful effects of light and shade. Closer to Vignola's ideal is the façade of Santa Maria in Transpontina on the Via della Conciliazione, designed by Giovanni Sallustio Peruzzi and completed in 1587 by Ottavio Mascherino. It is striking to see the extent to which, in this age, the church front becomes an autonomous work of art; in many cases it has no direct connection with the interior, taking on rather the nature of a rich wall decoration facing on the street or square. A typical example is the church of San Luigi dei Francesi, built by Giacomo della Porta and dedicated in 1589. The heavy, almost square façade does not in any way indicate the three-aisled internal structure.

Carlo Maderno (1556–1629) was a nephew of Domenico Fontana, brought up in the school of the Mannerists and a great admirer of Michelangelo. One of his most successful creations is the façade of Santa Susanna (1603), which has a more strongly modeled effect than the front of the Gesù and is far superior to it in its proportions. It is so designed that it can be seen either frontally or from an angle without losing effectiveness. The architect also shows his ability in the interiors of Santa Maria della Vittoria and Sant'Andrea della Valle, both designed after the pattern of the Gesù, but the decorative element here is of the essence of the architecture. In his controversial completion of St. Peter's, with nave and façade, he proves himself a true follower of Michelangelo. The façade design continues Michelangelo's solution, and in the nave he is faithful to the master's forms and ornamentation. The way in which he carried out this addition, prescribed by the altered spirit of the times, shows his great ability once again. Along with him, honorable mention should be made of G. B. Soria, whose work consists to a great extent of church

fronts, which he built with varying success. In the façade of Santa Maria della Vittoria (1626) he sticks close to Maderno's model at Santa Susanna. He is more independent at San Gregorio Magno, whose effect is largely due to the imposing flight of steps in front of it (1633) and in San Carlo dei Catinari (1636–38). By and large, it was the secondary figures, all artists of stature, who gave Baroque Rome its aspect: Flaminio Ponzio, Martino Longhi and his son Onorio and grandson Martino, Francesco da Volterra, Giovanni Vasanzio (the Netherlander Jan van Santen), Vincenzo della Greca, Alessandro Algardi, and many others. Algardi built the imposing façade of Sant' Ignazio (1642–45).

But the middle of the seventeenth century was completely dominated by two architects of genius, Gian Lorenzo Bernini (1598–1680) and Francesco Borromini (1599–1667); rivals and contestants, they both broke through the rigidity that still bound the Baroque to the prescriptions of classical architecture. Bernini was the architect of the papal Curia and the powerful Roman noble families; Borromini, visionary and religious, built mainly for the monastic orders. Bernini was a courtier; Borromini was something of a bohemian. Bernini knew how to go with the times, Borromini was a nonconformist, going his own way and finding his own forms, freer from tradition. For that reason he used to be denounced by classicists and esthetes, and just for that reason he deserves our praise. Moreover, the fact that Bernini was followed by lesser men, while Borromini inspired only the great, is in a way a measure of the two personalities and their genius. Bernini is a sculptor rather than an architect, but he is still an architect in his designs for monumental works of sculpture, such as fountains, altars, and tombs, while his architectural works have a sculptural character. His church architecture shows a marked preference for central plans. In Sant' Andrea al Quirinale

10. Interior of the Gesù, the prototype Jesuit church (see plan A). 11. The colonnade of Piazza San Pietro, completed 1667, is Bernini's greatest architectural work.

12. Piazza Navona, Rome, is a typical Baroque square, dominated by the façade of Sant' Agnese by Borromini and enlivened by Bernini's three fountains. 13. The surroundings of the Duomo in Catania (Sicily); the façade dates from 1736. The domed church to the left is reminiscent of Sant' Agnese in Rome.

14

15

14. *San Carlo alle Quattro Fontane, built by Borromini, 1640; façade also by him, 1667. 15. Sant' Andrea al Quirinale, by Bernini, begun 1658,* *shows how classicistic this master could be compared to Borromini, who always sought out his own way (see plan B).*

(1658–70) the plan is a transverse oval; for the two churches of Castelgandolfo and Arricia (1661 and 1664, respectively) he chose plans reminiscent of the early Renaissance, the first being a dome over a Greek cross, the second suggesting the Pantheon in Rome in form and aspect. His greatest work of architectural genius is the colonnade of Piazza San Pietro (completed 1667), whose broad elliptical form brings together the façade of the church and the Vatican palace. The largeness of the conception goes back to the ancient imperial fora (especially that of Trajan), while the trapezoidal shape of the forecourt in front of the façade may have been taken from Michelangelo's Piazza on the Capitoline Hill. In the play of perspective of the Scala Regia in the Vatican, too, Bernini builds on a discovery that his rival Borromini had made thirty years earlier in the colonnade of the Palazzo Spada, but he worked out Borromini's act of playful genius into a monumental rich ensemble. In 1665 Bernini was called to Paris to make a design for the rebuilding of the Louvre. He was treated like a prince at the court of Louis XIV, but the plan ended in failure, for the pompous Roman Baroque did not attract the French, with their rational and classicist tendencies. Back in Rome, he completed his most Baroque creation, the moving and radiant Cathedral of St. Peter, perhaps as a reaction against the cloudy atmosphere of Paris and its chill classicism.

Bernini is a preeminent builder of fountains. His Fountain of the Four Rivers on the Piazza Navona in Rome (1647–57) is an unsurpassed masterpiece, and would alone suffice to place him among the very greatest. In order to become acquainted with Bernini as a sculptor, one must visit Santa Maria della Vittoria (*Ecstasy of Santa Theresa*) and the Galleria Borghese (*Apollo and Daphne, The Rape of Proserpina, David,* etc.). His sculpture represents the complete victory

of the spirit over matter, and this is why his religious works are more spiritual than they were given credit for up to a short time ago. It is not merely amazing virtuosity, although that is what it becomes in the work of many of his followers, who are astonishingly numerous. That there were genuine artists among them can be seen from the funeral monuments of the Bolognetti family in the church of Gesù e Maria on the Corso.

The difference between Bernini's art and that of the rival genius, Borromini, can be seen most clearly in two small churches only a couple of hundred yards apart, Bernini's Sant' Andrea al Quirinale and Borromini's San Carlo alle Quattro Fontane (San Carlino). The latter church dates from about 1640, but the façade is a quarter century later. In contrast to the rich marbles of Sant' Andrea, the treatment of the material in San Carlo is extremely sober; over against Bernini's elegance and virtuosity is Borromini's almost convulsive expressionism. For him there were no conventional rules, for he followed his own inner urge. But he took the utmost care with every detail, as can be seen from his numerous studies, in which the motifs, sometimes repeated and sometimes altered, grow to maturity. The fact that he regarded the classical orders as an opportunity for creating new forms and fantasy was taken so ill by later classicists that they remained totally blind and insensitive to the unmistakable charm of his works. It is only in recent decades that he has been given his rightful place in the pantheon of the very great. His chief works in Rome are the Oratorio of San Filippo Neri (1637–52), Sant'Ivo della Sapienza (1642–61), the completion of Sant' Agnese on Piazza Navona (1653–57), the dome and campanile of Sant' Andrea delle Fratte (1653–65), and the Jesuits' Collegio di Propaganda Fide (1646–67). After an agitated life, Borromini committed suicide in 1667.

16. *Internally too San Carlo is original in plan and details. No costly marbles are employed here, but complex architectural forms. 17. Sant' Andrea is richly decorated. In contrast to the plan of San Carlo, the long axis of its oval runs across the church. 18. Sant' Ivo della Sapienza, Rome, by Borromini, 1642–61. The dome and lantern are topped by a spirally twisted spire.*

16

17

18

19

Second only to Bernini and Borromini is Pietro Berrettini, usually known as Pietro da Cortona, after his native town, who was distinguished as both architect and painter. Although less widely known than the other two architects, he was responsible for some of the most successful works of the Roman Baroque. SS. Luca e Martina (1634–50), near the Forum, is a domed church on a Greek cross, which yet gives a longitudinal effect. The façade is successful and original, and the same can be said for those he designed for Santa Maria della Pace (1656) and Santa Maria in Via Lata (1658–62). The first is elegant, and seems to have influenced Bernini in the churches of Sant' Andrea al Quirinale and Ariccia; this is surprising, for the two architects were not on friendly standing. Santa Maria in Via Lata is a great building in small dimensions, with its two superimposed colonnades.

Some echoes of Cortona's style appear in Santa Maria in Campitelli (1662–67), by Carlo Rainaldi, one of the most daring church designs of the seventeenth century. Both inside and out, freestanding columns are dominant; and the transept is shifted toward the middle of the nave. By this means (and the columns contribute to the effect), a perspective is obtained that is similar to that of Bernini's Scala Regia. Rainaldi has a marked preference for round or oval church spaces with chapels around them, as for example the two domed churches on the Piazza del Popolo. The first project for the Campitelli church was probably of the same kind.

Influences from Borromini can be seen in the work of Carlo Fontana, notably the façade of San Marcello, but the liberties taken there betray the approach of the Rococo, which emerges in the façade of Santa Maria Maddalena, designed by Giuseppe Sardi (c. 1680–1753) and erected in 1735. Ferdinando Fuga, too, is still striving for luxuriant decoration in some of his works, as in his Palazzo della Consulta (1732–37) and the façade of Santa Maria Maggiore (1741–43), but even by the end of the seventeenth century some Roman architects had already come to the conclusion that the Roman *gravitas* was hardly concordant with the drive toward movement and freedom that Borromini had released. This led to classicism, clearly seen in the work of Alessandro Galilei, as in his façades for San Giovanni in Laterano (1734) and San Giovanni dei Fiorentini (1734), where the straight line and flat surface reappear. Yet the Borromini tradition was anything but dead, as we can see from the outcurving front of Santa Croce in Gerusalemme, built in 1743 by P. Passalacque and D. Gregorini, which seems like the Borrominians' answer to Galilei's Lateran façade.

Tuscany, and in particular Florence, which had played such a dominant part during the Renaissance, was in the background in the Baroque period. The heritage of its great tradition worked against the infiltration of new ideas, and it was only toward the end of the seventeenth century that the international style developed in Rome gained the upper hand there. Bologna too was of less importance for great new architecture. Venice, on the other hand, was able as always to find a style of its own, and Baldassare Longhena (1598–1682) was a richly endowed architect of the same order of magnitude as the great builders of Rome. They did not influence him; he continued the Venetian tradition of Sansovino, Palladio, and Scamozzi, the great theorist, whose influence is unmistakable in Longhena's Pesaro and Rezzonico palaces; but Longhena's greatest masterpiece is undoubtedly the domed church of Santa Maria della Salute, in

19–21. The façade of San Giovanni in Laterano (19) by Galilei, 1734, is a product of classicism, in contrast to the fronts of Santa Maria Maggiore (20) by Ferdinando Fuga, 1743, and of Santa Croce in Gerusalemme (21), by Gregorini and Passalacque, 1743, both showing the influence of Borromini (all in Rome). 22. Guarini's Cappella della Santa Sindone, Turin, 1667–90, is reminiscent of Borromini in its fantastic forms.

which, following the precedent of Bramante, Michelangelo, and Palladio, he gave his own novel solution for the central plan (1630–82). On the exterior the dome is connected to the chapel-surrounded octagonal base by great upthrusting volutes, while the principal motif is repeated in a smaller dome above the choir, flanked by two

23

23. The Basilica di Superga, near Turin, by Juvarra, 1716–31, is a typical eclectic structure, showing the influence of Bernini, Borromini, and of classicism. 24. Santa Maria della Salute, Venice, by Longhena, begun 1631, dynamic and yet monumental, gives a new solution to the problem of the central plan. 25. Piazza del

Carmine, San Severo (Apulia), early eighteenth century. The Spanish influence on the architecture gives a Latin American aspect to the town. 26. The glorious façade of the Duomo at Syracuse (Sicily), probably by Andrea Palma, begun in 1728, is based on the contrasted play of light and shadow. 27. Palazzo Reale, at Caserta, near Naples, by Luigi Vanvitelli, an immense edifice on a square plan, begun in 1752. The classicistic façade is situated on a great forecourt, and is impressive for its mass and dimensions. 28. Palazzo Rezzonico, Venice, by Longhena, about 1660. The architectural detail and reliefs, characteristic of Venice, are enhanced by the moving, mirroring water. 29. Grand staircase of the University of Genoa, by Bartolomeo Bianco, designed 1630. The staircase, with its changes in perspective and play of light at every turn, is a typical Baroque construction. 30. Staircase of the Palazzo Braschi, Rome, by Cosimo Morelli, 1780. The architect rediscovers the great tradition of the Roman Baroque.

24

25

slender campaniles. Seen across the broad waterway, a rich silhouette appears that seems to link up with the outline of San Marco. Longhena's mastery can be felt when we compare his work, among which the church of the Scalzi should also be mentioned, with the façade of San Moisè, erected by Tremignon in the middle of the seventeenth century.

The most important Milanese Baroque architect is F. M. Ricchino, to whom we owe the fine court of the Brera with its paired columns. At Genoa, Bartolomeo Bianco is the most prominent master.

Of far greater importance is Turin, the Piedmontese capital, especially for the work of Guarino Guarini (1624–83) and Filippo Juvarra (1678–1736). Guarini's independent fantasy and the freedom of his forms remind us of Borromini (Capella della Santa Sindone, 1667–90; San Lorenzo, 1668–87; Palazzo Carignano, 1679). Juvarra, a Sicilian by birth, had been influenced in Rome by Bernini and Borromini and the other architects of the seventeenth century. Among the high points in his work are the domed church of the Superga near Turin (1716–31) and the Stupinigi hunting lodge (1729–33). His most gifted pupil was Benedetto Alfieri, who built the notable semicircular church of San Giovanni Battista at Carignano (1757–64).

In the south the situation is different again. Naples was under the direct influence of Rome, but Cosimo Fanzago (1591–1678), more than any one else, is the Baroque architect par excellence. Curiously

26

29

enough, all sorts of Mannerist elements persist in the Neapolitan Baroque, probably because most of the architects came from Florence or Tuscany. The man who marks the transition to classicism is Luigi Vanvitelli (1700–73), son of Gaspare Vanvitelli, the painter, under whom at first he studied. It is precisely in the direction of classicism that Naples has a special place, both in virtue of Naples' political importance in the second half of the eighteenth century and because of its contact with antiquity through the excavations at Pompeii and Herculaneum. Vanvitelli's masterpiece is the enormous royal palace at Caserta, begun in 1752 for Charles III of Bourbon. It is the Italian Versailles, and without imitating its illustrious model in any respect, it rivals it and in many respects surpasses it. The immense park was also designed by Vanvitelli.

Compared to Rome and Naples, the Baroque art of the further south of Italy has a provincial air. And yet Gregorovius, in the last century, called Lecce, in Apulia, "the Florence of the Baroque," and no one can escape the charm of Syracuse and Noto, in Sicily. The fact that one is sometimes irresistibly reminded of Latin America is due to the strong, sometimes overwhelming, Spanish influence that arose out of the political situation. This south Italian Baroque art is still too little known, and the traveler in that region sometimes comes across delightful surprises. In Lecce, Giuseppe Cino (early eighteenth century) and the Zimbalo brothers (seventeenth century) are the most important masters. The Zimbalo brothers (seventeenth

30

32

33

31

31. *Bernini's Fountain of the Four Rivers, 1647–51, in the Piazza Navona, combines the rich movement of its forms with the lively play of the murmuring water. 32. Bernini's representation of Santa Teresa, with* her heart about to be pierced by a burning arrow, illustrates his domination of matter by spirit (1645–52, Santa Maria della Vittoria, Rome). 33. The altar of St. Ignatius in the Gesù, Rome, by Andrea Pozzo, *about 1700, full of dynamic effervescence. 34. Apollo pursuing the nymph Daphne, by Bernini, 1622, is all movement and breathing life; the marble seems to have lost its weight and chill. 35. Santa Cecilia, by Stefano* Maderno, under the high altar of her church, Santa Cecilia in Trastevere, in Rome, 1600. The artist seeks beautiful flowing lines, that break the bulk of the volume but do not destroy the monumentality of the whole.

35

century) are the most important masters. The Zimbalos erected the façade of Santa Croce, which had been begun by Gabriele Riccardi, and the sculptor Cesare Penna made decorative sculptures of the utmost refinement in the easily worked sandstone. Noto was rebuilt closer to the sea after the disastrous earthquake of 1693, and became an entire ensemble of Sicilian Baroque. The Duomo in Syracuse, enclosing a fifth-century B.C. Doric temple to Athena, was given a grandiose Baroque façade, one of the handsomest of its kind (1728–37). Palermo too (San Domenico, 1637; façade 1726) and Catania (San Benedetto; Duomo, after 1693, by Fra Girolamo Palazzotto and G. B. Vaccarini), Acireale (San Sebastiano, 1705), Modica (San Giorgio, eighteenth century), Ragusa (San Giorgio, same period), and Trapani (Chiesa del Collegio, by Natale Masuccio, first half of

34

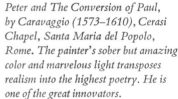

the living model, but there was also the danger of not getting any further than the given model and the reproduction of it: to avoid this, artists imitated the great masters; this explains Bolognese eclecticism, in which the models used were classical sculpture, Raphael, Michelangelo, Correggio, and the Venetians—but they were rather starting points than goals.

Michelangelo Merisi, called Caravaggio after his birthplace (1573–1610), was a greater artist than any of the Carracci and his influence reached further than theirs. He came to Rome as a young man and did most of his best work there. What influences he underwent are to be sought in northern Italy. In contrast to the Carracci, his nature and character make him one of the revolutionary painters who

41

42

40. *Bartolommeo Schedoni (about 1570–1615), The Three Maries at the Tomb. Schedoni's work is marked by plasticity created by effects of light and intense colors. He was active mainly in the province of Emilia, the birthplace of this trend.*

41. *Guido Reni (1575–1642), Aurora. The reputation of this master has faded somewhat, yet some of his larger works can still stir us, like this ceiling fresco of Aurora, who drives off the night and goes before the chariot of the sun.*

42. *Guercino (1591–1666), Aurora. This master, who chose the same subject for a ceiling fresco, interpreted it in a much more interesting manner. By juxtaposing patches of contrasting colors, he achieved effects that look modern to us.*

43. *Carlo Maratta (1625–1713), Pope Clement IX. This Roman follower of Sacchi was famous for his portraits.*

43

44

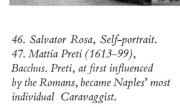

45

46

44. *Salvator Rosa (1615–73),*
Landscape with Bridge. The Neapolitan
school is many-sided. Rosa, of a
turbulent and adventurous nature,
was one of the greatest landscape
painters in Italian art. 45. Orazio
Gentileschi (1563–c. 1647), Annun-
ciation. He is a striking figure in Italian
Caravaggism.

46. *Salvator Rosa, Self-portrait.*
47. *Mattia Preti (1613–99),*
Bacchus. Preti, at first influenced
by the Romans, became Naples' most
individual Caravaggist.

renewed the art of painting. By means of a sober but always surprising choice of colors and a wonderful cool light, he transforms a
realism that sometimes seems crude into the highest poetry. His first
large commission, for the Cappella Contarelli in San Luigi dei Francesi, shows him at the full height of his skill. A first version of the
altarpiece in the Cappella Contarelli was removed from the church
by the spiritual authorities, because its nonconformism went counter
to the current taste of the faithful (it subsequently hung in the Kaiser
Friedrich Museum, Berlin, and was unfortunately destroyed during
World War II). His other paintings, too, some of which are among
the high points of world art, evoked lively and sometimes bitter
controversy. Shortly thereafter he reached his peak in the *Conversion*
of Paul in the Cappella Cerasi, Santa Maria del Popolo (1601). In
subsequent years the stormy painter got involved in a series of tavern
brawls, in one of which he killed a companion (1606), and only the
protection of his noble patrons enabled him to make his escape. He
turned up in Naples in 1607 where he executed a number of commissions; in Malta the year after; and then in Sicily, where he painted
one of his best works, the *Burial of St. Lucy*, for the church of Santa
Lucia in Syracuse. By way of Naples he came to Porto Ercole, on the
coast of the Maremma, from which he hoped to get back to Rome,
but he died of malaria in his thirty-seventh year.
The Carracci and Caravaggio gave rise to a broad stream in Baroque
painting, which calls for a few words. We begin with the followers
of the Carracci. Their influence is seen not only in Bologna and the
province of Emilia but also in Rome itself. In Emilia we should

47

48

49

50

48. *Andrea Pozzo (1642–1709), Glorification of St. Ignatius, Sant' Ignazio, Rome. Pozzo produced architectural illusionism in ceiling painting of extraordinary complexity. 49. G. B. Piazzetta (1683–1754), Glorification of St. Dominic, SS. Giovanni e Paolo, Venice. 50. Sketch for the ceiling painting in Palazzo Rezzonico, Venice, by G. B. Tiepolo (1696–1770). The art of the Venetian decorators is brighter, lighter, and freer than that of the Romans. Their virtuosity seems unbounded.*

51

mention Bartolommeo Schedoni, notable for his effects of light and intense colors, and Giovanni Lanfranco, best known as a fresco painter. Their reputations were overshadowed by that of Guido Reni, which has not lasted; modern criticism has found in his production too much false sentiment and too many airs and graces, and few works of genuine feeling; among the latter are the angelic musicians in the chapel of Santa Silvia in San Gregorio Magno in Rome and the *Aurora* ceiling fresco (1613) in the casino of Palazzo Rospigliosi. However, the most typical follower of the rules and regulations laid down by the theoreticians of the time was Domenico Zampieri, called Domenichino, who is now less famous than he once was but still can get through to us with his harmonious, though scholastic, colors and his landscape backgrounds. Francesco Albani is to be mentioned with him. Much more important is Francesco Barbieri, called Guercino (1591–1666), who modeled himself on the Venetians and Dosso Dossi. In the *Aurora* that he painted for the casino of Villa Ludovisi he obtained effects that strike us as modern by juxtaposing spots of color.

A group of painters was working in Rome at the same time who, although deriving their style from the Carracci, still had one eye on Venice; among them were Andrea Sacchi and his pupil Carlo Maratta, who was able to adapt to the taste of the time and became

a celebrity. Of his innumerable works, the portraits still have something to say to us.

Pietro da Cortona, whom we have met as an architect, was also a fresco painter; one of his works in this field was the enormous ceiling decoration in the Palazzo Barberini glorifying that family. As such, he prepared the way for the Jesuit Andrea Pozzo (1642–1709), who brought this art to fullest realization in the ceiling of Sant' Ignazio in Rome. He too was influenced by the Venetians, especially Veronese. Pozzo was also the designer of the splendid altar tomb of Ignatius of Loyola in the Gesù. Gian Battista Gaulli (Baciccio), the painter of the ceiling in the Gesù, deserves mention with Pozzo.

Caravaggio did not train students, as the Carracci did. His influence was based on the stimulating impression that his works made on his contemporaries, not only in Italy but far afield, even as far as the Netherlands. One of the most interesting figures among his Italian followers was Orazio Gentileschi, a painter of great grace and lyricism. Through his stay in Paris and then in London, he may have contributed indirectly to grafting Caravaggism on the stock of Netherlands art. This certainly was done by his daughter Artemisia for Naples, where she lived for twenty years. There Battista Caracciolo (Il Battistello) was one of the main figures, along with the Spaniard Jusepe de Ribera, whose Caravaggism has a very personal imprint with its intense effects of light and shadow. Neapolitan Caravaggism reached high points in the work of Massimo Stanzione and Mattia Preti, who was first under the influence of Guercino and Lanfranco.

The Neapolitan school had many sides. Along with those already named, we mention Luca Giordano, a virtuoso decorator who foreshadowed the eighteenth century, and the turbulent but extremely

51. *Domenico Feti (about 1589–1623), The Lost Talent. This work, full of atmosphere and pictorial charm, seems to have Netherlandish influences. 52. Giuseppe Maria Crespi (1665–1747), Confession. Reality, enchanted into poetry by a marvelous Rembrandt-like light. 53. Alessandro Magnasco (1667–1749), Monks in the Refectory. Expression carried to the point of dramatic hallucination.*

52

53

54. Pietro Longhi (1702–85), Venetian Maskers. A poetical, slightly caricatural interpretation of eighteenth-century Venetian life.

54

55. Carlo Dolci (1616–86), Madonna and Child. Sugary and sentimental.

55

gifted Salvator Rosa, one of Italy's greatest landscape painters (1615–73). There were thus painters in Naples that did not belong to either of the two trends.

The same was true in the rest of Italy, including Lombardy. There, a great still-life painter should be mentioned: Evaristo Baschenis attracts us today by his modern-looking compositions of musical instruments.

It is a proof of Tuscany's backwardness during this period that the best-known figure was the sugary Carlo Dolci. The foremost painter in Genoa, who incidentally ended his career in Venice, was Bernardo Strozzi, whose work is often reminiscent of the Netherlands realists. Also working in Venice was the Roman Domenico Feti, who came into contact with the early work of Rubens in Mantua, and was strongly influenced by it. Later he became famous mainly for his pictures of the parables of the Gospels, painted like genre scenes and full of atmosphere and pictorial charm. In the same trend, at the beginning of the eighteenth century, was the Bolognese Giuseppe Maria Crespi. In his best works he transforms reality into poetry by means of his marvelous light, which sometimes reminds us of Rembrandt. Related to him, but of a different nature, is the Genoese Alessandro Magnasco, who carried his expressionism to the point of dramatic hallucination.

In the eighteenth century, Venice consolidated its position of leadership in Italian painting. Sebastiano Ricci introduced the new revival at the end of the seventeenth century. His work is full of promise, which was to be fulfilled by Giovanni Battista Tiepolo (1696–1770): fluency of composition, joyful color and movement, lightness of touch, especially in fresco, and an incredible virtuosity which seems to know no difficulties. Tiepolo masters the vast surfaces of walls and vaults with sovereign ease. His path was made ready by Tintoretto and above all by Veronese, but his immediate predecessors (Ricci and his contemporary Giambattista Piazzetta) also contributed toward his formation. But Tiepolo soon broke free from any notable influences, and already showed his full personality in the great work that he did for the archiepiscopal palace at Udine in 1726. Thereafter his activity was amazing, in palaces and churches at Milan, Bergamo, and especially Venice: the church of the Gesuati, the Scuola dei Carmini, the church of the Scalzi, the Palazzo Labia; and also in the Villa Pisani at Stra, near Venice, and the Villa Valmarana at Vicenza. From 1751 to 1753 he worked for the prince-archbishop of Würzburg in his residence there. In the last years of his life, Tiepolo lived in Madrid, where he painted ceilings in the new royal palace, erected by his countryman Giovanni Battista Sacchetti from a design by Juvarra. It may be objected that Tiepolo was a great

decorator rather than a great painter, but it should be remembered that the two qualities may very well go together. It must be admitted that, especially in his religious pieces, a certain pathos sometimes takes the place of deeper feeling. All this does not remove the fact that he was a painter of genius, one of the figures who determined the culture of his period. The less monumental, more playful art of his son, Giovanni Domenico Tiepolo, should also be mentioned.

Rosalba Carriera was outstanding for her pastel portraits. Pietro Longhi (1702–85) is the poetical interpreter of the Venetian life of his time, like his countryman, the dramatist Goldoni. Longhi's son Alexander was an able and honored portraitist.

The Venetian *vedutisti* (painters of city scenes) are a group apart. Netherlands influences are present here. Caspar van Wittel (1647–1736), born in Utrecht, who Italianized his name to Gaspare Vanvitelli (and was the father of Luigi Vanvitelli, the architect), is the forerunner of Antonio Canaletto, Bernardo Bellotto, and Francesco Guardi. They play a poetical game with light and color, with the water and sky and buildings of Venice, the finale of a great art.

In Naples, Francesco Solimena continued the decorative tradition of Luca Giordano, with many borrowings from earlier masters, but without the transparent brightness and easy naturalness of Tiepolo. Of more importance is Corrado Giaquinto, who worked in Rome, Turin, and Madrid, and replaced the Baroque by the Rococo. In Rome, the caricaturist Pierleone Ghezzi is an interesting figure who illustrates the extent to which that city had lost its leadership in painting. It had an outstanding *vedutisto* in Giovanni Paolo Pannini. The most important Roman artist is Venetian-born, the engraver and etcher Giovanni Battista Piranesi (1720–78). The views of Roman ruins by this great, lone figure show him as a forerunner of the Romantic movement, who stands at the end of a period and shows the past and present greatness of Rome.

INTERIOR DECORATION AND FURNITURE   The dominant role that France played in the arts of furniture and decoration is sometimes exaggerated, to the neglect of Italy. Many of the motifs that the French employed in the seventeenth and eighteenth centuries appeared earlier in Italy. It is true, however, that the French cabinet-makers showed much more refinement in their work than did their Italian counterparts, and that motifs discovered in Italy were often fully developed in France, and sometimes brought back to Italy in their new form.

In Baroque furniture, Rome is predominant: heaviness, joined with strong curves, remained characteristic down into the Rococo. Ornament played a structural role: it furthered the logical structure of the

56

57

objects, by being applied to points at which emphasis was desired. Roman furniture does not have the easy slimness of French furniture; it has a slower and more stately sinuosity. Along with gilding, use was sometimes made of such precious materials as ebony, ivory, and variegated stones, which were combined in various tones and used as incrustations on cabinets and table leaves. Such figurative details as putti and fantastic animals were much employed on supports and entablatures, combined with acanthus motives and volutes. The cabinetmaking of the classicistic period, in turn, was influenced by the "Pompeian" style.

Along with Rome, Venice is important in this field. In the seventeenth century its furniture is, if possible, even heavier and more pompous, while the eighteenth-century work aims at the dashing and fantastic. Roman *gravitas* gives way completely; designs tend to undisciplined fantasy, kept only slightly within bounds by any feeling for measure, balance, or proportion, and producing the reproach sometimes made against Venetian decorative art, that it leans too much on instinct and not enough on intelligence. Venice shares with Rome a love for *chinoiserie* and the use of mirrors; classicism found few adepts there.

56. Bernardo Strozzi (1581–1644), Lute Player. This Genoese painter was influenced by the Netherlanders and the Venetians. 57. Canaletto (Antonio Canale, 1697–1768), Santa Maria della Salute, Venice. At the right is a corner of Sansovino's Library. 58. Giovanni Paolo Pannini (1692–1765), The Colosseum and the Arch of Constantine in Rome. This Roman *vedutisto had a romantic attachment for the remains of Rome's ancient greatness. 59. Jacques Callot (1592–1635), Pantalone, a character in the Italian folk drama (commedia dell'arte). Callot, a Frenchman, with his free and sharp etching technique typified the life of the Italian people, among whom he lived for many years.*

8

59

LOUIS XIV STYLE

POLITICAL AND SOCIAL LIFE   In October, 1652, Louis XIV made his entry into Paris. The *Fronde* was subdued but not forgotten—it was a time rich in lessons for the fourteen-year-old king. He had learned to distrust the people: with the complicity of the mutinous nobles, they had poured through his palace. He had learned to distrust the *parlements*. He had also learned that the unpopularity of a first minister could reflect upon the king. He therefore decided to rule himself. The death of Mazarin in 1661 was to give him the opportunity to do so. Mindful of the uprising of the *Fronde*, Louis XIV chose to live principally at Saint-Germain, and later Versailles, instead of Paris. He had unpleasant memories of his youth; and his extravagances were less obvious when they took place far from the city. The Louvre was all too open to the curiosity of visitors.

By assembling the elite of the French nobility around him in the enchanted milieu of the palace of Versailles, Louis XIV weakened their prestige in the provinces. By encouraging luxury, waste, theatrical performances, parties, and gambling, he made the nobility dependent on the royal generosity. For the same purpose, he chose most of his ministers from people of lowly origin. The administration of the kingdom was conducted by an army of functionaries, often derived from the bourgeoisie. For good and loyal service they could be raised to the nobility. The nobles had their eyes on the king, the bourgeois had their eyes fixed on the nobility. The entire society lived in an atmosphere of competition. Fénelon was to ridicule, in *Télémaque*, the princes who strove to have houses as rich as the immortals. The great nobles in turn imitated the king. After all, his own minister of finance, Fouquet, had set the example at his great château of Vaux-le-Vicomte.

The bourgeois did their best to ape the nobility. The plays of Molière, the satires of Boileau, and the character sketches of La Fontaine mock the bourgeois that has got rich by the development of commerce and industry. But thanks to this rivalry, the aristocratic ideal permeated the spirit of the French bourgeoisie.

RELIGION AND PHILOSOPHY   When Descartes wrote his philosophical works, between 1637 and 1649, he brought scientific knowledge within the reach of the mass of people for the first time; it was a development that was to be carried further in the eighteenth century. By proclaiming that common sense is the most widely distributed faculty in the world, Descartes established the rights of reason; but this hardly extended, as yet, to the fields of politics and religion, where conservatism reigned. Pascal freed the scientific method from theological and philosophical shackles by separating religion from science. His experiments on vacuum, air pressure, and the equilibrium of liquids helped to establish the victory of the scientific spirit over the prejudices of scholasticism. After the revocation of the Edict of Nantes (1685), financial difficulties and military reverses contributed to the formation of a critical spirit, which concerned itself with political and religious themes and reached its full development in the age of Voltaire and the *Encyclopédie*.

The Virgin Mary was zealously worshipped, even in the Jansenist convent of the Port-Royal, where they continued to use the rosary, practice the worship of Our Lady, and sing the Mass of the Virgin on Saturdays. But the Port-Royal and Pascal reacted strongly against exaggerations of the cult of Mary that furthered only the external ritual. The Virgin should no longer be represented only as a smiling, tender mother, but as the Mother of God, bowing before Him. It is noteworthy that Madame de Sévigné refused to have even a single picture of a saint in her chapel, with the exception of a picture of the Virgin and of course a crucifix, with the legend *Soli Deo Honor Et Gloria* (Glory and honor to God alone). At about the same time the question of frequent communion brought the Jesuits into conflict with the Jansenists, whose teachings in some respects resembled Calvinism, but for both the Jesuits and the Jansenists, piety concentrated around the idea of God. The final purpose of man is not only eternal bliss, it is also, and even primarily, the glorification of God. The priest now appears not only as confessor, shepherd, and servant of his faithful, but as a man dedicated to God. Of all the qualities of God, the seventeenth century placed most emphasis on His greatness. Religion had as its subject one God, in three persons, but most attention was directed as a rule toward the Word Become Flesh. The worship of Mary and the saints shared in this theocentric doctrine.

LITERATURE AND DRAMA   The writers of the new classicism of the seventeenth century put an end to the excesses of Baroque literature: the ridiculous intricacy of language, the crude realism, the plaintive or roguish spirits, the interplay of illusion and reality, the burlesque, the vulgarity, the unbridled romanticism, the exaggerated imagery and fantasy—all the qualities that the public took so to heart during the first half of the century. The classical writers dealt primarily with psychological and moral problems: the truth, and the way to reach it; the spirit that sees and links everything logically and mathematically; and the fine distinctions—the contrast between the heart and the understanding, between human freedom and its limitations, between heroism and human vanity and passions. By means of intellectual perception and probing, they expected to lay bare the lasting universal properties of the human soul. They cared very little for the picturesque. They ignored realistic description of strange lands, and were not aware of such feelings as were later awakened in the Romantics by long-past ages or far-distant peoples. Authentic reports of the exotic and of local color were seldom sought. These people were not concerned with the psychology of the child or of primitive man. They were unaware of the mysterious impulses of instinct, the unreasoned longing for the inconceivable

opera, but this art form was received at first with little enthusiasm. In the end, the public took to mythological spectacles, however, as well as to dramas sung from beginning to end. Music also was introduced into spectacles with machinery and apparatus. The failure of Perrin and Cambert, despite the success of *Pomone*, a pastoral drama in five acts, was to mark the end of the attempts to create a thoroughly French music drama, which was soon to be overshadowed by the works of Lully.

Jean-Baptiste Lully, a Florentine in the king's service from 1652 and naturalized in 1661, composed ballets and *comédies-ballets* and, with librettos by Philippe Quinault, created French opera. Once Molière had hit upon the idea of introducing *entrées de ballet* into his plays, music finally made its peace with the requirements of the intrigue. Lully was the creator of the classic type of *ouverture à la française*, which consisted of a slow stately part in accented rhythm and a lively fugal part, followed in turn by a partial repetition of the first part. The opera, which up to that time had been reserved for the nobility, became an official spectacle for which rules were established. In 1661 the ballet was accepted in the program of the Royal Academy of Music and Dance. The dance thereby attained a high level of technical perfection. At the end of the Renaissance and the beginning of the seventeenth century, that is, in the Baroque period of French literature, there was a revival in the domain of national folk dances: the Burgundian *branle* and the *branle* from Poitou, the gavotte, the Breton *triori*, the Auvergnat *bourrée*. From abroad there came the Spanish pavane, the allemande, and the galliard, a dance of Italian origin.

At the time of Charles Louis Beauchamps, dancing master of Louis XIV, and his pupil Raoul Auger La Feuillet, author of a *Chorographie ou l'art de décrire la danse par caractères, figures et signes démonstratifs* (1699), the art of dance was ordered into a vast system, under which detailed rules destroyed any form of spontaneity.

SPIRIT AND CHARACTERISTICS OF THE STYLE In art up to about 1660, the weight and somewhat stiff dignity of the Louis XIV style were reminiscent of the Louis XIII style. After that date the Louis XIV style was increasingly marked by royal dignity and an excess of ornament. From 1700 on, airiness and freedom already announce the style of the Regency.

The honor surrounding the person and the function of the king was introduced into the France of Louis XIV through the heroic and theatrical conception of life that found expression in the Spanish and Italian Baroque. Social life became a stage performance, with the king in the star role. Etiquette was governed by the rules of the court ballet. The king is a deity who needs servants and a temple for his worship. In Molière's prologue to *Amour Médecin*, he calls on drama, music, and ballet to leave off their idle rivalry and "give pleasure to the greatest king on earth." The heroic conception of life was to be embodied at Versailles with imcomparable magnitude and dignity. Gold and silver were lavishly spread: the purpose of wealth

and the unexpressed. They wanted to give pleasure, and this desire became stronger in them than the desire to keep to the rules. Their obedience to the rules was not slavish, but reasonable. Without being unfeeling for the charm of nature (some fables of La Fontaine and some letters of Madame de Sévigné), they did not go so far as to adore wild untouched nature, or to attribute souls to lifeless things, as the Romantics were to do.

With the exception of Molière, the great classical writers were very Christian and Catholic. Some of them had Jansenist sympathies, for example, Pascal, Madame de Sévigné, Racine, and Boileau. Saint-Evremond, Bayle, and later Fontenelle, held the middle ground between the Libertins of the first half of the seventeenth century and the daring thinkers of the eighteenth.

MUSIC AND DANCE Polyphony was given its last development in the fantasies of the lutenists, of the school of harpsichordists. The writing for both instruments is lively, even playful, and full of images, and was raised to a high point by the Couperin family. The Paris school had many organists, and the *Cérémonial de Paris* (1662) lays down the role of the organist during services. The organist alternates with the boy chorus, and plays the solo part at various parts of the mass and vespers. Nicolas de Crigny opposed the staccato style more characteristic of harpsichord music and developed the Gregorian themes in a more singing, more legato manner. Mazarin had undertaken to make the French public acquainted with Italian

2

3

was to compel respect. This heroic dynamism is suited only to exceptional beings; in this Olympian view of life the feeling for nature has only a very limited place. The picturesque and the realistic, still so much alive in the first half of the seventeenth century, gradually vanish. The vogue for the painting of the Le Nains is short-lived, as is the realism of the picaresque and "bourgeois" novelists Furetière, Scarron, and Georges Sorel.

Imitation of antiquity was still the rule. From it were borrowed columns, capitals, allegories, and mythology. The king was regarded as a sun god from Olympus (Apollo). Everything about him was on a heroic scale. This Baroque ideal was to disappear slowly, under the pressure of a specifically French rationalism. The need to impress was followed by the desire to please. The characteristic tension of the Baroque, as Heinrich Wöfflin has defined it, did not have the same intensity in France as in Italy, that is, there was less striving for the painterly at the expense of the linear, less contradiction between

depth and surface, shadow and light, or multiplicity and enclosed form. In the field of religion, the influence of Jansenism remained very strong. Cartesian rationalism, which matured toward the end of the seventeenth century, was extended to political and religious problems. After the worship of greatness, the price of which began to seem much too high around 1700, came a desire for a more peaceful, more rustic happiness, and this longing continued in the eighteenth century. The period of heroic deeds gave way to the period of feeling; the period of faith to the Enlightenment.

ARCHITECTURE In an era dominated by royal sensibility, it was normal that royal architecture should overshadow ecclesiastic and private building. The royal squares à la française serve to make the king's statue stand out better. The gates and triumphal arches are reminders of the feats of arms of the sovereign. The Hôtel des Invalides glorifies the fame of the conqueror and his providential

5

2. Château of Maisons-Lafitte, by François Mansart, built 1642–51. The height of the roofs and the weight of the ensemble are links to the Louis XIII style. 3. The Collège des Quatre-Nations, now the Institut de France, designed by Louis Le Vau in 1661–62 and completed by his son-in-law, F. Dorbay. The domed center is flanked by curved wings. 4. Interior of the church of Val-de-Grâce, designed by François Mansart in 1645, and completed by Le Mercier and others, shows the influence of the Italian Baroque but already foreshadows the Louis XIV style. 5. Porte St. Denis, Paris, designed by Nicolas-François Blondel, 1673. Blondel collaborated in changes of the plan of Paris.

10. Colonnade of the Louvre, 1666–70, by Claude Perrault. The expanse of paired columns, resting on a very simple lower story, was intended to give the building the harmony and solidity of an antique temple.

4

7

8

9

6. Garden façade of the palace at Versailles, 1669–85, by Louis Le Vau and Jules Hardouin-Mansart. The roof is flat and the projecting portions (avant-corps) with columns break the monotony of the ensemble. 7. The church of the Invalides, designed by J. Hardouin-Mansart and begun 1680.

8. Engraving of the Château Neuf at Meudon, by J. Hardouin-Mansart, 1706. The façade has no columns or pilasters. 9. Courtyard of the palace at Versailles, showing in right background the chapel, designed by J. Hardouin-Mansart and completed by Robert de Cotte, 1696–1710.

solicitude. As in literature, imitation of antiquity is the rule. But seventeenth-century literature, which meant to follow Aristotle's rules, usually was guided by the commentators of the Renaissance era. Similarly, the French architects believed they were working according to Vitruvius, when actually they were imitating Italian architects. But they never succeeded in taking over the construction in depth or the successive hidden masses of the Italian Baroque.

Classical French architecture is more concerned with surfaces, with stability, and with clarity. Its unity is Cartesian: it is built up out of clearly distinguishable parts. With Jules Hardouin Mansart, Claude Perrault, and Louis Le Vau, the traditional conception of classical French architecture is established.

Whatever the demands of climate or comfort may be, a theatrical and heroic conception of life predominates. The forecourt, the monumental staircase, the antechamber, and the bedchamber form the scenery in the heroic drama—to which the king's arising in the morning is the overture. The flat Italian roof triumphs at Versailles and the Louvre. Paired columns create greater emphasis, and the colossal order enclosing several storys comes into use. Façades are crowned with pediments. But just as the cult of the *honnête homme* slowly replaced the cult of the hero, and the desire to please finally supplanted the need to be imposing, the architects at the end of the Great Reign concerned themselves more and more with pleasing the senses and striving after comfort: the time of the Rococo was at hand.

10

11. Hôtel Rohan-Soubise, designed by P.-A. Delamair in 1704. The building was begun by him and continued by Gabriel and Boffrand after 1712. Although begun under Louis XIV, it was completed in the Louis XV style. The building, flanked by two low wings on the cour d'honneur, is notable for its fine proportions and its combination of dignity and grace.

At the beginning, open spaces around the château were still strategically important, in order to prevent a sudden assault. Under Louis XIV the gardens were completely subordinated to the architectural plan. The lawns, ponds, flower beds, walks, and terraces were subjected to a rigorous geometrical arrangement. The original strategic requirement was replaced by the desire for views, in as many directions as possible. Nature was chained by mathematical designs which prescribed a tremendous number of combinations of straight and curved lines. Perfect symmetry was desired. By clipping yews and boxwoods, nature itself was put in order. It became a maze, an arcade, a wall, a niche, a great hall, a theater.

SCULPTURE Sculpture is par excellence the art of a period oriented toward heroism and glory. It is the obligatory adornment of palaces and gardens. It shares in the prestige of antiquity and in that of the religious revival of the Counter Reformation. Although it is completely subject to an academic antiquarianism and is constantly tied down to rules and proportions of the human body, during the second half of the seventeenth century it finds many ways for expressing itself. Pierre Puget gives free rein to his southern creativity. Puget's striving for fire and movement shows the influence of Bernini, but to it is added the power, even the violence, of a Rubens. Long before Wölfflin gave his definition of the Baroque, Delacroix had made the accusation that the *Diogenes* of Puget was the work of a painter and not of a sculptor. It is true that Puget left his contours intentionally vague. He is the most original of French Baroque sculptors; as a result, he is a solitary figure.

Concern for psychological truth, and undoubtedly the influence of the theater as well, gave rise in some artists to a striving for dramatic composition, which we find both in Girardon's tomb of Richelieu and in his group, *Apollo Served by the Nymphs*, although the latter was later altered in arrangement. The power of life and the analysis of human feeling were soon to win over the abstraction and formality of allegory. Antoine Coysevox was the sculptor of busts in which the realism is striking. Whereas the academic canons of beauty bade the artist strive for absolute perfection and for the greatest beauty which could be drawn from the various living models, Coysevox was able to seize the most fleeting expressions. With Nicolas Coustou (1658–1733) sculpture became less grandiloquent, more elegant. Soon the witty anecdote and the graceful attitude were to be expressed in full freedom by Lemoyne, Bouchardon, Houdon, and Falconet, who belong fully to the eighteenth century.

12. Part of the gardens at Versailles, with the palace. The landscape architect André Le Nôtre worked on the gardens about 1662–90. Nature is subordinate to play of straight and curved lines. In this way, classicism seeks to establish the mastery of reason over the dark forces of instinct and imagination.

13. Tomb of Richelieu, 1675–77, by François Girardon, in the church of the Sorbonne, Paris. This sculpture shows the influence of the art of the theater. Richelieu wanted himself shown, not in a prayerful attitude, but as commending himself to God. 14, 15. Devotion to models from antiquity did not prevent Antoine Coysevox (1640–1720) from doing remarkable realistic work, as is seen in the irony and solidity of the scholar in the bust of Antoine Arnauld (14) and in the fire of the conqueror in the bust of Louis II, the Grand Condé (15).

14

15

16

16. Apollo's Chariot, by Jean-Baptiste Tuby, in the Bassin d'Apollon, in the gardens at Versailles.

17

17. *The King Takes the Government into His Hands, painting by Charles Le Brun in the Galerie des Glaces at Versailles. In this picture Le Brun enlists all the gods of Olympus. The cult of the monarch and the cult of antiquity merge in the mythological allegory.* 18. *Mary Magdalen Penitent, by Charles Le Brun. Such grandiloquence is in sharp contrast to the sobriety of the work of Philippe de Champaigne (see page 93).*

18

19

19. *Louis XIV and His Family, by Nicolas de Largillière (1656–1746). Largillière foreshadows the family portraits of the eighteenth century. The dog in the foreground gives an anecdotal element that contrasts with the pomposity, of Le Brun's work.*

20. Madame de Grignan, by Pierre Mignard (1612–95), a portrait not altogether free from affectation.
21. Madonna with Bunch of Grapes, by Mignard. The gracefulness of the conception shows Italian influence.

22. Camp of Louis XIV before Tournai, by Adam Frans van der Meulen, 1669. This court painter made a number of military scenes for Louis XIV, maintaining a calm narrative manner indicative of his Flemish origin.

PAINTING   Theories of beauty, in the reign of Louis XIV, reflected the heroic ideal of the time.

Félibien writes to Colbert that painting should "compete with poetry and eloquence to make great men immortal." Painting must be earnest; it must give moral support and above all be in the service of the king's policies. It must be subject to strict rules, respectful to antiquity, and in agreement with nature, truth, and the understanding. Even when Poussin is treating a biblical or religious subject, he tries to adhere to the aesthetics of antiquity, which is the official doctrine of the Académie Royale de Peinture et de Sculpture (founded in 1648). When he evokes Greece or Egypt, he gives the landscape a Latin cast, with only the slightest concession to local color. In his late version of *Eliezer and Rebecca*, he avoids painting the camels that the Bible mentions. The reason is that according to the French artistic principles of the seventeenth century, the camel signifies a concession to the picturesque, to local color, to the particular truth, which is less true than absolute truth.

Charles Perrault (brother of the architect) proclaims that it is not merely a question of imitating nature, "which is a talent in which there is no need to compete with the Flemish painters," but that French artists should try to go beyond this and attain something complete and divine that lies outside the individual. When conflict between the supporters of Rubens and of Poussin breaks out (1671), Poussin's partisans appealed to absolute truth.

Le Brun explains that drawing is to be given precedence over color, since drawing enables us to see the truth of things while color only shows single accidental aspects. Indeed, drawing seems to be nobler, especially since it can be considered a science, whereas color is bound to theory (Félibien). On the other hand, Rogar de Piles asserts that a good drawing, which is a product of diligent labor, becomes a question of habit, while chiaroscuro and harmony comprise endless reasoning. The effort is made, via the most rational byways of aesthetics, to raise painting to the dignity of a speculative science.

The engravers no longer have the realistic fantasy of a Callot, and still less the lofty nobility of an Abraham Bosse. What they lose in originality they gain in technique. Woodcuts are more and more neglected, in favor of copper engraving and etching. Jean Morin tries to get more depth into his prints by stippling. Most of the engravers that work for the king's collection illustrate his military campaigns and his festivities. Engraved portraits become more common. Edelinck of Antwerp makes his copper prints after pictures by Le Brun, Philippe de Champaigne, and Largillière. Naturally, the development of engraved illustrations is one reason for the flourishing of scientific and technical literature, and later on for the success of fashion plates.

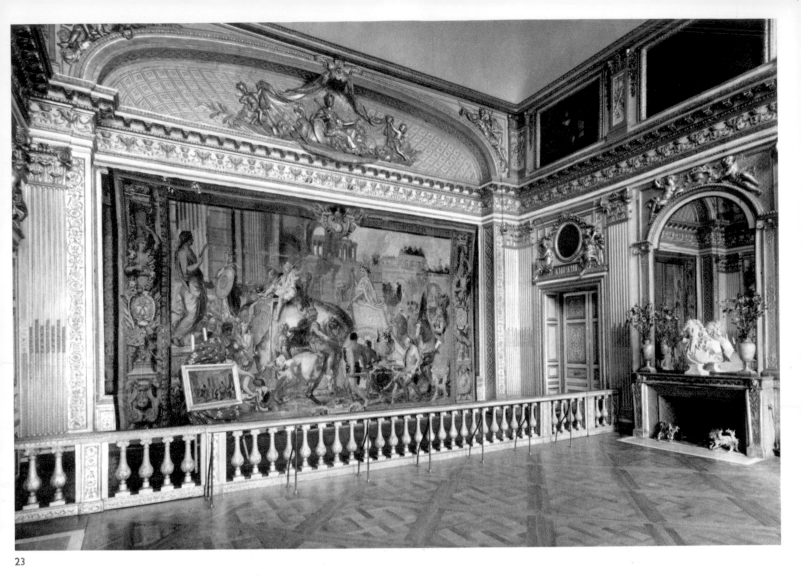

INTERIORS, FURNITURE, DECORATION, AND MINOR ARTS In the field of furniture, too, the Louis XIV style contrasts with the earlier stiffness of the Louis XIII and the subsequent refined elegance of the Louis XVI. This style is above all a matter of luxury and ornament. After the establishment of the Manufacture Royale des Meubles de la Couronne in 1667, furniture was made under official control. Colbert entrusted the management of the institution to Le Brun, and industry was brought under the authority of the Manufacture des Gobelins.

Mazarin had brought many craftsmen with him from Italy. Some of them, such as Cucci, Caffieri, and Megliorini, went into the Gobelins. They introduced into France a furniture style in the spirit of the Italian Baroque, with abundant decoration and variety of materials. Charles André Boulle gave his name to a characteristic style. He uses the most varied materials alongside each other, such as precious woods, copper, tin, tortoise shell, and mother-of-pearl. In one piece the background will be of tortoise shell with copper decoration, and in its companion piece the background will be copper and the decoration tortoise shell. Finely chased ormolu mounts serve to reinforce the joints. These decorations represent the most diversified objects: sphinxes, acanthus and other leaves, deer and goat feet, lion's claws. The vertical line still is clearly dominant. But the identity of the parts begins to fuse in the harmony of the whole. For

23. The Chambre du Roi in the palace of Versailles, used by Louis XIV from 1701 on, the background of the complicated ceremonies of his arising and retiring. 24. Chambre des Gardes de la Reine (1679–81) in the southern wing of the palace of Versailles. Geometrical decoration is dominant; the ceiling painting is by Nicolas Coypel. 25. The Galerie des Glaces, Versailles, 1678–84, by J.-Hardouin Mansart, 240 feet long, 34 feet wide, 43 feet high. Seventeen windows opening onto the garden face seventeen mirrors, the resulting reflections providing optical compensation for the enormous length of the gallery.

some commodes the curved line that foreshadows the Louis XV style is used, both in the shape of the chest proper and in the legs. Cabinets present a characteristically architectural appearance, with columns, arches, niches for statuettes, and false perspectives in which inlaid ivory and ebony imitate inlaid stone floors.

In the seventeenth century the bedchamber was a reception room. The bed itself was a luxurious piece of furniture, giving more prominence to the art of the upholsterer than to that of the cabinetmaker. The bed furnishings match the other furniture of the room, and consist, among other things, of the canopy, the back of which rests on corner posts or is suspended; sometimes it is in the form of a dome. In chairs, at the outset, the vertical line predominated, reminding us of the Louis XIII *fauteuils*. The back rises a yard above the seat, which is covered with brocade or velvet, and is now quite low. The connections between the legs are in the form of an X or an H. Toward the end of the seventeenth century, chair backs become lower. The line of the armrests and of the rungs becomes more rounded. Either side of the back of the *fauteuil* forms a wing, so that it becomes a forerunner of the *bergère*, the upholstered armchair of the Louis XV style. A large number of pieces of furniture were made of chased silver. In 1689 and in 1709, by order of the king, these were melted down, along with large numbers of other silver objects.

When piety reached the court, the art of the goldsmith enjoyed a new prosperity for religious objects. Tinware came back into fashion, after silverware was melted down. The bronze and copper in the Boulle pieces, on the other hand, were an integral part of the furniture, and made it very sturdy. The faïences of Nevers and Rouen tried to compete with those of Delft, but they too only flourished when the silver services were melted down. Moustiers and Rouen competed with the Netherlands in the imitation of Chinese designs. Leather was less used than it had been for wall hangings and upholstery, but took the place of parchment for most bookbindings. The binders of the age of Louis XIV are less original than their predecessors Clovis Ève, Le Gascon, and Florimont Radier, or those who followed them in the eighteenth century, as Pasdeloup, Derôme, and Dubuisson. Calf was used and, for expensive bindings, morocco. A form of bookbinding that was more and more used was the style *à la Du Seuil*, whose characteristic feature was a double fillet forming a rectangle, with flowers at the corners. The royal volumes, often made on the stamping press and in series, are provided with the royal arms, surrounded by a border of leaves. They are usually in red morocco.

Henri IV, who wished to reestablish the tapestry industry in Paris, renewing an old tradition, had workers brought to Paris from Flanders. Their ateliers maintained themselves during the reign of

26. Savonnerie pile carpet; composition typical of the age of Louis XIV: medallions, straight lines, and semicircles. One of a series of ninety-two for the Grande Galerie of the Louvre, ordered by the king.

27. Spring, wall tapestry, from the Gobelins factory, after a cartoon by Charles Le Brun. The heyday of allegory: even the rhythm of the seasons must contribute to the glorification of the warrior king.

Louis XIII and supplied Colbert with the first workers when the Manufacture des Gobelins was set up in 1662, with Le Brun as director. He gave his workers an extremely severe training, and by having them copy oil paintings, made the art of tapestry dependent on the art of painting. Thus *The Hunt of Meleager and Atalanta* (Louvre) was made as a cartoon for a tapestry. Many of these tapestries glorify Louis XIV. Toward the end of the seventeenth century tapestry managed to escape from under the thumb of painting. From 1664 on, Beauvais ateliers supplied works to private clients, while the Gobelins filled royal orders exclusively. The carpets of the Savonnerie and the wall tapestries of Beauvais broke free from painting and formed their own manner; symmetrical decoration becomes more and more important, at the expense of subject matter. This decoration comprises an enormous variety of motifs: birds, leaves, flowers, arabesques, and grotesques.

Page 93. Mother Cathérine–Agnès and Sister Cathérine de Sainte-Suzanne, by Philippe de Champaigne, 1662. With great sobriety, this Jansenist artist paints the calm piety of these two nuns of the Port-Royal.

Page 94. Above : Tapestry representing the visit of Louis XIV to the Manufacture des Gobelins. Below : Portrait of the painter and his family, by Nicolas de Largillière.

28

29

28. Taboret, Louis XIV style. The shell on the rung still has a stiffness that is to give way to greater fantasy and flexibility in the Louis XV and Louis XVI styles. 29. Settee with embroidered upholstery. 30, 32. Chest (30) and commode (32) designed by A.-C. Boulle (1642–1732). The rich metal trimmings and inlay are typical of Boulle furniture. 31. Armchair, known as a "confessional," with upholstered wings, a forerunner of the bergère of the Louis XV style.

31

32

30

33

34

35

COSTUME Up to the end of the seventeenth century, men's clothing was overloaded with decorations, such as gold braid, ribbons, and lace. The colors were violent. Until 1680 noblemen wore the *rhingrave*, a sort of wide short skirt covering the knee breeches, a fashion introduced in the Palatinate around 1660. The *justaucorps* was a kind of upper garment that as a rule likewise covered the breeches. Under the *justaucorps* was worn a sleeved vest, richly embroidered in front and of plain linen or laced tight in back. The whole costume was fastened with cords and knots concealed in a mass of ribbons. Men's wigs were no longer so capacious by the end of the century. The hats had straight brims, decorated with plumes and ribbons, until about 1700 they were replaced by three-cornered hats with turned-up brims.

Women's costumes consisted of a décolleté dress with short sleeves, a wide underskirt, and a long tight bodice. The underskirt was covered by a skirt with tucked-up hems, pleated flounces, and a train whose length was prescribed by etiquette. About 1665 women wore their hair longer, and about 1675 even down to the shoulders, *coiffure à la hurluberlu*. About 1685 the hair formed an elevation decorated with a *fontange*, a headdress named after Mademoiselle de Fontanges, a mistress of Louis XIV, and consisting of starched and pleated muslin or lace held straight on the head by copper wire, sometimes decorated with a ribbon. During the last years of the century various factors—political reverses, financial difficulties, the development of taste, and royal piety—caused aesthetic doctrine in the field of clothing to tend more toward simplicity.

33. Silver candlestick, Paris, 1717–18. A late work that still keeps the stiff baluster form. 34. Table, gilt wood with marble top, end of seventeenth century. Designed to be set against the wall, it was decorated on only

three sides. 35. Rouen faïence, decorated with the lambrequin ornament that came into use under Louis XIV. Blue on white background. 36. A la Du Seuil binding, with the arms of Louis XIV. 37. Title page by

Chauveau for Racine's Andromaque, in the 1676 and 1697 editions. The drapery gives an effect of movement that already announces the eighteenth century. 39. Engraving by Antoine Trouvain, showing Louis XIV with

members of the royal family and nobles playing billiards. Note the interior, the costume, and the low temperature that prevailed in the palace of Versailles (muffs worn by men).

37

38

EXPANSION OF FRENCH CULTURE ABROAD   The absolutism of Le Roi Soleil assured France of a hegemony that was hardly affected by the military and financial disasters of the end of his reign. What was especially widespread in Europe was not only the French language, which was spoken by portions of the aristocracy as far away as Russia, but French literature, wit, and art as well. The revocation of the Edict of Nantes had already caused the emigration of many French craftsmen. In the eighteenth century there were many Frenchmen among the goldsmiths of Amsterdam and The Hague, whose biblical given names betrayed their Protestant origin. After 1715 French architects spread out over Europe. French sculptors became more and more important, often overshadowing native sculptors in their own countries.

French painters worked in Madrid and in London (Montagu House). Watteau visited London the year before he died in 1721, though his influence on Gainsborough was to be mainly through Gravelot, who was in London later on. When the Academy of Fine Arts at St. Petersburg was founded in 1758, the instruction in painting was entrusted to Frenchmen. Many foreign artists got their education in France. Thus, the Europe of the Age of Enlightenment was penetrated with French influences. Many palaces were built abroad under the influence of Versailles: La Granja in Spain, Hampton Court (the Wren wing) in England, Het Loo in Holland, Potsdam and Hannover in Germany, Schönbrunn in Austria, and Beloeil in Belgium. The architects were no longer satisfied with imitations of the main palace at Versailles: they also copied the auxiliary buildings, such as Marly, the Trianons, and the Hermitage. Imitations of Le Nôtre's gardens were to be found in most countries of Europe, and especially in England, although many of these were later altered with changes in taste. Mention should also be made of the enormous popularity of royal squares *à la française* throughout Europe, whose architecture served as framework for the statue of the ruler. Those statues themselves, when they were made abroad, were the work of Frenchmen or copied French models. With these proofs of the spread of French art, the vogue for allegorical ceiling paintings, tapestries, and royal paintings should also be mentioned. Le Brun and Rigaud were to have disciples and followers almost everywhere: Louis Laguerre in London, Pesne at Potsdam, Silvestre in Dresden, and Chauveau and Fouquet at the royal palace in Stockholm.

We may well raise the question of whether the spread of French art in Europe had a beneficial effect on the other national schools. It is quite possible that in many cases it served to inhibit the spontaneous expression of a national spirit. In the eighteenth century many critics opposed the Gallomania of their contemporaries. But the influence of French art continued all through the Age of Enlightenment down to the French Revolution. And the Empire Style, though vastly different from the style of Louis XIV, maintained French influence down to the middle of the nineteenth century.

1

EIGHTEENTH CENTURY

POLITICAL AND SOCIAL LIFE The world of the eighteenth century was dominated by a few European kingdoms. France was governed, in sequence, by three Louis (with a regency intervening), by a committee, and by a consul who became an emperor. England was under William of Orange (who was also stadtholder of Holland, until 1702), then under Anne, and, from 1714 on, under three Hanoverian Georges. After the Peace of Westphalia (1648), Germany consisted of a large number of small states, with frequent wars of succession. Prussia became a powerful German state under King Frederick II (the Great). Hapsburgs bearing the title of Kaiser, inherited from Charlemagne, ruled in Austria; Maria Theresa and Joseph II ruled as despots "enlightened" by reason. Peter the Great (until 1725) and Catherine II (after 1762) were Russian rulers outstanding for their contacts with the West. In 1776 thirteen colonies in North America declared themselves independent of England. The Southern Netherlands passed from Spanish to Austrian possession in 1713. The Northern Netherlands were a football of international politics.

The middle classes gradually came to oppose the very narrow circle from which their rulers were chosen. Kings and princes had absolute power; even if Louis XIV did not say, "*L'état, c'est moi*," it was the maxim he applied. There were, to be sure, legislative bodies representing the people that could give advice, but neither the ruler nor his ministers were required to give public account of their actions nor to be responsible for them. After 1750, voices were heard that openly criticized this state of affairs. Victor Mirabeau in France demanded in a pamphlet, *L'Ami des Hommes* (1756), that Louis XV be a *roi pasteur* (shepherd) in place of an untouchable *roi soleil;* and in a book on taxes (*Théorie de l'Impôt*, 1760) asserted coolly that the position of a king as head of the nation was only justified so long as he was worth more than he cost. Frederick II of Prussia was probably fishing for compliments when he called himself "the first servant of the state." Along with the king, there were often prominent citizens who as ministers put their personal imprint on the government. In England, for example, there were William Pitt, and his son of the same name. In 1716 France called in the Scottish banker John Law to help put the public finances in order, an effort that ended in failure by and large. Jacques Necker, the French minister, was the first, in 1781, to publish a financial statement, which showed, to universal indignation, what enormous amounts the royal establishment at Versailles cost. In England the press published accounts of actions in Parliament from 1775 on.

Voltaire said, in a cosmopolitan way, that he would like to see Frederick II of Prussia as the head of the state and the English as its citizens. Montesquieu and Voltaire pointed out the limitations of narrow nationalism, and showed that climate and soil had a strong influence on the character of a people, and hence on its constitution and laws. François Quesnay and A. R. G. Turgot regarded agriculture as a purely productive human activity, and the only real basis for the economy and organization of the state. This school of thought, the Physiocrats, studied the circulation of commodities and opposed any artificial restrictions of it, for example, by means of import and export duties, as were applied under the mercantilist policies of Colbert. Agricultural methods in general did not undergo significant changes before 1800 from the age-old practices, except for reforms in England.

PHILOSOPHY, RELIGION, AND SCIENCE Culture was more and more the affair of the educated bourgeoisie, which strove to keep abreast of scientific research, theories, technological inventions and improvements, and the critical discussion of art and letters. French was read throughout the educated world, but the great majority of people were illiterate. Voluminous reference works were produced in order to satisfy the great demand for knowledge. One of the first was the *Dictionnaire Historique et Critique* of Pierre Bayle (Rotterdam, 1695–97). A copy was deposited in the Bibliothèque Mazarine in Paris, and it was said that before the library opened in the morning, a queue formed of people who wanted to study Bayle's work; but this may have been not so much for the sake of pure learning as for the piquant details and anecdotes that Bayle spiced his articles with. Much more universal in conception was the *Encyclopédie*, edited by Diderot and d'Alembert, for which Voltaire, Rousseau, Mirabeau, Montesquieu, Euler, Turgot, and Quesnay also wrote articles. The work was in 35 volumes, and appeared between 1751 and 1780.

1. *The Philosopher Monkey, or the Monkey Numismatist, 1740, by J. B. S. Chardin (1669–1779). This is how the sober citizen regarded the more learned occupations; perhaps a caricature of Voltaire is intended (cf. the statue of Voltaire by Houdon, Fig. 16).*
2. *St. Martin-in-the-Fields, London, 1721–26, by James Gibbs (1682–1754); combination of Gothic (tower), classic (columns, pediment), and Baroque (spacious hall interior) forms. 3. Interior of the Church of Ste. Geneviève (after the Revolution, called the Panthéon) in Paris, built 1760–90 by J. G. Soufflot (1713–80) and others. He tried to combine elements from the classic (giant Corinthian order), Gothic (open arches between cornice and vault), and Baroque (domical structure of Wren's St. Paul's). 4. The Circus at Bath, 1754, by John Wood (1704–54), a unit within a city plan based on classicistic uniformity.*
5. *Ecole Militaire, Paris, 1754–75, by J. A. Gabriel (1698–1782), a long Renaissance palazzo with the center emphasized by a typically Baroque projecting portico with pediment, and crowned by a four-sided dome.*

D'Alembert regarded the art of instructing and enlightening man as one of the noblest of human gifts; Diderot wrote in his article on *Encyclopédie* that "man is the only goal that we must have in mind and to which everything must be related." In Germany an even more learned and thorough work appeared, *Grosses vollständiges Universal-Lexicon aller Wissenschaften und Künste*, in 64 volumes, published at Halle, 1732–54. England published its *Encyclopaedia Britannica* at Edinburgh, 1771; Italy the *Nuovo Dizionario Scientifico e Curioso Sacro-Profano* at Venice, 1746–51; and Brockhaus's *Konversations-Lexikon* was published at Leipzig in 1796–1808. Periodicals, aiming to entertain as well as inform, were also established. In England *The Tatler*, *The Spectator*, and *The Guardian* appeared (in 1709, 1711, and 1713, respectively). Addison wrote in *The Spectator*: "It was said of Socrates, that he brought Philosophy down from Heaven, to inhabit among Men; and I shall be ambitious to have it said of me, that I have brought Philosophy out of Closets and Libraries, Schools and Colleges, to dwell in Clubs and Assemblies, at Tea-Tables and in Coffee-Houses." Following Addison's example, Justus van Effen founded *De Hollandsche Spectator* in 1731; *Le Spectateur Français* appeared in 1722; and in Germany appeared the exclusively literary *Briefe die neueste Literatur betreffend* (1759). Applied science and technology were made popular by the formation of societies which were connected with museums where machines, apparatus, laboratory equipment, and models for as yet unperfected inventions were exhibited to the public. The Teylers Stichting was founded in 1778 in Holland, the Conservatoire des Arts et Métiers in France in 1794, and the Royal Institution of Great Britain in London in 1799. Systematic attention was given to population density, with statistics mainly based on estimates drawn from samples of the numbers of births, deaths, and marriages. About 1780, the population of France was estimated at 25 million, and there were even statistics as to the distribution into the various classes of society. In 1801 Great Britain had 9 million, in 1750 Sweden had 2 million, in 1770 Russia 17 million, and about 1800 Paris had 500,000 inhabitants.

Consideration of the population figures obtained by statistical methods conjured up the specter of overpopulation. On the ground of estimates by Robert Wallace, a Scottish philosopher (that the population doubles every thirty-three years), Thomas Malthus, in the *Essay on the Principle of Population* (1798), came to the amazing conclusion that no matter how fast food production grew, it could not keep pace with the population: within the foreseeable future, the world would go down in a frightful war for food. An important gain in food production was the potato, which became the largest item of diet by the end of the eighteenth century. The rest of the basic daily menu consisted of beans, pickled vegetables, wheat bread, fish, dairy products, eggs, meat, and sugar, by now very cheap. In the course of the century the customary preserving techniques (drying, salting, smoking) were supplemented by new methods:

6. Stupinigi, hunting lodge of the royal court at Turin, 1729, by F. Juvara (1678–1736). Instead of a rectangular arrangement of buildings as at Versailles, the parts of the structure are grouped more playfully, around an inner square and the round main pavilion. 7. Church and monastery at Zwiefalten (Swabia), seen from the west. By J. M. Fischer (1691–1766); fancy-free Rococo architecture, with the main decorative elements of the church façade emphasizing the vertical. 8. Interior of the church at Zwiefalten; the curving lines running into each other and bounding the spaces and divisions are covered with festive decoration in light, gay colors.

6

7

8

9

9. Staircase of the episcopal Residenz at Würzburg, 1740–60, by Balthasar Neumann and J. L. von Hildebrandt, with a great ceiling fresco, 1750–53, by G. B. Tiepolo. Tiepolo constructed his composition partly on the basis of the architectural design of the staircase. 10. Staircase of the house at Lange Vijverberg 8, The Hague, designed by Daniel Marot, 1715, who introduced the stucco ceiling into Holland.

11. Royal Theater, The Hague, designed by P. de Swart as the Nassau Weilburg palace, 1763. The crescent-shaped forecourt shows a handling of space typical of the second half of the century.

11

evaporation, freezing, and canning, making it possible to transport many foods over long distances. In wealthier circles a fork had been used at table since 1750. Tea, coffee, and, unfortunately, gin, because of its very low price, were the usual daily beverages. In London the gin shops advertised, "Drunk for a penny, dead drunk for twopence." When people began to barter their clothes for gin, the municipal authorities tried to set up counterpropaganda, "Beer is best!"

Traveling was made more comfortable by improvements in the springs and cushions of coaches; the highest average speed, eleven miles an hour, was only reached by the big yellow mail coaches with green upholstery. In 1776 France projected its system of *routes nationales,* the width of the road depending on its importance. By 1800 the French road system had a total length of 25,000 miles. Around 1800, John McAdam, a Scottish engineer, developed an improved system of making roads. Paris had had the Ecole des Ponts et Chaussées since 1747, where practical road construction was studied. Everywhere the population had been required, for centuries, to work on the roads, supplying men and teams. The Alps could only be passed on foot or by pack animal; the monasteries on the St. Bernard and St. Gotthard passes sheltered yearly 30,000 pilgrims on their way to Rome. Most large cities had water supply systems consisting, up to 1760, of elm-wood pipes ten inches in diameter, and later of cast-iron pipes.

Care of the human body came to be of more importance after 1770. The German Johann Basedow founded a model school in Dessau where mind and body could be trained and hardened; he also sketched a method of teaching languages without grammar. Johann Pestalozzi, a Swiss, introduced a method of education in Zurich that included bodily exercises. Extreme, and famous, was the institution for body building at Pressnitz in the forests of Saxony, where at the break of dawn the pupils took a dip in the mountain brook.

There was great activity in the field of technology. In France, René Antoine de Réaumur worked on a method for producing steel. In Sweden, Emanuel Swedenborg and Christopher Polhem improved ore mining and metallurgy; Swedish iron production rose from 32,000 tons in 1720 to 51,000 in 1739. Especially in England, where the most important fuel, wood, was becoming scarce, coal mining was pushed. Abraham Darby, in 1709, first used coal instead of wood in smelting iron. Since many factories used water power for their machinery, these had been built in narrow valleys with rapid streams, and water power also gradually became scarce. At first, attempts

were made to improve the situation by using the steam pumps developed by Thomas Newcomen around 1700 to pump water up to higher levels for the watermills. At the same time, it had been calculated that no watermill could deliver more than five horsepower. On the basis of the scientific discoveries of Professor Black in Glasgow, James Watt replaced the reciprocating motion of Newcomen's steam machines by a powerful rotary motion. This opened the way to the rapid growth of industrial cities, preferably in the vicinity of coal-mining regions.

The contact seen here between scientific research and technological practice was characteristic of the eighteenth century. The scientists Antoine Lavoisier and Michael Faraday contributed greatly to technical progress. In order to determine the results of researches as accurately as possible, efforts were made to set up international units of measurement. Réaumur, Fahrenheit, and Celsius developed methods for measuring temperatures; the French Academy of Sciences defined as the unit of length the "meter," a ten-millionth part of a meridian. Radical improvements in large boring machines made it possible to make great progress in the construction of steam engines, by making the bore of the cylinders so precise that practically no steam could escape between the piston and the cylinder. The textile industry developed rapidly by the invention of spinning machines, satisfying the growing demand for yarn. Chemists, especially in Scotland, sought to produce the alkali, previously obtained from seaweed, that was needed for making soap. The buttermilk that had traditionally been employed for bleaching and dyeing textiles was replaced by sulfuric acid in 1750 and by chlorine after 1790. In 1783 Jan Pieter Minckelers, a Louvain professor, discovered the possibility of gas lighting.

The exact sciences were furthered, among others, by the Swiss family Bernoulli, their countryman Euler, and the two Frenchmen Lagrange and Monge (founders of descriptive geometry). The astronomers Newton and William Herschel developed the mirror telescope; Halley published an atlas of the southern constellations and discovered the comet that bears his name. Chaldni studied sound vibrations in rigid bodies. After Lavoisier and Black, Herman Boerhaave, professor at Leyden, studied heat; he composed a handbook of chemistry, *Elementa Chemiae.* Using a jar, later called the Leyden jar, Professor Musschenbroek of Leyden discovered that electricity can be collected and stored; he also studied the expansion of materials by heating. Inspired by observations of his countryman Galvani, Volta in Italy designed an apparatus that could deliver electricity

12

12. In the Seneffe Palace, Belgium, about 1760, by L. B. Dewez, classical decoration almost overpowers the simple building; giant pilasters enclose the two storys, and the central pediment rises against the balustraded parapet. Flanking Ionic colonnades form a harmonious extension of the building. 13. The façade of the Huis Osterrieth, Antwerp, by J. P. van Baurscheit II (1699–1768), shows a fine combination of playful Rococo decorative forms with strict, regular flat organization of the wall. The entrance is emphasized greatly by the heavy frame and crowning ornamental feature.

13

14. Winter Palace, Leningrad, by Rastrelli. The continuous undulation of the window heads is contrasted with the strong verticals of the attached columns. 15. Bronze portrait bust of Diderot, 1777, by J. B. Pigalle (1714–85). 16. Terracotta model for a posthumous portrait of Voltaire, about 1780, by J. A. Houdon (1741–1828).

Page 103. Above: Francesco Guardi, Departure of the Bucentaur. Below: Antonio Canaletto, View of Eton College.

15

16

17. Portrait of Voltaire, Seated Nude on a Rock, 1776, by J. B. Pigalle. Attempt at classical glorification, emerging as rather ridiculous because of Voltaire's meager physique. It is not known whether Pigalle's caricature was intentional or unintentional. 18. Bronze relief, about 1730–40, by G. R. Donner (1693–1741), The Judgment of Paris. Although elegant attitudes in the eighteenth-century taste are recognizable, the excessive attention to anatomical detail and the subject strongly suggest the sixteenth-century Mannerism of the school of Fontainebleau. 19. Pulpit in the Old Catholic Church, The Hague, by J. B. Xavery, 1729, altered 1742; very mobile forms, but with the rather heavy ornament of the Louis XIV style.

20. Portrait of Councilor Van Caversen, 1713, by M. van de Voort. The style is connected with French portrait style at the court of Louis XIV. The facial expression is very vividly rendered.

Page 104. Jean-Baptiste Oudry, Still Life with Pâté, 1743.

21. The Three Divine Virtues, by L. Delvaux. The intertwining forms are characteristic, and are found in the painting and graphic arts of the time as well. The group was made in 1767 for Robert de Bavay, Abbé of Villers.

22

(forerunner of dry cells and storage batteries). Coulomb in France studied the magnetic forces produced by electric currents. Linnaeus, the Swedish botanist, developed a consistent system of plant classification. Medicine profited by the results of Jenner's use of vaccination (England, 1796). Boerhaave tried to free medical science from mysterious and alchemistic quackery and fake cures. He made rational use of medicinal herbs, and also reorganized the medical faculty of the University of Vienna. J. Ingenhousz discovered the influence of light and air on the growth of plants (*On the Nutrition of Plants*, 1796). The psyche and behavior of man were studied (Condillac, Bonnet) and, along with them, human society; principles were deduced for increased well-being and welfare. Adam Smith was a pioneer in economics; his book, *Inquiry into the Nature and Causes of the Wealth of Nations* (1776), laid the foundations for the concepts and terminology of economic science. He regarded the division of labor as the prerequisite for the growth of industry.

Eighteenth-century historians became critical of their literary sources; quite independently of the differences among writers, they inquired into the intrinsic probability of the reported facts and events. Voltaire was one of the first to view the writing of history as more than a chronological listing of political events. He looked for a connection among happenings, not confining himself to the political domain but giving at least as much attention to religion, art, and finance. The Bollandists rendered service to the writing of history with their *Acta Sanctorum*. Art history, which since the sixteenth century had been limited to lives of the artists, was given an entirely new aspect by J. J. Winckelmann's *Geschichte der Kunst des Altertums* (1764). The forms of the works of art themselves were carefully described, and Winckelmann arrived at the theory that art itself went through an evolution, birth-growth-maturity-decay, of which the artists were unaware.

Philosophy culminated in the work of Immanuel Kant. In his *Critique of Pure Reason* (1781) he studied man's ability to know. In addition to knowledge from experience (which up to then had been regarded by humanist thinkers as the main source of knowledge), there was also knowledge that man can have without experience, knowledge not accessible by the understanding alone. As in the domain of worldly authority, the thinking portion of mankind became more and more critical of the authority of the Church, which strove to yield no ground. On the one hand there was increasing tolerance for the convictions of other people, and on the other in various countries certain religious groups were discriminated against. In England and Holland, Roman Catholics could not hold public office, nor could Protestants (Huguenots) in France. Except for Russia and Poland, the order of the Jesuits was suppressed throughout Europe; learned priests of this order had been all too

23

24

26

25

24. *Madame Boucher, 1743, by F. Boucher (1703–70). A good deal airier and less constrained in clothing and attitude, according to the style under Louis XV. The furniture is less heavy, and gracefully curved: side table with drawer, hanging wall shelves (with tea service and porcelain statuette of squatting Chinese), and footstool; the chaise longue, for reclining in a half-sitting position, is a discovery of this period's love of comfort. 25. Portrait of Johann Christian Bach, the composer, who lived for some time in London, by Thomas Gainsborough (1727–88).*

26. *Le Déjeuner de Madame Geoffrin, 1772, by Hubert Robert (1733–1808). This great lady, who set the tone in her time, was a protectress and friend of the circle of Encyclopedists; her furniture and interior are very sober.*

27. *Visitors at the Salon du Louvre 1769, where recent paintings were shown. Drawing by G. de Saint-Aubin (1724–80). The artist wrote little comments here and there, perhaps for painting from the sketch later.*

27

28

28. Presentation in the Temple, painting by Jacob de Wit, 1742, now in the Old Catholic Church of Delft. De Wit was a great admirer of Rubens, as can be seen from the spatial composition of this painting, and the postures and garments of the figures. 29. Country Life, by J. van Stry, 1790; one of five wall-paper scenes. An attempt to revive the late-seventeenth-century Dutch landscape style of artists such as Cuyp.

active in the secular aspects of government by way of their key positions as royal advisers. The declining respect for clerical authority was epitomized in the confiscation of all church property by the French National Assembly at the outset of the Revolution (1789); just as Joseph II of Austria had demanded ten years previously, people wanted the clergy to be officers of the state, paid out of the public treasury.

LITERATURE AND DRAMA Interest in literature increased tremendously. More and more books were published and bought. In many houses were found handsome bookcases or desks combined with bookcases, and a great deal of ingenuity was expended on all sorts of library ladders. Many works of French historians or thinkers could also be regarded as belles-lettres: Voltaire, Rousseau, and Montesquieu. Diderot also wrote voluminous art criticism, in which he showed his preferences for the sentimental and for the realistic; that is, for Greuze and for Chardin. André Chénier, under the inspiration of Greek poetry, was the only great French poet. Marivaux, with his polished, clever dialogue, was a successful writer of comedies. Beaumarchais's *Barbier de Séville* and *Mariage de Figaro* are best known in operatic versions, the one by Rossini, the other by Mozart. The improvised form of drama, the *commedia dell'arte*, for which Goldoni provided many subjects, was most in vogue at all the princely courts and in all the big cities at the end of the eighteenth century. The German-speaking regions produced some great poets: Lessing (with whom the *Sturm und Drang* period began), Klopstock, Wieland (*Oberon*), and Herder. The poems and dramas of Schiller and Goethe belong to the immortal heritage of Europe. England made many contributions to world literature: Defoe (*Robinson Crusoe*, 1719), Swift (*Gulliver's Travels*, 1726), Sterne (*A Sentimental Journey*, 1768), Richardson (*Clarissa Harlowe*, 1747–48), Fielding (*Tom Jones*, 1749), Goldsmith (*The Vicar of Wakefield*, 1766); Sheridan had great success with his comedies (*The School for Scandal*, 1777).

30. Self-portrait of J.-B. Suvée, a painter from Bruges, strongly influenced by the style of the young Frenchman J.-L. David, whose self-portrait in the Louvre shows strong resemblances to this work. 31. Wife of the Painter, by Alexander Roslin, a Swedish-born artist, in the fastidious style of French painters of the second half of the eighteenth century.

MUSIC AND DANCE   The eighteenth century was a high period in music in which was developed what we now call the classical style. Forms and practices in use today were perfected then: opera, symphony, sonata, concerto for solo instruments, string quartet. For one thing, the practice of music received great support from the many princes and kings; on the other hand, the public in the growing cities slowly came to take part in musical culture. The concept of chamber music is borrowed from the music of the courts; just as court dignitaries were entitled gentlemen of the chamber, the musicians in a sovereign's service were called chamber musicians. The instruments have remained in use almost unchanged in form and size since 1750. London, Paris, Vienna, and Hamburg were great international music centers. Among the opera composers were Rameau, Handel, Pergolesi, Cimarosa, Gluck, and Mozart. Religious music was dominated by the works of J. S. Bach and G. F. Handel, and later by the styles of Pergolesi, Haydn, and Mozart. Purely instrumental music grew more and more important; all the composers named wrote this kind of composition, as well as Domenico Scarlatti (545 harpsichord sonatas), Daquin, Couperin (harpsichord and organ), Corelli, Vivaldi, Tartini (these three particularly important for violin music), Marcello, C. P. E. Bach, J. C. Bach, Stamitz, Loeillet, Clementi (piano), and Quantz (flute). Many composers were outstanding performers, sometimes more honored as virtuosos than composers by their contemporaries.

The art of dance found a place in the opera, in the form of the intermezzo-ballet; Rameau even composed an entire ballet-opera, *Les Indes Galantes*, which is still played today. Many dance rhythms and dance melodies, strictly stylized, are to be found in the instrumental music of the eighteenth century (minuet, allemande, saraband, courante, gigue).

31

32. *Royal Family of Carlos IV, 1800, by Francisco Goya (1746–1828). Goya's art is unique. He was to become the only painter of the time who reacted strongly to the dramatic episodes arising out of war. This group portrait is vividly painted, with keen characterizations.* 33. *First plate of the book* Analysis of Beauty, *by William Hogarth (1697–1764). This plate illustrates the essence of Hogarth's attempt to find, from examples of all kinds, the one precise line that can be called "The Line of Beauty."*

STYLE AND CONCEPTION Naturally, the greater independence of people's judgments led to a great diversity in points of view. In the fields of science, art, human psychology, and social action, there arose a feeling for investigation that respected nothing and spared neither authority nor feeling. There were at the same time some sentimental impulses that were at least as powerful: love of nature, love for irregular forms (ruins, English gardens), tolerance, and social uplift for the masses (as yet based chiefly on sympathy).

ARCHITECTURE Great interest was shown in the architectural forms of antiquity. In addition to the ancient buildings of Rome, those of Pompeii, Herculaneum, Athens, and Paestum were measured and engraved. Then came an admiration for Gothic architecture, while Italian architecture of the fifteenth and sixteenth centuries was unquestionably admired. At the beginning, however, eighteenth-century architecture still showed the main characteristics of Baroque style: strong vertical links between parts of the structure, interpenetrating spaces, decoration unconfined by horizontal divisions. The century included buildings as diverse as Strawberry Hill (England, 1750–76), the church and monastery of Vierzehnheiligen (near Bamberg, 1743–52), and the Hôtel de Soubise (Paris, 1735).
A synthesis of these varying interests can be found in Soufflot, the

Parisian architect, in whose design for the Panthéon (before the Revolution, Ste. Geneviève) were combined the architectural forms of a Greek temple, a Gothic cathedral, and St. Peter's in Rome.
City planning continued the forms of the seventeenth century. An effort toward unity by grouping and proportion is seen in the Crescent at Bath, the Place Louis XV (since 1795, de la Concorde) in Paris, the Place Royale at Nancy, and the center of Turin.

SCULPTURE Sculpture was still under the influence of the works of the seventeenth-century Italian C. L. Bernini, as well as of the Greek and Roman statues discovered and recorded on engravings during and after the Renaissance. The Laocoön group in Rome was admired as one of the highest achievements of ancient sculpture; Winckelmann's description of it expressed the general admiration. Such sculptors as the Frenchmen Houdon and Pigalle made direct and intimate portraits.

PAINTING One readily tends to regard the festive atmosphere and delicate technique of the works of Watteau, Lancret, Fragonard, Boucher, and Guardi as the image par excellence of eighteenth-century culture. To do this is to ignore the simple, honest civic virtue that speaks from the works of Chardin; the melancholy

34. Copper engraving by G. B. Piranesi (1720–78), fancifully reworking motifs that he had observed in buildings of ancient Rome. 35. Bullfight, about 1816, aquatint by Francisco Goya. The cruelty of the sport is emphasized with great vigor. As the date of the work indicates, this aspect of Goya belongs to the nineteenth century.

35

atmosphere of the ruins in Piranesi and Hubert Robert; the passionate love of nature in Wilson, Crome, and, later, Constable; Hogarth's independent critical humor; the cool, classicist atmosphere of David's scenes of Roman history; Blake's fantastic visions; and Goya's savage satires. This period contains the contrast between the dashing, colorful ceiling paintings of the Venetian Tiepolo and the precise and accurate city views of Canaletto. In Piranesi and Goya the art of etching came to life again.

INTERIOR DECORATION The interiors and furniture in palaces, pavilions, and country mansions give an impression of the rapidly shifting fashion. The fashion came primarily from Paris; its stages are often named for French kings and systems of government. Decorators and furniture designers, in many cases known to us by name, were particularly able workmen. The furniture designs show not only a regard for handsome forms and soft colors, but also increasing adaptation to the postures and conformations of the human body. From the paintings of Chardin, Lancret, or Hogarth, and from innumerable eighteenth-century prints, we get a picture of the decoration and furniture of the homes of the wealthy middle class, in which the official forms of fashion were followed, either completely or very closely.

36. Opera Performance in Rome, painting by Pannini, 1730. The opera being given is La contesa dei Numi (Contest of the Gods), text by Metastasio, music by Leonardo Vinci (1690–1730), it consists of narrative recitatives, alternating with instrumental intermezzi illustrating the story.

36

38

37

37. Still Life with Fruit and Musical Instruments, by F.-A. Desportes (1661–1743). 38. Tea in the English Manner at the Prince de Conti's, by M.-B. Ollivier, 1777. While the gentry enjoy tea and dainties in the very rectilinearly decorated interior, little Wolfgang Amadeus Mozart entertains the gathering at the piano.

The eigtheenth-century taste for playful prettiness was expressed in the porcelain that was made in Europe after 1708 (Meissen, Sèvres), In contrast were the type-face designs, inspired by Roman capital letters, of John Baskerville and Bodoni; the forms were simple, clear. and legible.

COSTUME   The paintings of Watteau give us an idea of the finery of ladies and gentlemen: brightly colored, gleaming materials, broadly extended skirts, and fine laces. Chardin's works, and many contemporary prints, show us people in their everyday dress.
After the pompous, heavy clothing of the Late Baroque, the early eighteenth century accentuated the attractiveness of the figure; the shoulders were narrow and the forms spread out below, so that the clothing of both men and women showed a conical silhouette (Regency). In the case of women, this effect was obtained by stiffening the underskirt with a crinoline of whalebone or metal strips, or by means of a basket (pannier) of reed or whalebone resting on the hips. Women wore a loose robe over these, both in the house and out of doors. During the Rococo period, when the beauty of the figure was still accentuated, women's panniers were replaced by a hoop skirt up to four yards wide, over which the skirt (*jupe*) came.

The body was corseted. The loose upper garment (*robe*) gave the figure the mobility it needed. Such clothing was trimmed with lace, silk ribbons, pleats, and artificial flowers. The small headdress was now powdered white, the face painted in rather garish colors (men as well as women). The skirts of men's coats were made to stand out by the use of paper and horsehair. Knee breeches were fastened by buckles over long stockings. Lace cuffs fell down over the hands. The man's wig, likewise powdered, had rolled curls at the sides; the back hair was tied up. The favorite material for clothing was silk. During the last quarter of the century (Louis XVI) the first fashion prints appeared, as copper engravings. The hoopskirt and *jupe* became shorter, so that something of the leg could be seen. Over them was worn the *caraco*, a jacket or coat, with back pleats. Below, the figure fitting ended in the dome of the skirts; above, in the often enormous headdress, which sometimes served as the foundation for prettily arranged flowers and fruits. The French fashion, itself influenced by the English at one time, was followed by people of prominence over most of Europe. Men's clothing, which in the 1770s consisted of a *justaucorps* with wide cuffs, or coat, vest, and knee breeches, began in the 1780s to follow the more practical English model and became the prototype of present-day clothing.

39. Teapot, white Meissen porcelain with chinoiserie, by J. G. Höroldt, about 1728. 40. Tray, colored earthenware (faïence), made in Kiel. The landscape illustrates the popular taste for ruins.

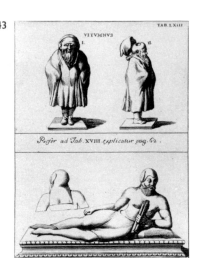

41. Print representing a shop making musical instruments, 1767. Illustration from Diderot's Encyclopédie. 42. Title page of an edition of the Works of Vergil, 1795, type face and typography by G. Bodoni (1740–1813).

43. Illustration from Museum Etruscum, by Gorius (A. F. Gori). This work on the monuments of the ancient Etruscans, published in Florence in 1737, gives an impression of the way in which historical works on ancient art were illustrated.

44. Title page of the first edition of J. J. Winckelmann's history of ancient art. This work, which appeared in 1764, for the first time gave the story of ancient art, as far as it was then known. His work is based on a biological vision of growth, maturity, and decay.

45

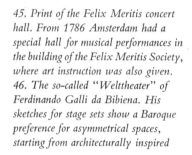

The mannish redingote (from "riding coat"), a long coat closed at the breast, was now worn by ladies too. At the end of the century came the revolutionary fashion: red cap, long red jacket (carmagnole), and long trousers (sans-culottes); the effort was made to design a true revolutionary mode of dress by adopting details of ancient costume (David). Ladies were dressed *à la grecque*: chemise with long train (*à queue de singe*), and sandals. Gentlemen known as the *incroyables* carried the masculine ideal to an extreme: the hair in disorder down to the shoulders ("hounds' ears"), high neckcloth, jacket with high collar and wide lapels, tight breeches, and oversize riding boots. The analogous female type was the *merveilleuse*.

45. Print of the Felix Meritis concert hall. From 1786 Amsterdam had a special hall for musical performances in the building of the Felix Meritis Society, where art instruction was also given. 46. The so-called "Welttheater" of Ferdinando Galli da Bibiena. His sketches for stage sets show a Baroque preference for asymmetrical spaces, starting from architecturally inspired compositions with lively effects of light and shade. 47. Library ladder that can be folded up into a table, after a design by Sheraton, 1791–94. 48. Masquerade à la Grecque, 1771, print by B. Bossi after a design by the architect E.-A. Petitot, ridiculing the solemn earnestness of reproducing precise antiquarian research in objects for decorative use.

46

47

48

LOUIS XV STYLE

GENERAL INTRODUCTION: POLITICAL AND SOCIAL LIFE Versailles had become the model for all of eighteenth-century Europe, but during the last years of the reign of Louis XIV taste in France was already turning away from official pomp. After the death of the king in 1715, some members of the nobility withdrew to their estates in the provinces, others to their *hôtels* in Paris. Groups formed around the regent and the Duchesse du Maine, and for some time there simply was no court. The life of the city supplanted the court life; intimacy came to the fore in society, and a new ritual was established, the ritual of private life.

In the salons of Paris, where financiers, rich bourgeois, writers, and artists mingled with the nobility, a brilliant, witty social life developed, with great freedom in thought, manners, and fashions. People regarded living as a refined art, and art as a higher form of decoration, of social play. Salon conversation set the tone for the expression of thought and feeling.

But underneath the surface a turn in the tide was in the making. Although absolutism remained the typical form of government on the Continent, the foundations of the traditional order were subjected to heavy criticism in every field; even by the beginning of the century the main lines of thinking that were to lead to the great change of 1789 had unfolded. After the death of Louis XIV, who had been able to keep the nobility under his control, the aristocracy reacted just at the moment when the bourgeoisie had become aware of its intellectual, ethical, and economic superiority. In the course of the century, the abuses of the regime by those who were privileged under it were endured less and less patiently; Louis XV, without the slightest concern for such matters, gave free reign to the intrigues of his favorites, the Marquise de Pompadour and the Comtesse du Barry. Meanwhile, important political changes were going on in Europe. During the reigns of Frederick I, Frederick William I, and Frederick II, Prussia became an important power, while Russia was despotically Europeanized under Peter the Great and his successors. The France of Louis XV was rivaled by England, which won commercial and colonial mastery in the course of the century; after the Glorious Revolution and the Bill of Rights of 1689 it had become a model of constitutional and parliamentary government. The hegemony of French culture in Europe reached its highest point about 1750, but from 1715 on, English influence was felt on the Continent, and in France itself.

SCIENCE, PHILOSOPHY, RELIGION The guiding force in culture was a sharpened rationalism originating in Descartes's "method." When freed from Cartesian metaphysics, it went much further and deeper. It now took on the form of free inquiry and subjected all things to analysis by critical reason. Reason, personal thinking, and experience attacked all authorities, institutions, dogmas, prejudices, or superstitions with a dynamic optimism. The new confidence in human understanding was so great that what was found to be rationally incomprehensible was simply denied; thus, any feeling for mystery was impeached. People had learned from Newton's discovery of the law of universal gravitation (*Principia Mathematica Philosophiae Naturalis*, 1687) that the heavens themselves are to be explained by reason. Experimental physics, based on mathematics and free from all metaphysical dogma, was identified with philosophical thinking. It was so much in keeping with the new spirit of the times that it became almost fashionable among intellectuals. Linnaeus and Buffon sought a rational classification of plants and animals, the latter venturing the remark (which he later withdrew) that if it were not for the express statement in the Bible, one would be inclined to look for a common origin for the horse and the donkey, man and the ape.

With the empiricism of John Locke (*An Essay Concerning Human Understanding*, 1690) a new psychology was born, which tried, in the same unmetaphysical spirit, to explain all mental life on the basis of sense experience of the external world. A new picture of man and the world was formed, in which nature, with its immanent laws understandable by reason, was recognized as the only and highest reality. True religion, they insisted, is identical with morality, and this "natural religion" (deism), based on reason and the feeling for good and evil, and common to all men, was contrasted to all dogmas, sacraments, and revelations, especially those of the Roman Catholic Church. A new virtue, that of tolerance, became a feature of the polemics of Montesquieu and Voltaire.

Natural law was opposed to written law and the divine right of kings, while society was reconstructed theoretically; the starting point in this enterprise was the natural state of man, and the structure was explained as a contract between the people and the sovereign. This picture can already be found in Locke, and via Montesquieu it leads to Rousseau's *Contrat Social* (Amsterdam, 1762). The critical spirit also reacted against the literary-rhetorical trend in the writing of history, and demanded scientific study of historical sources. Voltaire was the first to extend his interest to all aspects of human life and to all the world's civilizations. Secularized history became an ensemble of internally meaningful observations, and confidence in the capabilities of the liberated understanding, reinforced by the model of the sciences, aroused the idea of progress. All these ideas, at first mainly theoretical, took on a more and more aggressive tone toward the middle of the century, and the *Encyclopédie*, under the direction of Diderot and d'Alembert, applied them systematically in every domain, while empiricism, materialism, and atheism prevailed. A new type of man was born with the Enlightenment in France, the *philosophe*. As cosmopolitan as the thinking that he incarnated, the type spread throughout Europe.

1. The arcades flanking the Palais du Gouvernement, Nancy, form part of the so-called Hémicycle, one of the series of places of different shapes laid out along one axis by Emmanuel Héré de Corny, 1751–55. 2. The Amalienborg Square in Copenhagen, by Nikolai Eigtved (1701–54), consists of four similar palaces with low, short wings, forming an octagon around the equestrian statue of King Frederik V, where four streets meet. 3. The Place de la Concorde, Paris, 1755–75, an early work by Ange-Jacques Gabriel, is an open space with one axis extending between the Seine and two symmetrical palaces, and the cross axis linking the Tuileries Gardens with the long prospect of the Champs-Elysées. 4. The great stables at Chantilly, by Jean Aubert, are a

Esthetics and the philosophy of history owe much to G. B. Vico, who was the first to recognize the imagination as a specific activity of the mind, out of which myth and art arise; and he was the first to conceive of history as a cyclical evolution of spirit—intuitions of genius that were not to be understood until the Romantics. While criticism shook the objective dogmatic structure of religion by its mockery, true religious life found its refuge in subjective experience, which too belongs to the age by virtue of its individually feeling, mystically tinged character, and which, especially in German pietism after 1730, became a new force with a rich future.

LITERATURE AND DRAMA The intellectual and critical aspect of culture finds its most striking esthetic expression in the vivid clarity and simplicity of the French prose of Voltaire and Montesquieu, but it is likewise the cause of the equally significant dearth of true poetry. Poetry is only to be found where it tries to be nothing more than a witty game. While the old genres persisted, however exhausted, efforts were made to cast the new ideas into new forms. Thus, the novel, a genre for which no rules existed, had a great vogue. In it, the intrigue and the satirical, picturesque description of manners are as a rule more interesting than the depiction of character. The philosophes made use of the novel to give their criticisms an attractive form.

Montesquieu's Lettres Persanes (1721), which introduced the genre, also helped set the fashion for orientalism, feeding the fantasy with cheap exoticism and spicy stories of the harem. An equally beloved theme is the noble savage, the natural man who represents mankind. In the delicate, elegant dream world of his dramas, Marivaux combines intricate fantasy with fine psychological insight, so that feeling itself becomes intelligence. Life, lacking any sense for the tragic and the metaphysical, no longer provides material for tragedy. In Metastasio's librettos the tragic theme becomes idyllic, elegiac, even comic, and the speech dissolves into music: the dramma in musica triumphs.

The commedia a soggetto with its masks suffers a decline, while Goldoni rejuvenates the Italian stage with his comedies of character. In every realm, the new content demands freer forms of expression and a merging of the genres that classicism had so strictly separated; in this task English literature played a great role. Comedy becomes serious, even affecting. Where emotional life, too strongly suppressed by rationalism, can no longer be sublimated into spirituality, it seeks a more direct outlet; but since it remains subject to intellectual control, it tends to come out in a mawkish spectacle, in the rhetorical and moralizing sentimentality that marks the transition from the Rococo to the pre-Romantic. The most typical manifestation of the movement is the bourgeois drama.

MUSIC Perhaps no art is so typical of the Rococo as the Neapolitan opera. Where the drama dissolves into theatrical effects and bel canto,

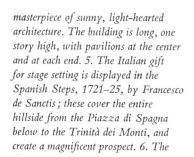

masterpiece of sunny, light-hearted architecture. The building is long, one story high, with pavilions at the center and at each end. 5. The Italian gift for stage setting is displayed in the Spanish Steps, 1721–25, by Francesco de Sanctis; these cover the entire hillside from the Piazza di Spagna below to the Trinità dei Monti, and create a magnificent prospect. 6. The

monastery at Melk, by Josef Prandtauer, 1701–38, has great three-dimensional movement; the church façade is flanked by monumental projecting wings, that are connected by a lower semicircle with a Palladian loggia opening on a view of the landscape. A. Plan of pilgrimage church at Vierzehnheiligen, near Bamberg, 1743–52, by Balthasar Neumann.

feeling finds an outlet in which it can reconcile itself with a strictly regulated formal construction. Play and inner emotion become one. Soon the freer, mixed forms of *opera buffa* and *opéra comique* arose (Pergolesi's *La Serva Padrona*, 1733, and Rousseau's *Le Devin du Village*, 1752). Rameau, who remained faithful to the more rigid tradition of Lully, reacted against the Italian exuberance and prefigured the reformation that Gluck was to introduce in the name of nature and simplicity. Toward the middle of the century instrumental music took on new importance. At Mannheim (Stamitz), Milan (Sammartini), Vienna (Cannabich), London (Johann Christian Bach), and Paris (Gossec) the classical forms of the future style came into being—the orchestral symphony, the sonata for solo instruments, the concerto for soloist and orchestra—and the new means of lyric expression that Haydn and Mozart were to bring into classical balance. It is no accident that this balance coincides with the end of Rococo art and the rise of Romanticism and *Sturm und Drang*.

The performance of music in large concert halls containing a much larger audience made basic changes in the point of view and in the very language of composers and performers.

SPIRIT AND CHARACTER OF THE STYLE Despite all the new features that appeared in the first half of the eighteenth century, the art of the Rococo is essentially a development of the seventeenth-century Baroque. It inherited not only formal principles but also basic elements determining the mental attitude of the artist. The Baroque spirit that saw a spectacle in every aspect of the cultural world, in the liturgy, and even in human life itself, persisted. It was only shifted from the heroic-stately plane to one that was more human, more intimate, more sentimental. In France the change sets

A.

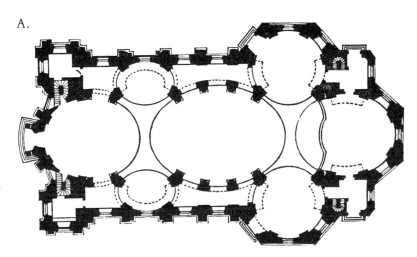

7

8

7 and 8. Two different aspects of the dynamic spatial effects of German and Swiss churches: 7. "Die Wies," Bavaria, 1746–54, by Dominikus Zimmermann: light, undulating fantasy. 8. Abbey, Einsiedeln, 1719–25, by Kaspar Moosbrugger: visual power and theatrical light effects. 9. Town Hall, Schwäbisch Hall, by Heim and Arnold, illustrating the gentle attractiveness of a more bourgeois conception of the Rococo.

9

in even before the end of Louis XIV's reign, so that the *Style Régence* begins about 1700. It breaks with the monumental stateliness as well as with the academic ideal of beauty; it demands elbow room for the fanciful and places new emphasis on everything relating to human life in society. A new urge toward comfort and graciousness is decisive for the development of the arts of furniture design and interior decoration, which now come to the fore. The forms bend and sway, flow over each other, and climb like ivy over the architecture, which gains in charm and movement what it loses in architectural weight and stateliness. The new principles of style come into full blossom in the *Style Louis XV*, which triumphed in the first half of Louis XV's reign, from 1725 to 1755, with the playful curling of capricious swirls pushed to the utmost. Mythology became *galant*; everything was aimed at the life of the salon with its witty conversa-

tion and manners. An extremely refined feeling for form, coupled with the realization that form can no longer be regarded as an absolute ideal of beauty in the sense of the Academy, led to the most intimate association of form and playfulness ever known in the history of art. Play, in the highest sense of the word, as the fusion of spontaneous free fantasy and strict regularity of form, is indeed one of the most typical characteristics of the Rococo. But just as noteworthy are its amazing spatial imagination and feeling for movement; these, combined with the element of play, give rise to the irresistible attractiveness of Rococo buildings in which the visual forms seem to pass over into pure music.

The Regency and Louis XV styles, strictly speaking, refer to French interior decoration and furniture. Rococo is often limited to the most Baroque-like manifestations of the Louis XV style, especially as interpreted in Central Europe. But broadly speaking it can be applied to the entire development of the Late Baroque in every field of art in the eighteenth century. Here France is outstanding, as it already was in the seventeenth century, for its traditional feeling for rational, classic equilibrium. But wherever the French influence spread in Europe, it came into contact with powerful Baroque impulses, especially in Central Europe; out of that contact arose a great and original synthesis.

The freer conception of art was reflected in art theory, which stressed fantasy, imagination, and good taste rather than academic rules and categories. Objective standards of art were supplanted by the subjective spiritual activity of the artist, although people were still unaware of the incalculable consequences of this change in the artistic center of gravity.

One factor that contributed greatly to lively and fruitful discussions of esthetic problems among artists, writers, and connoisseurs was the inauguration of regular *salons* of sculpture and painting, from 1737 on. Denis Diderot wrote important reviews of these salons.

ARCHITECTURE The principles that triumphed in France with Versailles influenced city planning everywhere in the eighteenth century. Perhaps the most noteworthy instance is Karlsruhe, an entire city designed in 1715 as a huge star, with the ducal palace at the center. The symmetrical royal square, built around the statue of the king, is another typical creation of the century. Among the most

celebrated examples are the complex of the Place Stanislas and the Place de la Carrière at Nancy (Héré de Corny); the former Place Louis XV, now Place de la Concorde, in Paris (A.-J. Gabriel); and the Amalienborg Square in Copenhagen (Eigtved). Terraces, fountains, and staircases provide fertile themes for spatial fantasy.

In France, the art of Jules Hardouin Mansart had a decisive influence on the architects who were to set the tone between 1700 and 1740: Robert de Cotte, Ange-Jacques Gabriel, and Gabriel Germain Bof-frand; Boffrand in particular helped to give Rococo architecture in the narrow sense its characteristic appearance. Church architecture, as a type, was in the background; the façades, in other respects kept strictly under control, were enlivened by a central portion projecting outward or inward, the hollow or swelling masses bound to the building at the sides, and by the double west towers. Internally, however, the decoration followed the rich secular fashion, quite in the manner of the salons. The most notable productions of French architects are in the field of city architecture, the palaces and *hôtels*. Here too the seventeenth-century type was taken over, the main building placed between the *cour d'honneur* and the garden. In the exteriors a degree of simplicity prevails; columns and three-dimensional ornament disappear almost completely. By the extreme refinement of their proportions, the façades combine a classic dignity with an attractive grace, to which a discreet use of trophies, masks above the windows, and trelliswork gave a witty accent. There was usually a protruding polygonal or circular central portion (vestibule and salon).

In the interior the stately, forbidding majesty of the Louis XIV style was replaced by finesse, by the new feeling for comfort and intimacy. The impressive enfilades disappear; in palaces, the *salon* rather than the gallery is chosen as the room for receptions and ceremonies. The rooms became smaller and were grouped into apartments; increasing specialization classed them as bedrooms, dining rooms, bathrooms, studies, *salons*, boudoirs, etc. Rounded forms, which had been objectionable under Louis XIV, were now preferred. The decoration of the interior became an essential element of the architecture, con-

10. The principal pavilion of the Zwinger, Dresden, 1711–22, by Mattheus Daniel Pöppelmann, combines, with its wide openings, an alert feeling for space and the Baroque fantasy of exuberant decoration.
11. Sans Souci, near Potsdam, 1745–51, by Georg Wenceslaus Knobelsdorff, after a sketch by King Frederick II, is a typical example of a Rococo Lustschloss (pleasure palace).
12. In the staircase, 1744–65, of the palace at Brühl, Balthasar Neumann succeeds in creating a movement in space that seems to suggest, as if in a scene, the mounting of the stairs by a gay company.

13

14

necting it, in a manner typical of the age, with the furnishings, in contrast to the sober, still classic-appearing grace of the façades.

In Spain, José Churriguerra (1650–1723) had worked out a typically Spanish version of the Baroque, in which exuberant decoration composed from every possible source masked the architectural structure. Churriguerrism is a kind of revival of the sixteenth-century Plateresque, that reversal of the strict structure of the Herrera tradition. The Bourbons reacted against the Baroque and, with the help of French and Italian architects, introduced classicizing taste (palaces of Madrid, Aranjuez, La Granja).

From 1680 to 1760 Central Europe witnessed an astonishing outburst of architecture, both church and secular. Two great trends developed side by side. One, the Italian influence, dominated exclusively in religious architecture, which had a splendid revival in Austria, Bavaria, and Poland. The French influence, which began about 1720, was naturally predominant in decoration and in secular architecture. But this second influence very soon underwent a radical recasting; fused with Italian Baroque in the furnace of German expressionistic tendencies, it produced German Rococo. The most prominent among a group of great architects are Johann Bernhard Fischer von Erlach, Johann Lukas von Hildebrandt, Mattheus Daniel Pöppelmann, G. W. von Knobelsdorff and, greatest of all, Balthasar Neumann.

Many monasteries were rebuilt on an enormous scale. The plan of these, with the church usually on an axis between two inner courts enclosed by the monastery buildings, goes back to the Escorial. As a rule, the churches have two western towers. In both plan and elevation the aim was a dynamic interpenetration of the spatial units. Although a central space emphasized the unity of the ensemble, the eye cannot rest anywhere; everything is transition and motion. Oval plans are preferred and every possible mode of fusing central and basilican designs. The decoration serves not only to conceal the structure, but also to conjure up an entire phantom world; the real space of the architecture is continued in fantastic illusory space, so

that the two merge and the spectator feels himself whirled along in a fusion of being and appearance, of sense and the supersensual, of heaven and earth, leading in certain cases to a true ecstasy. The play of light is used for opera-like effects, and architecture attains to the lyric enchantment of music. But no clear line can be drawn between *Ad majorem Dei gloriam* and wordly pride and pomp.

In palace design, French influences are found early in the period. One wing of the early Baroque hollow square structure drops away; the two side wings spread out, often in echelon, connecting the building with garden or court. There is also a preference for simple rectangular buildings with a central pavilion, sometimes with smaller pavilions at the four corners. Along with the development in breadth goes a decrease in height, leading to the typical Rococo *Lustschloss*, with a single story and a convex or polygonal center pavilion. Probably the most impressive element is the staircase, which is an occasion for the greatest spatial movement and stage effects. Those of Neumann at Würzburg, Bruchsal, and Brühl are masterpieces.

Russia, under Peter the Great, had broken with its own national tradition and had begun to be Europeanized. Empress Elizabeth continued the architectural development of St. Petersburg, and the Italian Rastrelli brought to it a curiously festive combination of Italian Baroque, German Rococo, and native elements (Winter Palace, Tsarskoe Selo); thereafter, French classicist ideas triumphed under Catherine II. Scandinavia, which was under primarily Dutch influence during the seventeenth century, went over to French taste during the eighteenth.

13, 14. The exuberant decoration of Churriguerrism is apparent in Ignacio Vergara's portal for the palace of the Marquis of Dos Aguas in Valencia (1740–44), and in the sacristy of the Carthusian monastery in Granada

(1727–64), by Luis de Arevalo and F. Manuel Vasquez.

Page 121. J.-B.-S. Chardin, Still Life with Pipe.

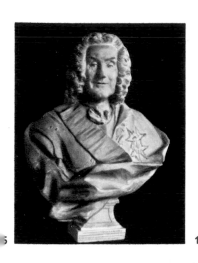

16

17

As during the Baroque period, landscape design is an indispensable complement to architecture, linking it to the surroundings. Here, too, the strictly geometrical French school of André Le Nôtre everywhere supplants the Italian school.

SCULPTURE Under Louis XIV, the Academy's classical ideal of beauty was consciously directed against Flemish and Italian Baroque. With the Regency there gradually came a trend toward movement and expression, toward suppleness and natural liveliness. Typical transition figures are Robert le Lorrain and Nicolas and Guillaume Coustou. The generation thereafter is completely free from the classicism of the seventeenth century. Laurent-Sebastian Adam and the Slodtz brothers produced work that looked Baroque, but its dramatic effects were mainly of decorative value. Edmé Bouchardon represented the continuance of classical taste, from the grandeur of the Louis XIV to the gracious sensibility of the Louis XVI. In the interiors, which had now become smaller and more intimate, there was no room for monumental sculpture; they required small-scale sculpture—portrait busts, statuettes, or little groups for salon and boudoir. These became more and more the fashion when particularly well-suited media of expression were found in terracotta and porcelain. Jean-Baptiste Lemoyne's busts caught with keen intelligence the passing moods of eloquent eighteenth-century countenances in a style that foreshadowed Houdon. Etienne Maurice Falconet, the favorite sculptor of Madame de Pompadour, made enticing marble statues of women in clearly modeled forms. Like Jean-Baptiste

Pigalle, who was inclined toward realism and pathos, Falconet in his mature works already belonged to the Louis XVI style. Sculpture in Central Europe was almost exclusively in the form of applied art, subordinated to architecture. Stucco plays a decisive role in the interior decoration, and figures are often half-modeled in stucco and half-painted. The altarpieces that resemble fantastic stage settings, are one of the most remarkable productions of the ecstatic German conception of the Rococo. E. Q. Asam's work at Rohr am Inn and Weltenburg uses trompe-l'œil techniques to sweep the spectator into supernatural visions. The sculptured figures themselves are assailed, as it were, by irresistible, unrealistic undulations, in which the expression, pushed to the utmost, attains ecstatic release. The slender figures by Ignaz Günther and Paul Egell, with their sharp, faceted accents, are reminiscent of the ambiguous grace of the Mannerists, while Georg Raphael Donner has a gentler, more classicistic charm.

In Italy too sculpture has a primarily decorative nature, for example, the monumental figures of the Apostles by Rusconi and others in San Giovanni in Laterano, and in the many altarpieces and fountains of the period. More in the spirit of the Rococo are the bozzetti of G. M. Morlaiter and the charming putti of Giacomo Serpotta. Naples developed a local specialty during the eighteenth century, many-figured scenes (presepio) of the Birth of Christ, represented by doll-like figures in a scene of little realism, and sometimes rather mannered; this art, under the Salzillo family, was to give a late impetus to Spanish polychrome sculpture.

18

15. The bust of Florent de Vallière shows the feeling of Jean-Baptiste Lemoyne (1704–78) for living psychological contact with the model. 16. Etienne-Maurice Falconet's Baigneuse (1757), with its fine tapering limbs, clean forms with slender proportions, and soft modeling, already prefigures the classicizing grace of the Louis XVI style. 17. The Horses of Apollo, 1740, by Robert le Lorrain, on the Hôtel de Rohan, Paris, combines decorative relief with the architecture in the manner of a painter, but maintains a degree of classical balance.
18. The seductive figure of a nymph by the Viennese Georg Raphael Donner (1693–1771), although conceived in a related spirit, has a more classical and balanced charm.

Page 122. Glory of the House of Pisani, sketch for a ceiling painting by G. B. Tiepolo, 1761.

PAINTING AND PRINTS Since the beginning of the eighteenth century, France was the scene of a vigorous reaction against the academic ideal of beauty and Charles Lebrun's dictatorship. The change finds expression in the quarrel between the "Poussinists," advocates of the traditional, intellectual school of painting, and the "Rubenists," supporters of a more colorful and sensual art. Rubens's Médicis gallery in the Luxembourg Palace induced an admiration of Dutch and Flemish genre painting as well. Jean-Antoine Watteau (1684–1721) created a poetical art, entirely new and all his own, appealing to the heart and evoking a light, melancholy, almost musical mood. His scenes based on the Italian comedy combine reality and the dream world. But his fame is due chiefly to his *fêtes galantes*, paintings with no precise subject, that represent amorous conversations in a dream park. Forsaking the intellectual mission of the previous century, painting shows an almost entirely decorative trend; it seems to have no other purpose than to be agreeable. Decorative painting divides into two traditions. Nicolas Lancret and Jean-Baptiste Pater turn the *fêtes galantes* into motifs that find a place in wall-decoration, while the Italianizing manner, with its mythological and historical themes, continues in the work of François Lemoyne, Jean-François de Troy, Charles-Antoine Coypel, C. van Loo and, above all, François Boucher. But historical subjects, treated in the spirit of opera, now take on a romantic tone. Boucher is typical of the taste that prevailed in the court circle surrounding Madame de Pompadour. In him, mythology is a refined but superficial salon game. Jean-Marc Nattier portrays the ladies of the aristocracy as

Flora, Hebe, or Diana, using external, formal, and decorative effects to mask any genuine contact with the human. But the later Hyacinthe Rigaud and Nicolas de Largillière begin to liberate their portraits from these formal poses; and with Quentin de la Tour and Jean-Baptiste Perronneau we attain a living dialogue with the individual. The healthy resistance of the French mind to the prevailing artificial frivolity found expression in the work of Jean-Baptiste-Siméon Chardin, a disciple of the Dutch masters, who discovered the human core in the simplest scenes of daily life and expressed it in sober painting, without the slightest concession to anecdote.

Toward the middle of the century a change was in the air. Jean-B. Greuze, reacting against the superficiality of Boucher, tried to raise genre painting to the level of the major subjects by treating it in a sentimental, moralizing manner. But his art, not without sensual charm, became false and anecdotal. His work is a remarkable counterpart to the bourgeois drama. Much more fruitful is the work of Fragonard, which combines the effervescent spatial fantasy, the playful elegance, and the erotic sensibility of the Rococo with an amazing, already Romantic impetuousness that announces the early nineteenth century.

The Italian school was overshadowed by the French. Naples still had capable ceiling painters in the persons of Francesco Solimena and Francesco de Mura; Giovanni Paolo Pannini in Rome introduced the landscape with ruins, a genre destined for great success; Alessandro Magnasco in Genoa combined an astonishing virtuosity of the brush with a special feeling for spatial fantasies, which are at once playfully decorative and dramatic in effect. But Venice, above all, still found strength enough to end its school in glory, in an apotheosis of light and color. Canaletto, and even more Francesco Guardi, were city

19. A Pilgrimage to Cythera, 1717, by Jean-Antoine Watteau. In the gently melancholy poetry of a dream landscape, Watteau develops, like a musical theme, the motif of the slow-moving couples who stand up and turn back for one last look, as if to say farewell, before embarking for the distant island of Venus. 20. Festival at Saint-Cloud, about 1775, is a

masterpiece of the effervescent light and space fantasy of Jean-Honoré Fragonard. 21. Dance before the Tent, by Jean-Baptiste Pater (1695–1736), still has great charm, but the dreamy poetry of Watteau is lost. The dance as a playful theme of movement is a favorite motif in eighteenth-century French painting.

22. In Still Life with Partridge, by Jean-Baptiste-Siméon Chardin (1699–1779), we admire the extremely refined intellectual geometry of the composition. 23. In Jean-Marc Nattier's (1685–1766) Duchess of Chartres as Hebe, psychological truth is crowded out by graceful convention and allegorical

painters of genius; Pietro Longhi an entertaining genre painter; and Giovanni B. Piazzetta and, especially, Giovan Battista Tiepolo, were great decorators. It is astonishing to see the virtuosity with which Tiepolo brings heroes and gods before us on walls and domes, in light streaming through unlimited ruins. He worked at Venice, Madrid, and Würzburg, leaving the Neapolitan, Austrian, and German fresco painters far behind (Maulpertsch, C. D. Asam, Spiegler, Zick).

The close link, so important for the Rococo, of painting, architecture, and the drama is illustrated by the Bolognese family of the Galli-Bibbiena, who specialized in stage decoration. Their ideas were widely propagated by means of their prints. Stately halls set obliquely on the stage, so that fantastic perspectives are suggested on either side of the corner pillars, are one of their favorite leitmotifs. Finally, the realm of actuality may be transcended for free fantasies in which the eye is lost. A masterpiece of this sort is the *Carceri* series of etchings of prisons (about 1745) by Giovanni Battista Piranesi, whose dramatic mood already gives a foretaste of the Romantic movement.

INTERIOR DECORATION, FURNITURE, MINOR ARTS The special importance of the interior in the eighteenth century is a result of the new demands for comfort, *commodité*, which freed architecture from pompous grandeur and enabled it to become part of daily human life. During the Regency, pillars and marble walls were supplanted by paneled wainscoting. Ornament became lighter and more mobile and consisted of straight and curved moldings that were soon reduced to lines embellished with foliage, shells, cartouches, and grotesques; tiny, fantastic figures were introduced in gallant scenes, idyls of shepherds and actors, *chinoiseries*, and *singeries*. Between 1715 and 1730 the *rocaille* arose, an abstractly decorative element marked by whimsical shell and rock formations in C- and S-shaped volutes that develop playfully into asymmetry, as if endowed with vegetative life. This completely original principle of form triumphed with G. G. Boffrand, J. A. Meissonier, and Oppenord, and by 1755 dominated every decorative domain. The style penetrated into Germany about 1720, and there was given a physiognomy of its own by the expressionistic tendencies of the German Baroque; it became harder in drawing and stronger in contrast.

The art of furniture had unprecedented development. Rapidly liberating itself from the old architectural or representational designs, it is the most striking reflection of the new art of agreeable living. For some time during the Regency it retained a remnant of the architectural aspect of the Louis XIV forms; but the Louis XV style is all feminine elegance. The walls of the commodes curve out, the legs of chairs and armchairs become slimmer and flow smoothly

costume. 24. Madame de Pompadour, about 1758, by Boucher. Everything here is typically Rococo: the setting, the clothing, and the composition, with its diagonals and spiral movement. The work gives us an entrancing picture of the life of the luxurious court. 25. Francesco Guardi (1712–93) reaches a high point of virtuoso play in his picture of Santa Maria della Salute in Venice, with whimsical boats, water, and architecture sketched in endless space.

over into the back and seat. Italian figured themes disappear; their place is taken by *rocaille*. Cressent was the first to give a major role to the ormolu (gilt bronze) ornament that winds its way over the surfaces of his commodes. From the turn of the century on, rosewood, lemonwood, and other exotic woods were used in place of ebony. Magnificent inlay work was made with the light exotic woods, and after 1748 Chinese lacquer was imitated with *vernis Martin*. Seats were upholstered with damask, satin, or Genoese velvet, sometimes with tapestry. A typical expression of the time is the cabriolet armchair, with a hollowed-out back that fits the contour of the body,

26

27

26. *The Golden Gallery of the Hôtel de Toulouse (now Banque de France), Paris, by R. de Cotte, shows the rounding off of the angles and the lightening of the architectural structure by F. Mansart, by the rampant, free decorations of the Regency style.*

27. *In the Cabinet des Singes of the Hôtel de Rohan, Paris, the light, swaying decoration of the mature Rococo dominates, while wainscoting with mirrors and painting replaces the classical pilasters. The paintings, 1745–50, are by Christophe Huet.*

and with flowing lines suggestive of female forms. The bergère is an upholstered armchair with enclosed arms; a bergère extended to form a chaise longue was called a *duchesse*. There were also credenzas, card tables, work tables, pedestal tables, *bonheurs du jour* (little desks for ladies), etc. With their slender, graceful legs they hardly seem to rest on the ground. The close connection between wall decoration and furniture can be seen best in the console tables, which have only two legs and lean against the wall. Great furniture makers, such as Cressent, Gaudreau, and B. V. R. B. (Bernard van Rissenburghe) were able to embody their personal styles.

Tapestry was still a flourishing art, but the slavish imitation of painting that was prescribed by Oudry, who became director of the Beauvais manufactory, constituted a decline in quality. The art of the goldsmith, although by nature conservative, adopted the formal language of the Rococo, but little French work is left, as much as was subsequently melted down at times of financial pressure. Ceramics developed enormously, thanks to being increasingly used in daily life. Princes were interested in ceramic manufactories. In Saxony, where the process was invented in 1709, hard porcelain was made with kaolin in the Chinese manner; Elector Friedrich August I founded the manufactory at Meissen, which produced splended vases and statuettes in the Rococo taste. Nymphenburg in Bavaria, and Rouen, Strasbourg, and Marseille in France, were flourishing centers. The Sèvres manufactory owes its first success to the support of Madame de Pompadour and the talent of her favorite sculptor, Falconet.

COSTUME Whereas costume under Louis XIV aimed at majestic pomp, the fantasy of the Regency created an elegant silhouette, which could suggest both vigorous design and poetic abandon. Male costume was mainly distinguished by a new type of *justaucorps*, with tight-fitting sleeves and broad stiff cuffs in the form of wings. The waist is slender, and the broad skirts of the coat spread out below. This mode continued until about 1750, after which it lost much of its

28

29

28. *The engravings of J. A. Meissonier show the inexhaustible fantasy of the great decorator and his delight in plastic forms.*

29. *The Library by Johann August Nahl (1710–81) at Sans Souci is a happy fusion of French art and German taste.*

30. *The Regency armchair has rich sculptured decoration, which lightens its severe framework; the legs begin to merge with the seat.*

31. *This commode in Louis XV style, with japanned lacquer work and rich ornament in gilt bronze with rocaille and flower motifs, was designed by Jacques Caffieri (1678–1755).*

30

31

32

33

34. The grand effect of this Beauvais tapestry, The Toilet of Venus, shows the remarkable decorative qualities of the style of Boucher, who made the cartoon for it.

34

32. The unbroken curves of the supple frame give this settee in gilt wood, by Nadal, its typical Louis XV charm.

33. The Louis XV cabriole chair is outstanding for simple elegance and living harmony of all its parts.

34. The grand effect of this Beauvais tapestry, The Toilet of Venus, *shows the remarkable decorative qualities of the style of Boucher, who made the cartoon for it.*

breadth. The Louis XV wig left the forehead free and was flat on top. The hair was curled at the sides (*ailes de pigeon*). In the back there was a distinction between the *perruque à bourse* (purse wig), with a bag of black taffeta silk to hold it in, and the *perruque à marteaux* (hammer wig), which formed three small tails on the neck. The three-cornered hat was usually held in the hand, because of the wig. For the ladies, the Regency created the skirt with Watteau pleats, i.e., folds down the back from the shoulders, merging in the wide skirt. The bodice was reinforced with whalebone and cross-laced in front. Dresses with reed or whalebone hoops, which the Renaissance had already seen, reappeared in 1718. The *robe volante* hung down wide and free, leaving room for the swinging of the panniers and presenting a typically négligé appearance. Later the waist again became fitted, while the material at the sides and back fluttered free. The sleeves opened out from the elbow funnelwise (*en pagodes*), and were adorned with lace. About 1740 the hoops spread out to the sides, while the *corps à baleines* was strongly reminiscent of the *corps piqué* of the sixteenth century.

35

36

35. *Paneled desk made about 1765 by Abraham and David Röntgen for the Elector of Trier. 36. Clock with rocaille ornamentation of gilded bronze, typical of the Louis XV period. 37. Footed soup terrine in Sèvres porcelain, with the irresistible elegance of the pure, flowing forms of the Louis XV period. Ornamented with rocaille motifs and gold trimming.*
38. Lidded jar in Mennecy porcelain. 39. The Mermaid, centerpiece from Count Brühl's porcelain "Swan" dinner service, by Johann Joachim Kändler (1706–75) and Johann Friedrich Eberlein (1693/6–1749) of the Meissen factory. 40. Louis XV-style goblet made in 1767 by the Hague silversmith Cornelis de Haan for St. Adrian's Guild in Scheveningen.
41. Capitano, porcelain Commedia dell'Arte figurine, by Frans Anton Bostelli (1723–63) of the Nymphenburg factory.

37

41

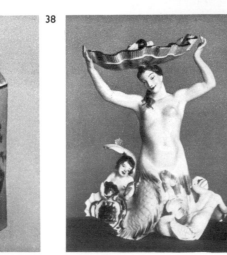

38

39

40

ENGLAND IN THE EIGHTEENTH CENTURY

INTRODUCTION   The example set by the French court, which the royal Maecenas had made a center of attraction for artists of every kind, was not followed in England. The eighteenth-century British sovereigns had little to do with the world of art, which developed independently of them, for the most part.

ARCHITECTURE   Architectural style changed in London during the half century following the Great Fire, when Christopher Wren (1632–1723) had accomplished so much. The style now often called English Baroque was superseded by a stricter ideal that reverted to Palladio and to Inigo Jones. From the late seventeenth century on, great country houses the size of palaces were built in the provinces: Chatsworth, by William Talman with later work by Thomas Archer; Holkham Hall by William Kent; Blenheim by John Vanbrugh; and many others. Important buildings included James Gibbs's churches, St. Mary-le-Strand and St. Martin's-in-the-Fields, Kent's Horse Guards building in Whitehall, and the Radcliffe Library at Oxford, by Gibbs based on a design by Nicholas Hawksmoor. William Chambers rebuilt Somerset House, and the Woods created, in Bath, a noteworthy model of town planning, especially the Circus and the Royal Crescent. Chambers' pupil Gandon did the best part of his work in Ireland. The brothers Robert and James Adam were among the best-known architects of the last third of the century. Contemporary with them were archaeologists such as James Stuart, but the real Greek Revival in architecture did not come until after them, in the nineteenth century. As well as these partisans of classical antiquity, certain patrons like Horace Walpole preferred a Gothic Revival, but this, also, flourished principally in the next century.

2

1. Street façade of the front quadrangle of Queen's College, Oxford, rebuilt by Nicholas Hawksmoor in 1709–34, inspired by French architecture of the seventeenth century. 2. Interior of hall of Castle Howard, Yorkshire, by John Vanbrugh; its height comprises that of all the storys, characteristic for castle architecture. 3. Hall of Holkham Hall, Norfolk, by William Kent, 1734, who combined in this staircase a reconstruction on the basis of Vitruvius and a design by Inigo Jones.

3

1

5

4

4. The Royal Crescent, Bath, 1767–75, by John Wood the Younger. England had a fondness for the crescent form; this case is a successful example of city planning. 5. The Long Gallery of Syon House, Middlesex, 1763–64, by Robert Adam. This Palladian style foreshadows the Directoire decor in France. 6. Marble bust of G. F. Handel, by L. F. Roubiliac (1702/5–62). 7. Marble bust of the architect James Gibbs, by J. M. Rysbrack (1694–1770). The work of these artists, Roubiliac from Lyon, Rysbrack from Antwerp, goes back to the traditions of the seventeenth century.

7

6

SCULPTURE Louis-François Roubiliac, a Frenchman, occupies the first place in English sculpture of the eighteenth century. Francis Bird, Thomas Banks, Joseph Nollekens, John Bacon, and John Flaxman were far inferior to their French contemporaries. Their modest achievements were amply made up for by the incomparable fame of British painting.

PAINTING In the eighteenth century painting had a phase of remarkable brilliance. Some few painters dominated the period, but it would be all too simple to attribute the character of the age solely to them, for the distance between the best masters and their contemporaries was not so great that the latter can be merely ignored. It might seem that we could leap from Van Dyck to Reynolds, as if the century separating them had produced nothing. The fact is that we do not find any artists of their magnitude, but the interval is more important than it may seem at first. After Van Dyck had been court painter for Charles I, and Peter Lely had held the same position for Charles's sons, another foreigner, Godfrey Kneller, held an outstanding position in the world of art, at first sharing the post of court painter with John Riley, but soon alone, until Kneller's death in 1723. The way to such a position was not by historical paintings or large compositions, as it was in France, but by portraits, which from the seventeenth century on were the most highly valued and frequently practiced genre. Strangely enough, foreign artists were favored in England and Scotland, with success and prestige that native artists could not hope to attain. Accordingly, the native artists imitated the foreigners, and painted what the public found beautiful. Kneller has been much criticized for the unequal quality of his paintings; on the other hand, it is clear that he made a deep study of the character of the people that sat for him. He never gave female models, however, the sensuous charm that appears so clearly in Lely. But he was preeminent in male portraiture, in the great portraits of representative Whigs, the members of the Kit Cat Club. Also important are his portraits of admirals for Greenwich Hospital, now the Royal Naval College.

Michael Dahl, a Swede who worked with Kneller, had originally a more attractive way of painting; but he soon began to work like Kneller, and by thus swimming with the fashion, he became the portraitist with the most commissions in the years after Kneller's death. Jonathan Richardson did better portraits of men than of women; finally he abandoned painting for esthetics. His writings made a great impression on Joshua Reynolds and influenced his career.

Charles Jervas, an Irishman, on the other hand, was more impelled to depict ladies, and rendered the precious materials of their garments in a way that was rare at the time. He opened the way for Reynolds by making friendships with writers and people in high society. He himself was able to follow Kneller as the first painter of the king.

The second half of the eighteenth century saw a real revolution. Painting, which had been partly conducted by foreign-born artists up to that time, was taken over by Englishmen, and technique underwent radical changes. The promoter of these alterations was William Hogarth (1697–1764), who in speech and writing agitated for a national art. He wanted to liberate painting from stifling conventions and give it more spontaneity and truthfulness. His own work

8. *Portrait of Charles Sackville, by Godfrey Kneller. His style is based on that of Van Dyck, but is less personal.*
9. *The Orgy, from the series The Rake's Progress, about 1734, by William Hogarth. Hogarth's intention of scourging sin is aided by the brutal realism of the composition.*

9

10. *Portrait of Captain Coram, by Hogarth. Hogarth's penetrating observation of his model permits him to reproduce the entire personality and thus to renew the art of English portraiture.*

10

11

12

13

11. Portrait of Dr. Mead, by Allan Ramsay (1713–84). We see here the resources of traditional portraiture in England, when practiced by a great painter.

14

12. General Lord Heathfield, 1787, by Joshua Reynolds. The technique of this fine portrait has the hallmarks of Reynolds's innovations in the distribution of light and color on the surface, under the influence of Italian art and Rembrandt. 13. The Duchess of Devonshire and Her Daughter, by Reynolds. This master of a thousand countenances paints equally well the woman's softness and gentleness and the awkward gestures of the baby. 14. Sketch in oils of Lady Hamilton as a bacchante, by George Romney, about 1786. Romney was famous for, among other things, his many portraits of this favorite model; she inspired him to mythological fantasies as well. 15. Mrs. Richard Brinsley Sheridan, by Thomas Gainsborough (1727–88). The expression lends her a provocative beauty like that of the Mona Lisa. 16. The Prince of Wales as a Colonel, by Thomas Beechey (1753–1839). His portraits echo the works of Reynolds and Romney.

15

16

was a model of the program. It includes portraits, some of which (those of his servants) are true to life, and compositions on religious subjects, which are less in his line. He shone, however, in a genre in which he remained unique, the portrayal of manners. The mastery that he displayed in composition and dramatic expression was the result of a long development in training as a book illustrator, for which he drew and engraved vignettes. Hogarth's satire undoubtedly influenced the savage caricatures that were later to make Rowlandson and Gillray famous. He took to prints when he wanted to express his opinions on current events, such as a threatened invasion of England by the French. In 1734 he succeeded his father-in-law Thornhill as head of an art school that prepared the way for the Royal Academy of Arts (founded in 1768). For thirty years the artist had a position from which to propagate his views. Because of his tireless fighting spirit, he made many enemies and his paintings received sharp criticism. It was more than a century before the true worth of his work was recognized.

On the other hand, everyone was immediately convinced of the great gifts of Joshua Reynolds (1723–92), the first of a series of portrait painters that was the pride of English art for three-quarters of a century. His career began early and brilliantly. His great talent and the value that it lent to his words and writings gave Reynolds an unprecedented prestige in his time. He was an intellectual painter; never satisfied and never misled by his success, he took no pleasure in easy routine. His life was a constant quest, and this differentiated him from his predecessors. He commanded a talent with inexhaustible reserves, as his rival Gainsborough openly conceded. His greatest fame came from his portraits, and in this genre he was an heir and successor to Van Dyck. He attracts our attention less by his psychological insight than by the completeness of his conceptions. The light effects in the portrait of Nelly O'Brien, a hundred years before the rise of Impressionism, are a measure of the originality of his painting. Unfortunately, the colors in his portraits have not

18

17

19

always retained their original hues; some of his subjects now have flat countenances, and something of the Venetian pictorial charm that he had intended to convey has been lost. The fact remains that he developed a portrait style of his own, by virtue of which he has a very special place; no matter how much he borrowed from his forerunners, including Rembrandt, he was one of the most notable figures in painting.

In contrast to Reynolds, Thomas Gainsborough was a much more lyrical painter. Gainsborough applied himself strictly to the practice of his art. He was not attracted by the social position of his calling, as Reynolds was, but he was much more sensitive to the character of his models, and thus his portraits are more moving. Also a good third of his work, in which a well-marked development can be traced but in which his clients showed no interest, consists of a set of landscapes that show him as the true forerunner of Constable.

A third artist, not so keen as Gainsborough and less interesting than Reynolds, shared in their success: George Romney, a man with a very special gift and enormous activity. He was the talented, irresistible painter of beautiful women. His drawing, color, and composition are admirable.

The new school hides artists from us that remained closer to the old ways. In the case of Allan Ramsay (born 1713), this circumstance proves most unjust. This Scot, ten years older than Reynolds, settled in London at a time when the fame of his rival was already established. However, he became the permanent painter of George III. His work had much in common with that of the French, in particular, Chardin.

Richard Wilson, likewise born in 1713, also made his career in portraits until, after years abroad, he was confronted with the favor that the other great portraitists enjoyed. Zuccarelli in Italy had already advised him to devote himself to landscape, for which he had special gifts. He decided to follow the advice. He has left Italian views that are in sharp contrast to those by French and Italian

17. Major Clunes, by Henry Rae-burn (1756–1823). Raeburn's manner is terser than that of Beechey. He authoritatively depicts the dis-mounted rider, who is almost over-shadowed by the gleaming rump of the horse. 18. The Calmady Children, by Thomas Lawrence (1769–1830). Lawrence, with his somewhat affected refinement, comes off best when depicting the theme of

childish or womanly grace. 19. Castle Pembroke and Pembroke Town, by Richard Wilson (1710–82). He makes of the atmosphere an important element and, as here, likes to use the diagonal in his compositions. 20. Landscape with Pines, by Alexander Cozens (1717?–86). Cozens is the first of the water colorists to seek inspiration in Swiss and Italian landscapes.

20

21

21. The Market Cart, by Thomas Gainsborough, 1786. A somewhat soft technique in his later landscapes foreshadows Turner. 22. The Departure of Regulus, by Benjamin West (1738–1820), an American painter who settled in England. This great historical painting, antedating David's Oath of the Horatii by 15 years, was commissioned by King George III. 23. In the Stable, by George Morland (1763–1804). This artist was successful with pictures of horses and with scenes of life at every level. 24. Landscape with a Gentleman Holding a Horse by the Reins, by George Stubbs (1724–1806). Stubbs was a tireless observer of nature, and especially of horses. He opened the way to the painting of sports that formed a favorite English genre in the nineteenth century.

Page 135. Portrait of Mr. and Mrs. Andrews in a Landscape, by Thomas Gainsborough.

23

24

22

painters of the time; his English landscapes are enlivened by expanses of clear atmosphere showing contrasts of light and reflection, and attesting a great feeling for nature.

A new generation of portraitists in the second half of the century continued the flowering of English painting: it begins with Hogarth and ends with Lawrence's death. The period is rich in talents, and the work of many painters is often confused with that of the greatest. There are three particularly representative artists: John Hoppner, Henry Raeburn, and Thomas Lawrence, who show the strong influence of their predecessors. Hoppner followed the style of Reynolds. He has a certain tendency toward softness that shows in his portraits of women. The personality of Raeburn appears in the manly strength of his broad, powerful touch. He is incomparable in male portraits, but some of his female models, like old Mrs. James Campbell and the young Lady Stuart of Coltness, inspired him to splendid paintings. Lawrence is a model of refinement. As an infant prodigy he was already supporting himself by painting portraits at the age of ten. His career was full of honors, and clients crowded his studio. His style has something unnatural about it, but that trait is shared by artists of the time on both sides of the Channel.

Both Wilson and Gainsborough had been landscape painters as well as portraitists. The English liked to have "portraits" made of their houses and parks. Many female figures are contrasted against a background of nature, and the men were often depicted in hunting clothing in the open air, with the landscape sometimes playing an important role. Other subjects, around the middle of the century,

sometimes include a broad landscape, as in the *Races on the Thames* by Griffier, or Samuel Scott's *Tower of London*.

The greatest landscape painter at the end of the century is John Crome, nicknamed Old Crome, the founder of the Norwich School, who enriched the technical knowledge he had won by studying the Dutch painters with an untiring observation of nature. With Constable and Turner, he is one of a brilliant trinity.

A few names would be enough to recall the historical paintings that are one of the weakest sides of visual art under the kings of the House of Hanover. One of the best representatives of this specialty, which incidentally was practiced with no success by painters of the caliber of Hogarth, was Hogarth's father-in-law James Thornhill.

The best genre painter after Hogarth was George Morland, whose work gained popularity through prints. The rural character of his works suggests themes of Greuze's; but although the sentimental and sugary note often appears, Morland does not have Greuze's theatrical bombast or sermonizing spirit. In addition, he was an outstanding painter of animals, as were Ward and Stubbs, who found the horse an inexhaustible subject. These painters initiated a genre that was to become one of the most characteristic specialties of English art. In addition to painters and watercolorists, engravers also flourished; they used chiefly mezzotint, a process that was widely employed in England. The miniature on ivory or enamel is an art form in which the English are unsurpassed. John Smart and Christian Friedrich Zincke are among the best-known names of the flock of artists that specialized in this domain.

INTERIOR DECORATION AND FURNITURE Under Queen Anne (1702–14), English furniture was close to that of the Netherlands; people liked supple, strong lines that were expressed, for example, in high backs with broad central panels, the leg thicker at the top and ending in a bear's paw below. In the Chippendale style (about 1730–60) the full, smooth forms used at the beginning of the century gave way to infinitely fragmented, openwork, or carved surfaces. The backs of the chairs became lower; the feet were often drawn from models from the Far East. Furniture was usually made of walnut, burr walnut, or mahogany. Inlay work and colors are much used in the style of Adam and Hepplewhite, which has more than one similarity with the Louis XVI style, namely, straight lines, practically no sculpture, geometrical or checkered forms on the backs, decorative motifs from the past, etc. Although English furniture-making followed national ideas, while developing along the direction of the French styles, there was one trend that slavishly imitated Louis XV furniture; in this trend, decorative inlay and finishing work in finely treated bronze played the most important part.

25. Walnut chair, reign of Queen Anne or George I (first quarter of eighteenth century). The middle splat in the back is still solid; there are shells on the knees of the cabriole legs, which end in ball-and-claw feet. 26. Chippendale armchair, about 1755. The back is not so high, the center splat has openwork. The arms bow out above the seat. 27. Lyre-back chair after design by Robert Adam, about 1775. The most striking features are the classicistic trend and the tendency toward slimness. 28. Wedgwood soup tureen, the so-called Queen's Ware, about 1770–75. The form imitates silversmith work. The bird decoration was applied in Liverpool by transfer printing. 29. Mantlepiece, pine, in the so-called Chinese style. We find here rocaille, and in particular the C-motif of the Louis XV style. 30. Crescent-shaped commode in Adam style, mahogany and other woods. Painted panels in the manner of Angelica Kauffmann.

25

27

28

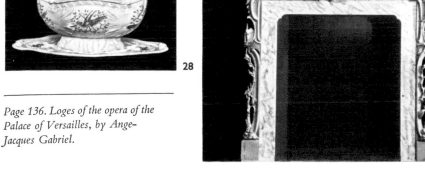

29

Page 136. Loges of the opera of the Palace of Versailles, by Ange-Jacques Gabriel.

30

LOUIS XVI STYLE

GENERAL INTRODUCTION The second half of the eighteenth century is so deeply marked by events of the greatest importance that every field of art shows their influence. Perhaps the most striking was the excavating activity, around 1750, in Pompeii and Herculaneum, where suddenly a civilization appeared before the astonished view of men who had only seen ancient objects in museum collections. An exaggerated interest in antiquity arose, expressed at the outset in architecture and decoration, and the *mise-en-scène* in theaters was revised; the mania even spread to everyday street clothing. The thoughts of the men who were preparing the Revolution and those that survived it were filled with Greece and especially with republican Rome. After the period during which the mind had free rein, in the discursive and sarcastic form in which Voltaire excelled, sentiment began to predominate in literature: the heart took the front of the stage, tears were *bon ton*, and the expression of states of mind went over easily from exaggerated sentimentality into the most theatrical of utterances.

Another very important gain of this century is the discovery of Nature, and the idea that peasants possess just the virtues that worldly life and its corruption had banished from society.

These discoveries led to the preference for English gardens with their rural character, as well as for insipid and artificial sheepfolds, in the world of the idle classes, such as the circle surrounding Queen Marie-Antoinette; in art, the rural melodramas painted by Greuze give a very good idea of the new fashion.

Music in France was represented by such composers as Grétry and Monsigny, but the finest works in this field were the operas of a foreigner, Christof W. von Gluck (*Iphigenia in Aulis, Iphigenia in Tauris, Orpheus and Eurydice*). Mozart was of greater interest to the French as an infant prodigy than during his early maturity.

The king was so completely indifferent to art that it is really ridiculous to refer to a style by his name. The queen, however, encouraged artistic activity by her numerous commissions; she had a marked preference for German artists, who held the foremost place in furniture design.

ARCHITECTURE The most outstanding works of the period were major buildings. Furthermore, architects, more than other artists, have always followed the whims of fashion with discretion; here too they gave little ground. They were already ahead of fashion when Ange-Jacques Gabriel (1698–1782) triumphed with the classical designs for impressive buildings, such as the Ecole Militaire, Paris, the Opéra at Versailles, and the Petit Trianon with its outbuildings, a masterpiece of taste and balance.

In church architecture, however, the Baroque style was firmly entrenched. It was weakening, though, and the most representative building erected was the church of Sainte-Geneviève by J. G. Souflot (1713–80) in a mixture of ancient styles, especially the Pantheon in Rome, after which it was renamed in the Revolution. Not much more church building was carried on, and as far as municipal architecture is concerned, Paris has nothing to show for the Louis XVI period that compares with the Place Vendôme and the Place des Victoires in the reign of the Sun King.

A great work, now unfortunately all but vanished, was undertaken at the initiative of the farmers general (tax collectors), namely a set of customs houses by Claude Nicolas Ledoux (1736–1806), forming a sort of belt around Paris. Two of these rotundas, in the Parc Monceau and in La Villette, are still standing.

The most frequent type of building has a rectangular façade with an arched opening in the middle, often flanked by Corinthian columns and with a triangular pediment above, decorated with sculpture. Splendid examples of this are the Hôtel de Salm by Pierre Rousseau and the Petit Pavillon de Bagatelle by François Bélanger, both in Paris, the Château de Bénouville by Ledoux near Caen, the Grand Théâtre by Victor Louis at Bordeaux, the Palais des Rohan by Salins de Montfort at Saverne, and the very fine water tower by J. A. Giral at Montpellier. In general, the buildings erected in the Louis XVI period can be described as masterful.

1

1. The Barrière de la Villette, one of the customs houses built in Paris, 1784–89, by Claude Ledoux, an instance of the sober, almost Roman style in which this forerunner of the architecture of the Empire excelled.

2. *Façade and dome of the Panthéon (Ste. Geneviève), by J. G. Soufflot, built 1764–89. His return to sober, antique tradition is visible especially in the interior. 3. Water tower at Montpellier, by J. A. Giral (1720–87). This architect too drew on antiquity. 4. The Pavillon Français in the garden of the Petit Trianon, by Ange-Jacques Gabriel. 5. Galleries of the Palais Royal, Paris, designed by Victor Louis and built 1786–90.*

SCULPTURE Edmé Bouchardon's nature led him to develop in the direction of the style of Louis XVI; because of his quieter expression and his gradual liberation from the dynamics and restlessness of Bernini, which were so powerful under Louis XV, Bouchardon may be regarded as a harbinger of the sculptors of the next period. Among them are latecomers, such as Caffieri, and vigorous innovators, such as Jean-Antoine Houdon, whose careers extend into the Empire. The activity of sculptors was intertwined with the erection of large architectural works.

Sculptors were not helped much by the church, nor did civilian architecture give them many opportunities: the exceptions are few pediments, like that of the Panthéon. By good fortune Count d'Angiviller, superintendent of works, provided commissions for a series of portraits devoted to national victories, which were designed for the great gallery in the Louvre.

As the careers of L. S. Adam, Guillaume II Coustou (mausoleum of the dauphin), and Louis-Claude Vassé (mausoleum of Stanislas Leszczynski, former king of Poland) were coming to an end, Jean-Baptiste Pigalle (1714–85) was at work, and continued virtually throughout the reign of Louis XVI. His tomb for the Maréchal de Saxe is already in clear reaction to the taste of the supporters of Adam and Slodtz.

In addition to these artists, new talents came forward: such names as Caffieri, Julien, Pajou, Clodion, and Houdon set the tone during the reign of Louis XVI. Jean-Jacques Caffieri remained an exponent of the lifelike style down to the eve of the Revolution. He excelled in such representations even when he made portrait busts of worthies whom he had never seen. Pierre Julien was much in favor with Count d'Angiviller, but the king preferred Augustin Pajou, who made the decorations of the Versailles Opéra and many portrait busts.

Jean-Antoine Houdon (1714–1828) was the most important sculptor of the age of Louis XVI. He was very acute in gauging the characters of his sitters, and thereby attaining great expressive power. His *Voltaire*, to name only one instance, is a type of the genre. Like Pajou, he worked in widely differing manners; his *Diana*, executed in the style of sixteenth-century Italian bronzes, is in diametrical opposition to the style of the portraits. Because of his faithfulness to truth, his collection of portraits is a historical document of the first magnitude.

The reputation of many artists of this time is based on their portrait busts of individuals. This activity may not have been in accord with academic dignity, but they earned their living from it rather than from official commissions.

One of the most gifted men of this time, Claude Michel, known as Clodion (1738–1814), did excellent work in the form of furniture ornaments and statuettes, mostly in terracotta. The sources of his inspiration, and his restless manner of working make him a second Fragonard.

Foreign countries had attracted French artists before, and this radiation continued under Louis XVI. Among the masters who spread abroad the reputation of the nation were Falconet, Marie-Anne Collot, Vassé, Saly, and Gillet, the founder of the St. Petersburg Academy.

7

6

6, 7. The decorations of the Hôtel Borély, Marseilles, and the former Hôtel de Fersen in Paris show how antiquity and its decorative motives came to permeate residences in the time of Louis XVI.

8

PAINTING Painting at the end of the reign of Louis XV and under his successssor clearly shows the two most important tendencies of the time, the increased receptivity to emotional impressions and the exaggerated admiration of antiquity. Among the many talented painters, some were highly regarded and have remained well known because they represented so completely the taste of their times, despite their various artistic merits: Greuze, David, Hubert Robert, and Madame Vigée-Lebrun. But the most faithful interpreter of the end of the *ancien régime* is undoubtedly Fragonard. He did not yield to the caprices of fashion, but his success shows that his manner met the actual aspirations of his clients and was not only a question of surface glitter.

Posterity has been much less kind to Greuze (1725–1805) than was Diderot, who saw in him the preacher of a morality which Diderot favored. Greuze's best-known works are the domestic scenes in which he extolled the harmony of family life, or portrayed with an avenging brush the punishment of an unworthy son. Prints at once gave these compositions wide distribution; they became, as it were, an antidote to the *fêtes galantes* and other trivial subjects to which the painters of the previous generation had been so addicted. Unfortunately, the good intentions are expressed in ostentatious gestures, so that we tend to pass over the painter's genuine merits. Greuze's penetration and knowledge enabled him to lay the subject bare; he

tried by means of exposed anatomy to interest those viewers who might not respond to other expressions of feeling.

Through prints, not only moralizing scenes were spread abroad; a copious repertoire of compositions signed by Pierre A. Baudouin, Lavreince, Schall, etc., showed for the most part scenes of various phases of undress, emphasizing suggestive insinuation. Yet Greuze in his portraits, the most traditional of French genres, rose to the level of the best artists; he was not distracted by the whims of fashion, and posterity came to regard him as the Largillière of his time.

The reign of Louis XVI has many portraitists who do not have the place in history to which they are entitled. Vestier is still too little known to be appreciated at his true worth; F. H. Drouais (1727–75) is interesting for his portrait of the elderly Louis XV and for his charming pictures of children. One of the best portraitists is undoubtedly Joseph Siffred Duplessis, famous for his portrait of Louis XVI as dauphin. Other portraits give a better idea of the artist's modesty; he liked to present his subjects in utter simplicity, trying to express the inner life of the person.

Portraits, too, are perhaps the best portion of the work of Jacques-Louis David (1748–1825). His brother-in-law and sister-in-law Sériziat are the subjects of handsome paintings, in which we can hardly recognize the stern maker of the *Oath of the Horatii* (1785).

11

12

*8. Jean-Philippe Rameau, bust by J. J. Caffieri
(1725–92). Caffieri obtained effects of remarkable life,
both in his busts of contemporaries and in those
prepared after old portraits. 9. Statue of Buffon, the
naturalist, by Augustin Pajou (1730–1809). Notable
for the sharply marked facial features; Pajou often
blurs a face, especially in the case of female portraits.
10. Bust of Cagliostro, by Jean-Antoine Houdon
(1741–1828). Great vividness, achieved by catching
a momentary pose. 11. The Citizen (1758–65),*

*allegorical figure, by Jean-Baptiste Pigalle. Here too
antiquity was the inspiration. The subject is unexpected
for a monument in honor of Louis XV, placed in Reims.
12. Dying Gladiator, by Pierre Julien (1731–1804).
This sculptor evokes a tragic theme derived from the
obsession with the past. 13. In the Young Bacchante
by Claude Michel, called Clodion (1738–1814),
there is the pleasant mythological note that inspired
the artist to so many gracious works.*

Color and glittering light are certainly not among the charms we expect in the artist who revived classical and academic painting in France. The drawing, which is very hard, forces itself on the attention. Some special works of his pre-Revolutionary period, such as the portraits of Count Potocki and of Philippe-Laurent de Joubert, make us regret not seeing more of that phase of his art.

Diderot had eagerly hoped for the return of the "great," stern antique style; David's *Belisarius*, and especially the *Oath of the Horatii*, exhibited in the Salon of 1785, fulfilled that wish to the letter. The movement had already been initiated by lesser artists. Hubert Robert (1733–1808) is not distinguished by the Spartan and Stoic inspiration that meant so much to David, but he had an unmistakable partiality for the antique. During a long stay in Italy he had made many splendid drawings, which he later used as the source of innumerable paintings intended to adorn dwellings in the new style. Robert is a connoisseur of antique objects rather than a fanatic for antiquity; what had impressed him during his travels in the peninsula was the picturesqueness of ruins, especially in combination with vegetation. Once the ruins had become a decor, many liberties can be taken with reality, and that is what Hubert Robert does.

Pannini and others had shown the profit that could be gained from ruins. Gaffoni, Lacroix de Marseille, and others have left us compositions that closely resemble such work. Italy also taught the French

13

15

14

16

14. *The Comte de la Bretêche, a portrait by Jean-Honoré Fragonard (1732–1806), one of his formidable sketches, "got up in an hour." Fragonard, painter of love, is also a wizard of light. 15. Gardens of the Villa d'Este in Rome, wash drawing by Fragonard. During his* *stay in Rome he was more interested in trees than in ruins. He draws nothing precisely but represents the foliage by suggesting the light falling on and through the leaves. 16. Bathers, by Fragonard. He was not afraid of daring subjects, and took pleasure in painting these soft bodies.*

landscape painters the decorative value of water and the enchantment of light. It would be unjust to these painters to dismiss them as merely decorators of talent: the French scene with its views of the Seine with its bridges, of the changes made in Paris and the park at Versailles, and of the antique monuments of Provence found in them interpreters of the first rank.

Joseph Vernet (1714–89) painted beautiful landscapes of Italian towns and the great French ports. His reputation as a specialist in sailing ships brought him many commissions for dramatic compositions. We should not forget that the men now moving with their times were full of sensibility when they could forget to be cynical. Although Vernet was not a wizard with light, he did much to inculcate a taste for genuine landscape, to which the French had been insensible for a long time.

Another artist, Louis-Gabriel Moreau (Moreau l'ainé, 1740–1806), treated landscape in a new spirit. People appear on a small scale and play no important part. Moreau's conception of nature, and of vegetation in particular, announces Daubigny and Théodore Rousseau.

Madame Elisabeth Vigée-Lebrun (1755–1842), a pupil of Greuze and the portraitist of so many pretty ladies of the end of the eighteenth century, became prominent early. She also liked to take herself as model, alone or preferably with her little daughter. She was the best-beloved portraitist of Marie-Antoinette, whose good qualities she brought out without stressing the defects. Her contemporary and rival, Madame Labille-Guiard, who had a more masculine talent, presumably handled her brush with less diplomacy.

Elisabeth Vigée's friendship with the queen brought her an enormous clientele. Fortunately for us, Madame Vigée-Lebrun (she was 34 when the Revolution broke out) usually did not paint her contemporaries in their ceremonial attire, but in simple, attractive dresses and soft straw hats, or in street clothing: a proof of good taste in the models and in the painter. Did all these ladies have such pretty faces? It is doubtful; most probably the artist helped somewhat to create the idealized types.

18

19

17. *Portrait of a Young Man (Saint-Just?), by Jean-B. Greuze (1725–1805), in an unconstrained posture. 18. Portrait of Babuti, by Greuze. This portrait of his father-in-law shows how skillfully Greuze adapted his style to his subject. 19. Young Girl with Doves, by Greuze, a model of the moralizing, prettified, or melodramatic works that were most appreciated in his own time but irritate us today. 20. The Dauphin and Madame Royale, the children of Louis XVI and Marie-Antoinette, by Elisabeth Vigée-Lebrun (1755–1842). There is a simulated naturalness, after the mode of the times. 21. Self-portrait with Daughter, by Vigée-Lebrun; she was a good pupil of Greuze, and confined herself to portraits. We need not ask what her models are thinking about— they are just pretty. Decorative values predominate.*

21

Jean-Honoré Fragonard (1732–1806) was the pupil and successor of Boucher. Virtuosity, restlessness, and brilliant improvisation are the outstanding features of his work. Young Fragonard's visit to Italy gave him, in addition to friendship with Hubert Robert, the most ravishing wash drawings of gardens, set down with a masterly hand. France imposed a genre on him to which his fame was to be limited; he became the painter of love, especially in its risqué eighteenth-century form. He was the favorite painter of Madame du Barry.

Fragonard also painted beautiful portraits of old men, but youth was his favorite theme. In drawings, in which the lines are barely suggested but nevertheless give brilliant life to the whole, he has sketched family scenes from various milieus, in an unforgettable manner. From the technical point of view, the great originality of this artist is that his works seem to be unfinished, contrary to the custom of the time. His brush strokes are as restless and certainly as strong as those of Frans Hals. His palette usually seems to have only

22

23

25

27

22. In the portrait of the aging Louis XV, F.-H. Drouais excelled himself. Here the king is alone, and this "snapshot" shows his human weariness and bitterness. 23. Portrait of the composer Gluck, by J.-S. Duplessis, 1776. A vivid portrait, as if the composer were awaiting inspiration. The painter obviously took pleasure in his treatment of the fabrics. 24. Portrait of Laurent de Joubert, by J.-L. David (1748–1825). David's work as a portraitist is entirely within the spirit of the eighteenth century, and he has left us some luminous and brilliant works. 25. Lot and His Daughters, by J.-M. Vien (1716–1809), David's teacher. He represents a style that draws on noble sources and classical models. 26, 27. The Storm and Ponte Rotto illustrate two aspects of the art of Joseph Vernet (1714–89), who put together either great dramatic compositions in the virtuoso manner, or admirable river views and seascapes, serenely painted in the tradition of Claude Lorrain.

yellow and brown, with a bit of red and white to give contrast. But with these very limited means he obtains amazing effects; the pictures seem to flame. His trees are surrounded by a special atmosphere, and his forms are more as if seen in a dream than in sharp presentation. Fragonard does not give detail; his image is vague or disappears in the half-shadow; he played with light as no other artist has.

Actuality and manners are sharply perceived by many painters and engravers, who became true historiographers of the reign of Louis XVI. They have one quality in common: the small format of their works does not preclude magnitude in the subjects they represented. Street incidents as well as weightier events of the day attracted their interest. A certain documentary dryness sets them off from their predecessors, the Flemish and Dutch genre painters of the seventeenth century, and their stature is not that of the French painters already mentioned.

When we consider it coolly, from a distance, we wonder whether the great artists of the period, especially those whose production was so large, were able to realize all their potentialities. Hubert Robert, Greuze, Joseph Vernet, Madame Vigée-Lebrun, and above all Fragonard himself, were victims of their own success, which nipped their curiosity, bridled their esthetic aspirations, and made them less able to renew themselves by exploring unknown territory. The work of these painters must often be regarded as decoration more than anything else.

While taking an interest in what surrounded them—woodwork, furniture, and *objets d'art*—the artists of the age of Louis XVI remain true to an established tradition of balance among all the factors that contribute to the beauty of an interior. There is no need to belittle these painters, theirs was no minor art. It may be that they provide little food for the spirit, but their works are a pleasure to the eye and leave behind them a memory of joy.

29

28. Replanting the Versailles Gardens, by Hubert Robert, about 1778. Robert himself made great changes in the gardens, and sketched the transformations realistically; he includes the royal family incidentally in his paintings. 29. Washerwomen at the Fountain, by Hubert Robert, shows another form of his talent, the combination of architecture and vegetation; for this genre Italy had provided him with perfect models. 30. Distant View of the Hills of Montreuil, by L.-G. Moreau (1739–1805). Moreau the Elder was particularly distinguished as a painter of trees. His canvases are small, and the human figures serve merely to bring out the height of the foliage.

30

31. The Awkward Confession, engraving after Lavreince, about 1787. In the reign of Louis XVI prints on risqué subjects were often made, many of them after Lavreince. 32. The Authors of the Encyclopédie, engraving by Augustin de Saint-Aubin (1736–1807), who succeeded in putting painterly nuances into his engraved work.

33. Promenade in the Palais Royal, 1787, by Ph.-L. Debucourt. Debucourt wittily sketched the idleness and absurdities of Parisians out for a stroll. His sarcasm precedes the caricatures of Rowlandson.

31

Charles Panckoucke aux Auteurs de l'Encyclopédie 32

33

34

PRINTS   The second half of the eighteenth century was very productive in the field of prints; this was of the greatest historical importance, since the old technique of the graving tool was enriched by a series of new processes for imitating drawings and watercolors. Public demand for the works of outstanding painters undoubtedly stimulated these inventions. One was what is called the crayon manner, the great archievement of Gilles Demarteau of Liège (1722–76), long resident in Paris; he realized that it was possible, using red pastel or three different colors, to make accurate reproductions of the most representative masters of the eighteenth century, especially Watteau and Boucher. His nephew, Demarteau le Jeune, enriched this repertoire with imitations of wash drawings and aquarelles, a process in which Janinet, Dagoty, Descourtis, and Debucourt (an engraver of his own works) made names. Pastels were also happily transposed by Bonnet.

The art of engraving also gave permanence to works from the reign of Louis XV. Engraving with the burin continued to be used as successfully as the new techniques. It provided book illustrations ranging in size from the vignette to the large quarto composition. The work of Eisen, originally from Brussels, remains close to Boucher, although he introduces a banal note; but above all he is the illustrator of La Fontaine's *Fables*, where his talent appears in the best light. His work is still linked with the past; he still represents the Louis XV style.

Jean-Michel Moreau the Younger, the younger brother of the landscape painter, did many engravings that show his mastery; but he outdid himself in the *Monuments du Costume*, incomparable scenes of elegant life under Louis XVI; the work is a source for everybody who wants to represent this period with the help of historical illustrations.

These were the greatest artists; in addition, there were many gifted people who would have had greater reputations had they lived in a time less favorable to able engravers.

34. The Little Godparents, one of the sheets of the Monuments du Costume, 1776, by Moreau the Younger, a masterful series of prints.

INTERIOR DECORATION AND FURNITURE In the field of decoration, the Louis XV style had gradually freed itself from its initial exaggeration; small leaves and very simple flowers began to drive out other motifs and give the style a typically French appearance, original in every respect.

Then the engraver Charles-Nicolas Cochin (1715–90) published his famous pamphlet, *Mercure de France*, in which he ironically summoned the decorators of every trade to abandon nongeometrical lines, especially the S-line which was the essential hallmark of this style. His narrow-minded opinion became a dogma, and an avenue became blocked when its potentialities were still unknown.

A general rigidity set in, and a rapid return to the entire gamut of the classical decorative repertoire. The works of the decorators, however, do not suffer by comparison with those of the first half of the century. Indeed, Pompeian paintings and varied mythological subjects inspired them to new themes. The Louis XVI style is never violent in color; sky blue, water green, pink, gray, and white dominate, whether in solid surfaces, striped panels, or in the figure compositions or cameo designs, often seen in textiles (*toile de Jouy*). The panels of woven fabrics on the walls were replaced by wallpaper.

The same mastery and sureness of touch is found in the furniture, where inlay work competes with painting: trophies, human figures, and views of ruins are set forth with exaggerated virtuosity on the panels; these in addition are loaded with geometrical combinations of cubes, lozenges, and curved lines, giving a somewhat more sober note. Rosewood often gives way to mahogany. The forms follow the feeling of the moment; the legs at first curve back under the bodies of the commodes, then curvature disappears, and is replaced by straight lines; legs with ball and pyramid forms are seen again, as in the *grand siècle*. Public taste prefers the rolltop desk, which supplants the flattop. In a remarkable way, the Louis XVI style has won its spurs and may well be regarded as a definitive national style, giving France works of art that often rival those of the previous reign.

35

36. Cabinet by Molitor. During the reign of Louis XVI, Molitor was already making pieces prefiguring the Empire, with their rigid forms and palmette decoration. 37. Secretary, with Sèvres porcelain leaf and side walls, by Martin Carlin (died 1785). Finesse and distinction are the hallmarks of most of his pieces.

35. Commode by J.-H. Riesener (1734–1806), the most representative furniture maker of the Louis XVI style. His pieces all bear the mark of his personality.

36

37

38. A bonheur du jour, a lady's desk, by R. Vander Cruze-Lacroix, who excelled in this form. 39. Arm-chair by Sené. This chair recalls the Louis XIV style, but the decorative motifs are completely Louis XVI. 40. Incense burner by Pierre Gouthière (1732–1813), a great master of bronzework. 41. Settee, 1790, approaching the Directoire style in the turned columns on back, arms, and feet, while the other motifs are Louis XVI. 42. Tobacco jar, by Leendert Brouwer, 1787.

EMPIRE

GENERAL INTRODUCTION: POLITICAL AND SOCIAL LIFE
The great change in France at the end of the eighteenth century had culminated in anarchy and the reign of terror. The interest of the substantial bourgeoisie in self-preservation and the security of their property, coupled with Bonaparte's genius, had enabled that dictator to found an empire on the ruins of the abolished monarchy. It had been seen where the power of the mob led to; there was now a longing for order and well-being. The hereditary aristocracy had been wiped out or had emigrated, and the Jacobin guillotine had thinned the ranks of the well-to-do educated bourgeois idealists who had unchained the Revolution but lost control of it. From among the newly rich adventurers, officers, and half-converted men of the people, the Emperor recruited his "aristocrats," laying much more emphasis on ability than on manners or a spotless past. Where the Jacobins had envisaged the Roman Republic as the model of civic virtue and freedom, the Emperor's subjects had the Roman Empire as their ideal, and identified him with Augustus. The Corsican could not but be pleased by the flattery; he played his role as this great man of antiquity flawlessly. His aim was a world empire greater than the Roman Empire, with a matchless art and culture to shed luster on it and a French-Augustan superliterature to perpetuate it.

Until the point was reached where the pressure of taxation and Napoleon's hunger for cannon fodder made his rule seem intolerable, people were content. Public works gave employment to huge numbers of men; unemployment was only local and sporadic. Commerce and industry received much government support in forms which also stimulated private initiative, already favored by the elimination of the last remainders of guild restrictions. Prosperity increased, one reason being the widened demand for luxury goods. The country's standing in the eyes of the world had risen; people sunned themself in the glory of the conqueror and in the prestige of their art, science, and way of life. Loosened guild restrictions and rapidly applied new inventions (Jacquard loom, 1800) foreshadowed the industrial revolution, but there was just enough industrialization to insure the manufacturer the key position that he later reinforced. It is true that the role of the nobility had not been exhausted; blue blood still opened the doors to high position. But manufacturers, great merchants, and bankers were indirectly the rulers of the century of the bourgeoisie. The people that were not "well-to-do" or "educated" were politically helpless.

The dark sides of industrial development only became visible under Louis-Philippe. For the time being the enterprises were small, and the personal tie between worker and employer was unbroken. The workers had been trained in the time of the guilds, for the most part, and the spirit of the craftsman was still strong; there was as yet little division of labor, and the public was demanding as to quality. Paris was already attracting manpower, but what agriculture lost went to local industries to a great extent. As yet depopulation of the countryside in France had not begun. In England, pauperization and the migration to the towns had already begun in the second half of the eighteenth century. Elsewhere it did not take place until the middle of the nineteenth century, and in Germany not until after the Franco-Prussian war. Although the balance of government in France swung from many-headed chaos to absolute rule, the achievements of the Revolution were not abandoned. The common sense of the solid bourgeois led him to expect Napoleon to provide a firm government that would discount the rights of the *homme et citoyen*, an expectation that was not disappointed. The Emperor's foreign adventures were accepted as long as France prospered from them, consoled by the realization that the days of adventure in internal affairs were over.

All this had its effect on manners and outward morality. Formality was adopted at the Napoleonic court, where laughter was not allowed and the bon mot perished in the atmosphere of chill majesty; and bourgeois manners had triumphed over both the frivolity of the *ancien régime* and the looseness of the revolutionary age; these factors cooperated to make the style of the Empire one of thoroughgoing classicism, with its special stamp of strict decorum. The excavations at Pompeii had brought a deeper knowledge of antiquity; when, in the middle of the eighteenth century, the Louis XVI style came as a classicistic reaction against the bizarre and swirling Rococo, it was already evident that antiquity was no longer seen through Renaissance lenses, but through a Romantic one.

SCIENCE, PHILOSOPHY, RELIGION The paradox of Romanticism is that, although freedom from restraint constitutes its essence, it still adapts itself to the limitations of a fixed form; this traditional formal language is based on the deeper paradox of a world view that still glorifies reason but is unsatisfied by its sobriety. Elementary outbursts of irrationality were detested after the Revolution, but people continued to cherish in their own spiritual lives what they feared as a mass phenomenon. The eighteenth century already knew the ambivalence of reason and sentimentalism, Enlightenment and Romanticism; when reasonableness destroyed spontaneous feeling, the way was always open to revel in sentiment, thereby proving oneself a chosen spirit, a *schöne Seele*, with finer feelings than the multitude. During the Empire, which marks the transition between the age of reason and the age of Romanticism, the cleft gradually spreads. But where reason lost ground in the field of art, it became for the first time dominant in science. The founder of experimental chemistry, Lavoisier, had fallen victim to the reign of terror; the Jacobin Carnot, however, became the greatest engineer of the time and Napoleon's minister; Cuvier, Geoffroy Saint-Hilaire, and Lamarck bring into biology the strictly inductive proof that arrives at general prin-

ciples by comparing evidence, without ruling out the converse procedure of deduction from the principle to interpretation of the evidence; Cuvier and Lamarck were the founders of the new sciences of paleontology and the theory of evolution, respectively. In philosophy France had not yet outgrown the Enlightenment, while German idealism, overlapping the Empire in part, had reached a synthesis of rationalistic and Romantic tendencies in Fichte and Hegel. Theology was still dominated by reason and had a theistic tinge; people believed in a Creator, who had called his creation into existence according to a rational plan and then left it to its fate without interfering further with natural laws. Outside of Germany the time was not yet ripe for Schleiermacher's mystical theology. Individuals and groups appeared here and there who vivified religion primarily by means of feeling, but for the majority of educated people, insofar as they had not broken with the church, its doctrine and ethics were more important than their immediate relationship with the divine.

LITERATURE AND MUSIC The Empire, carrying Louis XVI classicism to its utmost consequences, pretended to be even more faithful to antiquity. But it was not so classicistic, let alone classical, as it

made itself out to be; an unconscious Romanticism often was clad in antique forms. Many paintings by Ingres, Gros, or Prud'hon, statues by Canova or Thorvaldsen, poems by Willem Bilderdijk, de Chénier, or Foscolo, compositions by Beethoven, are Romantic in the Empire style; only later did the Romantic spirit find its own Romantic forms. It is no accident that the closing decades of the eighteenth century and the opening decade of the nineteenth are called the classical age in music, for Haydn, Mozart, and the young Beethoven reached a balance and a peak that was only possible as the synthesis of the innovations introduced by many predecessors. Nor is it an accident that toward the end of the Empire period that same Beethoven, who in his heroic solitude was already the incarnation of a Romantic artist's legend during his lifetime, went his own way so strongly that rigid form yielded to the expressive urge of his titanic personality. Haydn's cheerfulness and Mozart's grace had also concealed unsuspected depths, but a whole world lay between these artists, whose social function was to furnish musical adornment to festivals of the *ancien régime*, and Beethoven possessed by his art in the loneliness of his deafness. The characteristic Romantic composers did not drop from the skies, and Beethoven was the indispensable link to Romanticism in music. In the same way, the

1. The radiating lines around the arch and the medallions on the façade of the Hôtel Gouthière, Paris, foretell the tempered severity of the Directoire. 2. The Empire shop front of a pharmacy in the Rue de Gramont, Paris, shows symmetry, a linear design enclosed within an arch form, and winged Victories. 3. A typical Directoire façade, lighter in style than the heavy monumentality of the Empire, is that of the Folie St.-James of Bélanger at Neuilly-sur-Seine.

4. The Madeleine, Paris, a church in neoclassical style by Pierre Vignon. 5. Greenhouses of the Botanical Garden, Brussels, 1826, adorned only by the Ionic columns of the pavilions and its unity with the park around it : a masterpiece of the Empire style. 6. Under the influence of the Empire, the Baroque-classicist town hall of Groningen, 1793–1810, has a central portico, very rare in the Netherlands. 7. Arc de Triomphe du Carrousel, Paris.

5

generation of Chateaubriand and Madame de Staël prepared the way in literature for those who, with Hugo, Lamartine, de Vigny, and the Musset, dethroned classicism around 1830.

DRAMA AND DANCE   Although the Empire includes the time of the Napoleonic wars, which exposed innumerable people to conscription, invasion, billeting of troops, requisitioning, high taxes and prices, and commercial difficulties arising out of the Continental system, there was a lively social life all through Europe, a general thirst for pleasure and amusement. It was an age of great actors (Talma); the dramatic repertoire, still officially dominated by French classical tragedy, offered sufficient distraction in the form of sentimental comedies and all kinds of farces to attract full houses. The prosperity of the concert world was furthered by the rise of the virtuoso and by the modern symphony orchestra, which made performances for large audiences possible and put chamber music and small orchestras out of fashion. The ballet was in great vogue, and even more so new social dances such as the gavotte and the waltz. A man who could cut a good figure on the dance floor was sure of a bright career, and the dance mania was whipped up further by the part that Napoleon's officers played in social life. In ballet and in social

dancing, the public did not always distinguish between gymnastic and artistic feats; the cult for sensationalism was also expressed in the prominence of musical infant prodigies. Despite rigorously maintained decorum and the moderating influences emanating from the court circles and the wealthy bourgeoisie, with their long-standing ideas of propriety, manners were very loose, especially in France, in the pleasure-loving world of soldiers and parvenus; and ladies of quality competed with the demimonde in the daring of their dress, or rather undress, at balls and parties. But those who felt that a lack of suitable manners made them unacceptable could hire a dancing master or an impoverished *ci-devant* to give them some.

SPIRIT AND CHARACTERISTICS OF THE STYLE   The Empire style is subdivided into the Directoire style (1790-1800), and the Empire style proper (1800-30), the Directoire forming a transition from the Louis XVI to the true Empire style. The formal, representative, and static character of the Empire style and its conscious turning away fom nature were determined by the fact that it carries further an older classicism, while serving at the same time to glorify an emperor and an empire modeled on ancient Rome. Classicism aims at creating ideal, imperishable, timeless beauty on the basis of the stylistic forms

6

7

8   9   1

of some previous period held to be "classic," a permanent model. The best Empire has a character and shows an exquisite taste that becomes rare later on; bad Empire is associated in our minds with plaster instead of bronze and marble, is academic in the pejorative sense of the word, cold, rigid, lifeless, unoriginal, and uninteresting. Between the two extremes there are many possibilities. Classical art avoids the violent and titanic, seeking its power in Winckelmann's often-cited "noble simplicity and calm grandeur." It disdains the playful and amiable for the great, the stately, the noble, the majestic. No other style aspires less to being superficially attractive or is so completely devoid of humor and emotion. It aims at being impressive, but in a reserved way, with no trace of the excesses of the Baroque. Tall forms must not be lank and must have a certain volume, and in particular must not destroy the equilibrium between the load and the supporting parts, between horizontals and verticals. When space is scanty inside a dwelling, correct proportions and sparse furniture may give the impression of spaciousness; cool dignity is the main thing, with comfort and intimacy sacrificed.

ARCHITECTURE   No important public buildings were erected in the Directoire style; many of the smaller buildings that have come down to us have been modified in later modes.
Architects especially appreciated under the Directoire were François Bélanger and Claude-Nicolas Ledoux. Bélanger had built the small Château de la Bagatelle in the Bois de Boulogne and the Folie St.-James in Neuilly sur Seine; Ledoux had built the impressive tollhouses, or Barrières, of Paris, several of which still remain, in addition to some handsome, Italianate dwellings, now gone. These pre-Revolutionary façades have an air of cool calm, and serve to bridge the decorative equilibrium of the Louis XVI style and the majestic, pompous weight of the Empire. A favorite architectural ornament of the Directoire is the round medallion in relief with an antique scene. The creators of the Empire style in architecture are Charles Percier and Pierre-François-Léonard Fontaine. Their structures are often recognizable imitations of famous buildings of the Roman imperial time. Thus, one of their most important works, the Arc de Triomphe of the Place du Carrousel, is after the triumphal arch of Septimius Severus in Rome, although stones of various colors are used.
On façades, borrowings from the French and Italian Renaissance were often combined with strict antique pediments, pilasters, and

colonnades. The Madeleine, that seemingly austere temple in Paris, although not lacking in Italian details, became the model for many churches, including some outside France. From the point of view of color, an Empire building in the antique style has a different effect from its prototype since local stone takes the place of marble, to a great extent, and no other polychromy is employed. In Germany, Empire architecture is more Greek than Roman in character (Berlin, Karl Friedrich Schinkel; Munich, Leo von Klenze). In England too, where strict classicism antedates the Adam style (which corresponds to the Directoire) and where the acquaintance with Greek originals was fairly widespread, Greek forms and Roman mingle. Later in this period, Robert Smirke built the British Museum in a Grecian style. The French Empire style also set the standard for the Low Countries, Belgium producing more important work than did Holland.

SCULPTURE   Sculpture in France had excellent practitioners but no great men during the Empire: Jean-Baptiste Giraud, Antoine-Denis Chaudet, Joseph Chinard (portrait busts of Mme. Récamier and Empress Josephine), François-Joseph Bosio. More important than the French, and setting the tone for the antique forms of the time, softened by languid grace, were the Italian Antonio Canova (*Amor and Psyche*; *Perseus*) and the Dane Bertel Thorvaldsen (*Christ*; *The Lion of Lucerne*), both admired excessively at the time and unjustly belittled later on.

*8. L'Amour, by Antoine-Denis Chaudet, 1802; charm and delicate humor in the image of the winged god, symbolically kindling the flame of love by feeding the butterfly of Psyche.
9. Amor and Psyche, by Antonio Canova, 1793, feelingly reproduces the encounter of earthly and heavenly love. 10. Bertel Thorvaldsen, in his very Greek Christ, 1821, sacrifices power to an ideal quality, which is furthered by an almost symmetrical composition and careful drapery.
11. Discobolus, by Kessel, 1819, is an instance of classicistic representation of the athletic ideal, with more emphasis on refinement than on vigor.*

11

13

PAINTING AND GRAPHIC ART While Percier and Fontaine dominated architecture, interior decoration, and furniture design, a real tyranny was exercised in painting by Jacques-Louis David, a great realistic painter (*Death of Marat*), an excellent portraitist, and, by fits and starts, a great colorist who yet treated color as an unessential additive; a school was formed based on his contrived, antiquarian, programmatic mythological and historical pieces (*The Sabine Women*; *Oath of the Horatii*; *Brutus and His Dead Son*). The prevailing tendencies of the time were evident in the rational transparent composition à la Poussin and Raphael: smooth touch, sallow, dull color, emphatic drawing, careful drapery and *belle peinture*, and studied monumentality. His most important pupil, Jean-Auguste-Dominique Ingres, is a virtuoso of line; he too regards color as incidental, and yet makes fascinating, refined combinations of clear, cool tones; he too composes rationally, and yet is a remarkably penetrating portraitist of aristocratic refinement. "*Le trait c'est le tout*": even smoke follows a line in his art. The line fills empty spaces in arabesque fashion, and this *chiffre* character anticipates the Pre-Raphaelites. Other pupils of David's are François-Pascal-Simon Gérard and Anne-Louis Girodet. Mention should also be made of Horace Vernet; Antoine-Jean Gros, the first realistic historical painter, who has Romantic elements and a feeling for color and the dramatic; Antoine-Jean Gros (*Napoleon Visiting the Pesthouse at Jaffa*); and Pierre-Paul Prud'hon, who is closest to Romanticism in fantasy, grace, and chiaroscuro (portrait of Empress Josephine; *Abduction of Psyche*; *Justice and Vengeance Pursuing Evildoing*); finally, the portrait painter and incomparable miniaturist, Jean-Baptiste Isabey.

14

15

12. *Anne-Louis Girodet's Burial of Atala, 1814, is still classicizing in its restrained emotion, but entirely Romantic in spirit.* 13. *The Sabine Women Ending the Battle Between the Romans and the Sabines, by David, about 1783, has a statuesque pseudomovement, which cannot unbend even in the face of death.* 14. *Prud'hon's Abduction of Psyche, 1808, uses chiaroscuro to conjure up a dream world, typical of the new Romantic treatment of mythology.* 15. *David, Paris and Helen, virtually symmetrical composition à la Poussin in parallel planes, with the group before a caryatid porch.*

INTERIOR DECORATION, FURNITURE, AND MINOR ARTS The style of the interiors and furniture of the Directoire differs from the heavier Empire style in a certain cold grace and bright active colors, with curtains and hangings in black, chamois brown, or purple. Louis XVI motifs such as putti, and turtle doves billing and cooing are not yet ruled out. Antiquarian reliefs, in rectangular or medallion form, adorn the walls. Directoire chairs are not as heavy and imposing as Empire chairs, and have openwork backs with a palmette or stylized flower basket, curving out in a volute at the top. The woodwork is still painted light gray, the upholstery brown with a red, yellow, or green pattern, or red with black.
Percier and Fontaine are the legislators for the furniture and decoration of the Empire, and the brothers Honoré-Georges and Georges II

Jacob are its cabinetmakers; after the death of the latter the surviving brother called himself Jacob Desmalter. The basic material of Empire furniture is polished mahogany (solid or veneered on beech), heightened by sparsely used gilt bronze ornament. The seats do not have the look of comfort and intimacy that they had in the time of Louis XVI, but are square in form with almost straight backs. In addition to side chairs there are the chaise longue, the *méridienne* (sofa with slanting back), and the *chauffe-dos* (bench with low arms at each end but no back). Tapestry, silk, velvet, damask, and green leather were used for covering. Along with the expensive solid mahogany furniture and the cheaper veneered pieces, elm, lemon, and maple were also employed for everyday use. The use of marquetry disappeared. The tables are round or octagonal, with a pedestal or three legs, often in the shape of griffons. The low brick fireplace with a carved frieze has an open hearth or cannon stove, and is crowned by a mirror between pilasters. High windows, with deep reveals and window seats, have draped curtains. The walls often have a frieze above damask cloth or wallpaper, and walls in large rooms are broken up by ornamental moldings and panelwork. On festive occasions the room was illuminated by chandeliers hanging by chains hidden in garlands of crystal; for daily use, there were oil lamps, or five-branched candelabra with adjustable tops, the arms formed as swan or eagle necks.

The decorative motifs are borrowed from antiquity: sphinxes, chimeras, lions' heads, meanders, wreaths, garlands, etc.; they are used singly, very rarely linked together.

Goldsmiths' and silversmiths' work had practically no chasing, confining itself to chiseled cast work and cold mounting of matte

decorations on a polished background (Odiot). Jewelry followed ancient models; cameos were in vogue.

In ceramics, severe lines and sober decoration mark the Sèvres porcelain, and to a lesser degree all provincial French pottery. Sèvres in turn influenced English, Austrian, and Russian porcelain. Wedgwood pottery in classicistic style was already in fashion under Louis XVI and remained popular during the Empire.

16. In this drawing of the Stamaty family by Ingres, 1818, what strikes us is the flawless certainty of the beautiful thin line, of which Ingres shows himself a master, and his ability to characterize the personalities fully by very sparing contours, as well as his magnificent presentation of easy nobility. 17. A typically street scene, Louis-L. Boilly's Arrival of the Mail Coach, 1803, shows the costumes of travelers and bystanders at the coach stop and the happy scenes of reunion. 18. A dramatic historical picture by Antoine-Jean Gros, who knew war from experience, Napoleon at the Battle of Eylau, about 1807. In this work the painter pays tribute to Napoleon, but without empty pathos and with powerful realism, as in the soldiers' faces turning up to him.

16

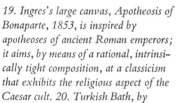

19

20

19. Ingres's large canvas, *Apotheosis of Bonaparte*, 1853, is inspired by apotheoses of ancient Roman emperors; it aims, by means of a rational, intrinsically tight composition, at a classicism that exhibits the religious aspect of the Caesar cult. 20. *Turkish Bath*, by Ingres, orientally voluptuous in atmosphere, but the figures statuesque and self-contained. With its Poussin-like composition in two planes, it is both Romantic and classicistic in nature, and suggests associations with Primaticcio, reliefs from India, and early Limoges ceramic platters. 21. Willem Bartel van der Kooi's *Love Letter*, 1808, a genre picture from Holland, distinguished in its types, light, and perception. 22. *Portrait of Mme. Rivière*, 1806, by Ingres, his ideal feminine beauty of the stout, luxuriant type. Note the attention to drapery. 23. In *The Lesson with the Angle Viewer*, about 1814, Adriaan de Lelie lovingly reproduces the grace and charm of the girlish figure bent over the instrument.

22

23

32

33

34

35

36

32. *François-P.-S. Gérard's portrait of Letitia Bonaparte, 1803, shows how the Empire costume flattered older women, in this case the emperor's mother. 33. Ingres, Bonaparte during His Visit to Liège, 1805, with his hand on a decree for the city. 34. In Gérard's Isabey and His Little Daughter, 1795, we are struck by the loving portrayal of the child.*
35. Abraham van Stry, The Weymans

Family, 1817, a very attractive group portrait that, for al its intimacy, still has the Empire suggestion of space in the interior; it gives a good idea of women's everyday dress, as contrasted with some of the gala costumes shown above.
36. Jewel cabinet of Empress Marie Louise, with amorous motifs, including Venus Anadyomene surrounded by cupids and nymphs.

37. *The chamber of Empress Joséphine at Malmaison, with ceiling decoration in medallions, has a Directoire character that makes it more intimate than true Empire. Its vaulted polygonal form suggests a costly tent. The details of the chairs are on the borderline between the two periods. 38. Despite the fact that the execution is simpler than the original design (by Prud'hon), this master copy by Odiot and Thomire of the cradle of Napoleon's son, the "King of Rome," is a masterpiece. 39. A pedestal corner table at Malmaison, mahogany, with a back wall of mirror glass, in which the Greek sphinxes are reflected. 40. Napoleon's desk at Malmaison, with chimera supports, a repeated chimera motif, and a carved, stylized branch.*

37

39

38

40

41. Prud'hon's paintings, separated by mirrors and Corinthian pilasters under a garland frieze in the Salon des Saisons in the hôtel of Eugène de Beauharnais. Rich effect of wall and ceiling decoration that is yet strictly controlled. 42. Anteroom looking toward the entrance hall of Syon House, Robert Adam's masterpiece, 1762; shows that at this early date the tendencies later known as Directoire were already appearing in England. 43. Empire clock, about 1800, ormolu; clock face framed with Empire motifs and flanked by caryatid figures with Egyptian heads of black enamel. 44. Dutch salon, Empire style, noteworthy for division of wall by Corinthian pilasters, with the capitals breaking a frieze of garlands. Note the mirror frame, the chimera legs on the tables, and the chandelier with garlands of crystal.

41

42

43

44

NINETEENTH CENTURY

GENERAL INTRODUCTION, POLITICAL AND SOCIAL LIFE Romanticism, with its paradoxes and contradictions, influenced all of the nineteenth century. Several European countries, such as France and England, developed colonial empires based on a nationalistic urge to conquest and on capitalism. On the other side, liberal and socialistic tendencies came more strongly into the foreground in Europe itself. The reaction against these liberal and revolutionary movements was especially strong in Russia, in Bismarck's Germany, in the France of Napoleon III, and in the countries of the Austro-Hungarian Empire. But even in the countries with more liberal governmental systems the right to vote was restricted to the propertied and educated bourgeoisie, who profited the most from the industrial and commercial development that marked the entire nineteenth century. The cities grew and flourished, and with them the middle class as well. The bourgeois is honest, since a good credit rating is the very foundation of his existence; he is tidy, hard-working, and liberal, but without excess. He is far from the noble-man, whom he despises for his idleness, and from the common people, whom he fears; he has no feeling for art, and is pleased with himself. He found his Homer in Balzac, who described him in the *Comédie Humaine*. Ingres immortalized him in the person of Bertin l'aîné. The Scandinavian and French dramatists directed their shafts against a certain sort of middle-class hypocrisy. The genuine bourgeoisie tries to outdo the old nobility in dignity and seriousness: this appeared in the works of Disraeli and Hendrik Conscience, Balzac and George Sand. A large portion of this bourgeoisie carried on the tradition of the Enlightenment, and made the transition from the rationalism of the *Encyclopédie* to the rationalism of Taine and Renan. However, the bourgeoisie could be reached by a sentimentality that is closer to the eighteenth century than to Romanticism. It read Goldsmith, Goethe, Rousseau, Bernardin de Saint-Pierre, and the novels of Fanny Burney and Jane Austen. It stood for the privacy of rural life, for the protected atmosphere of the home, for the simple pleasures of the family. It was the ideal purchaser of genre works, but it no longer had the good taste of the previous century. Industry developed, and with it the proletariat. In 1885, 28 percent of all dwellings in Vienna and Berlin were inhabited by two people per room (in Paris the figure was 14 percent), in St. Petersburg 48 percent). Slum housing in the cities was accompanied by drunkenness, theft, prostitution, and consumption. This was the field of observation of the naturalistic novelists.

After 1800 there gradually grew up a chasm between the public and the artist. We see the rise of the type of the rejected artist, the true pariah: Van Gogh, Jongkind, Toulouse-Lautrec, Gauguin, Albert Ryder. Some works submitted to exhibitions of paintings (Manet's *Le déjeuner sur l'herbe* and *Olympia*, Cézanne's paintings) were taken by both jury and public as mere acts of defiance. Among the refused artists are Pissarro, Seurat, Renoir, and Whistler. The word "artist" acquires an unfavorable nuance. He is regarded as a Bohemian or a charlatan. His field of work is more and more cut down by the progress of industrial technique (e.g., photography). His position becomes all the more precarious in that official commissions go for the most part to the academically trained and to the conformists.

SCIENCE, PHILOSOPHY, RELIGION The nineteenth century was marked by great discoveries in science and technology. Mathematics developed under the influence of Weierstrass, Hermite, and Kronecker. Henri Poincaré studied the connection between the phenomenon of electricity and the properties of light. Riemann, as early as 1854, formulated the conditions for a four-dimensional space, anticipated relativity theory and prepared the way for Einstein. Astronomy employed photography and spectroscopy. Maxwell showed the identity of electrical and light waves, and Hertz produced electrical waves. The ability to compress and liquefy gases brought the refrigeration industry into being. Chemists set about synthesizing methyl alcohol and acetylene. Thermochemistry soon took its place alongside thermodynamics. Nobel produced explosives and ozone. Darwin's ideas were generally accepted, despite religious opposition. Claude Bernard, Pasteur, Koch, Richet, Roux, von Behring, Nicolle, and Wassermann put medicine on a scientific basis. The use of chloroform made appendectomy and the Caesarian operation possible. Mental disease was studied by Lombroso and a beginning made in its cure. Freud founded psychoanalytic therapy on study of the unconscious and mental and emotional conflicts, and on the technique of letting "free associations" be expressed. In the twentieth century he was to have a profound influence on thought, manners, and art. He dispelled the suspicion that had surrounded sex. He justified in advance the efforts of the surrealists, who saw the automatic mechanisms of the psyche as the pure operation of the mind. He also began the psychoanalytic explanation of art and literature. Forms and images were thenceforth regarded as symbols of the unconscious, the richest region discovered by nineteenth-century psychology.

The amount of coal mined in 1900 was more than a hundred times that produced in 1790. Coal became the key material of industrial progress and hence of military power. The Eiffel Tower (1889) is the visual image of the "iron age". Soon new processes and new alloys were discovered. Brass replaced cardboard for making cartridges, tin was used in canning. Eastman employed cellulose for preparing photographic film. Oil lighting was replaced by electric light, which was soon to be fed by the power from waterfalls. Remington bought the patents of Scholes and Densmore, who had built the first typewriter (1867). Edison demonstrated his phonograph in 1877. In 1885 Peugeot brought out an automobile; it was equipped with a

1

2

5

3

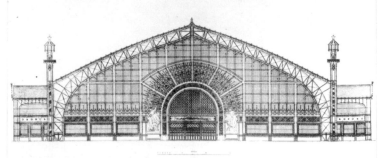

4

1. Grand staircase of the Opéra, Paris, by Charles Garnier ; building begun 1861, finished 1875. 2. Reading Room of Bibliothèque Ste.-Geneviève, Paris, by Henri Labrouste, designed 1843, finished 1850. 3. Original façade of the Gare du Nord, Paris, designed 1861. J.-I. Hittorf combines the use of steel and glass with an imitation of ancient columns and statues. 4. Eiffel Tower, Paris. Designed by Gustave Eiffel for the Exposition of 1889. 5. Hall of Machines, also for the Paris Exposition of 1889, by the engineer Contamin and the architect Dutert.

6. Buckingham Palace, London, east front by Sir Aston Webb, 1913. 7. British Museum, London, by Sir Robert Smirke, begun 1823. Neo-classic colonnade built 1842–47. 8. Houses of Parliament in London, by Charles Barry with the collaboration of A. Welby Pugin. Designed in an adaptation of the English Perpendicular style after the fire in 1834. (In the foreground, Westminster Abbey.) 9. Crystal Palace, built for the Great Exhibition in London, 1851. Constructed of cast-iron elements and large plates of glass.

10

1

Daimler motor and provided with solid rubber tires by Michelin. The bicycle, at first a means of recreation for the bourgeoisie, later became a means of mass transportation. While the inhabitants of rural areas were attracted to the "city with its octopus arms," city dwellers found the way to the country, to the shore and the mountains.

Sports became more and more popular. The rotary presses of Hoe and Maroni and the linotype made possible wide distribution of books and newspapers. Thanks to the development of press agencies the daily press could keep its readers abreast of developments throughout the world. Through the press, public opinion was influenced by political parties and financial powers. Popular novels and children's books became important. Before the century ended Röntgen discovered X rays, and Pierre and Marie Curie isolated radium (1898).

Romanticism stressed history; it rehabilitated the Middle Ages and at the same time supported religious feeling. The rediscovery of the Middle Ages sometimes was coupled with royalism (the *style troubadour* flourished in France during the reigns of Louis XVIII and Charles X) and with nationalism (Conscience, *The Lion of Flanders*; Walter Scott). History was still thought of as an epic.

During the Romantic period comprehensive philosophic syntheses were erected aimed at explaining the meaning of nature (Schelling) and of history (Fichte, Hegel, A. Comte).

From 1850 on, while realism was supreme in art and literature, rationalism spread to political thought and the science of history. Sober philology and historical criticism (Renan, Taine, Max Müller) worked toward making history an exact science. The historians now sought to establish the precise details, the reliable data, the significant facts. Jakob Burckhardt replaced the Greco-Roman civilization and the Renaissance in their historical connection; in the field of cultural history, of which he is one of the founders, he demolished the myth of spontaneous generation, the same myth that Pasteur was combating in biology.

Marxist socialism opposed not only the conservative Catholicism of de Maistre and Bonald, but also the prophesyings of Saint-Simon and Fourier. All through the nineteenth century there ran a pessimis-

tic current and an optimistic one. Philosophical pessimism conceived of humanity as going further and further away from the Golden Age, the Earthly Paradise. The pessimism is mythical rather than metaphysical in nature, and this explains the idyllic atmosphere in which Romanticism envelops earlier ages and distant lands. The myth of the "noble savage" comes to full expression in the paintings of Gauguin. The optimistic current is based on rationalism and science: Mankind was making progress from age to age, thanks to reason, science, and its technical applications. This optimism was encouraged by various political trends (socialism in 1848).

Nietzsche fiercely attacked the values on which the ethics and culture of the nineteenth century were based. Over against the Apollonian aspect of Greek art, which Winckelmann praised, he emphasized the Dionysiac aspect. He rejected art, which he considered an escape. He pilloried history as poison for a healthy being rejoicing in life. In contrast to the self-denial and brotherly love of Romanticism, he glorified theWill to Power of the Superman.

The supporter of Romanticism has intense religious feeling. He accepts the supernatural. He uses typically Christian language: God, love, heaven, sin, duty, angels, etc. But the meaning of the words is no longer checked by an objective religious and moral law. It is revised or altogether altered by his personal feeling or by a myth.

LITERATURE AND DRAMA Up to about 1845 Romanticism reigned almost everywhere in Europe, after having gradually overcome the resistance of neoclassicism.

In the writer's eyes, the world seemed to be an enormous and shifting drama, in which the interesting thing is to show the infinite number of changes in time and space. In order to be able to reproduce the "local color," the writer travels in foreign lands: Italy, Scotland, Spain (Mérimée, George Borrow), the Orient (Chateaubriand, Lamartine, Nerval). He discovers the people (Grimm and Brentano in Germany, Gogol in Russia). Even the most distant and the most primitive peoples seem to merit his interest. Romanticism implies feeling for nature, but not the exact reproduction of actuality.

About 1845 European literature freed itself from the Romantic and moved in the direction of a realism that in the end went over into

13

14

10. Letchworth Garden City, begun 1904. Model of a garden city following the ideas of Ebenezer Howard, who sought to combine the attractions of he city with those of the country. 11. Jumel Mansion, New York. Wood, with bands, coigns, and slender high columns, crowned by a Greek pediment with dentils. 12. Schauspielhaus, Berlin, 1819–21, by Karl Friedrich Schinkel. One of the great examples of neoclassicism. 13. Propylaeon, Munich, 1846–62, by Leo von Klenze. 14. Rathaus, Vienna, 1872–83, by Friedrich von Schmidt.

In Vienna, as in London, the Gothic style was imitated for its visual values and adapted, with more or less success, to the needs of modern life. 15. Neo-Romanesque castle of Neuschwanstein, designed 1867 by Eduard Riedel and finished by Georg von Dollmann for Ludwig II of Bavaria. 16. Wertheim department store, Berlin, by Alfred Messel. Begun 1896; façades illustrated added 1900–1904. Example of the new, simple monumentality. 17. Rijksmuseum, Amsterdam, 1877–85, by P. J. H. Cuypers.

16

15

17

naturalism. In his perception of the reality of daily life, the artist participates less deeply. When the writer finds his inspiration in suffering, he tries to recreate it with an almost scientific exactitude. The unbridled lyricism of Byron and de Musset is followed by a more objective poetry, which in addition gives more attention to technique. Novelists and poets lay more stress on form.

As for the novel, it tried, with Zola, to embody the positivistic and deterministic philosophy and constitute a scientific document. Under the influence of Poe, Baudelaire, and the German followers of Romanticism, poetry went in the direction of symbolism and tried to express the strangest of impressions. German Romantic poetry presents itself as a means to insight; it tries to restore the unity of man and nature, aiming at total resolution of the universe. It proclaims the omnipotence of the dream. Therewith it begins the investigation of the unconscious that was to be continued by Freud and the psychoanalysts.

In painting, symbolism derives from Romanticism. It sets its face against realism in art, against scientific positivism. The literary nature of its inspiration sets it in contrast with Impressionism. Even in the earliest days of the nineteenth century the Englishman Blake and the Spaniard Goya were interpreting their dream pictures with genius: the first his visions, the second his nightmares.

Gustave Moreau was influenced by scientific positivism, and set about bringing the past to life with the utmost attention to detail, in the manner of Flaubert and Leconte de Lisle. But the study of mythologies and religions brought him to an extremely personal conception of religion, based on secret doctrines and a chaotic mysticism.

Odilon Redon declared, before the Surrealists, that "everything is created by faithful subjection of the spirit to the thoughts that come to us out of the unconscious." His contemporaries showed more interest in his fanciful subjects than in his expert and vigorous technique.

Materialism and positivism were opposed by Carlyle in England, Tolstoi and Dostojevski in Russia, and Nietzsche in Germany. Over against the humanitarian evangelism of Tolstoi, Nietzsche upheld the cult of the Superman and an immoralism that was later expressed

very strongly in such writers as Gide and de Montherlant and in the nationalist mystics of the twentieth century.

The Romantic theater attacked the French classical tradition. It rejected the law of the three unities. No difference would be made any longer between the comic and the tragic. The Romantic dramatists were diligent as to "local color" and set great store by settings and costumes. Despite Dumas and Hugo, this drama did not triumph. The great theoretician of nineteenth-century eclecticism was François Ponsard, who wanted to use Racine to correct Shakespeare and Shakespeare to correct Racine. But Eugène Scribe was the playwright par excellence of the Restoration, the July Monarchy, and the Second Empire. He wrote more than 350 plays: light comedies, comedies of manners, and historical plays.

During the age of realism and naturalism, national traditions and stories of heroes were constantly put on the stage. The comedy of manners took on a social content, aimed at instruction; it developed into the play in which moral and social problems were discussed that arose out of the development of industry.

Emile Augier, in France, defended conservative and bourgeois ideas, while Dumas *fils* put his sometimes swollen eloquence in the service of noble thoughts. Becque and Mirbeau delivered powerful attacks on bourgeois society and pilloried the dishonesty of businessmen.

Drama in the northern countries reached its high point with the Norwegians Henrik Ibsen and Björnstjerne Björnson. At first Ibsen wrote national and Romantic dramas, later developing, in *Brand*, in the direction of realism, and, with *Peer Gynt*, emphasizing the ethical nature of his work. Subsequently he turned to denunciation of social abuses and petty hypocrisy. But he was more interested in stating the problems than in trying to solve them, and finally ended up in a symbolism foreshadowed in *Peer Gynt*.

Björnson too was inspired by the manners of his time and by history to write dramas in which he took up the most diverse subjects: faith, miracles, miraculous cures, the demands of workers.

Johan August Strindberg, a Swede, reinforced the realism of Ibsen and Björnson. He was influenced by Nietzsche, preached antifeminism and the cult of the Superman, and finally broke with naturalism. He wrote mystical and symbolic dramas, meanwhile

18. H. P. Berlage's original design, 1897, for the Amsterdam Exchange, now the Commodity Exchange. 18a. Berlage's Exchange as built 1898–1903. 19. Palace of Justice, Brussels, 1866–83, by Joseph Poelaert, embodying many styles. 20. Town house, Avenue Louise, Brussels, by Victor Horta, one of the creators of Art Nouveau; begun 1895. 21. House at Tervuren, Belgium, by Henry van de Velde (1863–1957), who had great influence as architect, furniture designer, and teacher. 22. Victor Emmanuel II Monument, Rome, by G. Sacconi. Ornament overwhelms the underlying structure.

20

continuing to produce dramas in which he depicted the history of Sweden.

The Germans Hebbel and Hauptmann brought social problems on the stage. Hauptmann posed the problem of hereditary alcoholism, which Zola had already treated in the novel. In the end, naturalistic truth and social problems outlived their time. Toward the end of the nineteenth century, under the influence of Maeterlinck of Belgium and Claudel of France, a reaction began to form against naturalism, in plays and production. Maeterlinck's plays evoke a somber feeling of fatality; time and place are left indeterminate. The characters awkwardly stammer out words fraught with mysterious forebodings.

MUSIC AND DANCE Music now was directed more at the masses. The number of concert halls increased rapidly. Singing and piano lessons brought music into every home. Music criticism had its specialists, chroniclers, and newspapers. The artist expressed his innermost feelings, passions, and sorrows; the virtuoso enjoyed unprecedented prestige. Schubert and Schumann, sensitive to the poetry of lyric minor art, revive the lied. Weber and Berlioz exploit the descriptive possibilities of music. Music had a tremendous influence on the poetic esthetics of the last partisans of Romanticism and the first Symbolists. Baudelaire, the defender of Wagner in France and one of the founders of music criticism, replaces the rhetorical development that is still so clearly to be seen in de Musset and Hugo by subtler effects that are closer to musical harmony. Under the influence of Verdi and Italian verism, the opera no longer deals with mythological themes, and lays more stress on action and reality. But the Italian opera, of remarkable virtuosity, airiness, and glamor, lacks the spark of genius. Richard Wagner, who had a great gift for synthesis, strove in his musical dramas to unite poetry, dramatic art, music, and mythology. In Debussy (Pelléas et Mélisande) the music holds the entire performance together and nonetheless remains independent. The expression of escstasy becomes, in Claude Debussy, the most important if not the only aim of music. Many of his contemporaries tried to imitate his fascinating tonalities, but did so with much less spontaneity (Ravel, Dukas, de Falla, Schönberg).

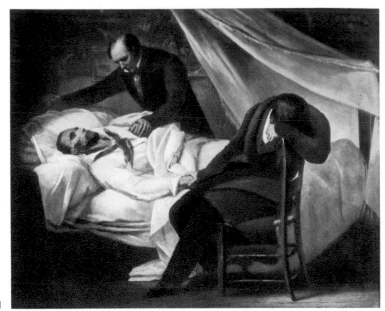

built in neo-Gothic style but also such public buildings as city halls, hospitals, post offices, and even railroad stations. The architect attempted to work historically but not originally, let alone functionally.

After 1830 French architecture went through a serious crisis. However, the development of technology created new possibilities. Baltard was one of the first to employ steel and glass (Halles Centrales, Paris). The Gare du Nord (Hittorf) is well adapted to its function by virtue of the spacious design and good access. Eclecti-

cism was the basis for the design of the Paris Opéra (1861–75); in it Garnier used various styles, materials, and techniques to create what he called a Napoleon III style.

Léon Vaudoyer imitated Romanesque and Byzantine art, more or less successfully (Marseilles Cathedral, begun 1852). Abadie adopted a Romanesque style for the Basilica of the Sacré-Cœur in Montmartre.

Haussmann, inspired by Napoleon III, drives the great boulevards through Paris. A new sort of dwelling appears, the "barracks for

36

31. *Riderless Horses at the Start in the Corso at Rome, by J.-L.-A.-T. Géricault (1791–1824), who liked to draw his inspiration from subjects rich in dramatic complications. 32. Death of Géricault, by Ary Scheffer (1795–1858), whose Romantic conceptions and literary effects relate him to both the Nazarenes and the Pre-Raphaelites. 33. In The Massacre of Chios, of 1822–24, by his quest for local color and the dramatic intensity with which he depicted the struggles between Greeks and Turks, Eugène Delacroix (1798–1863) gave form to Romanticism. Under the influence of Constable, he made painting more intense in color. 34. Amateurs de Peinture, by E. Meissonnier (1815–91), expresses a love for the anecdotal. 35. A falconry scene by Eugène*

37

38

Fromentin (1820–76). The Romantic school's love for local color was succeeded by a preference for realistic perception, which Fromentin brings to the fore with the elegance and distinction of an artist capable of remaining within the limitations of his ability. 36. Bridge at Narni, by Jean-Baptiste-Camille Corot (1796–1875). Before he became the painter of forest scenes and ponds, Corot excelled in harmonious architectural compositions, with light effects. 37. Noonday Rest during Haying Time, an example of the simple and realistic manner of Gustave Courbet (1819–77), which in its time constituted a revolution in painting. 38. The Little Shepherdess, by Jean-François Millet (1814–75).

rent,'' with the ground floor for shops. In Paris, as in London and Berlin, avenues appear on which all the buildings are identical.

England was the promised land of the neo-Gothic. Many influences converged in this direction: Walter Scott, Ruskin's ideas, and the national conservatism.

Building in steel and glass developed fully in the Crystal Palace, built for the 1851 Great Exhibition. However, the most interesting expression of English architecture was later, in the planning of the garden cities. They constitute a return to nature, from which

industrial civilization had banished man. They honor an individualism not to be seen in Le Corbusier's "radiant city."

In Bismarck's Germany, glorification of national feeling was especially strong, as a reaction to the liberal and revolutionary movements. The desire to produce a purely German art is expressed in architecture as well as in Wagnerian drama. Unwieldiness, overemphasis, and imitation mark the works of Raschdorff and Paul Wallot (Reichstag, 1884–94), while Bavarian neo-Romanesque sets the tone at Neuschwanstein.

39

40

41

In Holland, Petrus J. H. Cuypers made neo-Gothic imitations (Rijksmuseum and Central Station, Amsterdam) but, like his teacher Viollet-le-Duc, he has a feeling for space and dignity. Hendrick P. Berlage was able to free himself from the past; after paying tribute to eclecticism, he was attracted to the severity and sober functionality of Romanesque art. He reached the twentieth century without being led into Art Nouveau.

In Belgium, Joseph Poelaert built the enormous Palace of Justice that dominates Brussels with its mass and combines so many styles that it is hopeless to try to list them all. This prodigious structure attests the lyrical power of its creator, and at the same time the inability of the nineteenth century to achieve an original style of its own. Victor Horta (Hôtel Solvay) and especially Henry van de Velde were important influences in the Europe of the "modern style."

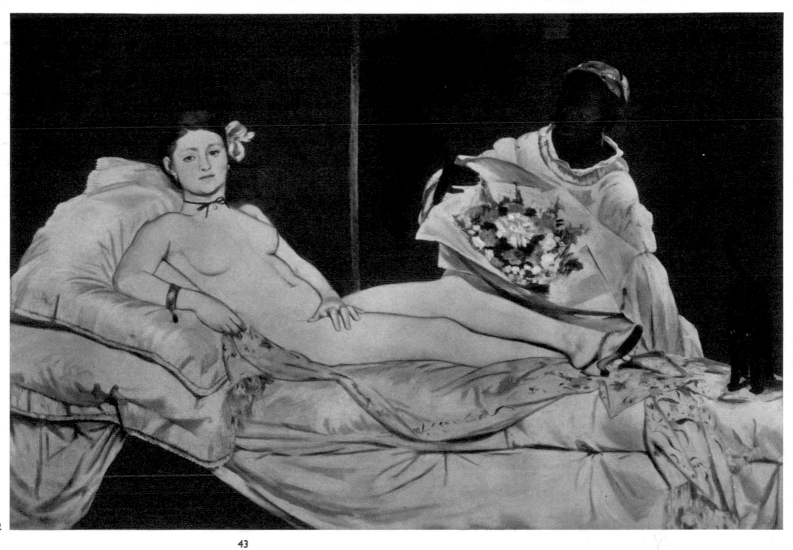

43

44

47

45. *Snow Scene at Argenteuil, by Claude Monet (1840–1926), outstanding Impressionist painter of landscapes. 46. View of the Town between Trees, by Paul Cézanne (1839–1906). 47. The White Horse, by Paul Gauguin (1848–1903). 48. Ta Matete, by Gauguin. Living in Tahiti and the Marquesas, Gauguin arrived at a static manner of painting far removed from the mobile transience caught by the Impressionists.*

SCULPTURE The neoclassic tradition held its own better in sculpture than in any other branch of art. James Pradier of Geneva was strongly influenced by Canova. The Romantic sculptors do not achieve eminence; Jean Du Seigneur, David d'Angers, and Préault have more ideas than talent. François Rude made his debut in Paris when he was forty-three (1827); the Revolution and the Empire inspired him to works of impetuous lyricism. Daumier alone manifests originality and talent to an outstanding degree; by carrying his caricatural view into sculpture, he created statuettes of daring expressionism. Carpeaux had a great reputation during the Second

Empire, but was eclipsed by Rodin and Constantin Meunier, the Belgian. Rodin freed himself definitively from the classic influence, while giving moving expression to human heroism. He did not seek an example in the stiff academicians that tried to imitate the art of antiquity; he studied the problem of the light that played over the forms. His book on the French cathedrals, which appeared in 1914, shows that he was well aware of the splendors of the Gothic, and that many of the sources of his extremely expressive art are to be looked for there. The figures of Rodin emerge from the modeling clay in such living reality, but from such a powerful and unexpected

49. *Le Chahut*, by Georges Seurat (1859–91). *He juxtaposed small spots of pure unmixed colors, which merge when seen from a certain distance; one of the directions taken by Post-Impressionism.* 50. *Under the Trees*, by Paul Signac (1863–1935); *Post-Impressionism.* 51. *Chocolat, Dancing in the Achille Bar*, by Henri de Toulouse-Lautrec (1864–1901), *an example of the numerous paintings and drawings he made in the bars and cabarets of Paris.* 52. *Orpheus*, by Gustave Moreau (1826–98), *a forerunner of the Surrealists.*

psychological point of view, that we can well understand why conservatives were shocked when his *Victor Hugo Nude* and his *Monument to Balzac* were shown.

Constantin Meunier dealt mainly with man's sorrows and labor. In him, the working man gained citizenship in the world of the visual arts. Above all, Meunier sought to translate the new and fruitful themes that working life gave him into a sculptural language of uncommon worth.

54

53

53. *St. Anthony, by Odilon Redon (1840–1916). 54. The Snake Charmer, by Henri Rousseau (Le Douanier). In protest against the immoral world that Degas and Toulouse-Lautrec had depicted, Rousseau glorifies an improbable naïve paradise, in which men and animals live in brotherhood. 55. The Lawyers, one of Honoré Daumier's famous caricatures. 56. Portrait of Countess Ehrenburg by Wilhelm Leibl (1844–1900). 57. Hans Thoma*

(1839–1924), in this portrait of his mother and sister, has got rid of the sensibility characteristic of the Biedermeier period and focused on realism. 58. Fish Market at Ostend, by Andreas Achenbach (1815–1905), one of the best-known members of the Düsseldorf school, a tendency in German painting that was characterized by a mixture of idealism and realism. 59. Naïads at Play, by the Swiss Arnold Böcklin (1827–1901).

PAINTING AND PRINTS In accounting for the revival of interest in the art of the Middle Ages, mention must be made of the German Nazarenes and the English Pre-Raphaelites. They imitate the Italian painters of the quattrocento. The Germans Cornelius, Overbeck, Pforr, and Schnorr established themselves around 1812 in the Sant' Isidro monastery in Rome. Their technique is marked by a love for details, paralleling the naïveté of the drawing and color. The Germans were dominated by the story, and this is true both for the Nazarenes and their followers, such as Böcklin and Feuerbach. Menzel portrayed the age of Frederick the Great with a vignette-like precision, until under the influence of Daumier and Manet he developed in the direction of naturalism. Leibl and Hans Thoma fall into an awkward photographic realism. Winterhalter settled in France, where he was to become the official painter of the imperial court. Von Lenbach, the portraitist of Bismarck and Wilhelm I, was influenced by the Flemish masters, the Venetians, Rembrandt, and Velazquez. Hans von Marées conjured up mythological pictures, with figures painted in a naturalistic technique. Max Liebermann painted workers and craftsmen realistically, proving himself a bold innovator in the way he placed his figures in space and illuminated his interiors. Lovis Corinth was already developing in the direction of expressionism.

English painters formed the Pre-Raphaelite Brotherhood (1848). In the anecdotal and "literary" work of Hunt, Dante Gabriel Rossetti, Burne-Jones, and Millais, we find a religious yearning that is made still more languorous by a sickly sensualism.

The Belgian François-Joseph Navez, a pupil of David in Paris and in the Brussels atelier of the refugee French master, was the first of a series of Belgian painters who gave new life to the national school. Antoine Wiertz tried to imitate Michelangelo, Raphael, and Rubens, but finally succumbed to empty bombast. Charles de Groux gave impetus to social realism. Leys, from Antwerp, with his able coloring, was an expert in historical reconstructions. Henri de Braekeleer depicts old interiors, furniture, and Cordovan leather with an

55

58

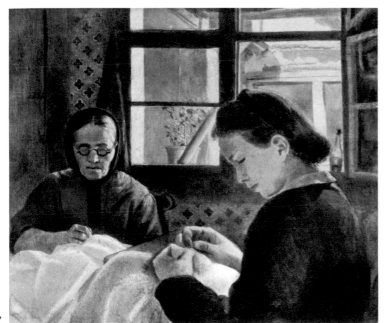

59

antiquarian devotion, but his paintings have an intimate atmosphere that recalls the seventeenth-century Dutch masters.

The *Mouvement des XX* and the *Salon de la libre Esthétique* brought outstanding talents together, fully open for the influence of the French realists and impressionists. Theo van Rysselberghe was to go over to pointillism in Paris. Willem Vogels, an impressionist, gave himself to browns and grays, to mist and rain. Claus, Verwée, and Courtens are strong landscape painters. Alfred Stevens (a Belgian, not the English sculptor of that name) became the painter of elegant

Parisian women, while his brother Joseph continued the animal-painting tradition of Verlat and Verwée. Laermans is full of humanitarian problems, and paints figures that anticipate expressionism. Evenepoel, who died at 27, was a delicate brilliant portraitist.

Félicien Rops was a witty etcher, full of creativity of Baudelairean and satanic inspiration. But the master figure of the end of the nineteenth century and the beginning of the twentieth was that of James Ensor, from Ostend, in turn impressionist, symbolist, and expressionist. He was the painter of masks and street scenes whose fairy-

60

61

60. *Salisbury Cathedral Seen from the River, by John Constable (1776–1837), renowned for his landscapes, in which the interest is centered on the effects of light. He was the first to set up his easel in the open air. 61. The Cornfield, by Constable. 62. The Harvest Moon, by Samuel Palmer (1805–81). 63. Venice, by J. M. W. Turner, the English painter and watercolorist (1775–1851). The lines flow and the volumes disappear.*

62

63

like lights, red, blue, and yellow, are forerunners of the Fauves. He carries on the mocking and fantastic tradition of Bruegel and Hieronymus Bosch.

By virtue of his romantic conceptions, sentimentality, and striving for literary effects, Ary Scheffer is related to the Nazarenes and the Pre-Raphaelites. The transition from Romanticism to realism in painting is marked by Bosboom, who came into his own in impressionism, via realism.

It is understandable that in 1846 Jongkind got the idea of leaving a country where a scholastic neoclassicism reigned that ran counter to the basic principles of the national tradition. From 1856 on his manner of painting with a stippled shimmer announced pointillism. He was to show Boudin and the Impressionists the brilliant play of light. Jozef Israëls, who discovered in Rembrandt the importance of light effects, set his face against the idealism of Kruseman and Pieneman. Later, he too found a suitable technique: a misty grayish color, with which he pictures the lives of simple folk. The oversensitive but balanced Anton Mauve preferred to use silvery and unobtrusive tones. Via the Barbizon school, J. H. Maris found the way back to the great tradition of the seventeenth century. He too was under the influence of the German Romantics and the French realists, but was above all the poet of home life.

Two trends can be distinguished in the renewal of the Dutch tradition in the nineteenth century: the literary trend, related to the Nazarenes and the Pre-Raphaelites and enriched by the discovery of social problems; and the search for new techniques.

Van Gogh's powerful personality enabled him to assimilate the tendencies of his time, to master them and go beyond. He freed himself from social art and naturalism. He discovered Impressionism without renouncing form, and finally found in Expressionism the vehicle for his inner drama, caused by a heartrending loyalty and a pathetic devotion to the values of the spirit.

The expanding feeling for nature in the nineteenth century produced a radical change in the vision of the artist, his themes, and his technique. Constable was the first to set up his artist's easel in the open air, aiming at reproducing the most fleeting impressions. As early

65

66

64. Annunciation, by the Pre-Raphaelite Dante Gabriel Rossetti (1818–82). 65. Christ in the House of His Parents, one of the best-known works of John Everett Millais, the foremost English Pre-Raphaelite. 66. Woman's Figure, by James McNeill Whistler (1834–1903).

leading up to the Impressionist revolution. Delacroix is still Romantic in some of his subjects (*Liberty Guiding the People*), but his technique is revolutionary; to a great extent he is indebted to Rubens for this. Color gets the upper hand of drawing. His stay in Morocco and Algiers enabled him to see new color harmonies.

Corot's Italian landscapes show that his only interest is the solid structure of masses and the balance of volumes, as they appear in the radiant atmosphere. In his French landscapes he shows himself more sensitive to the infinite mobility of the landscape.

In Barbizon, Millet devoted himself more to painting man's hard labor and sorrow than to landscape.

In the spring of 1874 a number of painters showed their canvases at the shop of the photographer Nadar in Paris. A shocked journalist gave the group the invidious name of "impressionists," after a painting by Monet with the title *Impression—Rising Sun*; the description was fully in accord with the deepest purposes of the artist. His purpose was not a precise awareness of objectives and means, but an explicit will to free himself from current conventions and make a fresh start, on the basis of direct and felt perceptions as he viewed nature.

Impressionism did not trouble much with theory; its theory was only erected after the fact. The only aim was that the work, and its maker, should be spontaneous.

Fifteen years previously Darwin had published *On the Origin of Species* (1859). The significance of the book, which suddenly established the idea of a world committed into all eternity to a permanent condition of change, only emerged much later. Almost forty years were to elapse until Chevreul's theories of simultaneous color contrasts were embodied by Seurat in the neoimpressionist mode of painting.

Perhaps the heroes of the new painting reflected on the words of Baudelaire: "If it were possible, I should like to prove that colors, no

as 1830 the germ of Impressionism can be seen in his painting. Turner went still further. In him all of nature was transformed in a bewitchment of the senses, in which lines flow and volumes disappear. He willingly sacrifices actuality to the inspirations of a palette with enchanting colors.

France was far in the van in the development of painting during the nineteenth century. Although Géricault felt the inspiration of subjects that are rich in dramatic developments (*The Raft of the "Medusa,"* 1819), he could also use a sharp eye to investigate everyday reality (*The Madwoman*, 1822). His love of life and feeling for movement make his work breathe with a powerful spirit. The work of Delacroix and Corot brought about a basic change in painting techniques,

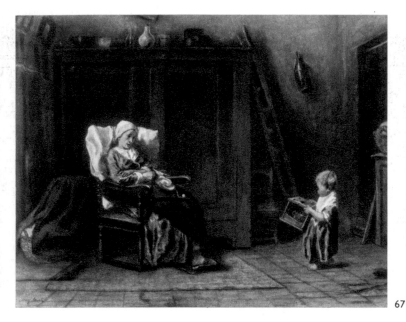

67

68

67. *Domestic Scene, by Jozef Israëls, who discovered the effects of light via the work of Rembrandt. In many of his works he depicts the life of simple people.* 68. *The Unwelcome Guest, by Jacob Maris (1837–99).* 69. *The Small Bridge, an example of the wide, flat landscapes of H. J. Weissenbruch (1824–1903).* 70. *In The Damrak, by G. H. Breitner (1857–1923), we see his great love of the sights of Amsterdam.*

69

matter how many there may be, when logically put together, merge of their own accord by virtue of the laws that govern them. Chemical affinity is the reason why nature can make no mistakes in the arrangement of this kind of color nuance; for her, color and form are one." The impressionistic technique is implicit in these rules. Impressionism abandons contours; the pure colors are used primarily as transitions, at the expense of grays and browns; the palette becomes lighter, and even the shadows acquire color; light, elevated into the guilding principle, reigns supreme from now on. In order to reproduce this light, the touch is fragmented, obedient to the impulses of the hand. As a reaction to the historical subjects, stiff academicism, and literary inclinations of the Romantics, the new painters, under the influence of Millet and Courbet, turn first to naturalism and later "purify" their spirits completely, painting only themes from

nature, in which flowing water and racing clouds, set down in their transparent motion, predominate. These painters drew their models from the water colors of Jongkind and Bonington, and from Boudin's seascapes.

After 1860 Monet, Renoir, and Sisley, soon joined by Pissarro, knew what they had to do and enthusiastically went in the new direction. The 1874 exhibition signified the beginning of a heyday that was to last for ten years. Monet, Renoir, Pissarro, Sisley, Cézanne, Degas, Guillaumin, and Berthe Morisot were among the exhibitors. Edouard Manet, the pathfinder, who fully sympathized with them, later joined them. Monet (who died in 1926), the painter of white water-lilies, is the Impressionist par excellence. He restored to painting its independent manner of expression, and exultant freedom to which the painter gives himself again in full at each new act of creation.

72

74

71. *Garden at St.-Rémy, painted in 1889, gives clear expression to the powerful personal manner of Vincent van Gogh (1853–90). 72. Hemptinne Family, portrait by François-Joseph Navez (1787–1869). 73. Battle between Greeks and Trojans over the Body of Patroclus, an enormous canvas by the Romantic, Antoine Wiertz (1806–65). 74. Antwerp Cathedral. Henri de Braekeleer (1840–88) paints old-fashioned interiors, with an atmosphere suggesting the Dutch masters of the seventeenth century.*

This trend in art opened many eyes. Impressionism comes to mind when we speak of Debussy, Marcel Proust, or Henri Bergson. The intuition of the painter introduced a new era in thinking.

Edouard Manet, a substantial citizen, pupil of Thomas Couture, who was regarded as a hopelessly old-fashioned painter, undertook to set the Impressionist revolution more or less in motion. This role came to him, most probably, because of the fact that he was the oldest (he was some ten years older than his young brothers in art), but also because of the vigor with which he attacked stereotyped notions of composition. His *Déjeuner sur l'herbe* and *Olympia* caused scandals. In them he showed a realistic vein too outspoken for the current taste.

Manet prefers a brighter manner of painting, rather than deep blacks in the manner of Velazquez or Frans Hals. As a painter of "modern

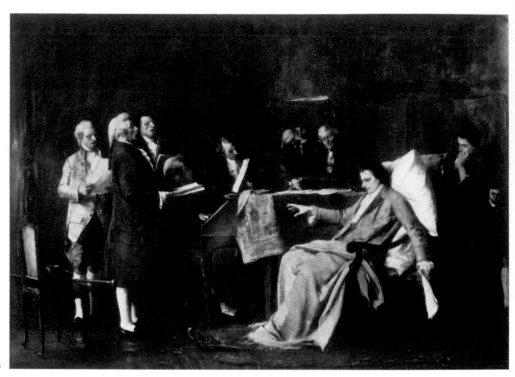

75

7

life," he maintained connection with objective reality in his motifs (which Baudelaire set such store by). He did not by any means give up the narrative element. This sets him in a sense somewhat apart from the rather ascetic dedication with which the first Impressionists set about depicting nature, a nature in which we should not dream of complaining, as Baudelaire still did, of the absence of man. Manet, the "Spaniard from Paris," as he has been well called, is as French as it is possible to be, assuming that the French nature comprises intelligence, lightness of foot, and controlled mastery.

"As far as I know myself," said Claude Monet, "I have always been an impressionist." Monet is the direct heir of Jongkind and Boudin. "Perfection, which flees, which always flees . . . Nature, which I constantly observe, without seeing it . . . I look at the light pouring over the earth, vibrating on the water . . . and my head spins when I see how much genius is needed to overcome so many difficulties." Monet could have made these words of Boudin his own. It is the credo that he was to be faithful to down to the *Nymphéas* that he painted at the end of his life. His numerous views of the Gare St.-Lazare and Rouen Cathedral, his surfaces of drift ice, his haystacks, and his poplars are always series of the same subject, tirelessly studied at every hour of the day and attesting the tireless curiosity of his painter's eye.

It has been said of him that he "was all eye." Since then, we have realized that Monet introduced an unsuspected spiritual dimension into painting: the concept of time, which was perhaps the most important of conceptions around the turn of the century.

Paul Cézanne was born in 1839 in Aix-en-Provence, and took part in the Impressionists' show at Nadar's in 1874. Refused in the official salons, laughed at when he exhibited with the Impressionists, and hurt by the failure of Zola to understand, he went back to Aix for good, leaving it only for short visits to Paris. He had years of rich harvest between 1885 and 1895. He kept only that in Impressionism which he could use. He wanted to "do something that would last, like the paintings in the museums." He arranged his color in large patches, searched again for space, and fled from the impressionistic reproduction of the atmosphere, "which chews things up." A sort of cosmic architecture shimmers before his spirit, in which he gives volume to everything, even air and water; "cylinder, sphere, and cone" become his standards. Cézanne introduced a new classicism, but one which no longer appealed to the past but inaugurated the future: he was a forerunner of the Fauves; the Cubists invoked his name later and, still later, the geometrical abstractionists.

Degas is the only one of the Impressionists who had little to do with nature unadorned. He painted the opera, ballets, dancers, and, toward the end of his life, female nudes at their toilet. Although he is related to the Impressionists in the way in which he depicts the glittering bits of material, his primary object is to capture movement, the passing moment. With Monet, he helps introduce a new conception into painting, which went further than the realization of light and movement: the concept of time.

Gauguin was originally influenced by Pissarro, later by Cézanne, still later by divisionism. He used the process of what is called

75. *Perfect Happiness, by Alfred Stevens (1817–75).*
76. *Mozart's Death, by the Hungarian painter Mihaly von Munkacsy (1844–1900).*

Page 183. *Above: Caspar David Friedrich (1774–1840), Bohemian Landscape.*
Below: William Turner (1775–1851), Interior at Petworth.

80

81

78

79

77. *Dancing Death, etching by Félicien Rops (1833–98).*
78. *March Revolution, Berlin 1848, woodcut by Alfred Rethel (1816–59). 79. Adoration of the Magi, etching by Henri de Braekeleer. 80. The City Mouse and the Country Mouse, by Gustave Doré, woodcut ilustration for the Fables of Jean de La Fontaine. 81. Woman Asleep, by the German graphic artist Adolf von Menzel (1815–1905). 82. Creation of Eve, from the Paradise Lost series by William Blake (1757–1827). 83. Dame aux Camélias, by Aubrey Vincent Beardsley (1872–98).*

82

83

Page 184. Above: Claude Monet, La Gare St.-Lazare.
Below: Vincent van Gogh, Vase with Flowers, 1890.

84

85

86

87

88 AN INITIAL WORD FROM THE "CHAUCER"

cloisonnism, which consists in painting in flat tones, in the manner of Japanese prints, and then using hard lines to give the colored spots a contour.

In his manner of working and in his message, Gauguin stood apart from the Impressionists. He saw art as the visible expression of a thought. He set his face against European civilization, against the Greeks "who understood everything." He proclaimed the return to the animal condition, to the origins of civilization. Thereby he took part in the effort of the nineteenth century, as it neared its close, to break through the limitations of a thinking stuck fast in rationalism, in order to rediscover the childhood of humanity and the elemental processes of the spirit.

89

INTERIOR DECORATION, FURNITURE, AND MINOR ARTS

Around 1820 the arrangement of furniture changed; the effort was now to enhance sociability by fitting out separate "corners." Knick-knacks increased in number. Furniture became less massive and easier to move. People remained faithful to mahogany, but lighter woods were also used, such as cherry and lemonwood. Bronze ornaments disappeared. Glass-fronted cases have pointed arches as frames, and the lines lose their purity. A new type of chair is used more and more: with or without arms, completely upholstered, with pleated flounces underneath and seat and back in piled fabric. Chairs become more comfortable. The semicylindrical backs are curved inward. Sometimes an openwork portion is decorated with cross-tying. The Empire decorations gave way to simple volutes that were strong but not pretty. The *style Troubadour* and decoration *à la cathédrale* found application in gewgaws, bookbindings, clock decoration, and knick-knacks.

Toward 1840 the interior lost its light color. Dark walnut or mahogany was preferred, upholstered in dark-red or dark-green velvet or repp. The pieces of furniture became heavier, and there were more of them. The general line was inspired by the Louis XV style, but it is heavy and bourgeois, although livelier than the preceding period. Much furniture was mass produced.

The furniture of the period between 1840 and 1870 consisted of mahogany chairs with red or green velvet or repp, a round or oval table on a central leg ending in volutes, armchairs known as *bergères*, suggesting the rococo style, a sofa often in the form of a double chair, and many low stools called by such names as toad, baby, or tuffet.

84. Title page of Franz Schubert's Am Grabe Anselmo's. 85. Page from Lesage's Gil Blas, with illustrations by Gigoux. 86. Illustration by Eugène Delacroix for Goethe's Faust. 87. Title page of W. J. Hofdijk's Kennemerland Balladen. 88. Page from The Golden Legend, drawing by William Morris. 89. Interior of Schubert's room in Vienna. 90. Bible Reading, by Alex. Hugo Bakker Korff (1824–82), example of a typical nineteenth-century interior.

90

91

92

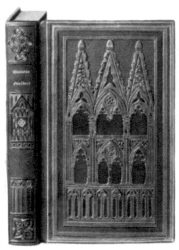

93

94

95

96

The study had a secretary with drawers, the upper portion having a lid coming down to form a writing surface almost unchanged from the Empire secretary. The bookcases were in two parts, with three or four glass doors above and drawers below.

The *étagères*—sometimes with twisted columns—were filled with knicknacks, and photographs in their ormolu frames. The clothes cupboard in the bedroom now had only a single door, whose panel held a mirror. Everywhere the same curves, more or less suggesting the rococo style. Everything is solid, somewhat bourgeois, but the chairs are well fitted to the shape of the body and meet a demand for comfort.

Thanks to the progress of industry, carpets were seen more and more in the homes of the less well-to-do. Printed cloth was popular because it was economical. Although wallpaper was widespread, cloth was still used as a wall covering. Velvet and repp were used for furniture, velvet and silk for curtains.

Industrial production made glass more common. Milk glass was fashionable; small objects, vases, and drinking glasses were made of opaque crystal. Paperweights (millefiori) were made in thousands by Saint-Louis, Clichy, and Baccarat.

Electroplating, which was discovered by Elkington in England, was spread in France by Christofle and Ruolz. That allowed silver-plate to replace pewter tableware. Pretty metal objects competed with porcelain. The so-called imitation porcelain (*pâte tendre*) was replaced by true porcelain (*pâte dure*). Decorated porcelain was fashionable. The form is still reminiscent of the Empire style of the eighteenth century. More and more excessive use was made of gilding. China and silver were decorated with landscapes and flowers. The work of religious goldsmiths suffered the influence of archaeologists, leading to imitations of the Gothic style. The way to Charles Cahier was shown by his brother P. Cahier; to Poussielgue-Rusand by P. Arthur Marten and Viollet-le-Duc. Armand of Lyon copied Romanesque models. Imitation of the Middle Ages and the Renaissance extended to jewelry. The chatelaine that hung on the belt consisted of a hook with various pendants and medallions hanging by chains of different lengths. During the Second Empire the frippery became richer. As a reaction against the imitations of the Middle Ages, and undoubtedly under the influence of archaeological discoveries and the introduction of archaeology into novels, Egyptian, Estruscan, and Byzantine models were imitated.

The long coat is still fitted closely at the waist, but the collar is lower. 99. Female fashion in 1836 was in full revolt against the simple line of the Empire period. The curved line supplanted the vertical line, and is reminiscent of the Louis XV style. 100. Costumes of 1865–66, with braided ornament in the front, suggesting the passementerie of the imperial guard.

7   98   99

91. Glass vase, with typical fin de siècle flower decoration, about 1900, by Gallé. 92. Silver plate, 1899, by Christofle. 93. Binding à la cathédrale. Bookbindings and small objets d'art brought out the Romantic artists' preference for the Gothic style. 94. Neo-Gothic mill of gilt bronze, with sails adorned with purple glass and set in motion by a mechanism. 95. Neo-

Gothic chair. The chairs were so uncomfortable because of their sharp points and ornaments that they were used only to a very limited extent. 96. Romantic trinkets, called chatelaines. 97. Around 1829, country dress consisted of a long frock coat of fine cloth, linen trousers, a batiste shirt, and a high hat.
98. Town and fancy costume, 1841.

100

101. Empress Elizabeth of Austria, by Franz Xaver Winterhalter (1805–73). 102. Portrait of a lady, by Jan Adam Kruseman (1804–62).

101

102

COSTUME Women's clothing was completely altered from the Empire line, which had been influenced by antiquity. Skirts bellied out. The waistline dropped. The illusion of a "wasp waist" was accentuated by a sharp point downwards (*ceinture à la Maria Stuart*). The leg-of-mutton sleeves fitted tight at the wrist; there were also slashed sleeves, reminiscent of the Renaissance. Pleated collars appeared in England ("betsies") and France. Muffs grew longer and larger. During the Second Empire the crinoline appeared. Originally, a stiff material with a horsehair weft was used to make the sleeves and petticoat stand out. Around 1856 corsets began to be fastened with a number of metal hooks and eyes connected by cloth strips. Travel by rail and ship and in the mountains called for more functional clothing. From 1856 on the crinoline was flat in front.

Men's clothing showed more fantasy and more refinement in France than in other countries. It served to bring out the literary, political, and social aspirations of the wearer. Men wore the republican vest, *à la Robespierre*, or taken in at the waist, suggesting the doublet of the Middle Ages. The frock coat with bell-shaped skirts is tight around the waist, and the neck opening very wide. A monumental stock supported the chin. The trousers were light in color. About 1830 a black coat was worn in the evening, a white vest with gilt buttons, and a lace jabot. From 1850 on men's clothing became simpler. The striped or checked trousers still had no crease.

Frock coats were somberer in color, very often black. The jacket and bowler hat made their modest entry about 1870.

The strife over the performance of *Hernani* had set the cool heads of the well-shorn classicists against the luxuriant hairdos of the bearded Romantics. In Germany and Austria sideburns were allowed to flourish freely. Napoleon made the mustache with twisted points and goatee fashionable. Little by little industrial civilization excluded all individuality and fantasy.

TWENTIETH CENTURY

POLITICAL AND SOCIAL LIFE   The development of imperialism, capitalism, and industrialization begun in the nineteenth century continued up to 1914. World War I showed how important the role of nationalism was. Distrust among peoples caused the spread of the conflict, limited at first, over a large part of the world. In Russia the Soviets came to power in 1917; the New Economic Policy (1922–27) and five-year plans were needed to stimulate agriculture and industry. Central Europe was split into small states after the war in order to give national minorities their rights, with the result of producing new minorities. The League of Nations, to which the United States did not belong, could only give advice and had little success; for one thing, because at first only the victor nations were members. The workers assumed political responsibility (Labour governments in Great Britain). Economic difficulties (unemployment, pay cuts) enabled Fascism and National Socialism to take power in Italy and Germany.

Between 1929 and 1935 international economic conditions were bad. Among the causes of this prolonged depression were the fact that the production of finished products lagged behind raw material production, and the economic structure was deranged by the increasing use of credit. Constantly falling prices upset international economic organization and made smooth commercial and trade operations impossible. In order to support the world economy, Roosevelt's New Deal in the United States tried to make good the losses of the community. Unemployment insurance was introduced and legislation was passed to regulate banking and the stock exchange.

The blitzkrieg attacks of Nazi Germany preluded World War II (1939–45). After the war, in which Fascism and National Socialism were annihilated, the United Nations was organized (October 24, 1945), with almost all nations represented in a General Assembly and a Security Council dominated by the five largest powers. The Technical Commissions, UNESCO (educational program), and the ILO (international labor organization and social legislation) were under the Economic and Social Council. The International Court of Justice in The Hague, although set up under the League of Nations, was continued. In 1948 the *Rights of Man* was prepared, asserting the equality of all men in the world.

After World War II the policy of colonialism was done for. In 1946 Egypt became independent, followed by a large number of new states. This trend is continuing. The world is now divided into a Western and a Communist sphere of influence, with the neutralist Afro-Asiatic countries in between; in addition, there are the nationalist revivals in the Mohammedan world and among the Negro peoples.

During the twentieth century efforts were made to find a solution to the problems of society. For one thing, the workers got the right to strike, to petition, and to hold mass demonstrations. One point of dispute is whether a new society must be achieved parliamentarily or by revolution. The Marxists believe that to improve living conditions does not lead to that goal; at best, the worker becomes a bourgeois. In Russia it is said that the "dictatorship of the proletariat" is to be followed by "proletarian democracy." The socialism of the West is democratically organized, with the leadership having executive functions; in the Russian Communist party the leadership has the power. In countries ruled by authoritarian methods, art is in the service of the state (U.S.S.R., Nazi Germany).

Since 1931, planned socialism has been developed, in part as a reaction to Fascism and Communism, in an effort to set up a cooperative organization of social life.

Community life is more important than ever in the twentieth century, and increasingly takes place outside the home. Among the causes are: better organization of work (shorter working hours), general welfare, easy communication. Manifestations of this are the development of sport, travel, cinema, theater, and music. Rapid communications lead to continual exchanges, so that a world culture is being gradually attained. The influence of the press, radio, films, and television is of the greatest importance. Communication has become so intensive in the Western countries that concentration on individual values is possible only by means of great effort. The influence of literature, for better and for worse, goes much deeper than before, largely due to modern production facilities; never before has such a mass of literature been poured out over man, often to the point of confusion. The high point of the process of making things easy is the comic strip, in which the written word may be omitted. Much the same is taking place in music (radio, recordings).

One new aspect of this era is the democratic effort to bring culture to the masses (popular concerts, libraries, museums, expositions). The necessary task of proper preparation of the public is now more and more understood by school administrations, youth organizations, and sometimes broadcasting companies.

Social changes, among which one of the most deep-reaching is the emancipation of women, could be traced directly in the external changes in customs. Social fluctuations can be followed in fashions.

COSTUME   After 1900 there was a movement to reform clothing, aimed against the unhealthy constriction of the body. Corsets were less used and later abandoned. Around 1910 trimmings were inspired by Art Nouveau. Van de Velde also designed women's clothing (streamlined forms, retaining the tight corset). In 1913 the form of women's clothing was dominated by the Japanese kimono; the abdomen was accentuated. In the middle 1920s people spoke of the "functional" style: skirts hardly reached the knee, the jumper had a chemise form without sleeves and a low waist; the hair had a boyish cut; hats were cloches. The arms and legs were uncovered;

3. Les Fauves: four states of a painting by Henri Matisse, Odalisque, 1936. The strong colors and firm contours are characteristic; the contours were more and more accentuated as the work advanced. Upper left dated Jan. 23, 1936; upper right Jan. 14; lower left Jan. 25; lower right, the definitive canvas. 4. Analytical Cubism: Les Portugais, by Georges Braque, 1911. The dark and light flecks in gray, green, and brown, whose sharp boundaries form the structure of the painting, are free of spatial forms.

1. Jane Avril, one of Henri de Toulouse-Lautrec's first posters, powerful and expressive in form and color, lithograph, 1889. 2. Expressionism: Csardas Dancers, by Ernst Ludwig Kirchner, a vigorous picture of the demimonde, in which the emotion of the painter is translated directly into line and color.

3

hips and bosom were taboo. The visibility of the legs made the stocking industry more and more important. In 1947 the "New Look" was introduced (Dior). Also after World War II came slacks, turtleneck sweaters, and, even for men, colored shirts. Functionalism was manifested in the short skirts and the growing use of trousers by women (for sports since 1910, for house wear since 1930, as work clothing since World War II). Men's clothing showed no essential changes in this century. It was more and more designed for comfort, and has become somewhat more colorful in recent years. One might say that feminine clothing has become more masculine and masculine clothing a little more feminine.

PHILOSOPHY At the beginning of the century, Henri Bergson attacked intellectualism and overemphasis on scientific thinking; it is intuition that must be relied on to fathom the reality of life (vitalism). Neo-Kantian philosophers (Rickert) asserted the need of separating the natural and the social (mental, *Geistes*) sciences: on the one hand, those that lay down laws (nomothetic); on the other, those that describe (ideographic).

In contrast to classical philosophy, existentialism saw the littleness of man. This trend, a form of the German philosophy of existence (Heidegger), regards human existence as the subject par excellence of philosophical thought (Sartre). Existentialists believe that it is not the individual who determines his own existence, but that our being is determined in existence. According to Sartre, man possesses absolute freedom. Whereas he starts from the standpoint of atheism, other existentialists seek association with Christian thought. Gabriel Marcel, since his conversion to the Catholic Church (1929), has been the most prominent representative of a Christian existentialism. He stresses the distinction between "problem" and "mystery." According to him, a man is a being-in-the world, which at the same time rises above the world into a being-to-God.

Bertrand Russell and A. N. Whitehead are representatives of the philosophy of logical analysis, which starts from experimental thinking and mathematical and natural science. Since 1950, many philosophers have engaged in the study of language.

RELIGION The Roman Catholic Church works in its way toward solving social problems. Pope Pius XI drew up, after World War I, a program for the future (in 1929 an encyclical on education, in 1929 and 1930 encyclicals on the family and marriage and on the social situation). *Catholic Action*, established in 1922, seeks to give the laity independence under the leadership of the hierarchy. It is a religiously and socially oriented movement; it starts from the proposition that the layman must bear responsibility for lay matters. In the church he

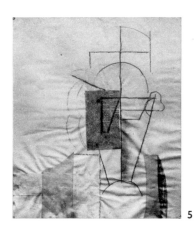

5

6

5. Synthetic Cubism: Tête d'Homme, by Pablo Picasso, 1913. Only the essential forms are represented, and various materials (including newspaper, here) are used to enhance the distance between the natural form and the image. 6. Plastic treatment of sheet metal under the influence of Cubism, in Woman with Mirror, 1937, by Julio Gonzalez. 7. Experiments in the field of graphic form from Nu, by W. J. H. B. Sandberg, 1959. 8. Surrealism: The Persistence of Memory, by Salvador Dali, 1931. The painting is a psychoanalytical interview, in which forms rising from the subconscious without the control of the understanding are represented (e.g., the malleable watches, immeasurable perspective).

is asked for liturgical participation. In connection with this are the novenas (explanation of the service) and the activity of the layman in the field of religious art. Modern art too is enlisted in the service of the Church. A strong need is felt for an Ecumenical Movement, a spiritual trend that aims at a better understanding of what is believed in common (prayer for unity, Abbé Couturier). In this way Protestants and Catholics could grow closer to each other.

Protestantism was marked by an enhanced missionary zeal, which resulted in the formation of many "young churches." The problems of Europe, set forth in many a confessional writing, seemed irrelevant for non-European Christians; a dialogue arose that led to the emancipation of the African and Asian churches and to a revaluation of their own religious tradition, as against the Bible and scientific knowledge. A basic division—God as the Completely Other—was proposed by Barth. The distress of the missionary regions and the dechristianization of workers and intellectuals revealed the necessity for the churches to speak out on the problems of society.

7

Out of the conviction that the cleavage in the church is a sin, and contrary to the will of Christ, there arose the ecumenical movement. It is held that the Churches must respect one another; the attainment of a single Christian Church is set as the ideal. The World Council of Churches was set up as a permanent organization (1948) which, with the exception thus far of the Reformed Churches, comprises all the important Protestant denominations, the Anglican Church, and the Eastern churches. Protestantism and Catholicism look for new forms in liturgy, and in connection with that, of church architecture and church interiors.

In Islam the powerful missionary vocation has fallen off in recent decades. Women are acquiring a less subordinate position in the Mohammedan world (working women, in Egypt). Some Neo-Buddhist sects have arisen in Western Europe since the beginning of the century, but we cannot speak here of the influence of Buddhism.

8

9. Expressionist art: water color by Wassily Kandinsky. 1910. Moving colored abstract forms are able, for this painter, to express emotions more purely than can images taken from nature. 10. Peace Column, abstract sculpture by Antoine Pevsner, bronze (53 inches high). 11. Bauhaus, Dessau (established there in 1925), during the 1920s an important art school for architecture, interior decoration, photography, and industrial design. Building designed by Walter Gropius, who founded the institution in 1919. 12. A rhythmic composition of firm flecks of color. Parable, 1958, an abstract painting by Ernst Wilhelm Nay. 13, 14. Two of the 63 illustrations in the picture novel Le Soleil, by Frans Masereel, 1920, who rejuvenated the art of the woodcut. In this series, man's desire for the light is expressed.
15. Sculptor and Model and a Sculptured Head, etching by Pablo Picasso.

9

11

SCIENCE Science has developed so rapidly since the turn of the century that a new picture of the world has come into being. In the nineteenth century the cosmos was regarded as a machine functioning according to fixed laws of nature; today the perceptible universe is seen as the picture of a succession of events, of which classical mechanics can give only an approximate explanation. Mass can be converted into energy and energy has mass; space and time are no longer regarded as independent of each other.

Physics no longer sees the electrons as particles having at each point of their orbits in the atom a determinate position and a determinate velocity, both of which can be precisely calculated at every instant; rather, within a given region the presence of energy (the electron) is more probably than at other points. Newton had said that the planets are diverted from motion in a straight line by the attraction of gravity. The conception now is that the curved paths of the planets around the sun are due to the metrical properties of space, which is curved in the neighborhood of concentrations of mass. There are no isolated

12

13

14

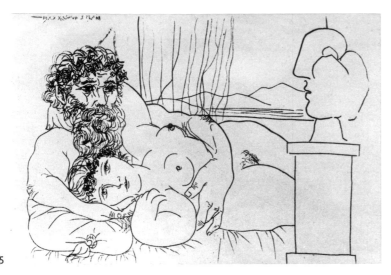

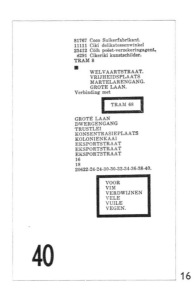

16. *Typographical experiment: a page from the Vademecum for the Young Suicide, by Kurt Köhler.*

17. *Book jacket for Die Wolkenpumpe, Dadaist poems, 1920, by Jean Arp.*

particles or moments of time; in the relativistic world picture (Einstein), space and time together are regarded as a single four-dimensional structure, in which events occur.

Man uses the annihilating power of the atom, released by nuclear processes that go forward in a way such as occurs inside the sun. The most spectacular results of technical development are the launching of artificial satellites and photographing of the back of the moon. Mechanization and automation play an important part in daily life. Man's actions are restricted as far as possible to throwing switches and pushing buttons. Twentieth-century man has more energy at his command than ever before.

PSYCHOLOGY Art has been greatly influenced by the ideas of Freud concerning the forces and drives that lie hidden in man and that, unknown to consciousness, determine the actions of the individual (depth psychology). Freud attributed the greatest importance to sex drives and aggression, Adler to the drives toward self-assertion and power, Jung to determinate reaction patterns (archetypes).

Behaviorism concerns itself with the behavior of man and animals with reference to determinate situations (Thorndike). Social psychology (after 1908, McDougall, Ward, Allport) regards the individual as a part of the community and as a member of a determinate group, and studies the interaction between man and the group.

STYLE AND CONCEPTION After the mechanical picture of the world had proved to be inadequate, the visible world was regarded as the reflection of events. A yellow square that is given a different motion relative to a spectator can become a red rectangle for him (Doppler effect, Lorentz contraction). In general, exact representation of the subjective world of perception is no longer striven for as the ideal. The classical conception that art forms must be adapted to natural forms gave way in the twentieth century to greater freedom for the artist in respect to the object. Descriptions of local color and material disappear (Expressionism), along with photographic illusions of space (Cubism), and the structure of the human body was dissolved (Picasso's metamorphoses). Experiments were directed primarily against bourgeois conventionality and academicism.

Art Nouveau (1890–1920) was a reaction against the repetition of earlier style forms. William Morris's work had a powerful influence. Gracefully curved lines were used in both architecture (Van de Velde) and arts and crafts.

Expressionism (1890–1930) tried to translate an emotion immediately into form, words, color, or sound. No effort was made at classical beauty; there was no hesitancy in distorting natural forms. An analogous drive toward expression is found in the art of primitive peoples, in children's drawings, and in the art of the Middle Ages. Les Fauves (The Wild Beasts; 1902 on), as they were called, were a group of painters for whom the use of fierce unmixed colors, often accentuated by mobile contour lines, was more important than form. The paintings were often composed without any effects of light and shade, and every color was raised to the highest possible intensity. Large surfaces were often filled with arabesque-like linear ornament (Matisse). No atmosphere was given, no effects of depth. After 1907, only isolated painters were still working along these lines. The Cubists accented the volumes at first, using local, natural color (after 1907, influence of the retrospective shows of Cézanne's work). The perspectivist view of an object, using transient illumination to represent something as an accidental appearance at a single moment and from one point of view, no longer gave any satisfaction; it was too photographic an idea. People wanted now to penetrate into the essence of an object by showing it, without perspective, in several characteristic views at once. This is the meaning of the saying by the painters Gleizes and Metzinger: "The cubist must be able to move around his object, in order to set down the successive aspects of it together in a single picture and so to express time." The term "cubist" was used in the sense of "spatial." However, the surfaces were soon detached from the spatial forms, brought on to the surface of the canvas, and composed into a single picture. In the painting, then, they are partially superposed, and the alternation of dark parts and light depicts the changing play of light (Analytical Cubism, 1910). The actual colors of the natural forms are no longer used, giving way to constructive grays, greens, and browns (Picasso, Braque). Synthetic Cubism (1913 on) reached its climax in 1921–22 in the works of the same painters. Since the emphasis was now placed on the essential forms, the subjects were treated in a more real fashion. Vivid colors were now also used, and foreign materials, such as colored and printed papers, were pasted into "collages." The intention was that the applied objects should accentuate the painted surface and in-

18

19

23

2

18. *Siegfried, 1924, by Fritz Lang, a film of stately static rhythm, in which more emphasis is put on the monumental composition of the picture series than on the expression of movement, which older films gave.*

19. *The cabinet of Dr. Caligary, 1919, by Robert Wiene, the first Expressionistic and original Literary film composition, that had great influence on cinema art.*
The forms are adapted to the unreal action.

25

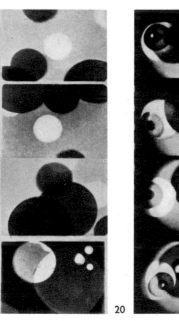

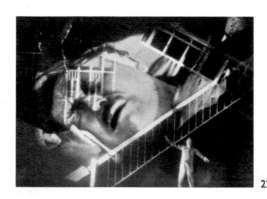

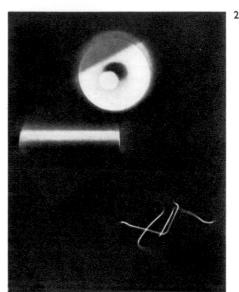

22

20

21

26

20, 21. *Film Study, 1927, by Hans Richter, an example of "absolute film art," in which an optical rhythm is created by means of camera technique. 22. A frame from Geheimnisse einer Seele, 1926, by G. W Pabst, which shows the influence of Surrealism. The camera tries to penetrate the interior of man. 23. Le Merle, 1958, by Norman MacLaren, an instance of cinépeinture : drawing, engraving, and painting directly on the film strip. 24. Charlie Chaplin, The Great Dictator, 1940. 25. Photogram by Laszlo Moholy-Nagy, about 1922, abstract image (Constructivism) produced by letting light fall on sensitized paper through more or less transparant objects and cut off by opaque objects, thus avoiding the use of the camera. Light is the image-forming*

Page 197 : James Ensor, Carnaval, detail.

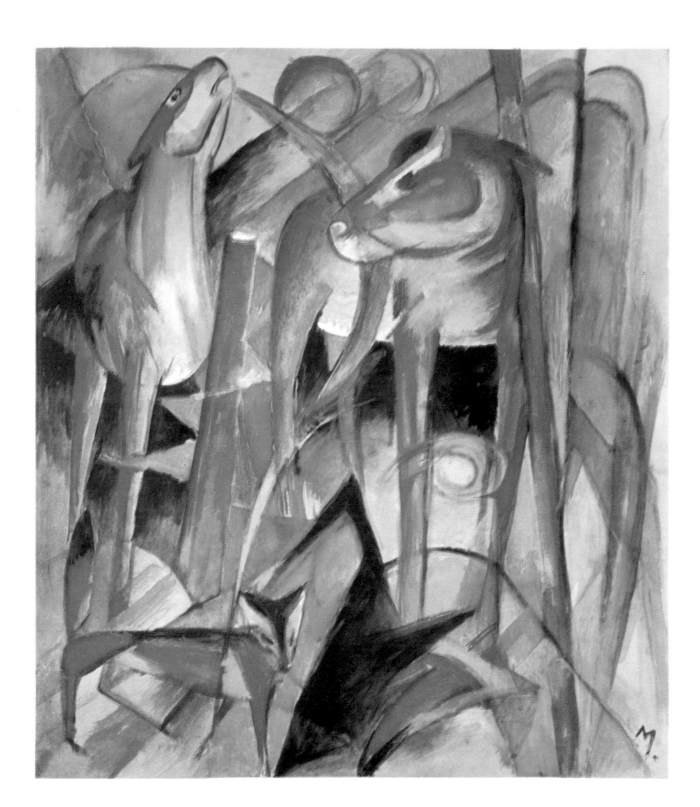

7

0

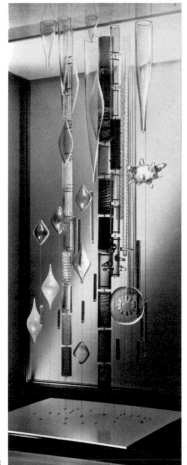

28

29

27–30. Industrial design: The forms of useful objects come from their materials and functions. 27. The simple but purposefully constructed Barcelona chair, designed in 1925 by Mies van der Rohe, is still being manufactured. 28. Glass composition from Orrefors (Sweden), one of the centers of contemporary decorative art. 29. Chair by Arne Jacobsen (Denmark). 30. Streamlined forms of the French SE–210 Caravelle.

element, as color is in painting and tones are in music. 26. The Three-Cornered Hat, by the Nederlands Opera Ballet during the Holland Festival, 1958, with décors by Picasso, Leonide Massine in the principal role.

crease the distance between object and representation. Cubism, at first rectilinear, became curvilinear as well, after 1923.

Futurism (1909–19) aimed at depicting the passage of time in the movement of modern life ("the thing is not any longer to represent a speeding car, but the car's speed"; Severini, 1914). Successive phases of a movement of the body or of emotional life were combined into a single picture. The tendency was influenced by Analytical Cubism, which was rejected, however, because it is static. We cite from a manifesto of the writer Marinetti (1909): "We wish to celebrate war —the only hygiene of the world—militarism, patriotism, the destructive movement of the anarchists, contempt for women," and "Museums are cemeteries, where the spirit is numbed in a funeral urn." Futurism came to an end shortly after World War I.

Neoclassicism (in Picasso about 1920–24) drew its origin partly from Diaghilev's ballet. Picasso made illustrations for the *Metamorphoses of Ovid*; Braque illustrated Hesiod's *Theogony*. The compositions and the types suggest those of Greek art. Dadaism broke all bonds with the past. (The name was found, in 1915, by opening a dictionary at random.) After World War I the theses of the movement were propagated by manifestos (*Dada* magazine), lectures, and expositions (Tristan Tzara). Dada was hostile to all earlier theories of art and to bourgeois culture. Forms borrowed from nature were used subjectively. Useful objects were also exhibited as works of art (readymades). In addition to paint, nails, streetcar tickets, and iron wire were also used in paintings. A combination of Dadaism with the Constructivism to be discussed below appeared in Kurt Schwitter's *Merzbau*, built up out of rubbish (see *Merz* magazine, 1923–32). Most of the Dadaists later joined Surrealism (about 1924). Surrealism 1920s) arose out of the popularization of psychology and psychoanalysis. The direction in which it evolved was also determined by the writers Guillaume Apollinaire and André Breton. An art work came to resemble a psychoanalytical session. Breton wrote, in the *Second Surrealist Manifesto* (1930): "It is no longer primary to create works of art, but rather to bring the dark sides of our being to the light." The content of the unconscious that was thus tapped was represented as without any control by reason. Some used the symbolic forms of the dream (Max Ernst, Yves Tanguy). Others let themselves go passive and followed every passing impulse, as in automatic writing (Joan Miró): "The artist must strive to encompass the entire psychophysical terrain, of which consciousness is but a small segment. In this bottomless depth, as Freud has shown, freedom from all the bonds of inhibition prevails, a timeless condition.

Page 198: Franz Marc (1880–1916), Blue Roes, about 1909.

31

32

3

34

35

3

37

38

3

31. The first skyscrapers were erected in New York and Chicago. In the Guaranty Building of 1895 in Buffalo, N.Y., Louis Sullivan aimed at a form suitable to the structure, even the ornament, in which he created a personal Art Nouveau. 32. Sullivan's disciple Frank Lloyd Wright aimed at an "organic architecture," organic likewise in the spatial connection between interior and exterior (Falling Water, Pennsylvania, 1936). 33. Antonio Gaudí used organic shapes in both ornament and construction in the Batlló house, Barcelona, 1905–7. 34. Applied, unnecessary ornament was completely rejected by Berlage. In the Amsterdam Exchange (1898–1903), his aim is clear, visible construction and the incorporation of monumental art. (See also previous chapter, Figs. 18 and 18a.) 35. In Erich Mendelsohn, the form becomes expressionistic in the Einstein Observatory Tower at Potsdam, 1921. 36. The Schröder house, Utrecht, 1924, by Gerrit Rietveld, exemplified modern architecture in an open plan and windows extending to the corners in order to unify inside and outside. 37. Ludwig Mies van der Rohe's Farnsworth house, Fox River, Illinois, designed 1946, built 1950, presents a synthesis of the dematerialized art of space. 38. Van Nelle Factory, Rotterdam, 1926–30, by Brinkman and Van der Vlugt, early example of the completely new, businesslike architecture in factory construction. 39. Consistent use of

40

Automatism brings us directly to these regions" (Breton). Surrealism does not confine itself to the realm of art; it aims at being a world view, a campaign against the dominion of logic.

The partisans of the abstract trends (1910s) were of the opinion that forms and colors that were independent of natural models could better express man's emotions.

The experience of beauty found expression in abstract images of splendid colors or word sounds (Delaunay, Apollinaire). Or else the "ballast" of natural forms was thrown overboard, and a start was made on the basis of "pure" forms: circles, rectangles, and crosses (Suprematism). The name is directed at the supremacy of pure feeling. The starting point could also be the surface to be painted,

high dwelling houses was first achieved in Sweden, e.g., by S. Markelius, who has also designed lofty office buildings (1959) for the center of Stockholm. 40. Prestressed concrete was developed by Eugène Freyssinet in France. Daring use of reinforced concrete was made by Robert Maillart in his bridges with a strong expressive effect, as in this bridge over the Arve, near Geneva, 1936. 41. Pier Luigi Nervi, Palazzo dello Sport, Rome, 1957. Since 1926 Nervi has been using his characteristic constructions in reinforced, prestressed, and shell concrete for all sorts of structures (hangars, churches, offices, stadiums). 42. South American architects adopted the use of concrete with the support of Le Corbusier, and under the leadership of Lúcio Costa and Oscar Niemeyer, who collaborated on the Ministry of Education and Health, Rio de Janeiro, 1937–43.

using rectangles and confining oneself to simple surfaces (De Stijl). In doing so, the act of painting was seen as an inseparable part of a complete, harmonious future society.

In Tachism (abstract or nonabstract, since 1950), the painter applies his colors in the form of flecks, or permits the paint to run, and thereby to act as arranger. Other painters leave the result to chance as far as possible (random art). In Action Painting the painters work dynamically. Experimental art (since 1940) seeks to represent the inner contact between the artist and the world by way of association. The experimental artists oppose any intellectual art such as Cubism and Surrealism. In 1948, the Internationale des Artistes Expérimentaux (Cobra) was founded in Paris; it was dissolved in 1951.

42

43

Some tendencies relate to painting alone (see the section *Painting*, below), but in general they comprise many arts, or more broadly, manifestations of culture, as will be seen from the descriptions below of the several domains. The surveys of the traditional "major" arts (architecture, sculpture, and painting) given below treat them in more detail, in their historical development.

43. In Russia after 1923 and in Germany after 1933, a reaction set in that led to colossal monumentalism with classical borrowings, such as Troost's Haus der Kunst, Munich, 1936. 44. Woodland Crematorium by Eric Gunnar Asplund, near Stockholm, 1940. Functional architecture first achieved equilibrium with its surroundings in Scandinavia. 45. All conscious monumentality has vanished in Arne Jacobsen's City Hall, Rødovre, 1952. 46. Norwegian Exposition Pavilion, by Sverre Fehn, 1958. Use of wood and glass combined the natural materials with spatial connection. 47. An elementary school designed by the architects of the London County Council, 1957. Functional traditions have been carried out in England chiefly in school buildings. 48. General Motors Technical Center, Warren, Mich., 1950–56, by Eero Saarinen. American perfectionism and style favored an architecture of geometrical relationships.

44

45

46

47

48

50

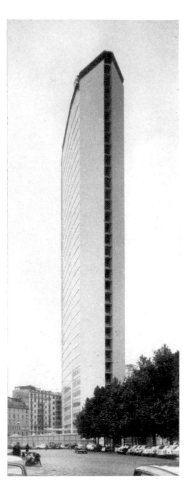

51

52

49. Free interpretation in a school in Florida by Paul Rudolph, 1959. 50. Nervi's construction is to a great extent determinative of the form of the Pirelli Building, Milan, by Giovanni Ponti, 1955–58. 51. Model for hangar by Konrad Wachsmann, 1959. Research into complete prefabrication by Wachsmann and Buckminster Fuller led to tubular constructions capable of roofing over large areas. 52. Union Tank Car Dome, Baton Rouge, La., 1958, by R. Buckminster Fuller.

LITERATURE At the beginning of the century the most important trends were still realism and naturalism. As a reaction against them, neoromanticism arose (1910): the beautiful was accentuated, in sonorous language. Expressionism developed in Germany (1910, Trakl, Stramm, Werfel; in Flanders, Van Ostaijen and Gijsen). Expressionism had less chance in France (Claudel, Apollinaire, Romains). Cubism and Futurism manifested themselves in typography, and by means of suggesting movement (rhythmical repetition of the same sounds, Van Ostaijen). Apollinaire called typographical experiments *calligrammes*.

After the hard reality of World War I, people were very hostile to any kind of Romanticism and sought after objective construction. Van Doesburg, the Neoplasticist, wrote in 1916: "We no longer long for the wilderness and fairy tales, since we possess the order of the engine room and the fairy tale of the modern mode of production. The longing for heaven has given way to the flight of the airplane into the heavens with its calm pilot."

The war novels written after World War I somewhat displaced the family chronicle which had been a favorite form since the beginning of the century (Thomas Mann, Jules Romains, John Galsworthy, Hugh Walpole, Roger Martin du Gard). Dadaism was a literary movement as well (Tristan Tzara). In 1913 the Cabaret Voltaire literary club was founded; in 1918 the magazine *Littérature* appeared (both Dadaist; Breton, Soupault).

In Surrealist literature automatic writing was done, as well as images rising to consciousness. A poetic Surrealism is found in Apollinaire. The first sentences of André Breton's novel *Poisson Soluble* (Soluble Fish, 1924) give the same sort of image as a Surrealist painting by

Salvador Dali: "At this hour of the day the park spread its blond hands over the magic fountain. A castle without meaning rolled on the surface of the earth." Paul Eluard and David Gascoyne are Surrealist poets.

André Gide's novel *The Counterfeiters* (1926) had great influence because of the originality of its structure. François Mauriac wrote psychoanalytic novels (*Thérèse Desqueyroux*, 1927) and set the tone for the literature of the Resistance during World War II. André Malraux strove for human dignity (*La Condition Humaine*, 1933), and also wrote philosophical art criticism. Albert Camus was related to the existentialists (*Le Mythe de Sisyphe*, 1942).

After World War II experimental writers attacked fixed form, meter, and words. People put themselves in the hands of free associations, trying to awaken the reader from the trance into which he is put by the flood of newspapers and magazines. In Germany M. L. Kaschnitz worked in the abstract manner (*Genazzano*, 1955); the verbs have no tenses and are used only for the purposes of rhythm and sound. Paralleling the studies in communications and linguistics (cybernetics, communications techniques), an associative formation of word images was developed (Dylan Thomas). In France this was seen primarily in literature for the stage.

DRAMA At the beginning of the century the stage presented realistic dramas with social significance (Ibsen) and symbolic dramas (Strindberg). Under the influence of Bergson, George Bernard Shaw expressed his philosophy of life (vitalism). In particular, the French stage led the way to renovation (Hervieu, Bernstein).

In the 1920s the influence of the Russian Expressionist theater on

204—TWENTIETH CENTURY

Western Europe was important, via Germany (Piscator, Proletarische Theater and Volksbühne, Berlin). Poetry was rejected; the effort was toward didacticism.

Surrealist drama was developed after World War I (*Les Mamelles de Tirésias* [*The Breasts of Tiresias*], Cocteau, 1917). After World War II, Anouilh wrote *pièces roses* (nominally comedies, but with a melan-

53. Frederick Kiesler's "Endless House" project, 1959, a reaction against industrialization, although use was made of sprayed concrete, a recent invention, for forms like this. 54. University of Mexico, 1950–55, by a group of architects headed by Carlos Lazo. The walls are decorated by enormous mosaics. 55, 56. La Tourette monastery, Evreux, France, 1960, by Le Corbusier. 57. Unité d'Habitation, Nantes, 1958. Le Corbusier created architecture having strong personal design based on a system of measurement (the Modulor), on dramatization of concrete construction, and on the autonomous dwelling unit as a machine for living.

choly aftertaste) and *pièces noires* (somber and often bitter). Sartre wrote plays based on his philosophical principles (Existentialism; *Huis Clos* [*No Entry*]).

An automatism influenced by Existentialism and in part by Surrealism, which led to quasiabstract drama, was introduced by Ionesco, Beckett, and Adamov.

In East Berlin, Bertolt Brecht (director of the Berliner Ensemble) was opposed to all emotion; he made use of alienation between actor and role, between audience and presentation. His earlier works show Impressionist elements as well.

At the beginning of the century stage settings were designed by Redon, Vuillard, and Toulouse-Lautrec. In 1912 Kandinsky wrote on the subject of abstract settings. Adolphe Appia and Gordon Craig chose abstract spaces, enlivened by lighting effects, for their settings; this principle was applied in its most extreme form in the recent Bayreuth style of Wieland Wagner. In Russia after World War I

the peoples' theater was developed (Kegentsev and Evreinov), in which Meyerhold and Tairov used blocks, cranes, and elevators (Constructivism). The Futurist painter Depero designed settings for Rodolfo de Angeles. Around 1930 the members of the Bauhaus at Dessau created settings (Gropius, Moholy-Nagy, Schwitters). Stern and Pircham worked for the producer Max Reinhardt in the 1920s. Among the stage designers of the United States were Simonson, Bel Geddes, and Oenslager. Igael Tumarkin's settings for Brecht are a mixture of realism, photomontage, and mechanical constructions. After World War II experiments were also made with the form of the theater itself. In the theater in the round, in Paris and elsewhere, the performance takes place in the midst of the spectators, virtually without props; at Tampere (Finland) the spectators are in the middle of the stage, on a turning platform following the course of the events.

59

60

58. Design for a model village near Moscow, by Miasto-Projekt, Kraków, 1959. 59. An almost naturalistic concrete structure by Eero Saarinen: TWA Terminal at Kennedy Airport, New York, 1960. 60. Apartment house, Antwerp, 1947–59, by Maes, Braem, and Maremans.

A

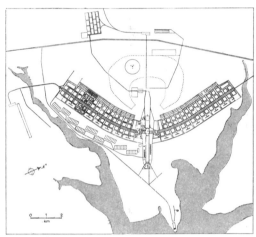

A. Plan of Brasilia, under direction of Lúcio Costa. New communities, in Europe limited to residential districts of small area, are erected in Asia and America as provincial and national capitals all at once.

61

61. The Lijnbaan, Rotterdam, by City Planning Service, 1949–56, has been influential in solving the problem of shopping centers inside cities. 62. Municipal Orphanage, Amsterdam, 1959, by A. van Eyck, member of Team Ten, an international group which advocates clear characterization of district, neighborhood, and residence. B. Recognizability in an architectonic conception has been most intensively and impressively used by Oskar Nikolai Hansen for the Auschwitz monument, a granite concrete road 60 meters wide that runs

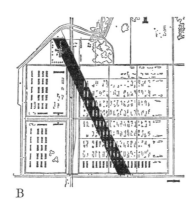

B

62

MOTION PICTURES Motion pictures (since about 1895) can evoke a shadow world in which the dream wishes of the public acquire a certain reality, but they can also confront men with actual problems. Early in the century films were used as carnival attractions or, as "art films," reproduced stage plays. In the 1920s the avant-garde took the possibilities of film technique as its starting point, and liberated motion pictures from the stage. Various schools of art can be encountered in the cinema. Expressionist experiment was seen in *The Cabinet of Dr. Caligari* (Robert Wiene, 1920). Eisenstein's *Potemkin* (1925) and Joris Ivens's *The Bridge* (1928) show that the cinema, by means of camera technique, can possess a language of its own. Cubism and Futurism are recognizable in the *Ballet Mécanique* by the painter Fernand Léger. Dadaism was applied in the *Dadaïstischer Filmversuch* (Dadaist Film Experiment) of Hans Richter and Viking Eggeling, and in *Dadascope* (1957), also by Richter. Surrealist films are *L'Etoile de Mer* (The Starfish) of Man Ray, *Chien Andalou* (Andalusian Dog) by Luis Bunuel, and *L'Age d'Or* (Golden Age) by Bunuel and Salvador Dali, all made between 1924 and 1930.

In abstract films rhythmically moving lines and surfaces were employed: *Rhythme 21*, by Richter (1921), and *Opus I*, by Walter Ruttmann (1923). Oskar Fischinger used moving geometrical figures synchronized with music; Norman MacLaren (Canada) is now working abstractly in color (*Boogie-Woogie*). Political films were produced: *400 Millions*, on China, by Ivens (1938), and *Yellow Caesar*, a montage of new films about Mussolini, by Cavalcanti.

Sound was added in the 1930s as a new expressive possibility; at the present time color is sometimes a gain. In addition, painting, drawing, and engraving are done directly on the film strip (*cinépeinture*): Norman MacLaren (*Love on the Wing*, 1938; *Blinkity Blank*, 1955) and Rolf Engler [*Traum in Tusche* (Dream in Watercolor), 1952]. Another procedure is to allow light to fall on the sound track, so that it is reproduced as sound (Film Exercise, G. Whitney). Motion picture companies, however, produce almost exclusively film plays of varying quality, making skillful use of the cult of film stars. The survival of the cinema depends on its function as a mass medium. Tragically or comically, the social problem of man in the mass is posed (Chaplin, Clair, Italian neorealism) or other primary human problems (religion: Bergman; sex and fate: France, notably by the *nouvelle vague*; power: the United States, e.g., Orson Welles). Emile Cohl is a pioneer in the field of the animated cartoon. Other important figures are Dubout (*Anatole à la Tour de Nesles*) and Walt Disney (*Snow White and the Seven Dwarfs, Fantasia*).

PHOTOGRAPHY Photography, which at the beginning of the century was often used to reproduce romanticized landscapes, is also searching for new ways. The same kinds of experiment are being conducted here as with films. Photography is conceived of as a form of art that makes pictures, with or without the use of photographic apparatus, by means of a sensitive film. Some remarkable abstract experiments were made in the twenties by Man Ray and Moholy-Nagy (Bauhaus, "photograms" and photomontage, Constructivism).

MUSIC Late Romanticism continued into the twentieth century, especially in Germany (Strauss, Mahler), and there led to Expressionism, while in France it appeared as Impressionism (Debussy, Dukas, Ravel). Thereafter there was a reaction, following the reali-

63

64

diagonally through the ruins of the Nazi extermination camp, 1958. 63–65. Impressionism and naturalism were maintained in sculpture well into the twentieth century. 63. Standing Nude, by Aristide Maillol. 64. Pegasus, by Carl Milles. 65. Domestic Cares, by Rik Wouters, 1913. 66. The Fountain, by George Minne, 1898. 67. Kneeling Woman, by Wilhelm Lehmbruck, 1911. 68. Singing Man, by Ernst Barlach, 1928.

65

66

67

zation of the crisis in tonal-functional harmony (after Wagner's *Tristan und Isolde*) and of the Romantic-literary load that the musical material was bearing. The trends may be classified as follows:

a. There was a return to the pre-Romantic period: the "neo" styles, such as neoclassicism, neo-Baroque (Stravinsky between, say, 1920 and 1955), and neoromanticism (Poulenc);

68

69

70

72

73

74

75

69–76. *Expressionistic sculpture presents many forms and personal conceptions. 69. Horse and Rider, by Marino Marini, 1947; inspired by Etruscan art. 70. Devastated City, by Ossip Zadkine, 1947; Expressionism. 71. Figure of Musician, by Henri Laurens, 1938; Cubism. 72. Recumbent Figure, by Henry Moore, 1921; primary forms. 73. City Square, by Alberto Giacometti, 1949. 74. Glenkiln Cross Group, by Henry Moore, 1956; inspired by prehistoric art.*

77

78

75. Bird in Flight, by Constantin Brancusi, 1919; influence of (and later, on) nonrepresentational art. 76. Seated Pierrot, by Jacques Lipchitz; influence of Cubism. 77, 78. Sculpture without relation to visual reality is not prominent as compared with painting, before World War II. 77. Construction in Wood, by Jean Arp, 1917; Dadaism. 78. Construction, 1957, by Naum Gabo; Constructivism. Even after World War II the persistence of

b. A neotonality was sought, and the effort was made to treat the material strictly musically, unliterarily: the new objectivity, which in the end glided into the neostyles (Hindemith, Hartmann, Badings); *c.* The effort was made to infuse new life into tonality by using several tone centers at the same time: polytonality (Satie, Milhaud, Pijper); *d.* The melody and the harmony inherent in folk music was used as a basis (Bartok, De Falla). This may be taken to include the adaptation of jazz (Milhaud, *Création du Monde*; Stravinsky, *Ragtime*, 1911); *e.* Tonality was thrown overboard altogether (Schönberg's strictly atonal period, about 1910–20).

Of all these trends, only the last seems actually to contain new possibilities. For the time being, it was rather negative. Schönberg was able to convert it into something positive by a system based on the negation of tonality: the twelve-tone system, or dodecaphony (only a technical innovation). The aesthetic innovation was brought about by his disciple Webern, in an analysis of the musical material into its four essential components (pitch, duration, volume, and timbre).

The most recent generation, since 1950, has from the technical point of view relied chiefly on a borrowing from dodecaphony (serial technique, or seriality) and combined this with Webern's theories, by means of which the four musical components are tied into a single initial series. The need to organize completely the four parameters led to electronic music, in which the technical apparatus makes possible exact mastery of the material. As a reaction to this, and paralleling other random art, such as Action Painting, the aleatory element was introduced into music (Cage).

The latest development presents a mixture of serial and aleatory principles (improvised accompaniment within strictly ordered interconnections), produced sometimes with a mixture of traditional and electronic means, and with reference to space as the fifth musical component (stereophony) (Stockhausen, Boulez, and Berio; Stravinsky since 1955).

79

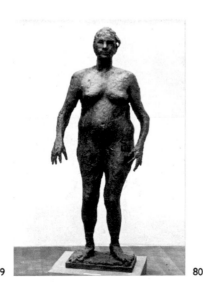

80

81

impressionistic-realistic design is still very common, and more brilliant than in painting. 79. Dockworker, by Mari Silvester Andriessen. 80. Hurricane, by Germaine Richier, 1949; Expressionism. 81. Sculpture B, by Roel d'Haese, 1959. Free from the problems of figurative versus nonfigurative, a concrete, spontaneous art developed, often under the influence of Henry Moore.

82

85

82. *Lunar Landscape, 1956, by Shinkichi Tajiri. 83. Inward Eye, by Lynn Chadwick, 1952. 84. Wire Sculpture, by Alexander Calder (mobile). 85. Spatial Plastic, by Robert Jacobsen, 1951; abstraction. 86. The Kiss, by Gustav Klimt, 1908; Art Nouveau. 87. Nude, by Pierre Bonnard; Nabi. 88. The Rumanian Blouse, by Matisse; Fauvism. 89. Paddock at Ascot, by Raoul Dufy, 1935.*

In opera many stage plays and novels were used almost complete as librettos (by Berg, Einem, Liebermann, Britten, Blacher, Klebe, Henze, Poulenc, etc.), and the *bel canto* element retreated into the background. An identical tendency emerged in the reproductive style: the staged opera became dominant. The clearest representative of the tendency (which is called *Musiktheater* and seeks dramatic truth in the interpretation) is Walter Felsenstein; Günther Rennert is an important related figure. The general inclination toward abstraction struck root in Bayreuth, where Wieland and Wolfgang Wagner presented their grandfather's works as static manifestations; lighting took on a new dramatic function.

DANCE By the end of the nineteenth century the art of the ballet had grown rigid in Western Europe, but had retained its vitality in Russia. The appearance of Serge Diaghilev's Ballets Russes in France (1909) brought about a revival there, in which young choreographers (Fokine, Massine, Lifar, Balanchine) participated, along with composers and painters. For example, there was the ballet *Parade* (1917), book by Cocteau, music by Satie, curtain and costumes by Picasso (partly in a Cubist manner), choreography by Massine, performed by dancers of Diaghilev's group. Apollinaire wrote the introduction to the program, in which the word *sur-réalisme* was used for the first time.

The influence of the Diaghilev group was international, and so strong that when the core fell apart at his death (1929), groups could arise in many countries that proved to be viable, and could even add new stylistic elements of their own to the classical art of ballet. To a great extent these were derived from the antitraditional art of dance: for example, Isadora Duncan, from about 1900. Taking her inspiration from the ancient Greek art, barefooted and in a loose-fitting tunic, she liberated the movement of the body from the often oppressive bonds of classical technique. From this came the free dance trend of Rudolf Laban and Mary Wigman and the ballets of Kurt Jooss, and in America the art of Martha Graham (Expressionism and influence of depth psychology).

After World War II the traditional ballet seemed to meet needs best, whether rejuvenated in antinarrative, musical-abstract form (Balanchine) or by assimilating nonclassical elements: jazz, revue, folklore, and even the free dance of movement (Robbins, De Mille).

ARTS AND CRAFTS, AND INTERIOR DECORATION At the beginning of the century the arts and crafts were under the influence of William Morris and Ruskin and the English Arts and Crafts movement. Attention was devoted to the function of ornament.

The graceful curved lines of Art Nouveau were adopted both in interiors and in useful objects, as well as on posters (Hillebrand, Steinlen, Toorop). In Holland, Berlage went on to reject any ornament that did not arise out of the structure and the material. After World War I interiors and furniture came to be regarded as a totality. The abstractionist trend (from 1917) was influenced by, among other movements, Neoplasticism (*De Stijl* magazine). Every piece of furniture, every utensil, must have a harmonious effect in the taut interior.

In the instruction at the Bauhaus at Weimar, later at Dessau (founded 1919, by Walter Gropius), the accent was very soon placed on the arts and crafts (functional style, since 1920). The school's experiments were published in the *Bauhausbücher*. Forms were sought that connected the uses of the objects with the nature of the material employed (industrial design, since 1925). For example, the steel chair made of a single tube was designed (Mies van der Rohe, 1925). Seats were designed to fit the form of the body, tableware to eating habits.

As time went on, forms were influenced by the use of new materials, such as plywood (which makes curved surfaces possible) and plastics (Jacobsen, Berthoia, Eames, Saarinen, and Knoll).

In France, Cubism recurs in the art of the poster, in the adoption of a constructive division of the surface. This trend also influenced the revival of tapestry weaving in France (Marcel Gromaire). Jean Lurçat's wall-hangings can in some cases be called Surrealist.

ARCHITECTURE   Although historicism and eclecticism persisted well into the twentieth century, the turn of the century showed the first efforts to find a new language of space. Originally, the language was concerned chiefly with the exterior: in Art Nouveau, ornament predominated. This movement was a protest against limitations on style and bad industrial products; it began in England with Morris and was taken over in Belgium (Horta, Van de Velde), France (Guimard), and in particular Germany and Austria (Olbricht, Hoffmann). Berlage, the most important architect of the period around 1900, stood apart from it from the beginning. A distinctive figure is Antonio Gaudí, the Spaniard, the only man who enriched Art

86

87

88

89

Nouveau structurally (Barcelona: Sagrada Familia, Parc Güell). There were many sources to this protest: social stirrings, mystical ideas, *l'art pour l'art*, and "decadence." Art Nouveau attained its most important results in the field of the minor arts. No investigation was made into the problem of space, and this condemned the movement to sterility.

The next movement was directed chiefly against ornament, which the Austrian, Adolf Loos, called a crime. In 1909 he designed the Steiner house as a smooth cube. In Germany, Peter Behrens found his way in the same direction (AEG turbine factory, 1909). Even earlier (about 1900), architectural composition in structural masses had been advocated by Frank Lloyd Wright in the United States.

90

91

90–94. Expressionism. 90. Blue Colts, by Franz Marc; Blaue Reiter. 91. In the Lemon Grove, by Emil Nolde, 1933; Die Brücke. 92. Double Portrait, by Oskar Kokoschka, 1919; Der Sturm. 93. Demoniacal 1916, by Paul Klee; Blaue Reiter. 94. The Fencers, by T. Makowski, 1936.

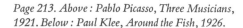

Page 213. Above: Pablo Picasso, Three Musicians, 1921. Below: Paul Klee, Around the Fish, 1926.

92

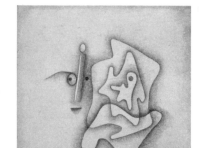

93

94

style (Stockholm City Hall, by Ragnar Oestberg). Both reactions, against ornament and against the concealment of construction, were decisive in architecture down to World War I.

The most important impulse came from Weimar, where Van de Velde reorganized the Kunstgewerbeschule and directed the students toward the investigation of materials. Among the most important works of this period are Berlage's Amsterdam Stock Exchange, Max Berg's Jahrhunderthalle in Breslau (1912), an apartment building (Rue Franklin, 1903) and the Théâtre des Champs-Elysées (1913) by Auguste Perret in Paris, the works of Behrens, the Werkbund-theater (1913) in Cologne by Van de Velde, Gropius' Fagus Factory (with Meyer, 1911) and Bruno Taut's Glass Pavilion (Cologne Fair, 1914). Mention should also be made of Otto Bartning's design for the Sternkirche (not built). A number of these structures had an Expressionist element as well. This tendency is found most outspokenly in Gaudí and in the early work of Erich Mendelsohn; the most important buildings are Mendelsohn's Einstein Tower at Potsdam (1920) and the church of the Sagrada Familia (from 1884) by Gaudí in Barcelona (see also the discussion of Expressionism in the section *Painting*).

When the architects could resume activity after World War I, the prewar conceptions could not provide a solution, although they had made their contribution. But a substitute for Renaissance civilization could not be found in new structures or new ornaments. The artists were compelled to start from scratch: the creation of an adequate space. To this end, the first step was to define the practical needs that any space must meet; studies were made of the functions of dwelling, work, recreation, and commerce. The effort was made to arrive at a purposeful, objectively functional development of space. At first, of course, aesthetic considerations still played an important part: in particular, Cubism and De Stijl (Oud, Van Eesteren, Rietveld) sought an abstract visual pattern. The Weimar Kunstgewerbeschule, renamed the Bauhaus after the war, later moved to Dessau (1925–27) and, led by Gropius, aimed at reviving the guild communities by a rehabilitation of instruction in craftsmanship.

Outside the group were various architects in search of the nature of space: Frank Lloyd Wright, Gerrit Rietveld, Mies van der Rohe, and Le Corbusier. Wright first, but after him and independently of him Rietveld and Mies, discovered the necessity of opening up the space formerly enclosed in rooms, and of giving the rooms a freer connection with the entire internal space (and with Wright, the external space as well). Le Corbusier carried skeleton construction on *pilotis*, or free-standing columns, to its logical conclusions. An isolated figure in France, he fought for the new art by means of his magazine *Esprit Nouveau* (1920–26).

While the external aspect of architecture was thus altered, construction too brought about as yet invisible revolutions. Cast iron, then steel, and reinforced concrete, were already in use in the nineteenth century for bearing structural loads. Art Nouveau started using steel as a decorative element. In reaction against that, people sought to use materials "honestly." Berlage was of decisive importance. His Amsterdam Stock Exchange had great influence, primarily on his fellow-countrymen and in Germany. Subsequently, this influence was to be combined with that of the nationalized Scandinavian

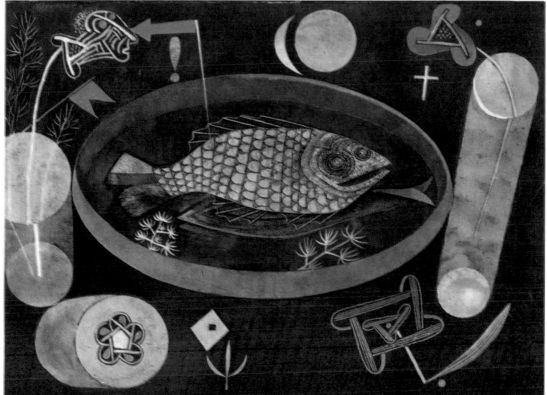

96

98

95. *The Power of the Street, by Umberto Boccioni, 1911 ; Futurism. 96. Large Winter Landscape, by Jean Brusselmans, 1939 ; Primitivism. 97. Ave, by Ben Shahn, 1957 ; social realism. 98. Italian Square, by Giorgio de Chirico, 1915 ; metaphysical art.*

97 *Page 214. Shooting Star, 1947, by Jackson Pollock.*

The most important trends in the 1920s were the Neue Sachlichkeit and Expressionism. The latter struck deep roots in Germany (Poelzig, Taut, and Bartning). In Holland Expressionism was represented by the Amsterdam school (Van der Mey, De Klerk, Kramer, etc.). It emerged from Berlage's conceptions, but in making the construction visible, the objective now became to make it dynamic, with a primarily external aesthetic purpose to which the space behind the façade was completely subordinated. Dudok too, on the basis of Wright's early monumental, heavy structures, had a connection with this group for some time, but he later turned to a strongly Cubist division of volumes. His chief work is the Hilversum City Hall. Expressionism in Italy appeared under the name of Futurism. The most important architect, who died young without having any of his plans materialized, was Antonio Sant' Elia. The Futurists aimed at a completely mechanized society and urbanism. Their anarchist-revolutionary ideals were stated in the *Manifesto of Futurist Archi-*

tecture (1914). They were important for later developments, since they introduced the dynamic element into modern architecture.

The Neue Sachlichkeit (New Objectivity) rejected beauty as an independent value of architecture, and held that the practical was also beautiful. It divided the building into a number of rooms each adapted to its purpose, and it was thus the counterpart in space to the "crossword" paintings of Mondrian's early period. The purest works in this style are the Van Nelle factory in Rotterdam (1927), by Brinckman and Van der Vlugt) and the houses in the Weissenhof (1927) in Stuttgart, designed by Le Corbusier, Oud, Stam, Taut, etc., under the overall direction of Mies van der Rohe. The Neue Sachlichkeit was given an organizational and theoretical basis with the establishment of the Congrès Internationaux d'Architecture Moderne (CIAM). The first of these congresses was held at La Sarraz, Switzerland, in 1928. Many of the outstanding architects of the world met there. They stated the requirements that architecture, and in particular

99

99. *The Night Is Setting Up Rhyth-mically*, by Joan Miró, 1954; Surrealism. 100. *Fruit of Long Experience*, by Max Ernst; psycho-analytical style. 101. *Praying Mantis*, by Graham Sutherland, 1949; Surrealism or transparent realism. 102. *Adam and Eve*, by Fernand Léger; Purism.

100

101

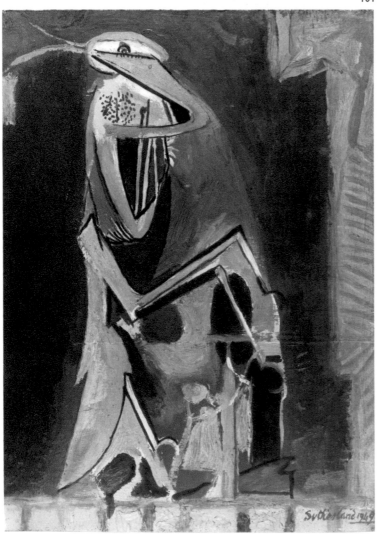

102

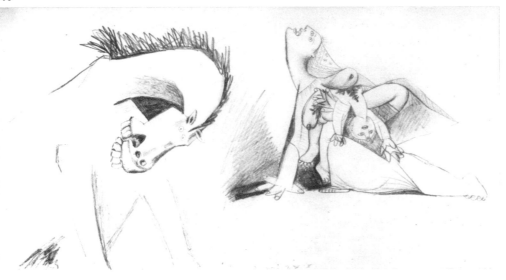

103–110. Forms of Expressionism. 103. Woman of the Streets, by Frits van den Berghe; social Expressionism. 104. The Sow, by Constant Permeke, 1929; animal Expressionism. 105. The Old Actor, by Chaim Soutine; pictural Expressionism. 106. Study for Guernica, by Pablo Picasso; political Expressionism.

city planning, must satisfy a rectilinear, materialistic program, which was of incalculable value in forming an architecture adequate to our time.

The heyday and decline of the Neue Sachlichkeit both came in the 1930s. As a transitional phase to the purely functional style, it constituted a period of inquiry and reflection on the primary task of architecture.

The full flowering of the new architecture began after 1924 with the work of the four men mentioned above. In that year Rietveld built his Schröder house in Utrecht. But the German Pavilion of Mies van der Rohe at the World's Fair in Barcelona in 1929 was more immediately influential. In this work the new space can be seen in its purest form. Rietveld and Mies held the same basic principle: the new style is one directed toward human uses, and it is on the human scale; it differentiates between public and individual actions, suppressing neither for the sake of the other, but giving each its own space. Thereby it is highly democratic. But its respect for individual free-

dom does not lead it to neglect the wider links by which individual freedom finds its full meaning and fulfillment. Spatially, this is achieved by the principle of differentiation without separation. As in the Neue Sachlichkeit, the functional style stresses unmistakably the function of each space. But with this analysis there is synthesis: the interpenetration of the spaces, made possible with the lavish use of glass, the reduction of structural portions to their smallest dimensions, and partial enclosure by partitions. In the Barcelona pavilion the functional style exemplified in the utmost perfection and subtlety. Mies made use of various kinds and colors of glass; his walls are detached marble slabs; curtains suggest privacy without enclosure. Reference should also be made to the work of northern European architects. Markelius in Sweden; Aalto and Eliel Saarinen in Finland; Jacobsen in Denmark: all made substantial contributions by their subtle use of natural materials, including wood and brick, and by their great sensitivity in the internal and external execution of their buildings. They avoided the dogmatism of CIAM, and were

107

108

109

110

exemplary practitioners in urbanism, of which more will be said. Wright had the same kind of feeling for materials; he also used the interpenetration of space, as the functional "pattern" was named, for the inside-outside relationship.

In architecture, to be sure, the boundaries were not so sharply drawn as might appear from differentiating the tendencies. Still, in the early period of modern architecture, compromise was hardly possible; one was either for or against it. This was brought home to Oud, who seemed to join the forces of reaction with his Shell Building in The Hague (1938-41). This reaction arose partly under the influence of the nationalistic tendencies then rife in Europe. What was said to be characteristic of the land and the nation was glorified, and varied only by the "classic." A similar tendency had already come into being in Russia in 1923, where it had put an end to Constructivism and substituted for it a monumentalism of the most inhuman kind. This monumentalism consistently revived the axis of symmetry, and built screening façades and huge entrances. Monumentalism was also practiced in democratic Europe, especially in France (Musée d'Art Moderne, Paris, 1937, by Aubert, Dondel, et al.) It found entry in the Netherlands, where it was grafted onto the historic

107. *Church at Halle, by Lyonel Feininger, 1930; Bauhaus.* 108. *The Lovers, by Marc Chagall.* 109. *Girl with Neckerchief, by Amedeo Modigliani, 1918.* 110. *The Battle, by José Orozco, 1920; social monumental art. In Mexico art was entirely in the service of the left-wing political struggle for liberty. The great monumental artists are Diego Rivera, David Siqueiros, and Orozco.* 111. *Winter (detail), 1940, by Jean Lurçat. Lurçat gave the impulse to the revival of the art of tapestry, at first chiefly at Aubusson.*

111

national style and its "eternal Christian values," and thus seemed suitable for church buildings (Delft school, under the influence of Granpré-Molière).

The following tendencies can be distinguished in post-World War II architecture: dogmatic functionalism, geometrical functionalism, expressive functionalism, the fashionable, and the "informal."

Dogmatic functionalism retains the position of the CIAM, which incidentally was dissolved in 1959.

The geometrical functional architects are followers of Mies and Rietveld. The style can also be seen in the late work of the founders themselves. A high point is the Farnsworth house by Mies (Plano, Illinois, designed 1946, built 1950). Of Rietveld's buildings in Holland, mention should be made in the first place of the Sonsbeek Pavilion (since demolished) for a sculpture exposition near Arnhem in 1954, and dwellings at Bergeijck and Ilpendam. Reference may also be made, in this connection, to the extension of the Kröller-Müller Museum at Otterlo by Van de Velde (1951). The style of Van de Velde, one of the masters of Art Nouveau, digested and inspired all the phases of modern architecture. His influence was felt by the younger Belgian generation. This geometrical functional trend is undoubtedly powerful the world over, including such large firms in the United States as Skidmore, Owings and Merrill, and Harrison and Abramovitz; Drake and Lasdun, Fry and Drew in England; and many architectural firms in Germany, Scandinavia, Switzerland, France and Italy.

Expressive functionalism is found chiefly in the Latin and the Latin American countries. The difference is mainly in temperament. The southern dramatic feeling can find only limited satisfaction in the severe lines of geometrical functionalism. Although there is thus no difference in principle, considerable changes may occur in the spatial development. For example, in Latin countries the equivalent spaces are often replaced by a dominant principal space.

Naturally, a single determinate space may dominate because of its function. It is precisely in this kind of commission—convention halls, stations, stadiums, churches, factories with undivided working space—that the high points of this trend are to be found. The most important design consultants and engineers are Pier Luigi Nervi (Italy), Pietro Belluschi (U.S.A.), Felix Candela (Mexico). They limit themselves chiefly to the design of vaulted structures at the commission of other architects. The best-known architects are: Reidy, Costa, and Niemeyer in Brazil; Villanueva in Venezuela; Eero Saarinen and Paul Rudolph in the United States; Ponti and Castiglione in Italy; Gillet and Zehrfuss in France; Torroja in Spain; and Jorn Utzon in Denmark.

Although mathematically and structurally their structures are very rational, the personal aesthetic approach plays a preponderant part in designing the form. Another group, some of whom do not even call themselves architects, deals exclusively with the possibilities of prefabricated structural elements. Practical results have been achieved in the United States (Buckminster Fuller with geodesic domes, Konrad Wachsmann with his modular tube constructions and in England with school construction. Research in Germany and Poland is still theoretical.

Popularity is the proof of the acceptance of functional architecture: especially in the United States, the battle has been won, but clients want some distinctive dressing up in addition to the functional spaces; this desire is met by architects such as Edward D. Stone and,

to some extent, Marcel Breuer. The same phenomenon is encountered elsewhere, especially in South America.

The informal school is the architectural parallel of *peinture brute* or Action Painting. The impulse came principally from Le Corbusier, although his chapel at Ronchamp of 1950–54, the first work in this direction, was still completely faithful to functionality of space, and was "informal" only in the plastic structural forms. Informal architecture tries to stick close to nature: the snail-shell, trees, caves, the peeled orange. Its most important representatives are the Americans Bruce Goff and J. M. Johansen. This tendency is the source of the renewed interest in Art Nouveau.

Another name for informal art is *art brut*. A number of architects are sometimes included in the informal school whose use of materials is sometimes extremely primary and rigorous, but who are followers of the CIAM (which they put to death) in their spatial conceptions. The post-war congresses were dominated by the rebels, who in 1956 were entrusted with reorganizing the CIAM. They advised the Tenth Congress (hence the name Team Ten) to disband the CIAM.

In the meantime, they formed a closed group, consisting of Team Ten and some others, who met in Otterlo (1959). The group calls for a new attitude toward the community on the part of the architect. Architecture must be the expression of the community on the human scale, and hence buildings must be united in neighborhoods and districts, the latter being the largest unit that can be sensed at a single viewing. The dwelling must once more be recognizable as independent. Architectural form must be given to the boundaries between isolation and neighborhood, between interior and exterior. One of the members (Aldo van Eyck) is especially enthusiastic about the indigenous city structure of North Africa, the complex within an enclosure, or casbah idea. In practice, attention is paid particularly to inner and outer communications as expressions of group living. Up to the present time the most important works in conformity with these requirements have been erected in Holland: the Municipal Orphanage by Van Eyck in Amsterdam, and the Wereldomroep in Hilversum by Van den Broek and Bakema. Bakema was the initiator of the meeting in Otterlo. Further members of the Otterlo group are, among others, Zoltan and Hansen (Poland), the Smithsons (England), Voelcker (Germany). The tendency in question is found outside this group (monastery at Bismarck, by Breuer). The group will accept no distinction between architecture and town planning, since the architecture of the individual can only manifest its identity in the larger unit. An example of this interrelationship was given by Van den Broek and Bakema in their plans for Noord-Kennemerland and for Marl (West Germany, 1962).

CITY PLANNING   City planning is very backward. The materialistic program of the CIAM still partly dominates the subject. Although sufficient light, air, and space are present in new projects, resulting in an unprecedented improvement in workers' districts, many new schemes are rigid, rectilinear, and unimaginative. A contrast is the other conception, that of garden villages, but this too offers no way out because of the enormous demand for living quarters on sites as small as possible. New ideas have been realized only in the last few years, chiefly following the model of Scandinavia. There, as early as in the 1930s, tall buildings were used in the main, making possible a free arrangement in the landscape. Bringing nature to the feet of the

113

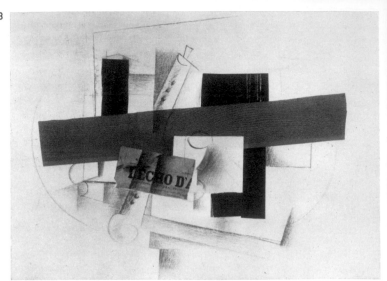

112

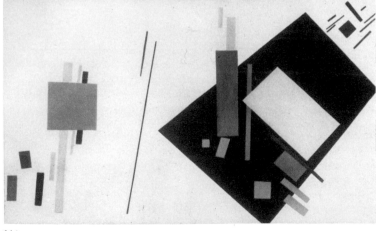

114

The transition to nonrepresentational art :

112. L'Estaque, 1908, by Georges Braque. The influence of Negro art (stronger in the art of his colleague Picasso) and of Cézanne. 113. The Clarinet, by Braque ; Cubism.
114. From Girl to Woman, by M. Duchamp, 1912 ; Simultaneism and Orphism.
Nonrepresentational art came from De Stijl in the Netherlands, Constructivism in England, Suprematism in Russia, and the researches of Kandinsky in Germany (also at the Bauhaus).
115. The East, 1913, by Wassily Kandinsky ; lyrical abstraction.
116 Suprematist Composition, by Kasimir Malevich ; Suprematism.
117 Composition 1931, by Piet Mondrian ; Concrete art, De Stijl.
118. White Relief, by Ben Nicholson ; Constructivism.

115

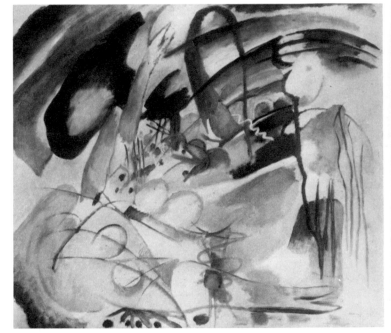

116

118

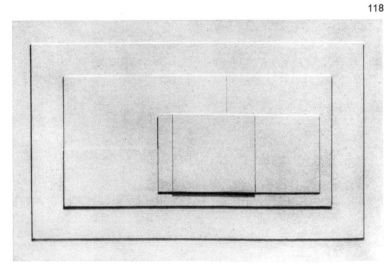

117

dwellings in the outskirts, coupled with the complete urbanization, and hence denaturing of the centers (Stockholm, by Markelius), does away with the unsatisfactory mixed conditions. A complete elaboration of this system is found in the above-mentioned plan of Van den Broek en Bakema. Cities designed on a large scale were commissioned from Le Corbusier (Chandigarh, the capital of the Punjab, India) and Costa (Brasilia, the new capital of Brazil, most of whose buildings were designed by Niemeyer). Traffic has become more and more important in planning, as well as menacing the viability of the centers of cities. The problem has been dealt with, more or less sucessfully, by means of pedestrian districts (Victor Gruen's shopping center near Detroit), by curved and narrowing streets and automatic slowing down (Reichow in Germany), rings of parking garages, garages on shop roofs (Coventry), satellite cities as dwelling places (Great Britain's New Towns) or as maintenance centers (suburbs of Paris).

SCULPTURE The development of art in the twentieth century has not reached fulfillment in sculpture. It seems to be hard to realize the new ideals in volumes. In addition, it is clear that in this region the classical tradition is very stubborn and keeps reestablishing its grip on sculpture. The individualism of Jacob Epstein in England comes to mind.

This resistance was manifested in particular after World War II in the design of the innumerable war monuments. Almost without exception we find human figures, male or female, standing, lying, or gliding. This of course is not a value judgment: such sculptors as, in Holland, Mari Andriessen have reached great heights in this style (*The Dockworker* at Amsterdam and his monument to the Resistance at Enschede).

Naturally, too, elements of the progress of style are found here as well, such as Impressionism in Maillol and Despiau, Art Nouveau in Lehmbruck and Minne, Expressionism in Kolbe, Haller, Fiori, and Marini, and Cubism in Leinfellner, Wotruba, Heiliger, and others. But pure representatives are much rarer. (For descriptions of the various trends, see the section *Painting*). Expressionism, under the influence of Negro sculpture and Expressionist painting, was the trend best able to develop in sculpture (Picasso, Schmidt-Rottluff, Modigliani, Laurens, Zadkine, Lipchitz, Gonzalez). Germaine Richier was another who later worked in this style. An element of social or political accusation is evident: it is also found in the Netherlanders Kneulman and Lotti van der Gaag. There are, too, the independent artists: Duchamp-Villon, Lipchitz, and Belling. Some of them, such as Gonzalez and Lipchitz, represent the Surrealist phase of these trends. Genuine nonfigurative work is found in several Constructivists. Vantongerloo belonged to De Stijl. Carel Visser still adheres to that movement. A more spatial direction brought the most important "sculptors" forth: Gabo, Pevsner, Hepworth, Brancusi, Bill, and, later, A. Volten. Their work approaches architecture, in the sense that they work on surfaces spanning, separating, and enclosing space, and representing mathematical or scientific formulas that may or may not be capable of scientific calculation. Some of their work along this direction was also guided by natural forms, elaborating them Surrealistically or even Dadaistically (Brancusi, Arp, d'Haese).

An important phenomenon of twentieth-century sculpture is the supremacy of England. Assuming that art can only arise and flourish when the spiritual conditions for its formation and character are present, the explanation for this phenomenon might be as follows. Down to the twentieth century the sculptor was bound to the human figure and had an explicit function in depicting it: to make a man, or group of men, "eternal," or rather untemporal, by representing them in a durable material. Sculpture did not exist primarily for the artist or the client, but was offered to third parties as an inescapable, space-occupying volume. This glorification of a person or a group is not in the tradition of the English, nor of the Netherlanders. When the art work became autonomous, this implicit requirement imposed on it fell away. Sculpture became more exclusively the expression of the artist, while its monumental character linked it to "monumental" subjects, and especially to the primary force and form of nature. And thus it now became possible for nature-loving England, before all others, to realize in sculpture its emotional relationship with nature. It was on this basis that the work of Henry Moore and of many sculptors after him took form (Chadwick, Butler, Armitage, etc.). A new element in art, a fourth dimension in the shape of movement, found embodiment in the "mobiles," of which the American Calder is the most notable innovator; he designed constructions of metal that can be moved by a touch or by the wind. The latest development, action art, can not be followed as sculpture; the first prerequisite of the genre, the concentration of the creation in a momentary irrevocable action, has not yet found sculptural form. The art of this tendency seems to come remarkably close to Impressionism, and may even perhaps be regarded as its nonfigurative phase (Ferber, Hajdu, Lippold, Lassaw, Pomodoro, Tajiri, and many others).

PAINTING In 1900 an international exposition was held in Paris which included a survey of one hundred years of French art, concentrating particularly on its most recent phase. It was likewise the year in which Picasso first came to Paris. From 1900 to about 1950 that city was the center of world art.

It was not primarily the French but the foreigners attracted to Paris as a center of communication and culture that determined the currents which led to the subversion of the Renaissance-oriented culture predominating at that time. Up to 1918, it is true, other centers can be taken into account, but later all the artists, with the exception of the architects, are to be found in Paris at one time or another. Confused as the evolution of modern art may seem to be, a fairly constant line can be drawn for it. It can be formulated as the process of making forms and visual means independent of visible reality. Freedom was sought along two lines: Expressionism, and then the direction that completely rejected visible reality as a source of inspiration, that is, nonrepresentational art. Since it is impossible, in this survey, to give a succinct history of art proceeding from year to year, the development and the phases of both paths will be described one after the other, down to World War II.

At the beginning of the century Art Nouveau had been dominant in Europe for a short time. Almost all painters were gripped for a time by the symbolic linearity of this movement. Mallarmé had formulated the ideal: the object must not be named, but suggested; that was the dream. The artistic attitude was more important than art (Oscar Wilde). As a matter of fact, people had no interest in the renewal of the language of art, and the movement ended in bloodless symbolism (e.g., Denis, Hodler). In France, people had joined the group of the Nabis, the prophets. Some, including Bonnard and

119

The role of optical realism was played out after World War II, except in countries with totalitarian forms of government. Of the prewar currents, chiefly Expressionism and, to a lesser degree, Surrealism remain alive. 119. Memory, by René Magritte. Later nonfigurative Expressionism, under Kandinsky's influence, came to the fore. The painted "touch" (Tachism) and calligraphy in enlarged form became of the greatest importance. 120. T 1956–59, by Hans Hartung. 121. Flying Thought, 1958, by K. H. R. Sonderborg. 122. Calligraphy Buddha, 1957, by Yuichi Inoue. 123. Composition 1957, by Roger Bissière.

121

122

120

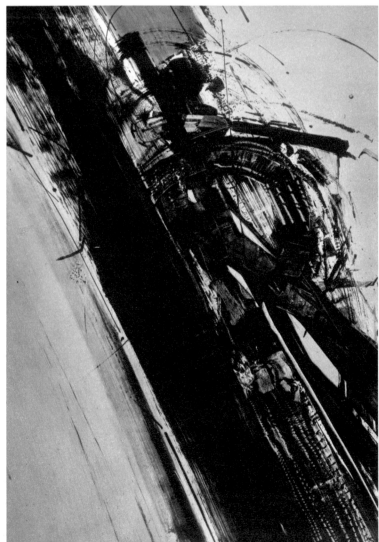

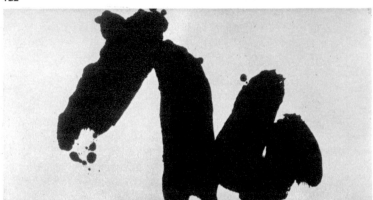

123

124

Vuillard, tried to suggest the symbolism by means of painting alone. In that way they prepared the path for Fauvism (Matisse, Vlaminck, Derain, etc.), a trend in which color was more important than the subject. The Fauves juxtaposed colors without regard to the composition. In Germany, artists had united to form a Künstlerbund (Munich), which organized the first large Van Gogh exposition. A year later, a more revolutionary group was organized in Dresden, Die Brücke (Kirchner, Schmidt-Rottluff, Nolde, Heckel), which put color and form in the service of a militant socialism. Malcontents in Munich founded the Neue Künstlerverein (Jawlenski, Kubin, Münter, Kandinsky). This gave rise to a group surrounding the almanac *Der Blaue Reiter* (1911). The most important members were Macke, Marc, Kandinsky, and Klee. Great differences marked the work and the conceptions of the members. Macke and Marc sought for constants of coloring and composition in nature, Kandinsky sought harmony of surfaces and lines, which was later to lead to his nonrepresentational style, and Klee developed a visual language of his own in which actuality is reduced to a childlike simplicity, an enigmatic, somewhat melancholy, but also visionary runic writing. Along with the artists of the groups that have been mentioned, such artists as Kokoschka, the Polish Makowski, the Swedish Zorn, and some Dutch painters (Wiegers, Werkman, etc.) may also be included in German Expressionism. Expressionism was encountered in Holland and Belgium, e.g., by Sluyters (with a strong Fauvist tinge) and Chabot. The latter was influenced by Permeke, the Belgian painter, who shows a set of themes firmly linked to the soil. De Smet and Van den Berghe, the other members of the "second Latem group," are more spiritual. Van den Berghe forms a link between Ensor (*Christ's Entry into Brussels*) and Surrealism, which is suggested by his later fever fantasies. The first Latem group, Van de Woestijne, De Saedeleer, and Minne, had preceded this, but had still remained strongly symbolistic. In addition to the work of Van Gogh, Munch in Norway, and Gauguin had great influence on this group.

At the time that emotional, unconfined Expressionism was coming into flower in Germany, some artists in France were returning to a more constructive composition. A "landscape" by Braque (1908) was called a composition of cubes by an insulting critic; from this the trend got the name of Cubism. To a great extent it derives from the work of Cézanne, who received great attention from 1907 on. He had sought after the formally constant in nature, instead of the Impressionists' emphasis on the fleeting. After 1909 Braque worked together with Picasso, whose *Les Demoiselles d'Avignon* (1908) had shown the influence of Negro sculpture. In Cubism, to which Gris also belonged, among others, various phases can be distinguished, from the dogmatic to the free. By its search for a new constructivity in composition, Cubism was of tremendous importance for art in an age of desperate seeking.

It had direct influence, however, by way of a new technique: collage, in which all sorts of materials, from wood and paper to iron and, later, even plastics, were used in the composition.

The Expressionist direction rests on still other, and different, starting points. In Italy it took the form of Futurism. In 1909, the poet Marinetti published the first *Futurist Manifesto*. This trend declared war on everything that was conservative or had to do with museums, and fought for advance, for violence, for technology, for speed.

130

Representative figures are Boccioni, Russolo, Balla, Severini, Carrà, and, in France, Duchamp. Rayonism in Russia was of the same nature, (*Rayonistic Manifesto*, 1912, by Larionov). The effort was made to express speed by presenting consecutive movements in a single image, which gave rise to the name of Simultaneism.

Before going on to describe the sequel to these primary modern trends, it must be kept in mind that some artists do not come under

For a large group, the problem of representational versus nonrepresentational art has ceased to be relevant. 127. Letter to My Son, 1949, by Asger Jorn; Cobra group. 128. Woman and Ostrich, 1957, by Karel Appel; Cobra group. 129. Woman II, by Willem de Kooning. 130. Parc des Princes, 1952, by Nicolas de Staël. 131. Painting, 1958, by Antonio Tapies. The progressive, transforming movement has been acquiring influence for some years. 132. Tropicalism, 1948, by Mark Tobey. 133. Composition, by Victor Vasarély.

any catalogue heading, although they can be classified in the Expressionist school: the primitives, such as Henri Rousseau; some Russians, such as Soutine and Chagall; and the melancholy elegance of Modigliani.

After 1912 the most important trends are: Orphism, advocated by Apollinaire, which revolted against the gray tones of Cubism and against rigidity (painters: Delaunay, Léger—who took over Futurism's glorification of materialism—Villon, La Fresnaye, and Picabia). Simultaneism also went far in this direction (Delaunay, *Les fenêtres simultanées*); Vorticism, around Ezra Pound and the magazine *Blast* (painter: Wyndham Lewis); Dada, formed around the Cabaret Voltaire in Zürich, founded by Arp, to which Picabia, Tzara, Schwitters, and others also belonged. Art was reduced to the abolition of existing culture (Futurism) by means of compositions of primeval forms, and also by improbable machinations. This

131

132

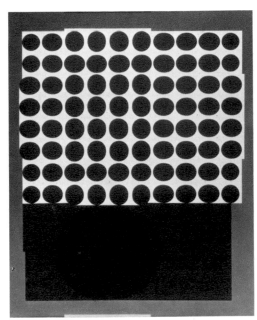

133

general discomfort finally took shape in a pronounced Expressionism, a conscious deformation of actuality (Picasso, Beckmann), and eminently in Surrealism, which made psychoanalytic use of the forms and objects of visible reality for Freudian dream pictures (Ernst, Klee, De Chirico, Miró, Dali, Tanguy, etc.). Characteristic of most Surrealists is the smoothness of the technique, the invisibility of the brushstroke in very precise painting. This is also found in the Belgians Delvaux and Magritte, and the Netherlanders Hynckes, Kock, Ket, and Willink. Delvaux may be classified as a pure Surrealist; Magritte strives for a more fantastic and quiet suggestion of space; the Netherlanders try to intensify the (psychic) reality. This last school is known as Magic Realism. Art after World War II hardly added new facets here; only the influence of nonrepresentational art is visible.

Where representational art in the twentieth century is conspicuous for its constant variation of style, nonrepresentational art follows conscious lines. There are two directions: geometrical and dynamic or expressive nonfigurative art. Geometrical art has a strong pantheistic or at any rate universalist trend; it is based on a future reign of peace, in which all the arts will work together in harmony toward an ideal environment, and in which any separate artistic aim is superfluous. The harmony of creativity is coupled with a harmony of culture, in which space, volume, surface, and line will have their evident places. Imitation of nature is rejected in principle; in art, the relationships of colors and surfaces are the prelude to an eventual utopia. This vision is found most forcibly expressed in De Stijl. The spokesman, Van Doesburg, spoke of the New Imagery. It was, according to him, a concrete art, in which the intention of the artist was made concrete directly on the canvas, and not by means of motifs, ideas, or objects that are intrinsically extra-aesthetic, borrowed from visible reality. Piet Mondrian was the most important figure.

Van der Leck belonged to the group for a short time, along with Huszar from Hungary and the Russian Lissitzky. In 1917 Victor Servranckx of Belgium had already begun his geometrical-constructivist compositions; in so doing he was a pioneer of abstract art. In Russia we find Suprematism (Malevich), in France Purism (Ozenfant and Le Corbusier), in England Constructivism (Nicholson), all of which led to equivalent results.

Along with this is a different trend, the dynamic direction, which intends to bring forth images (not represent) of the emotions by means of line and color. Kandinsky was its forerunner. Both tendencies found a synthesis for a time in the Bauhaus (e.g., Schlemmer, Vordemberge-Gildewart); likewise, a synthesis with representational art was also attempted here (Itten, Klee, Feininger, Schreyer). The expressive direction continued after World War II and became the most important style (e.g., Hartung, Soulages, Kline, Sonderborg, De Kooning, Manessier, Bazaine, Bissière). There is a notable upsurge of Spanish painting (Tapies, Feito, etc.). It is above all Expressionistic in its close bond with the earth, in both color and form. Art as a representation of visible reality is, for many artists, such an outworn point of view that they can even work with visual elements in nonfigurative art (e.g., Appel in Holland). This may be called the triumph of nonrepresentational art. Then comes Action Painting, or *peinture informelle*: a method of working in which the act of making also determines the result, and in a certain sense the content. The harbingers are the American Jackson Pollock and the German Wols (W. Schulze); there are many others. The most recent development is in the direction of an art of movement that is related to the researches into the possibility of psychosomatic structural changes in animals and men by means of changes in the sensation of experiences that can revolutionize the pattern of behavior (Vasarély, Tinguely).

4

4. Relief on the wall surrounding the Bharhut stupa, 2nd century B.C. The ancient Indians regarded the world as peopled with semidivine spirits of nature. A number of them are present on the fence at Bharhut as guardians of the entrances. In this initial period of stone sculpture and architecture, the work is primitive in part, but often suggests clever ivorywork and jewelry.
5. A medallion with a Jataka relief, on the same fence. The scene is viewed from an elevated point; the same person is represented two or three times; tree trunks are bent in order to improve the composition.

5

of good deeds has a definite quantity of good effects. If this fruit is used up, a new birth follows, pursuant to the actions performed in between. And the existence of each created thing is also a sequence of falls and rises, a cycle of becoming (*samsara*) of which Buddha says: "All existence is suffering." It is the effort of every Indian to be released from this cycle. In Buddhism, however, there is a basic difference between older Buddhism, continued in the Hīnayāna, and the Mahāyāna. Wereas the first aims at individual salvation, the latter is directed toward the salvation of others, that is, toward redemption. What the Mahayanist envisages is the state of Buddha and of a Bodhisattva.

In older Buddhism, a Bodhisattva was a future Buddha, such as the historical Buddha was in his previous incarnations. The Jātakas (stories of incarnations) give accounts of this in words and images. In later Buddhism (Mahāyāna) every believer who strives to obtain the highest wisdom, love, and power that are necessary for the salvation not only of himself, but also of others, is also in principle a Bodhisattva, and thus a potential Buddha. After uncounted lives and along a clearly outlined path, the Bodhisattva goes on step by step until he has reached the stage of the great Bodhisattvas that stand directly below the state of Buddha and are greatly revered in later Buddhism. Above all is Avalokiteshvara, whose compassion for creatures was so great that he refused the state of being Buddha so long as there was still a single living being that was not saved and could stand in need of his help. Here a conception arises that is absent in older Buddhism: that it is possible to partake of salvation by the grace of a higher being. The loving veneration that is an important aspect of this is the *bhakti*, the devout dedication to a special divinity. In Hinduism too, especially with reference to such figures as Krishna and Rāma, incarnations of Vishnu, this *bhakti* plays an important role. Image worship is, naturally, the frequent evidence of *bhakti*.

The striving for salvation, *moksha*, is in general characteristic of the Indian world. Many paths are traveled to that goal. One Buddhist will seek *moksha* by the attainment of insight, another by good deeds, a third by refraining from actions, by strict asceticism, by definite practices and training. This effort also contains the conviction that in addition to this world in its largest sense, including heaven and hell, there must be another still higher reality. This highest reality can also be regarded as the "true nucleus," present even in this world of appearance and forming its deepest background. For this the Indian uses such terms as the world soul, which is likewise the deepest core of ourselves. But there are also other possibilities of less impersonal nature. This often presents us with conceptions that seem totally contradictory at first sight. The Indian mentality sees no difficulty in this, however. Thus, in the domain of ideas about divinity, a great diversity of possibilities was admitted. At most we must strive to bring them into accord with each other (syncretism). On the highest level all gods are one, since indeed they are aspects of a single highest deity, whom we can think of personally as the All and One, or impersonally as Total Unity, the Total, the Absolute. The multiplicity of the cosmos is to be reduced to a number of apparently contrary, but actually mutually complementary groups of phenomena, which together form a higher unity. Unity in duality, dualistic totality.

In this way we come, in art too, to such ideas as God and *shakti* (female energy), which together form this totality in that they bind

man die only once, but an endless number of times: as man, as animal, as divinity. There is nothing arbitrary about his birth, but rather a stern law of cause and effect (*karman*). But these consequences, the "fruit" of actions, are not permanent: a definite amount

6. The great stupa of Sañchi, 1st century B.C.; a massive structure, derived from a burial mound; a reliquary and, especially later, a symbol of Buddhism. The base and surrounding wall are circular, the decoration confined to the gates. 7. Borobudur, a remarkable development of the stupa, Java, about A.D. 800: square base built up of terraces, each terrace surrounded by a fence with gates, the central hemisphere or bell likewise divided into terraces with smaller bells in circles and one in the middle. This is the view of the shrine from the air; seen from the ground, the silhouette gives the impression of an overturned bowl. 8. Relief at Amaravati in South India, 2nd century after Christ, with the image of a stupa as object of veneration, even for the inhabitants of Heaven. Despite obvious resemblances, this stupa differs in various respects from the one at Sañchi: for one thing, the lowest part of the stupa body is covered with reliefs, including the Buddha legend. A similar wealth of narration is to be seen at Borobudur, on the square terraces. 9. One of the mighty gates of Sañchi, richly decorated with symbols and edifying stories.

10

11

10. Relief on the Sañchi stupa, of an event in the life of Buddha, seen from a very high standpoint, with all the trees and figures placed above one another, flat on the surface. Every detail is carefully depicted, but the protagonist, the Buddha, is missing. The seat under the tree, at right, represents him. 11. A relief from

Amaravati, about three centuries later, full of action and emotion, as we always find there. The elephant is represented twice, and those who subdue it, the Buddha and his monks, are now also shown. The creation of the figure of Buddha in art dates from the period between Sañchi and Amaravati.

together the two great aspects of the cosmos, the male and the female, as two figures that together form an invisible unity. Or the two figures, Shiva and his wife Pārvatī, united in a single figure Ardhanāri, half male and half female. Both representations thus might be anthropomorphic, but it was also possible to present the same principle in an abstract form: the *lingam*, the symbol of Shiva's creative power, originally phallic, become an abstraction in a sequence of cube, octagonal prism, and hemisphere, each given a symbolic significance and contained in a pedestal, the female element. Another anthropomorphic combination is that of Shiva (Hara) and Vishnu (Hari) into a single figure of Hari-Hara. Actually, Vishnu and Shiva are one. "He who knows you, knows me too. There is no difference between us," says Vishnu to Shiva in the *Mahābhārata*. And thus the Trinity (Trimurti), too, is an attempt to combine in a system the three principal figures of Hinduism. But they can also be regarded as three aspects of a single higher god: Shiva as the Great

God, Shiva as Vishnu, Shiva as Brāhma. This highest god, under whatever name he may be worshiped, is called Ishwara. However, there are also forms of religion that do not recognize a highest god, but rather an impersonal principle.

Later Buddhism, too, knows a highest being or a highest principle. It can be a Buddha thought of as personal (Adi-Buddha), sometimes in combination with a *shakti*, just like the Hindu god. From the Adi-Buddha there radiate the various other figures of the Buddhist pantheon and the various aspects of the world. But there can also be an impersonal, unthinkable, unimaginable "body" (Dharmakāya), as the highest member of a system of three bodies (Trikāya), which comprises both the world of visible and invisible forms as well as Buddha, who descends into this world in a number of forms, each form comprehensible to the dwellers in that phase.

The Indian mentality is more strongly aware than is any other that the Highest—Highest Deity or Highest Principle—belongs to a "totally other" category than anything there is in this world. This "totally other" cannot be given or expressed by any human term or conception, no matter how abstract. It is neither beautiful nor ugly, good nor bad: "either . . . nor . . .," as the Indian formulation runs. A very negative formulation, apparently, when the All-Highest is described as "nothing" and the Highest Good as a nirvana ("being blown out," that is, extinguished), therefore as complete "nothingness." Actually, it is a completely positive conception. When we start with the proposition that the world is appearance (Māyā), a game of the deities, we come to the conclusion that what is the complete contrary and denial of this appearance is in reality the completely

12

14

15. In Northwest India and its surroundings much work was done in stucco: a young man or a spirit, from Hadda (Afghanistan), 5th century after Christ.

13

15

12–14. The Buddha image probably arose more or less simultaneously in two places. Into the northwest of India (Gandhara) came Central Asiatic tribes who were in contact with the Greco–Roman Asiatic world, and who put into the service of the Buddhist doctrine, from the first century B.C., a great abundance of iconographic forms, scenes, and motifs (fig. 12). The Greek ideal of beauty was united with the figure of the Buddhist monk: the Buddha of Gandhara, which had great influence in India and outside (fig. 14). In Mathura Indian sculptors, on the basis of earlier statues of dynamic nature spirits, created a Buddha figure of a more Indian type (fig. 13).

16

17

18

16. *Buddha of Sarnath. Throughout the history of Indian art can be traced iconographic traditions to which each era gave its own content and forms. The Gupta period (300–600) created a Buddha figure that is stylized, despite all its refinement of detail; this preaching Buddha from Sarnath is perhaps the handsomest instance. 17. Buddha Between Two Bodhisattvas, Pala period, 11th century. Pretty, but often rather superficial, sculpture. 18. Façade portion of Borobudur, with a niche containing one of the five hundred, more or less, Buddhas in sculpture in the round that decorate this monument. The clothing, only indicated by a few lines, and the sublime calm in the midst of a wealth of ornament, kept apart from the figure, are reminiscent of Gupta art. Three*

examples of hand positions (mudras): fig. 16, preaching; fig. 17, touching the earth, fig. 18, protecting.

19–21. Here, too, we have an iconographic tradition: Buddha Between Two Bodhisattvas, on the reliquary of Peshawar, 2nd century after Christ or later (fig. 19), and in the interior at Mendut on Java, about 800, the grandest instance of this motif (fig. 21). In various ways, including the unusual position with legs hanging down, the central figure shows great similarity to the Buddha in one of the Ajanta caves (fig. 20), a columned hall with a stupa, and the Buddha enthroned against it, as the object of veneration.

19

20

21

positive, the Completely Real about which nothing more can and need be said than that it is the "Being-so." What in Buddhist philosophy is still referred to by another term as the Empty (Shunya) has here become Fullness. And, strangely enough, the world of appearance in which men and gods (other than the Total Deity) live, and which is a reflection of the real world like an image in a mirror, is likewise as great a reality as that which it reflects.

Here the transcendent god, or reality (sharply distinguished from the world of appearance), approaches the other conception that is typical of the Indian mind, the idea of the Immanent God. God is in this world, God *is* this world—personal in that the body of a divine primeval giant was made into a world, impersonal as the All-Soul that permeates the world. The consequence is that our personal soul is likewise one with the All-Soul. Or, God is immanent *and* transcendent, partly in the world and partly outside it. According to one of these ideas, the world has the form of the primeval giant. And likewise the image of this world, the temple in which the deity lives as he too lives in the world, corresponds to his body in its essential parts. The ground plan is regarded as that of the giant lying with his face down. The intersections of the parts are the joints of his limbs. Another way of expressing the unity of temple and cosmos is to give the temple the form of a mountain—the world mountain, center of the cosmos—and to lay out the temple precincts according to cosmographic conceptions.

With reference to religious conceptions, the idea of the inconceivable provides little or no basis for an iconography—that is, for images. The multiplicity of images of the gods, so typical of Indian art, is to be explained by another aspect of the Indian mentality, which seeks to describe the indescribable. By means of a multiplicity of heads, arms, attributes, and auxiliary figures, in a profusion of statues, reliefs, motifs, and symbols, Indian art floods us with the magical world of appearances, which is our world and that of the gods. Since the purpose of the images is worship, the establishing of contact with the divinity represented, it is strictly necessary that the images agree in every detail with the true outer aspect and inner essence of the god. The Hindu finds the data on this in the holy scriptures and, in more compact form, in the special texts compiled for architects, sculptors, and painters: the *shilpashāstras*. It must be realized and stressed that tradition plays a great part in Indian art. Where tradition did not become mere convention, it was the force on which the artist drew and it gave direction to his inspiration. Working in the service of religion, he created the requisites for worship and for personal contact with the divinity. His knowledge of tradition formed the basis on which he constructed his relationship to the god to be represented, and out of this identity with his subject, what he created became a work of art. Indian art is no model of *l'art pour l'art*; it was not intended to be art, but it is, nonetheless.

SCULPTURE   The uninterrupted history of Indian art begins in the time of the Maurya dynasty, and especially of Emperor Ashoka (third century B.C.). He and his Maurya predecessors found inspiration in the great kings of ancient Persia; and for their works of sculpture, too, they made evident use of foreign artists (from Susa, Mesopotamia, or Bactria). Native sculptors worked with these, dealing with subjects of more local nature and using, for the most

22. Head of a fifty-foot recumbent statue of Buddha, with a standing disciple, in Polonnaruva, Ceylon; 12th century. The massive and powerful character typical of some Hindu statues was not unknown to Buddhism.
23. Shiva in Battle, from one of the Elura temple grottoes, about 800.

24

25

24. *Three Aspects of Shiva as the Highest God, in the three-headed bust in the cave temple on Elephanta Island near Bombay, with scenes from his myth cycle, which make the cave a sculptured song of praise to this god. 8th century.* 25. *Funerary statue of an East Javanese princess (14th century) as Parvati, Shiva's wife, with her two children. She is standing on her mount, the bull Nandi.*

part, rougher workmanship. The earliest artistic productions subsequent to these are the *stūpas* of Bhārhut (second century B.C.) and Sāñchī (second and first centuries B.C.). It is typical of the earliest Indian sculpture that the life of the Buddha was represented without showing the protagonist himself, except as a symbol (a tree, a footprint, etc.). The reliefs are synoptic (various scenes are presented in a single relief). The picture is given, especially at Bhārhut, as if seen from a very high point of view; in other words, the figures are placed above one another, those in the highest positions being farthest away.

The first centuries before and after Christ produced the earliest cave temples (Kārle, Nasik); later, in the seventh century, came the important monuments of Elūrā and Ajantā, where we also find mural paintings. In the second and third centuries after Christ the *stūpa* of Amarāvatī in southern India was erected and, somewhat later in the same time interval, the temples of Nāgarjunakonda. In the meantime the Buddha image had made its entry into Indian art, probably at about the same time in the Greco-Buddhist art of Gandhāra (Northwest India) and at Mathurā. The first instances date from the reign of the Indo-Scythian ruler Kanishka (second century after Christ). They also usher in the beginnings of Greco-Buddhist, or perhaps more accurately Romano-Buddhist, art, which derives its origin from Greco-Roman influences and Buddhism, under the patronage of Central Asiatic conquerors. The influence of this art

was considerable, chiefly perhaps in the direction of Central and Eastern Asia, but also in India proper. More important than the stone sculptures are the works in stucco, known from those found at Taxila in the Punjab and especially in Afghanistan. The first point of contact in India for the Greco-Buddhist influences was at Mathurā (between Delhi and Agra), an old religious center which transmitted the new artistic and iconographic elements to the rest of India.

During the time of the Gupta dynasty (about 300 to 600), Hindu (Brahmanist) art also came into its own. In all aspects of cultural life, this period was one of the summits of Indian history. The spiritualization and at the same time the refined detailing of the ornament appears best, perhaps, in the Buddha of Sārnāth. Its serene calm is reminiscent of the Buddhas of Borobudur and Mendut, where, however, the fine carving of the nimbus and back-piece do not appear. To that extent the latter are more like those in the cave temples that date from the Gupta and post-Gupta eras. Iconographically, too, the type of the Buddha was more closely delineated, especially by fixing the positions of the hands (*mudrās*), which are connected with events in the life of the Buddha. Thereafter definitively set *mudrās* were characteristic of what are called the Dhyani Buddhas, manifestations of the Adi-Buddha in a transcendental sphere. During this period the Bodhisattvas also became more important. To a certain extent this was at the expense of the previously well-beloved episodes from the life of the Buddha, which in the

Gupta period are restricted to series of four or eight principal scenes, at least so far as sculpture is concerned. The Ajantā murals often deal precisely with the stories of the Buddha and his previous births (Jātakas). In the Hindu temples, freestanding or carved out of the rock, the dominating themes are large-scale scenes from mythology, showing the might of Shiva or related to the incarnations (avatars) of Vishnu. Most of them, however, belong to the art of the post-Gupta era. These are marked by a less gentle, more powerful and violent character; in contrast to the serene calm of the Gupta period there is often a superhuman motility. The foreign influences that India had received before the Gupta period, and had subsequently elaborated, were fully digested by this time and had grown into an organic total. To that extent the Gupta art may be considered "classically Indian." In northern India there followed a period (about 600 to 800) of second blooming and then, for several centuries, under the dynasty of the Pālas (until about 1200), a last period of sculpture, technically perfected but conventional and cold. For northern India, Islam meant the end of temple building and hence of sculpture. Painting persisted in the courts of Rājputāna and in the mountain areas outside the realm of the Great Moguls.

Mention should be made of the bronzes of southern India, whose figures of the dancing Shiva, personifying the movement and rhythm of the cosmos, are unsurpassed.

Ceylon was subject in many respects to the influence of southern India, not always in peaceful ways. However, other parts of India also had their share in the formation of the culture and art of Ceylon. Buddhism made its appearance there in the third century B.C. It is still actively alive in Ceylon, with the result that most of the monuments have been repeatedly restored until they are unrecognizable. The old atmosphere comes out best in some freestanding statues. The principal centers were Anurādhapura and Polonnāruva. Paintings are to be seen at Sīgiriya (sixth century).

By way of Gandhāra and Greco-Buddhist art, the influence of Indian art found its way to Central and Eastern Asia. And once again Buddhism brought Indian forms to Nepal and Tibet (after the seventh century and even more strongly after the ninth). The magical practices that had been developed in India by that time struck fertile soil in Tibet. The extensive pantheon of Tāntra Buddhism is reflected in the Tibetan bronzes and paintings on linen. The influence of the traditional prescriptions was so great that no stylistic differences can be seen between old pieces and new. Chinese influence is also to be noted.

Farther India and Indonesia, in the first centuries after Christ, gradually came into contact with the culture of the Indian subcontinent. Even in prehistoric times a diversity of styles must have been present there, expressed in buildings, utensils, megalithic monuments, pottery, and metalwork. Both in the Neolithic period (from the second millennium B.C.) and in the early Age of Metals, migrations had taken place from South China. The rise of work in bronze in South China and North Indochina was stimulated by new elements from Southeast Europe and surrounding lands. Eventually, this culture spread to Indonesia too. Its most important expression was in the bronze kettledrums of the centuries immediately before and after the beginning of our era. They show an outstanding technical mastery and feeling for harmonious decoration. Apart from this

26

26. Shiva Nataraja, bronze, 12th century. The renewing, creative— and hence often destructive—force of Shiva is expressed in many ways, including representation as the cosmic dancer: in the cave temples in enormous reliefs, and in the bronzes of South India, after about the year 1000, in unsurpassedly beautiful and majestic figures. Height about 60½ inches.
27. Vishnu, too, is a creator, in that the initiative for a new creation of the world must emanate from him after the expiration of an age of the world. Between two eons, he rests on the world snake. High relief on the Dashavatara temple at Deogarth (Northeast India), about 600.

27

28   29

30   31

32

28–30. Three Old Javanese bronze figurines, 9th to 10th century: Padmapani, Mañjusri (two important Bodhisattvas), and a third with a chain as attribute. 31. Head of a sleeping Vishnu, Khmer, early 12th century. Remains of an entire figure. 32. The Bodhisattva Padmapani, a fresco at Ajanta, 7th century.

noteworthy visual gift for decorative art, contact with Indian culture was never so fruitful here. Indian art had again come into a new milieu, which gave a different turn and content to its forms and traditions. One important factor was the adaptation of ancestor worship, in the Hinduized societies, into a cult of the dead ruler. Many temples of the gods served also as funerary monuments for the rulers that had been incarnations of the god while they were alive. These cannot be called mausoleums, strictly speaking; rather, they were monuments that helped to reunite the ruler with the deity, that gave his soul eternal life and at the same time made it possible for the deceased to descend to earth for a time in an image amid his descendants and their vassals. Further, the temple also served as a replica of the abode of the gods. This does not mean that all the temples were "funerary temples" and all the statues "funerary statues." There were also numerous ordinary temples and images of the gods. In the third century after Christ, the kingdom of Fu-nan in Farther India comes to the fore, replaced about 550 by Cambodia, the kingdom of the Khmers, with a capital that changed several times. A *lingam*, which symbolized the kingship, formed the principal element in the central shrine on a hill, the visible image of the world mountain. After the end of the ninth century, the most important monuments were built in the neighborhood of Angkor, including Angkor Vat, under Sūryavarman II (1113 to after 1145), and Angkor Thom, restored under Jayavarman VII (1181 to after 1200). The center of Angkor Thom forms the Bayon, a structure with towers in the form of enormous heads; the snakes belonging to this world mountain, named Meru, are carried by gods and demons, and extend to the approach bridges. Khmer art continued until into the fourteenth century, when the capital was devastated by the Thais, or Siamese, and Pnom-Penh became the center of the kingdom. Subsequent art is strongly under Siamese influence.

In early times the kingdom of Champa extended along the east coast of Southeast Asia. For a long time it was exposed to the attacks of the Chinese and then of the Annamites, who completely expelled the Chams from their original territory in the fifteenth century. Despite the turmoil, the Chams still managed to keep alive an art of their own. The temples here were all of brick, a material that was also used in Cambodia at the outset and is familiar in Indonesia (Sumatra, East Java, Bali). Siam (Thailand) likewise was subject to a variety of foreign influences, along with the stimulus received from India. For a long time the influence of the Khmers was predominant; in the thirteenth century the Thais poured in from the north. Gradually a national style took form in architecture, which made much use of wood, and in the other arts. An untold number of Buddha images were made in metal The *stūpas* here became giant bells with pinnacles soaring upwards.

The oldest inscriptions that show the existence of Hinduized kingdoms in Indonesia date from the fifth century after Christ. They are found in West Java and East Borneo, but parts of Sumatra too must by then have been under Indian influence. A large stone statue of a standing Buddha in Palembang may date from the same period, as may a bronze statue from West Celebes. Both show the style of

Page 237. Head of Buddha, Thailand, bronze, 15th–16th century.

35

33

34

36

33, 34. Two reliefs from Central Java: a dancer with orchestral accompaniment, Borobudur, about 800 (fig. 33), and a scene from the tale of Rama (Ramayana), Prambanam, early 10th century (fig. 34). Illustrations of texts of Indian origin, linked with Indian art developed into something quite individual.
35, 36. Reliefs of the Chandi Djago and the Chandi Panataran, East Java, 14th century. Relief art as continued on Java has an entirely different atmosphere, despite the fact that stories of Indian origin are still being depicted. We speak of a Wayang style: in fig. 35, figures show the same characteristics as wayang puppets, with the twisted stiff position of the body and the same headdress. Fig. 36 shows the comical servant types of the wayang shadow theater.

Amarāvatī in South India and attest Buddhist activity in the archipelago. The oldest statue in Java is one of Vishnu, probably dating from the seventh century and in the style of the South Indian Pallava kingdom. The oldest existing fixed monuments are those of Central Java, dating from the beginning of the eighth century. For the chronology of the Middle Javanese period (to about 930), we must rely on stylistic criteria, for which no thorough studies have yet been made. The most important monuments of Central Java are either in the plain of Kedu (for example Borobudur) or in the plain of Prambanam, and are sometimes large complexes. Smaller temples are to be found in the mountainous regions in North Central Java and at the rim of the Southern Mountains. Two dynasties reigned in Central Java between about 750 and 850, the Buddhistic Shailendra dynasty and the Shivaite dynasty of Sanjaya. Some monuments of Central Java were built by co-operation of the two. About 930 the political and cultural center of Java shifted to the east. After the powerful monuments of Central Java, built in its most recent period, an era of relative quiet ensued, with no great monuments being built. It was only in the time of King Erlangga (eleventh century) that we get some monuments, cave temples and what are called

grave baths, water works that served as funerary monuments. The most important shrines date from considerably later, during the dynasty of Singhasāri (thirteenth century) and that of Mojopāhit (fourteenth and fifteenth centuries). Other important structures of the era include Panātaran.

Characteristic in the reliefs of the fourteenth century is what is known as the Wayang style, so named after the fantastically drawn forms, like puppets (*wayangs*) and clowns, that accompany the heroes and heroines in the reliefs. A common phenomenon in the East Javanese era is the emergence of other elements of the population, who had better preserved the old indigenous ideas and traditions, which increasingly predominate over the tendencies and forms of Indian origin. Likewise in the terrace shrines in the mountains, dating from the latest Hindu-Javanese period, which are closely tied to the old indigenous ancestor worship and to the prehistoric monuments related to it, the same development is clearly to be seen.

Outside Java, we know of old monuments on Bali, such as the Gunung Kawi at Tampaksiring. Sumatra has a few: the most important groups are at Muara Takus (Padang Highlands) and Padang Lawas (partly thirteenth and fourteenth centuries).

Only incidental discoveries have been made on the other islands, Borneo and Celebes. The coming of Islam brought not only a change in religion but also the end of an art completely tied up with the old religions. However, the old culture and art still are notably

Page 239. Polychrome wood statue, probably North India, about 18th century. Depicts a woman playing the bin, a stringed instrument.

39

37–46. Indian architecture presents, on the one hand, a definite trend toward horizontals : the temple is divided into foot, body, and head (roof), and the head is in turn divided horizontally. On the other hand, its creations often take the form of high towers, in which the rising lines break through the masses built up of many layers, seeming to strive upwards. 37, 38 .Temples at Bhuvaneshvara and Khajuraho (East and Central India), 11th century. The buildings, assembled into complexes, have only small interiors, but above the statues of the gods that they contain, the shikharas rise tower high, consisting of many horizontal members and yet with a supple, high-rising silhouette. 39. The Raths of Mahamallapuram, South India ; 7th century. Many temples were cut out of cliffs or rock masses, sometimes in such a way that a cave was formed to correspond to the interior of a temple, in other cases to form the exterior of a temple, a massive structure that could be hollowed out. Also compare fig. 41. In the first Rath the forms of the building are repeated as roof pinnacles along the horizontals.

41

40

40. A pagoda on a relief at Chandi Djago, East Java ; 14th century. In the far northern part of India proper, in the Himalaya region, and far to the east, in old East Java and even today on Bali, we find the pagoda-shaped piled-up roofs, erected in many stories, in wood or other light materials. 41. The Kailasanatha temple of Elura, entirely cut out of the cliff.

43

44

42–44. *The Shiva temple of Pram-*
banam, the main temple of a great
complex in Central Java, early 10th
century. The restoration of this
mighty structure, under study since 1918,
was carried out between 1937 and
1953 by the Archaeological Service.
Here, too, we have marked horizontal
divisions of the roof portion with a
shikhara-like contour line and, by
way of roof pinnacles (cf. fig. 39), a
repetition of the crowning top portion
in bell forms. The fact that the temple
is an abode of the gods, a heaven
mountain, is accentuated by the
heavenly dancers, keepers of the
winds, and other cosmic motifs, such as
the trees of heaven (figs. 43 and 44),
with which the temple is richly
adorned. Each panel and figure is a
precious witness of the decorative value
of Old Javanese art. 45. Temple
façades hewn out of the rock, reminiscent
of the Indian cliff temples, are found on
Bali: Gunung Kawi, Tampaksiring;
11th century. 46. Small auxiliary
temple of the Panataran complex,
East Java, dated 1369, restored in
1917–18 by the Archaeological Service.
It was one of the first of the many
restorations undertaken by this service.

45

46

active, even down to the present, not only on Bali, which had taken much of Hinduism into its religion, but on Java and Sumatra as well.

ARCHITECTURE A brief account of architecture should begin its general survey of the many structural forms of Indian art by first drawing a distinction between freestanding, constructed buildings and those carved out of the living rock. In the hilly regions of India the number of the latter is very large. They are modeled on the free-standing buildings, in one of two ways: either an artificial cave, cut into the rock, imitates the interior and the façade of a temple in the open air, or enough of the cliff is cut away so that the external form of a building is created, sometimes with an interior carved out and sometimes not. In both cases the correspondence is carried so far that the type of construction and even details of freestanding wood structures are copied in the native rock. Sometimes wooden beams are inserted into windows or ceiling to make the correspondence even more faithful. Imitations of this kind also give us some idea of the freestanding architecture of the centuries immediately preceding and following the beginning of our era although virtually no examples, apart from the *stūpas* to be discussed below, now exist. The oldest rock temples belong to the first of the two types in question, with some of the second type also occurring after hte seventh century A.D. (Kailāsanātha temple at Elūrā, and the so-called Raths of Māhamallapuram). The first category, again, falls into two groups, one with a square ground plan and the second with a design reminiscent of a basilica: a central nave separated by columns from side aisles which form a semicircle at the end of the hall around a *stūpa*; temples in this group are called *chaitya* halls.

The oldest freestanding temple types must likewise have been divided into these two groups. All that has come down to us, however, are some *stūpas*, and representations of *stūpas* on reliefs. The oldest examples are those of Bhārhut (second century B.C.) and *Sāñchī* (second and first centuries B.C.). The *stūpas*, the most typical structures of Buddhism, are a genre apart. They evidently developed out of a burial mound surrounded by a wooden fence. In the oldest

47

48

47. *Gopura (porch tower) of Ramesh-
wara, 17th century. We find the same
construction in horizontal layers, once
again of tower height and covered by
sculpture with schematically suggested*
*temple replicas on the roof cornices, in
the gate buildings of the South Indian
temples, built on a rectangular
ground plan. 48. Angkor Vat,
funerary temple of one of the*
*Cambodian rulers, first half of 12th
century; a remarkable complex of
towers connected by galleries, composed
in concentric squares rising in terraces,
the whole being a replica of the world*
*mountain, the shrine as center and
replica of the cosmos, of which the
Meru, or world mountain, constitutes
the nucleus.*

specimens preserved, however, they are all made of brick with a
stone railing, although traces of the old wood construction are still
to be seen. The great hemisphere, the most important element of the
stūpa, is crowned by a smaller balustrade with a sun-screen. Monuments of this kind were originally erected above the remains of a
saint, and later over other sacred objects as well. In the long run,
though, so much symbolic significance was attached to the building
itself that even without relics it was erected as an independent object
of veneration. The decoration was originally concentrated on the
fence and doors, but later spread to the base and a part of the central
hemisphere. This base, originally circular, changed to a kind of step
pyramid on a square ground plan, in Greco-Buddhist art; the central mound was sometimes raised to form a rounded-off cylinder;
the crowning pinnacle assumed enormous dimensions. But many
other variants also proved possible. In Ceylon and Siam the bell form
is usual for the *stūpa* body. The most complicated form is probably
that of Borobudur, where a diversity of old elements are meaning-
fully applied in a large and highly original conception (about 800,
Central Java).

One of the characteristic features of Indian architecture is its tendency to repeat the same elements—to an ever-increasing degree—
and pile them up one on the other. Replicas of the cubic temple body
are superposed as if they were building blocks. This continues until
the top is reached, after an accumulation of pseudo-stories in this
manner has sometimes reached tower-like proportions. By this
means the multiple roof lines give a strongly horizontal character.
Despite the many horizontals—partly concealed behind an overwhelming multiplicity of statues—a powerful upward-striving
effect is often obtained. This is visible in particular in what are called
the *shikharas*, towershaped temples on a square or polygonal ground
plan, with slightly curved contours, which are found chiefly in the
northern areas of India. The most striking instances of this manner of

building are to be found at Bhuvaneshvara and Khajurāho (eleventh
century). Outside India, it was primarily the southern storied style
of building that spread abroad, although the effort was made to
combine this with a *shikhara* type of contour. Even the ornament
that is not purely architectural gets its power in Indian art in part
from repetition: for example, in the more than five hundred
Buddhas and the countless *stūpa* motifs of Borobudur, the many
bells of Prambanam, etc. Indeed, repetition is an aspect of "eternity."
This multiplicity may appear in the form of heavy masses (as in the
temple doors of South India), and is then related to the earth's mass
(as in the powerful solid blocks of the monuments carved out of the
rock). Continued repetition may also create an atmosphere of rest
and silence.

Roof forms typical of the Himalaya region are the piled-up roofs of
the temples of Nepal. These also appear in old East Java, old and
modern Bali, and in Javanese mosques. The name usual on Bali is
"Meru." Actually, people saw in the levels of the roof the articu-
lations of the world mountain, or Meru, which forms the center of
the cosmos. Every temple, in principle, has more or less the character of a Meru, which can be accentuated in many ways.

Indian temples served to accommodate ritual statues and a few
officiating priests at ceremonies. In general, the interior is small.
Moreover, the construction, of courses of heavy masonry with no
true vaults, and only limited use of columns, did not permit any large
interior spaces. The multitudes gathered in the temple precincts
around the buildings. When more than a ritual statue had to be
accommodated, the solution was sought in auxiliary spaces or
pavilions, and, in South India, in great complexes with gates and
galleries.

On Java we sometimes find very extensive complexes with many
subsidiary temples, while those in Farther India have passageways
and towers.

CHINA

The history of China, extending over more than four thousand years, is the longest in the world; others have been known that were older, but they have long since disappeared, while China exhibits a vital force that continues down to the present. The country has gone through periods of power during which it expanded and grew rich with the winning of distant regions; it has also experienced years of trouble and penury, but through the most chaotic revolutions it has remained true to the traditions of its ancestors, and thereby has maintained a very original civilization. This is reflected in a beautiful and moving art.

The history is divided into periods as follows; it should be kept in mind that down to 841 B.C. there is no agreement as to the chronology:

1523–1028 B.C.	Shang-Yin Dynasty (including An-yang period)
1027–256 B.C.	Chou Dynasty: 1027–c. 900, Early Chou; c. 900–c. 650, Middle Chou; c. 650–256, Late Chou
221–206 B.C.	Ch'in Dynasty
206 B.C.–A.D. 220	Han Dynasty
221–316	Three Kingdoms ⎫ also called Six Dynasties
316–581	Northern and Southern Dynasties ⎭
581–618	Sui Dynasty
618–906	T'ang Dynasty
907–960	Five Dynasties
960–1297	Sung Dynasty
1260–1368	Yüan Dynasty
1368–1644	Ming Dynasty (1426–36, Hsüan-tê; 1465–88, Ch'eng-hua; 1522–67, Chia-ching; 1573–1620, Wan-li)
1644–1912	Ch'ing Dynasty (1662–1722, K'ang-hsi; 1723–35, Yung-cheng; 1736–95, Ch'ien-lung)

ARCHITECTURE A Chinese building, whether it be a temple, a palace, or a simple house, consists chiefly of a roof carried on wooden columns rising out of a terrace or floor of beaten earth. Consoles inserted above these columns carry the main beams and the over-hanging portion of the roof, which often covers a gallery running around the building. A number of stories can be erected one above the other by having the columns in each case rest on the beams of the floor below. In this way high pagodas are erected. The spaces between the columns are filled with stones, planks, or clay; the windows are formed by openings left free, often decorated with finely carved trellis work.

An important temple comprises various buildings: rooms for the ritual proper and for prayers, a library, a pagoda, rooms for the monks, storage space, etc., assembled in an enclosed space surrounded by a wall; the entrance is through a more or less monumental roofed gateway. The same is true of palaces and large family dwellings; in these a common fence surrounds the dwellings of the individual families, which are separated from each other by inner courts and gardens. The door to the street is wide open all day, but it is closed at night, when the family has come together.

In a country that is subject to frequent monsoons, wood rapidly disappears; very few old wooden monuments are left in China. Certain buildings were made of durable materials, such as many pagodas that indicate where relics or sacred texts were kept in the inner courts of the temples. Pagodas are massive monuments on a square or polygonal ground plan, with a number of apparent stories that decrease in size and end in a spire with rings around it, symbolizing the parasols of state.

But stone and brick were used mainly for such major works as bridges, docks, and monumental gates; arches and window openings were made with bonding stones, and from about the beginning of the Christian era, graves were provided with bonding stones cut in a special ingenious fashion to connect the arches. Stone and brick were used largely for military structures, as revetments for walls and towers of tamped earth, and for superstructures. The most famous work is the Great Wall of China, with a total length of over two thousand miles, reinforced at regular intervals with towers, and protecting the country from incursions by the nomads of the steppe.

1. Painted ceramic model of a house, funerary offering, Han period, 1st century A.D. Copied presumably from a contemporary many-storied house in wood and wattle.

1

2. *Grave furniture of reddish terra-cotta with green varnish, representing farmhouse buildings surrounded by an enclosure. This 4th-century farmhouse is identical with those of North China today. 3. Pagoda of Sung-yueh-ssu, in Honan, one of the oldest that have come down to us. Towers like this were erected in the courts of great temples to hold relics or sacred texts. 4. In the 3rd century B.C. the Ch'in emperor Shih Huang-ti had the sections of tamped earth wall protecting the northern regions of China made into a great fortification. It became the Great Wall of China, on which hundreds of thousands of workers—convicts and prisoners of war—were engaged. The wall extends from the sea to the western frontier. 5. A p'ai-lou, or entrance gate, on the grounds of the Summer Palace in Peking. P'ai-lou were erected in honor of a person who had rendered great services or who was much loved as official or wife. They are made of wood, brick, or stone.*

7

6, 7. The imperial palaces in Peking, built under the Ming emperors (1368–1644), were constructed around broad paved inner courts. One of the principal buildings (fig. 6) contains one of the throne rooms. 8. Interior, with the throne of the *emperor, in the Temple of Heaven, Peking. The colors are dark red and gold. 9. The Temple of Heaven, a structure of perfect proportions on a terrace with several levels, located in the temple complex where the emperor made offerings on the high holy days.*

8

9

T'ang periods harbor a whole miniature world of high officials, soldiers, servants, and dames, the tenants of the great feudal lords. The little statuettes were mass-produced, but modeled with great naturalism, and give us a remarkably good picture of the upper-class life of the T'ang period, the most brilliant that China has known. In the fifth century the Wei people from Central Asia had invaded the country. As ardent Buddhists, they had a great influence on the world of thought and on art. Buddhism had been known in China since the first century of our era, but its spread was slow; during the Wei Dynasty, however, it became the state religion; all over the land underground temples were hewn out of the cliffs and decorated splendidly with frescoes and sculpture. Scrupulously interpreting an iconography that arose in the Greco-Indian world and had been changed under Persian influence, China created an art that was

SCULPTURE The oldest known sculptures in China are the marble carvings from An-yang; they are highly stylized human and animal figures, apparently bases for columns and related to decorative sculpture. Similarly stylized and decorative are the little heads and animal figurines with which certain bronze objects of the Shang and Chou periods are adorned.

At the time of the Han Dynasty there appeared handsome sculptures, very powerful in outline, realistic in design, and with strong plastic qualities. This art consists of bronze figurines of human beings and animals that are probably reproductions on a small scale of larger statues which, as the texts inform us, adorned the palace terraces. Great stone monsters, motifs of Achaemenid origin, flanked the paths leading to the burial mounds of important persons; this tradition continued down to the sixth century.

Stone slabs incised or carved in low relief, from tomb chapels, as well as the molded bricks of the tombs, are decorated with scenes from history, mythology, or daily life, thereby forming a rich source for studying the life and beliefs of the Han period.

The custom of surrounding the dead with representations of things out of his former life has left us a picture, in the form of small soberly modeled terracottas, of the ordinary environment, including persons, animals, houses, and utensils. This custom lasted for many centuries, and the necropolises of the Wei (Northern Dynasty) and

10. Stylized female figurine, time of the Chou Dynasty.

10

11

12

archaic in aspect, more linear than plastic, but displayed a profound mysticism. Toward the middle of the sixth century, however, the striving for plastic quality is seen, and the tendency becomes still more prominent during the Sui Dynasty, in static works, full and often great in form, which become more supple under the T'ang Dynasty, embodying a new doctrine of form. The high point of Chinese sculpture occurs in the early part of this dynasty.

Under the influence of sects that left more room for the intervention of beneficent deities, sculpture soon became less strict; lifelike and superficial works attest a feeling that is worldly rather than religious. During the Sung period handsome figures were carved of wood and dry lacquer. The small works of art during the Ming Dynasty are still interesting, but in the eighteenth century decadence is irrevocable; the many figurines of wood, ivory, and hard stones still bear witness to great skill, but their prettiness cannot make us forget their artistic poverty.

PAINTING Painting is the art in which the Chinese artistic endowment appears at its loftiest and most original. It differs greatly from our painting and is never conceived of as a means of representing visual reality, but rather as a manner of expressing ideas or feelings in perceptible form; it does not seek a direct reproduction of nature, but forms it in such a way that painting becomes related to writing. This comparison is facilitated by the nature of Chinese writing, in which signs represent not sounds, but ideograms, i.e. pictures that indicate concepts and become abstractions in the course of time. The characteristics of the brush strokes are to be found in both arts; and calligraphy and painting are equally honored. Not only in its fundamental conception, but in its technique as well, Chinese painting is at variance with ours. The Chinese artist paints on silk or paper and uses only a sort of gouache, that is, an opaque watercolor, or more or less diluted ink.

There are no shadows, and perspective is obtained by means of diagonal views from a great height, with the "vanishing lines" parallel. In a landscape represented vertically, these views are placed one above the other on surfaces connected by single elements. This system makes it possible to survey enormous vistas.

These works are framed in ribbed silk and hung on the wall; they are stretched smooth from below by means of a stick on which they can be rolled up when not being shown. Other paintings are made on long rolls, like ancient papyrus rolls: a landscape or the episodes of a story can be followed by unrolling from right to left. Still others, of smaller dimensions, are often collected in book form.

11. The phoenix bird, the fong, on a pillar on the tomb of Shen (Szechwan). Pillars of this kind were set up at the entrance to the path to tombs of exalted persons. The force and elegance of the bird of the sun are typical of the summit of Han art. 12. Sitting Bear, bronze. The latent power and intense vitality of the *massive animal are given in simple and expressive forms. The many statues of bears from the Han period may well be linked to ancient religious conceptions. 13. Interior of Cave VI in the rock temple of Yün-kang, second half of 5th century after Christ. The walls of the Buddhist caves were covered with sculpture and had un-*

3

14

15

16

17

18

*counted niches with statues of gods.
14. Relief in the Ping-yang cave of
Lung-mên, Wei period (Tartar
Dynasty in North China). The
emperor, surrounded by courtiers
carrying palms and lotus flowers,
advances with dignity. The robes have
heavy, supple folds. The composition
is remarkable for its suggestion of
space and movement. 15. Bodhisattva
of Pai-ma-ssu, 5th century, Wei
Dynasty. The elongated figure has lost
all plastic quality. The humble
gentleness of the face, and the form
seemingly disengaged from mere matter,
give the statue a mystical character
that speaks directly to the soul. 16. Stone
statue of a Buddhist monk or priest,
Sui period, 6th century. The statue
has great dignity, conveyed by the
proud bearing of the head, the simplicity
of the volumes, and the straight folds
of the monk's robes. 17. Bodhisattva,
dated 593, part of a bronze group of
the Sui period. A gracious charm
emanates from the elegant statuette,
standing on a lotus, with joined hands,
half-closed eyes, and a smile on the
lips. The rich aureole is striking.
18. Head of a Bodhisattva, stone, Sui
period. This is a masterful example
of sculpture in the round; the sculptor
had a feeling for beauty of form. The
expression on this face is at once mild
and tense with inner power.*

19

20

21

22

23

24

19. *Relief on the tomb of the T'ang emperor T'ai-tsung (627–49), who had his six beloved horses depicted in the vestibule of his tomb. An officer is drawing an arrow from the chest of the horse, wounded in war. A strong sober piece, showing careful attention to anatomy. 20. Terracotta figure of a woman playing polo,*

T'ang Dynasty. Women were emancipated in ancient China and took part in sport. 21. Terracotta soldier. However luxurious and refined life was at the time of the T'ang emperors, there was need for great watchfulness on the country's borders. 22. Camel, colored terracotta. Camels carried the products of the entire

empire and those from far countries along the caravan routes to Ch'ang-an, the capital of the T'ang empire. 23. Shakyamuni in Meditation, dry-lacquer figure, Yüan Dynasty. There is nothing hieratic about this image; the flexible material permitted great freedom of form. These little figurines, very light in weight, were intended to be carried in processions. 24. Kuan-yin, the Bodhisattva of mercy who deferred his redemption to help men, seated in relaxed position; wooden statue, Sung period. The opulent forms and elegant play of the scarf already anticipate the goddess that he later became.

25

25. Warrior figure beside the approach to the luxurious tombs of the Ming emperors, an avenue flanked by large figures of animals and warriors.
26. Toilet Scene, detail of a roll painting by Ku K'ai-chih, period of the Six Dynasties, 4th century. The charming picture illustrates the

saying: Men and women know how to adorn their bodies, but few know how to make their souls beautiful.
27. Scholars on a Broad Bench, Comparing Classical Texts. Sung copy of a work of the T'ang period. The scene is very lively, the discussion vehement.

Old texts speak of edifying scenes that adorned the walls of palaces. The only mural paintings that have come down to us are in temples; they were not done in true fresco (that is, pigments integrated with the plaster wall) but simply applied to a polished surface of stucco. The incised stones and bricks cast in ornamental forms from the Han Dynasty graves mentioned above give us an artisan-like idea of the painting of the time; in them can be seen the abiding characteristics of Chinese graphic art. The same can be said of the famous roll that Ku K'ai-chih illustrated in the fourth century with a series of drawings done with a fine brush and a firm hand. In addition to pictures in the Buddhist grottos, which maintain the Indo-Iranian traditions that were introduced by Buddhism, all that we have of the painting of the T'ang Dynasty (618–906) are a few fragments of originals and some copies; Chinese tradition regards this era as the Golden Age of the portrait and the genre piece. Landscape, one of the most interesting productions of the art of the Far East, is, however, a creation of the T'ang period; we see in it a search for essential characteristics, brought out with intensity by powerful brush strokes. During the Sung Dynasty this art finds its highest expression in monochrome paintings in ink, attesting a remarkable impressionism. These were the work of painter monks who lived in mountain temples around the lake of Hangchou; inspired by Ch'an (Zen) Buddhism, they presented, in a few strokes or with a few spots, an impression rooted deep in their minds by intense contemplation of nature. In its beauty, spiritual content, and technical perfection, this school of painting remains one of the most moving expressions of human feeling.
The art of the Ming period goes back to older traditions in genre pieces that are often anecdotal, while landscape tends to confine itself to formulas; yet gifted artists continued, down to the end of the empire, to produce extremely successful works.

26

27

28

28. Ironing Silk. Detail of a painting of the T'ang period, in a copy by Emperor Hui-tsung or one of his court painters. Silk culture goes far back into the antiquity of China. The irons were heated with burning charcoal. 29. Deer in an Autumn Dell. Ink and colors on silk, period of the Five Dynasties. In this picture we can clearly see the great love of the Chinese for nature.

29

APPLIED ART   The Chinese craftsman's astonishing dexterity and artistic taste brought all applied art to a very high degree of perfection. Europe first learned of Chinese art through its silks, and much later, during the Yüan and Ming dynasties, its celadon ware and its more developed silk weavings, especially its brilliant brocades; in the eighteenth century, through its fine porcelain and its wondrous lacquer work—the final result, and in many cases the last expression, of long artistic traditions.

Bronzes. The Chinese evolved a magnificent art in the working of bronze. We do not know its origin and formative period; at An-yang (fifteenth to eleventh centuries B.C.) the art was already fully developed. The arms, wagon furniture, harness pieces, sometimes inlaid with turquoise or colored paste, and the brilliant vases for ritual and household use, cast in molds or by the lost-wax process, all show a technical perfection that has never been rivaled.

The types of vases used at ceremonial banquets or for the various offerings to the souls of ancestors were strictly prescribed. The great variety of their forms indicates an intricate social and religious ritual; they become fewer in number in later centuries.

The motifs with which the bronzes were decorated recur throughout Chinese history; we can recognize the *t'ao-t'ieh*, an animal mask with huge eyes, the *kuei* dragon in various forms, the owl, the snake, etc.; the *lei-wen*, a play of spirals, often forms the background of the decoration. We are still in the dark as to the religious significance of these motifs.

Page 251. Buddhist Lion, porcelain. Famille verte, K'ang-hsi period (1644–1722).

30. Detail of the work, Eighteen Songs of Wen-chi, by Chen Chü-chung: the return of Wen-chi to her family from Mongolia, where she had been held as a hostage. Clear picture of the inner court of a great *family's house with many buildings, and a vivid set of many scenes, including one of the military escort at ease, buying fruit from the merchants.*

Page 252. Porcelain dish, so-called Swatow porcelain, 17th-century folk art. Decoration in red, green, and turquoise enamel under greenish-gray glaze. The medallion on the bottom shows the fabulous ch'i-lin animal, a luck symbol for illustrious posterity. On the rim, fabulous animals: fêng-hwang or fong (phoenix) and ch'ing-lung (dragon), symbol of the bride and bridegroom.

31. View of Rivers and Hills, by Hsia Kuei, ink on paper, Sung Dynasty. The fantastic cliffs through which the river flows recall the wild landscapes of South China. 32. Imaginary portrait of the poet Li T'ai-po, by Liang K'ai. A few strokes of the brush present the great poet of the T'ang court in a state of almost intoxicated inspiration.

33

33. *Birds, Hawthorns, and Bamboo in a Garden,*
painting in ink on paper by Chang Yen-fu (1280–1367),
dated 1343. Bamboo is one of the favorite subjects of
Chinese painters, and stone formations selected for
their form play a decisive part in garden composition.
34. *Lady with Servants Walking in a Palace Garden,*
by Lêng Mei. Early 18th century. The scene gives a
good picture of clothing, and of garden design with
remarkable rock formations. In the distance is the
palace, overlooking a landscape of lakes and mountains.

34

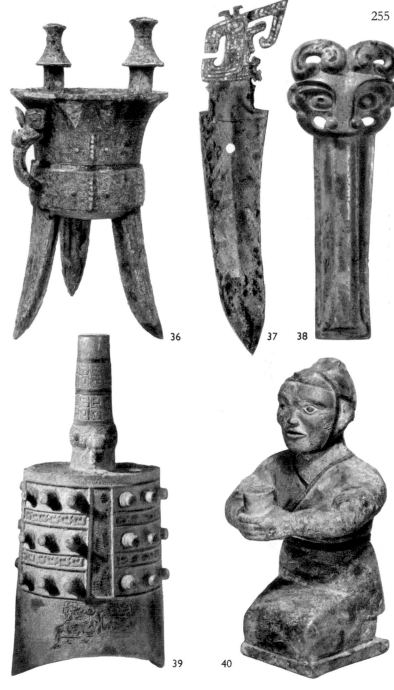

The quality of the bronzes was maintained during the first centuries of the Chou Dynasty. The art degenerated toward the ninth century B.C.; during the era of the warring kingdoms, it had a brilliant revival, accompanied by new techniques for inlay with precious metals; these techniques reached their highest point of perfection during the T'ang Dynasty. Down to the nineteenth century of our era this art continued to attest the great ability of the Chinese craftsman.

Ceramics. The Chinese have always been skillful potters. In prehistoric times there was, along with fine decorated work related to the ware of all Europe and Asia, a gray earthenware whose forms are the prototypes of the various vases of the historic periods. Under the royal dynasties of the historic periods decorated earthenware disappeared, but in the Shang-Yin Dynasty (fifteenth to twelfth centuries B.C.) fine incised white pottery was made, and at the end of the Chou Dynasty, around the fifth and fourth centuries B.C., potters succeeded in baking ware containing kaolin at 2400° F, covering it with a glaze containing feldspar. This process was perfected during the Han Dynasty, while at the same time, probably derived from the Near East, a lead enamel appeared, baked at low temperatures and colored by the addition of metal oxides.

During the T'ang Dynasty this technique was improved and enriched with various colors; the splendid decoration is in combinations of brown, yellow, green, and blue. But the most interesting creation of the T'ang period was the *grand feu* ceramics, ringing clear and a translucent white in color, that correspond to our definition of porcelain. With the enormous extent of the Chinese empire and trade, the products of Chinese kilns were spread all over Asia. In succeeding centuries, during the Sung Dynasty, the most beautiful pottery was produced that the world has ever seen, as to purity of form and beauty of glaze and color: the *Kuan* ware with the thick white layer of glaze, the *Ju* ware with delicate lavender-blue tints, the bluish *Chün* ware with wine-red areas, the dark brown *Chien* ware with an endless variety of shades, the soft green celadon ware, the white *Ting* ware, the bluish *Ying-ch'ing.* They are works of art of unsurpassed beauty, the reflection of an extremely refined civilization. The production of various types continued during the Yüan period; celadon was exported in great quantities, especially to the

35. Bronze li-ting, a vase of the Shang-Yin period, about 7³/₄ inches high. This vessel was used to prepare the sacrificial food, and stood on the altar. 36. Bronze chia of the Shang-Yin period. A wine dish used in ceremonies in which cups were exchanged. 37. A ko or dagger, with turquoise-inlaid handle, Shang-Yin period. Length about 13 inches. 38. Ornament of a horse's bit, bronze. The cavalry was of great importance under the Chou rulers, and harness fittings were often of great luxury and beauty. 39. A bell, end of the Chou era, bronze, about 11³/₄ inches high. Ritual ceremonies were accompanied by the rhythmical sounding of bronze bells. The composition of the alloy was very carefully studied. 40. Kneeling Man, bronze sculpture of the Chou period. 41. Bronze mirror back, diameter about 8¹/₂ inches, end of Chou period. The mirrors of this period are little marvels. The mirror side was carefully polished and the back beautifully decorated, with a bored knob in the middle for a cord or handle to pass through.

42. Mirror back, T'ang period. Sea creatures playing among vine tendrils; on the border, butterflies and birds. The motifs show a distant relationship with Hellenism, having traveled through Iran and all of Asia to flourish again in China. 43. Bronze clasp, inlaid with jade, end of the Chou period. 44. Ornamental cooker, Han period. Bronze, inlaid with gold and silver. Decoration of leaping animals in mountains. 45. Bronze vessel, Han period, decorated in gold and silver.

42

43

44

45

Malay Archipelago and the Near East, where it was greatly prized by the local rulers, as it was believed that by means of it poisoned food could be detected.

But slowly the preference shifted to a blue underglaze technique that was brought to a high point of perfection during the Ming Dynasty. This was primarily the period of polychrome porcelain. Ching Te-chên, close to the rich kaolin beds, became more and more the center of the porcelain industry. After manufacture had been stopped for some time because of the disturbances connected with the fall of the dynasty, it was revived at the end of the seventeenth century. Emperor K'ang-hsi realized what wealth could be brought to his country by trade with the West; it expanded greatly with the progress of navigation and the establishment of great shipping companies. Europeans took at once to Chinese textiles and lacquers, but above all to the fine glazed porcelain decorated with polychrome enamel: the *famille verte* with brilliant colors; then, during the Yung-cheng Dynasty, the *famille rose* with pale and tender colors. During the Ch'ien-lung Dynasty the enamel became darker, the drawing more negligent, and mass production impaired the quality of the

goods; the decadence became more noticeable in the nineteenth century, but the extremely fine things that were still being created for the imperial court as late as 1912 show that the Chinese craftsmen had lost none of their skill.

Textiles. Silk is the Chinese textile par excellence. According to tradition, the breeding of silkworms was introduced by the Empress Hsi-ling, the wife of the legendary ruler Huang-ti; down to the last days of the empire, ceremonies of worship to her were conducted. Fragments of silk, adhering to the surface of Shang bronzes when these were excavated, show the same sort of decoration as the bronzes, obtained by artful weaving methods. As early as the third century B.C. the precious material reached the cities around the Mediterranean by what was called the "silk route," a long caravan trail crossing Central Asia; on its arrival it was unraveled and rewoven to meet the tastes of the Roman ladies.

During the T'ang Dynasty weaving techniques were greatly improved; in the Sung period they reached a high point of perfection, and by the eleventh century there were many workshops in the large

46

47

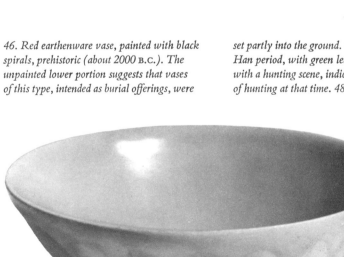

48

46. *Red earthenware vase, painted with black spirals, prehistoric (about 2000 B.C.). The unpainted lower portion suggests that vases of this type, intended as burial offerings, were* *set partly into the ground. 47. Hu vase of the Han period, with green lead glaze. Decorated with a hunting scene, indicating the importance of hunting at that time. 48. Oil lamp in the* 49

form of a duck, with a flower in its beak; yellow, green, and brown glaze, T'ang period. 49. Urn of white earthenware with gray enamel, T'ang period. Its elegance suggests the Hellenistic influences that reached China in the T'ang period. On the other hand, the handles end in typical Chinese dragon heads. 50. Delicate green celadon cup in the form of a lotus, Sung period. 51. Tz'u-chou vase, Sung period. The decoration is incised in the thick layer of glaze, allowing the white undercoat to show through. This forceful method of decoration was still esteemed down into the Ming period.

50

51

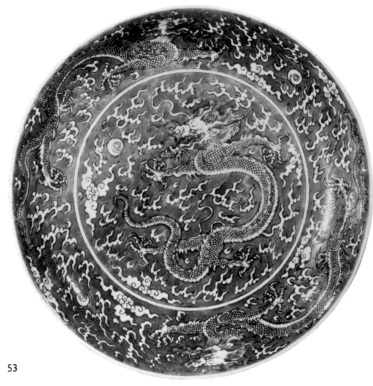

52

53

52. *Plate with blue underglaze decoration, Ming period, Wan-li porcelain. The technique of the "Chinese blue" was already known in the Sung era, but was perfected under the Ming Dynasty. A very pure cobalt was imported from Iran*

and mixed with somewhat grayer Chinese minerals. Wide borders of this kind were not used on the plates for Chinese tables, but were made for export (diameter about 19 inches). 53. Plate with yellow dragon on blue background, K'ang-hsi period.

The decoration of the five-clawed dragon was used exclusively on imperial objects. 54. Plate in "eggshell" porcelain, famille rose. The decoration is adapted to the taste of 18th-century Europe, but the symbolism is Chinese, nonetheless: storage jars, long-lived

mushrooms, lotus flowers, and woman with children all symbolize wealth, long life, community, and numerous progeny. 55. As early as the first centuries of our era, lacquer technique was highly developed, as is seen from this lacquer plate of the Han period.

54

55

57

cities, where thousands of workers labored. The conquest by the Yüan Dynasty, and the great economic development that the Mongol conquerors brought about in China, contributed to the spread—even to countries in the West—of damask silk, embroidered satin, and gold and silver brocade, whose technical qualities and beauty of decoration have never been surpassed; pieces of these textiles are carefully preserved in European collections of valuable church furnishings. The tradition was maintained during the Ming period and throughout the eighteenth century, although without any great renewal of inspiration. For everyday use the Chinese wove other materials, such as hemp and, in the eleventh century, cotton; the wool that came from Mongolia was used only for carpets. Little is known of the early history of Chinese rugs; there were important workshops during the eighteenth century, and their production was very large in the nineteenth.

56. Detail of an imperial robe, k'o-ssu, with a dragon and waves, mid-19th century. 57. Damask with the chou character, signifying long life, Yüan period. The piece, dating from the 13th century, was found in Egypt, which shows the extent of trade with the Near East during this period. 58. Ivory statuette representing Lao-tzu, god of longevity; early 17th century. 59. Plate of cloisonné enamel, vine-tendril decoration, 15th century. One of the handsomest pieces in a technique that was taken over from Iran but reached a perfection in China that was unknown in its country of origin.

59

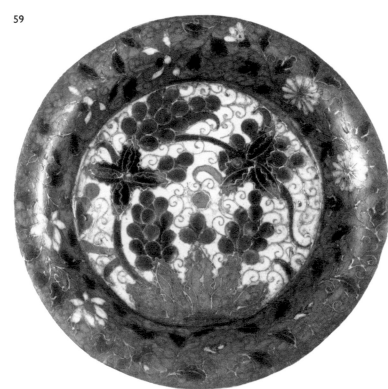

Lacquerwork. Lacquer, which forms an excellent protective layer and is heat- and moisture-resistant, was used to coat utensils, furniture, and wooden structural panels.

Painted lacquerwork of the end of the Chou Dynasty (fifth century B.C.), the oldest that has come down to us, attests an already highly developed craftsmanship. New techniques were developed in succeeding centuries; specimens are rare from the T'ang and Sung periods, but under the Ming Dynasty there was a brilliant period of black or vermilion sculptured lacquer, delicately painted with gold and inlaid with mother-of-pearl or semiprecious stones. In the seventeenth century appeared what is called Coromandel ware, after the region in India through which it was exported to Europe; its sunken decorations are colored in gouache. In 1680 the Emperor Kang-hsi founded the School of Craftsmanship in Peking. He particularly encouraged the production of vermilion lacquer, and had complete sets of furniture for his palace made of it.

Chinese lacquer became very fashionable in Europe, and imports of it created a mode of furniture there, especially for cabinets with lacquer panels.

Jade and Semiprecious Stones. Jade is a hard translucent stone that feels cold to the touch. For the Chinese it is the most precious of materials, the gem held to be endowed with essential virtues. Among the oldest jades, of the Shang and Chou dynasties, we find certain ritual objects: the *pi*, a disk with a round hole in the middle, the symbol of heaven; the *ts'ung*, consisting of a squared tube representing the earth; symbols of the chief winds; badges of office; amulets used in burials. There are also objects of adornment and decoration: earrings,

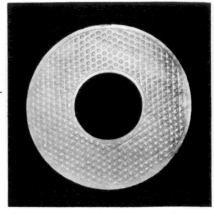

60. Throne of Emperor Ch'ien-lung (second half 18th century), of sculptured vermilion lacquer. This emperor had many luxurious pieces of furniture made. 61. Jade ritual pi, late Chou era. The pi, placed on the altar, symbolized heaven. 62. Mythological Horse on Waves, brown and white jade, Ming period, about 1500. The figurines are made with great attention to the picturesque. The artists make splendid use of the variations of color in their material.

61

62

60

pendants, small dishes. At the end of the Chou Dynasty jade-working attained a remarkable degree of perfection. In the T'ang and Sung periods figurines were carved in jade; this custom was very fashionable from the seventeenth to the nineteenth centuries, along with the custom of carving figurines in other stones, such as amethyst, cornelian, agate, turquoise, etc., pretty trinkets that were also exported during this period and enchanted everyone in the West.

JAPAN

1

INTRODUCTION   The adoption of models, styles, techniques, and forms from China, with or without Korea as a way-station, has been a very important element in the history of Japanese art.

In its fully developed form, however, Japanese art shows that no matter how much is taken over, the vigorous native taste, added to the typical mentality of islanders with powerful links to the sea, very soon brings about changes in the exact, in fact initially slavish, copying. Archaeological finds as well as the application of Chinese art show that the Japanese had artistic taste and sound aesthetic perception. In the nineteenth century Japanese art opened the eyes of European connoisseurs to the art of the Far East and gave strong impetus to the development of Oriental studies in general.

PREHISTORY TO A.D. 552   It is well established that the Japanese people stemmed from two groups, the pit dwellers, who probably came from the mainland, and the lake dwellers, who probably came to the islands from the south. They drove out the original Ainu inhabitants, twelve thousand of whom still live on Hokkaido, the northernmost island of Japan. We know that they baked pottery with a decorative corded pattern (jōmon), and that they modeled clay figurines, possibly of religious significance. Lacquer technique was very early adopted from China. Several centuries before Christ the typical elements of Japanese life appeared: their paddy rice culture, their bronzes, their characteristic earthenware, their military spirit, and their clan system (Yayoi culture). For the following centuries, we mention only the period of the great tumuli (third to sixth centuries A.D.), from which come the haniwa: these are clay images, of houses, human beings, animals, and other grave offerings, that crowned the cylinders supporting the outside of the mound. In the bronze technique taken over from Han China, we have mirrors and dōtaku (bells), which were first used as bells and later as symbols of power. Their frequently rich decoration, of contemporary scenes, in itself makes them valuable. We get an idea of the oldest forms of building through the Isé Shrine, which has been rebuilt every twenty years from time immemorial in its ancient form, which must

date from the third century B.C. In general, it is believed that the most common architectural style of that period is one with curved overhanging gables, as seen in the haniwa of the period.

SUIKO (OR ASUKA) PERIOD   The Suikō period (552–645) is named after a celebrated empress of that time. Buddhism, introduced from Korea in A.D. 552, made its influence felt in every sphere, although opposition to it went on for some decades. Romantic and narrative poems have come down to us from this time, and, at the end of the period, compilation of the oldest Japanese history was begun. In art, Chinese style predominated.

Architecture is known to us in part from the several structures of the Hōryū Temple complex, or Hōryū-ji, built in the seventh century, and from the wooden model there of a portion of a palace, which was fitted up as a domestic altar, the Tamamushi Shrine. *Sculpture*, exclusively religious, was initially entrusted to Chinese and Korean artists brought in for the purpose. The first statue of Buddha made by a Japanese dates from 587.

Painting: the panels of the Tamamushi Shrine just referred to have been preserved, on which are represented scenes from the life of the Buddha. We also have some fragments of a large tapestry, done from a painting. As for other textiles, fragments show that silks and

2

1. Prehistoric jomon pot from the collection of the Kokubon Temple, Tokyo. Earthenware with the so-called cord pattern (jomon). 2. Model Neolithic house, reconstructed after earthenware grave offerings and remains that have been found. It is set up in the Kyokodan, Musashino. 3. Female Head, baked clay, belonging to the so-called haniwa, the grave offerings that have been found, often in large numbers, at the mounds of important graves. They appear from the 3rd to the 6th century.

3

4

7

5

6

By this time, however, the art showed that although it was modeled on the Chinese, it took a successful line of its own. Literature flourished, and a number of anthologies and historical works have come down to us, along with a book of laws; much of this is written in the Chinese style.

Buddhism suffered at first under the reformation, which was on a Confucian basis, but it soon recovered. By the end of the seventh century there were already twenty-four established monasteries, some of which are still in existence, although fires and destruction have destroyed all of the original buildings. Drama and dance were combined, and down to the present time the *kagura* dance is performed at certain Shinto shrines, and the *bugaku* at the imperial court, all in ancient costumes and equally ancient masks.

Architecture was modeled entirely on the Chinese. We know from old descriptions that the palaces, temples, and monasteries were of enormous dimensions. Trees of a size to supply lumber for these structures are much more scarce today in Japan. Emphasis was placed on symmetry, following the Chinese ground plans; the buildings were put up on level sites. In any case, the main hall must have been massive, forceful, and above all impressive.

Sculpture was the art most strongly influenced by native taste, style, and aesthetic feeling. The finest statues date from the end of this period; in addition to the bronze, which had been used exclusively hitherto, there was clay, lacquer, and (in one instance) stone. Priests and figures from the Indian pantheon were represented, as well as Buddhas.

Painting. We have a good idea of painting, for a number of pieces have been preserved. It is hard to determine whether they are all indigenous, but it is certain, from catalogues and other works, that a purely Japanese school originated in the eighth century.

Arts and crafts. Ceramics were improved by the use of colored glazes, learned from T'ang Chinese models. Lacquerwork was perfected: gold, silver, and mother-of-pearl were applied in thin layers as decoration, and gold dust was also mixed in with the lacquer. Brocades reached a high point of technical perfection and beauty. (Until recently, it was believed that it was impossible to imitate them, despite Western technical resources.) Batik, tie-dyed, and stenciled textiles have come down to us; later, the first two methods went out of use. We still know something of the costume of the early time, from a single painting; by and large it is much like that of later periods.

brocades were of high quality, as well as the *kasuri* (resist-dyed or reserved-thread) technique.

Although virtually no ceramics have been preserved, comparison with previous and subsequent periods suggests that it was of good quality. The metalwork was of high quality, as shown by some crowns and a nimbus on statues of the Buddha.

NARA PERIOD The Nara period (645–794) is named for the site of the imperial palace, which became the center of cultural and political life. The period is dated from a political reform that took place in 645, in which political and social changes were introduced on the Chinese model. As it was difficult or impossible to apply these ideas to existing economic conditions, little came of them in practice, and the principal result was that the culture of T'ang China was more generally introduced, applied, and copied.

8

11

9

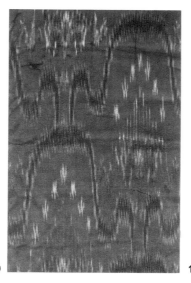

10

12

13

4. Model of a house, earthenware, grave offering, 3rd–6th centuries. Stylized model, whose oversailing roof indicates Indo-Malay influences. 5. Warrior in Armor, haniwa figure, possibly 6th century. Height about 24⁸/₄ inches. The helmet and armor show Chinese influence. 6. Bronze object (dotaku) after Chinese-Korean model. Dotaku are found in prehistoric tumuli. 7. Main building of Isé Shrine. Uji-yamada. It is rebuilt every twenty years without change. It may be assumed that this complex presents the oldest Japanese architecture known. It is the central national shrine of Shinto Japan. 8. Amitabha (Amida) with Two Bodhisattvas: bronze, about 13 inches high. The sculpture stands in a miniature house and must have belonged to Lady Tachibana, end of 7th century. Now in Horyu-ji, Nara. 9. The Maitreya (Miroku) Buddha,

carved in camphor wood, now a brilliant black; about 52 inches high. Suiko (Asuka) period (552–645). The statue is in the Chugu Temple, Nara. 10. Detail of the so-called Kanto Brocade, Suiko period; in kasuri technique, an ikat (reserved-thread) process. 11. South main gate, on the central axis of the Todai Temple group, Nara. 12. The oldest pagoda of the Horyu Temple group. With the main building, it lay on the north–south axis of the entire complex. 13. Detail of side panel, bronze lantern in the Todai Temple. It shows influences from both India and China. 14. Mask used in the so-called gigaku, and old dance, from China, probably performed in the open air within the temple precincts. These masks, sometimes grotesque, cover the entire head.

14

15

16

17

In 756 a collection of contemporary works and antiques belonging to an emperor was made, and stored in the Shōsō-in, a log-built court storehouse at Nara, which is still virtually complete. The objects themselves and old inventory lists are of incalculable value, and have provided us with the basis for much of what we know of old Japan.

HEIAN PERIOD The Heian period (794–1185) is named after the city (modern Kyōto) to which the imperial capital was removed in order to escape the pressure of the clergy. It was an age in which influential families competed for the emperor to chose his wife and prime minister from among their own ranks, a time of great land-holdings and agrarian revolutions, of bitter strife to the death between powerful clans, and of the rise of professional soldiers and armies of monks. Economically the country drifted into poverty. And yet this is regarded as a classic period for Japanese culture. Literature flourished; for the first time women, too, were writers, and with remarkable success. Many collections of poems were still in the Chinese style, but a purely Japanese style arose as well; garden parties with poetry competitions came into fashion. In prose, the novels and diaries written by women are renowned. Along with the Chinese characters, used for writing Japanese, a simplified set of forty-eight characters was developed for the syllables. This was used chiefly by the female authors.

The music taken over from China and Korea merged with the native music, and the *gagaku*, court music dating from the ninth century, is still played today. The instruments were flutes, the mandolin-like *biwa*, the cither, cymbals, and drums.

Philosophy was still derived entirely from China. The influence of Buddhism increased greatly, with new sects being formed. There was a strong shift to the Amida sect, since the country was sinking into an economic swamp and an immediately understandable ideal of salvation had to be found for the simpler people; it was a religion stated in simple language, without philosophical subtleties and not requiring the mediation of priests. The flight to Amida took place

18

particularly in the eleventh and twelfth centuries; the influence of the sect has persisted down to the present. The nobles of the court also took to the Amida sect, for entirely different reasons. The national Shinto cult dragged on its existence by virtue of Buddhism's great tolerance and a certain adaptation to it. Under the influence of the court, drama and dance were highly developed, while retaining old forms.

Architecture followed the tendencies in Buddhism. At first, to meet the needs of esoteric Buddhism, temples and monasteries were built, with the housing of the priests quite apart from the central hall. The pagoda was an indispensable part of the temple group, although from this period we possess only a single twelfth-century copy in which, with difficulty, the elements of the *stūpa* can be identified. In the ninth and tenth centuries especially, palatial richly decorated temples and monasteries were built, after the pattern of the Paradise of Amida. The main structure was square or rectangular and harbored a number of statues of Amida. The most notable shrine is the

20

19

21

22

15. Part of the Kako Ingakyo, the sutra of the former incarnations of Buddha Sakyamuni. Part of a narrative and illustrated scroll painting (makimono, or handscroll). 16. The Tamamushi Shrine in the Horyu-ji, Nara. On the pedestal painted scenes from the life of the Buddha. 17. Detail of one of the Six Beauties of Nara, six-leaved screen, preserved in the Shoso-in. It shows the influence of T'ang China. 18. The Shoso-in, imperial storehouse of Emperor Shomu (died 756), in the grounds of the Todai-ji, Nara. In it are thousands of objects, many of them from T'ang China, which the emperor owned during his life. 19. Pot with three-colored glaze, a technique taken over from China. Nara period. 20. Sacred gate (torii) standing in the

sea before the Itsukushima Shrine, one of the five principal Shinto shrines of Japan, on Miyajima Island. Oldest portions 12th century, most recent portions 16th century. 21. Sculpture of Kichijo-ten (originally a Hindu deity); cypress wood, about 35 1/2 inches high; Joruri Temple, Kyoto. Listed in the temple annals under the year 1212, but probably older, because of its Heian style. 22. East pagoda of the Yakushi Temple, Nara. Base about 22 feet square, height about 112 feet. Built in late 7th century, brought to its present site in 710. 23. Detail of the Kongo-kai mandala now in the To temple of the Singon sect, Kyoto. Probably 9th century. Gold and silver on purple background. A concentration object, or aid to meditation.

23

24

25

26

27

24. Amida, wood sculpture, by the sculptor Jocho, dated 1053. The statue is in the Ho-o-do, or Phoenix Hall, at Uji.

25. Ju-ichi-men Kwannon, eleven-headed deity (Chinese Kuan-yin), painted on silk with sumi, colors, and gold leaf. 10th century. 26. Fragment of the first roll of a makimono painting in four parts, with a total length of 36 feet. Late 12th century. Collection of the Kozan Temple, Kyoto. 27. Detail from a series of three makimono. The set tells the famous tale by the novelist Lady Murasaki, The Tale of Genji. Attributed to the Fujiwara (late Heian) painter Takayoshi; first half of 12th century. 28. The Shari-den (reliquary hall) of the Engaku Temple of the Zen sect, at Kamakura;

Hō-ō-dō, or Phoenix Hall, of the Byōdō-in (1052), resembling both in elevation and plan a huge bird hovering over the earth.

Sculpture at first followed the requirements of esoteric Buddhism and gradually abandoned all materials except wood, either native species or sandalwood. The sandalwood statues are in one piece; those in other woods usually have the hands and ornaments attached. The style is completely Japanese; the frontal aspect and the stiff resemblance to relief have disappeared. In later years, the trends followed the requirements of the Amida sect.

Painting. Here, too, the number of religious subjects increased. As the new sects required occasional changes of the central icons, paintings were more practical than statues. The *mandala*, a diagram in the form of a painting, became the fashion, depicting in geometric patterns the various series of Hindu gods incorporated into Buddhism, in both their contemplative and fierce aspects. In later centuries the decorative element became more important, as evidenced in brilliant colors and exuberant ornament. In the realm of secular art, scroll paintings appeared; the subjects were illustrations of novels of the time, of sutras (narratives of Buddha), and of marvelous histories of monasteries. Some have been preserved in which men and animals appear in caricature or comical situations. This is the beginning of the *Yamato-e* a purely Japanese school of painting, in which one outstanding feature is the omission of roofs and parts of walls, in order to be able to portray the inhabitants of rooms and palaces as if obliquely from above. The outline was drawn first, and the colors filled in later. A few screens and panels in *Yamato-e* have been preserved, and give us an idea of how the grandees of the country must have lived. Chinese influence diminished in all fields of art; native taste emancipated itself. To some extent this came about because of the decline and fall of the T'ang Dynasty in China, which resulted in a great decrease in contacts with China; in part, it was the result of increasing self-consciousness.

Arts and crafts. Ceramic production reached enormous dimensions; to this day porcelain is called *setomono* in Japanese, after the Seto region of this period. Porcelain in three and five colors predominated. Lacquer technique reached a peak of excellence, and for the first time a Japanese art product was appreciated and sought for on the mainland.

Costume. Although not a single piece of cloth has been preserved, we know, chiefly from paintings, that marked changes in costume occured; the Chinese style was abandoned and clothing became longer, pleated, and in several layers. The colors and patterns became simpler; batik, tie-dyed, and stenciled decoration disappeared almost

about 33 feet square and 33 feet high. The temple was founded in 1282 and the building must have been erected shortly thereafter.

28

Page 267. Colored woodblock print by Kitagawa Utamaro (1735–1806).

30. Detail of the Portrait of Yoritomo, painting on silk attributed to Fujiwara Takanobu (1142–1205). Collection of the Jingo Temple, Kyoto. 31. Fragment of the Yamai-no-Zoshi, or Scroll of Diseases : the man with loose teeth. Early Kamakura period.

31

entirely. Ordinary citizens all wore the kimono by that time; it is still the national costume, although printed with a larger and freer pattern.

The Heian period marks emancipation from the source that for centuries had given models and inspiration, namely the mainland: China, India, and, in a sense, Korea. Although most art and all art appreciation centered in Kyōto, the capital, the style was not a local one and it contained all the elements that a nature-loving people with a feeling for beauty could supply.

KAMAKURA PERIOD   The Kamakura period (1185–1338) is named after the place in the vicinity of present-day Tōkyō where the military government of the shogun was established. This last was the result of fifty years of strife among a trio of provincial families for influence at court, which they wrested from the urban, luxury-loving, effeminate court nobility.

The emperor retained his status as nominal head of state, but actual government was in the hands of the shoguns. Various shogunate families followed one another in power. The struggle brought misery and poverty, which contributed greatly to the spread of Amida Buddhism. Literature took a sharp turn, developing the heroic romances that had come into fashion at the end of the Heian period; women writers were relegated to complete obscurity, although their works from the Heian period were frequently depicted on picture scrolls. The poems were epics. Some sixteen collections of poems were published. Chinese, which for many centuries had been a special language for the learned, was Japanified, and used mainly for powerful heroic tales.

Architecture. Two styles came to the fore, both taken over from China. The first was called the Indian style, although it had no special connection with India. The second style, known as the Chinese style, was a consequence of the rise of the Zen sect, which had many followers among the military and the ruling families.

Sculpture. The Sung realism was adopted. Unkei and his family are among the most famous Japanese sculptors.

Painting. The first relatively realistic portraiture came into being, along with impressionistic pictures of poets and poetesses.

29

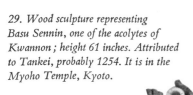

29. Wood sculpture representing Basu Sennin, one of the acolytes of Kwannon ; height 61 inches. Attributed to Tankei, probably 1254. It is in the Myoho Temple, Kyoto.

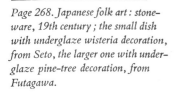

Page 268. Japanese folk art : stoneware, 19th century ; the small dish with underglaze wisteria decoration, from Seto, the larger one with underglaze pine-tree decoration, from Futagawa.

Arts and Crafts. As could be expected, the art of weapons and of ironwork rose to new heights; much of the finest work was already being sold to Chinese collectors in those days. The art of ceramics declined, with only a few centers remaining active. Enormous quantities of Sung celadon ware were imported from China and used by the aristocracy; some kilns began to imitate the process.

Costume, too, changed to meet the needs of the warrior and his campaign travels and marches. Emphasis was on surface pattern, embroidered rather conservatively with birds and flowers or done in *ikat*, that is, reserved-thread work. The quality was undistinguished and the work uninspired.

MUROMACHI (OR ASHIKAGA) PERIOD   The Muromachi period (1338–1573) gets its name from the districts in Kyōto where the Ashikaga shoguns had their headquarters and palaces. The period began with sixty years of bitter fighting over the imperial succession, followed by a time of relative peace and a stable government, then by a century of constant civil war and social unrest.

In literature a sharp division took place between the spoken and written languages; a few heroic tales appeared, and various historical works. A sort of popular literature also appeared. Poetry continued to be much practiced; regular poetry competitions were held and chain poems became fashionable. Zen priests were outstanding in prose and poetry. A pantomime that was performed at a religious

32

32. Fragment of one of the nine paper scrolls from the collection of the Kitano Shrine, Kyoto; height about 20 inches, total length about 22 feet. The picture represents the banishment of Sugawara Michizane (845–903) to Kyushu. The year 1219 is given in the text and it is assumed that the picture dates from that year. Ascribed to Fujiwara Nobuzane (1176–1265).
33. One of the pair of temple guardians standing on either side of the South Gate of the Todai Temple, Nara. Wood sculpture, 26 feet 6 inches high, by the sculptors Unkei and Kaikei, 1203.
34. Winter landscape, by Sesshu (1420–1506), hanging scroll painting, ink on paper, about 18 x 11 inches.

33

34

festival grew into the *dengaku*, which gradually led to dramatic lyrics; out of the comic pantomime there developed the *sarugaku*, a sort of picaresque or funny drama. On the model of the Chinese drama with its dialogues, which flourished in the thirteenth and fourteenth centuries, a primitive opera developed at the end of the fourteenth century: the *nōh*, with the *kyōgen* as a comedy interlude. The classical repertory contains 264 plays, all composed between the late fourteenth and late sixteenth centuries. The stage, which has remained unaltered down to the present time, strongly resembles the Chinese stage of the Yüan Dynasty. The Zen sect had great influence in every sphere. Not only were the simple way of life and the sobriety of Zen attractive to the military caste, but the samurai (knights) had a contempt for learning of any kind and were more than willing to leave diplomatic relations, negotiations, and even the management of finances to Zen priests. The third Ashikaga shogun restored normal commerce with China and, with Zen priests acting as go-betweens on both sides of the water, the influence of China in the field of art was renewed.

Architecture. An eclectic style developed that has given us the most beautiful temples of present-day Kyōto. The country residences of the lords and the design of gardens changed in style, following Zen aesthetic influences.

Sculpture. The same influence, Zen, was the cause for the partial recession in sculptural production; since Zen had no need of statues and the Amida tradition in sculpture was dying out, the art became sterile.

Painting. The painters took enthusiastically to the ink monochromes that they had become acquainted with from Sung China; the handsomest works in the medium were imported. (Much has been preserved in Japan that has been lost in China.) The first Japanese painters to use this technique were Zen priests; at the end of the fifteenth century there was Sesshū, who had studied in China for years and produced superb works. His followers formed the Kanō school and for four centuries were protected and encouraged by the shoguns. The *Yamato-e* declined, but got new life from the painters of the Tosa school.

Arts and Crafts. A very important development was the tea ceremony, which raised the drinking of tea and the meeting in harmonious, aesthetically cultivated surroundings to a point of cultural importance in life. The architecture of the tea pavilions, the ceramics, metal utensils, flower arrangements, and the garden design all entered into the art. Ceramics revived, under the inspiration of the Sung models and the requirements of the tea masters, who valued simplicity and naturalness above all other things. In textiles too, which had decreased somewhat in quality and taste, there was a revival to meet the needs of the tea ceremony. Muromachi lacquerwork followed the style of the ink monochromes and became simpler, under Zen influence. Lines and motifs became simpler generally, and the bright colors of previous periods were avoided.

MOMOYAMA PERIOD The Momoyama period (1573–1615) is named after a hill near Fushimi, where Hideyoshi had a palace built. He was the second of three generals who subdued the local military feudal lords dominating at the end of the Muromachi period, and restored national unity; the first general was Nobunaga and the last, Tokugawa Ieyasu, moved the capital to Edo (present-day Tōkyō). This period brought about a lasting internal peace, and during it occurred the first contact with Europeans (1542). With the inception of peace there arose a class of *nouveaux riches*, who were unable to appreciate the subtle and refined tastes of earlier times, and sought for large and spectacular effects. Gold, gold lacquer, and the color of gold were predominant; color and contrast became the criteria of good taste.

Architecture. The need for ramparts, donjon keeps, and citadels was emphasized by acquaintance with European firearms. The castle at Himeji, one of the many built at that time, has come down to us intact. Such castles were very spacious; sculptors worked on the decoration of pillars, beams, and eaves, and painters decorated walls and screens. Backgrounds became golden, and even the ink monochromes became deeper, darker, and sometimes of enormous size. Kanō Eitoku was the leader of the Kanō school, and produced large works. Along with this established school there were others which worked after Sung models, and were therefore more spirited than the official Kanō school. The Tosa school declined at the outset, but got new vigor from Sōtatsu.

36

37

35

38

39

40

41   42

43

EDO PERIOD The Edo period (1615–1868) is named after Edo (present-day Tōkyō), where Tokugawa Ieyasu set up his capital. After overcoming all resistance, he had absolute power in Japan. The emperor remained nominally as the descendant of the gods, and the owner of the land; Ieyasu and his descendants ruled with an iron hand. Confucianism, which was best suited for inculcating obedience and reinforcing the Tokugawa government, became the official philosophy. Gradually the country was shut off from all foreign influences, with small doors left open to Nagasaki in the form of the Dutch factory on Deshima Island and the Chinese settlement on the mainland. A century later this Dutch factory was used to introduce Western science, and a school of Japanese scholars was formed to speak and study Dutch. After the fall of the Sung in China, many men of learning fled to Japan from the Manchus, and helped to spread Sinology and Chinese art. Peace and relative prosperity gave rise to the class of merchants and financiers, along with the warrior class (samurai) to which they remained subject; the third class was that of the artisans.

A gradual conversion took place. Rich men began to take an active part in furthering the arts, and the whole nation participated in such forms as the *haiku* (verses of seventeen syllables), *kabuki* (popular drama), *ukiyo-e* (the art of prints, produced by artists of and for the people), and such minor arts as the *inro* (medicine boxes) and *netsuke* (decorative toggles). In literature novels were written, often illustrated by famous artists; the dramatist Chikamatsu wrote texts for *bunraku* (marionettes) and *kabuki* that achieved an importance there akin to Shakespeare's in the West. After 1854, Tōkyō was reopened to commerce; Japanese art reached Europe and was greatly appreciated there—Japanese prints inspired the French Impressionists and Van Gogh. The strong emphasis that Confucian ideas placed on emperor, state, and loyalty gave rise to a school of national historians and led to a revival of Shinto, while Buddhism underwent no new impulses and continued its calm subsistence. Toward the end of the period, it

Arts and Crafts. Textiles and lacquerwork followed the taste for bright colors, and gold and silver. In ceramics, tea porcelain was in demand; Chinese influence had vanished. *Oribé* and *Raku* ware were typical Japanese developments at this time. Contact with Europe led to copying and imitation of Western decorative motifs on purely Japanese materials, such as lacquer boxes, screens, etc.—one dandy even wore breeches and jacket of European cut.

44

45

45. *Portrait of the actor Onoe Matsusuke as samurai, woodcut by Toshusai Sharaku, about 1795. Mica worked into the background.*
46. *Woodcut by Suzuki Harunobu (1725–70), from the series Furyu Yedo Hakkei (Eight Modern Views around Tokyo). This print is entitled Sunset on Ryogoku Bridge.* 47. *Painting (nikuhitsu) on paper, mounted as a kakemono, by Isoda Koryusai. About 1780.* 48. *Woodblock print by Katsushika Hokusai (1760–1849). Mishima Pass in Kai Province, one of the series, Thirty-Six Views of Mount Fuji.*

46

47

39. Drip plate for an oil lantern. Oribé earthenware, folk art, about 1750. 40. Page from the illustrated book Buta Ogi (Theater Fans) by Tani Buncho, 1770, showing a contemporary actor. 41. Porcelain vase from Kutani, early 19th century. 42. Puppet for the marionette theater: bunraku from Awaji Island, about 1800. 43. Six-leaved screen by Ogata Korin (1658–1716), painted on paper, 59 inches high by 11 feet

8 inches wide. The colors are green and blue on a gold background. The subject, iris, is taken from a poem from the Isé Monogatari. 44. Three-part inro (medicine box) in boxwood, lacquered, with landscape and river. The cord passes through an ajime (slip ring) of stone to the netsuke (knob or toggle). The netsuke is in the form of two turtles. End of 18th century.

48

was the same national consciousness that advocated the restoration of the emperor as actual head of the state; this, coupled with the uneasy realization by some great figures that Japan was becoming backward in its isolation, finally led to the downfall of the Tokugawas and the restoration of the emperor, and opened the land to foreign commerce and intercourse.

Architecture, Sculpture, Painting. No great peaks were attained in architecture and sculpture; style was eclectic. In painting, the old Kanō school split into several branches having their own style and themes. In the eighteenth century the Okyō school pleased the views and taste of the merchant class; it was a naturalistic school with an assured, decorative realism. In reaction to it was the *bunjingwa* school, consisting of amateurs from learned circles, high functionaries, and literary men, who worked after Chinese models but entirely by inspiration. In prints and paintings the *ukiyo-e* depicted the floating life of every day—women of all classes (not least the professional women from tea houses and other places of amusement) and actors in their roles—and later the beauty of landscape as well. In a word, there is no facet of the Japanese life of those days that cannot be found and studied in the woodcuts.

Arts and Crafts. In the porcelain industry, glazes and decoration were of a quality that has never since been attained. Yet in the long run, here too, as in all the other arts, excess and overrefinement of decoration were deleterious influences.

The luxury-loving life affected textiles. Gold and silver threads were woven in, sometimes so thickly as to resemble embroidery. In lacquerwork splendid pieces were produced by such universally admired masters as Kōrin; but here, too, technically perfected workmanship led to rigidity.

MEIJI PERIOD (1868 to the present). The opening of Tōkyō had enormous influence in every domain of Japanese life. Compelled to adopt the Western pattern politically, militarily, and economically, this imitative people took over the Western tendencies in art as well. Only in an undercurrent was the beautiful and traditional retained and upheld in periods of doubt and wavering. A great deal of tasteless stuff was produced for the export market, but it was accepted by only a part of the ultramodern Japanese for their own use. Conservative and modern trends are both reflected in the public taste of today's Japan. Considerations of utility predominate in everyday practice.

50

49

51

54

2

53

55

49. Colored woodblock print by
Hokusai from the series, Six
Pictures after Poems, about 1835.
50. Triptych of three woodblock color
prints by Hiroshige (1797–1858),
representing a portion of the Kiso
Kaido, the great northern highway
from Kyoto to Edo. 51. Cat Washing
Itself, painting by Takeuchi Seiho
(1864–1942), an eclectic with a strong
sense of representation. This painter
was well known in Japan, at a time
when the modern Japanese style was
being formed. This work dates from
the 1920s. 52. Seated Nude, by
Umehara Ryuzaburo (1888–).
The work dates from the 1940s and
shows a powerful symbiosis of Post-
Impressionism and traditional Japanese

style. The painter went to Paris in
1908 and was influenced by his
teacher Renoir, as well as by Cézanne,
Van Gogh, and Gauguin. 53. Painting
in modern Japanese style by Kobayashi
Kokei (1883–). Combination of
elements of the old styles and modern
conceptions; this is clear in the subject
as well as the style. 54. Painting in
Western style by Yasui Sotaro (1888–
1955). In Paris he was strongly
influenced by Pissarro, Cézanne,
and others. In his later work, such as
this one, he returned to Japanese
elements and color harmonies.
55, 56. Museum of Modern Art at
Kamakura, Kanagawa Prefecture,
1952, by architect Junzo Sakakura,
a former pupil of Le Corbusier.

56

15

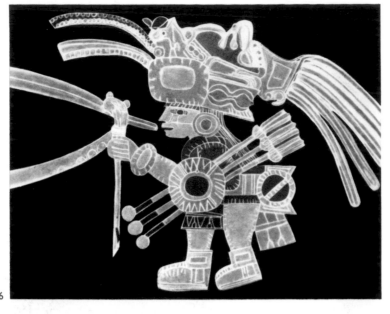

16

17

15. Prisoner, one of the very few free-standing statues from the Mayan region. Uxmal, Yucatan, eleventh-twelfth centuries. 16. Wall painting, bird-hunter with his prey. Colors on blood-red background. Barrios house, Teotihuacán, Mexico. 17. Standing figure with stone sacrificial knife. The "laughing" facial expression is typical of the Totonac region. Cerro de las Mesas, Vera Cruz, Mexico. Height about 12¹/₂ inches. 18. Vase in form of seated figure with feather headdress; gray earthenware. Zapotec region, Mexico. Height about 11³/₄ inches.

19

18

20

Figs. 19 to 36 are objects from the Peruvian culture region. 19, 20. Chan-chán, the central point of the kingdom of Chimu. 19. Detail of adobe wall with reliefs: fish and birds. Walls like this were covered with stucco and painted in colors. 20. Air photograph of Chanchán, area of about 11 square miles. Foundations of groups of adobe houses, surrounded by heavy walls, with graveyards, fields, and reservoirs also inside the precincts. The kingdom was conquered by the Incas. Northern coast of Peru.

Page 281. Pectoral in the form of a two-headed snake, mosaic technique on wood. Mexico, Aztec period. Width about 16¹/₂ inches.

21

Guatemala) exemplify the architecture of these Indians. Such buildings, erected on pyramidal or terraced mounds, were long narrow structures with false (corbeled) vaults of stone, and wooden beams. As the beams decayed, the roofs did not remain intact as a rule. The walls were richly decorated with reliefs or mural paintings. On the Mexican plateau step pyramids are the chief types of architecture. At one time these were crowned by temples, foundations of which are sometimes still preserved. Some famous pyramids are at Teotihuacán, Cholula, Tollan, and, on the coastal strip, Papantla, a pyramid with niches over its entire surface. We know the palaces of the Aztecs only from the descriptions by the conquistadors, who were deeply impressed by their splendor and stateliness.

In Peru, the architecture of the Incas culminates in the last centuries before the Conquest. In the old capital of Cuzco there are still many palace and temple walls that have survived centuries and earthquakes, and in the Andes are many border fortresses of the same period. Both cut stones (ashlar) and irregular, so-called Cyclopean, blocks were used, carefully fitted together. On the coast, where stone was lacking, temples and fortresses were built of sun-dried bricks, or adobe.

22

SCULPTURE Sculpture flourished under the Aztecs. Imposing colossal statues of gods with their attributes, usually of stone but sometimes of clay, give an impression of this art. The statues were usually colored. In addition, work in semiprecious stones, such as jadeite and nephrite, formed some fine figurines and plaques which have come down to us.

The Mayas in particular were great masters of the art of relief. A horror of empty space characterized their work. Wood too was worked, but this material survived only rarely in Mexico. In Peru, in the dry semidesert coastal region, however, many handsomely worked cups, boxes, spoons, etc. have come down to us. Stone sculpture is rare in Peru. Work was also done in bone and shell.

PAINTING Mexican and Mayan drawing and painting appears in the hieroglyphic books. These books were in accordion form, painted on two sides, of deerskin or paper made from agave (maguey) plant fiber. The books of the Mayas were less colorful than those of the other Mexican tribes, which employed red, blue, yellow, and green in bright hues. These colors included vegetable dyes (blue), mineral dyes (yellow), and animal dyes (cochineal red). Temple and palace walls were also brightened with paintings. For example, beautiful murals have been found at Teotihuacán; those of the Mayan region (at Palenque, Chichén Itzá, and Bonampak) are certainly at least as good. In Peru, adobe reliefs on walls in the coastal region were colored, but only traces are left here and there of such perishable materials. Remains of wall paintings have also been found.

walls, up to about 13 feet high, of Inca palaces, dry masonry of evenly dressed stones. 23. Machu Picchu, Inca border fortress in the high Andes. Urubamba Valley, Peru.

24. Zigzag wall of the fortress of Sacsahuaman, above Cuzco, of irregular stonework, known as Cyclopean construction.

23

21. So-called Gate of the Sun, monolithic lintel decorated in relief. In the center a figure with two staffs, enthroned among rows of winged beings. Tiahuanaco, Bolivia. 22. Street in Cuzco. On either side, remains of

24

25 26 27 28

29 30 31 32

25–29. *Five vases with handle spouts, Mochica period, north coast, Peru. 25. Portrait vase, painted reddish brown on cream-colored background. Height about 10¹/₂ inches. 26. Vase in form of warrior with shield and club; painted in reddish brown on cream-colored background. Height about 9³/₄ inches. 27. Vase in form of squatting figure with owl face and wings. Height about 11 inches. 28. Vase, with brown painting, on cream-colored background, of geometrical decorations in horizontal*

bands. Height about 10¹/₂ inches. 29. Vase in form of squatting man, asleep. Height about 7 inches. 30. Flask-shaped vase, reddish-brown earthenware decorated in relief; background painted. Style related to Tiahuanaco, i.e., the plateau. Central coastal strip (Supe Valley?). Height about 11 inches. 31. Spherical vase with two joined spouts, characteristic of the Nazca valley. Painted in blood red, reddish brown, and dark gray; theme, a demon with an animal head, the so-called "cat-demon." Height about

7¹/₂ inches. 32. Vase in form of seated flute player, with handle spout,

black earthenware, typically Chimu. Northern coastal strip.

MINOR ARTS Pottery was made in all regions. Along with domestic utensils and vases made for ceremonial purposes, such as grave offerings, many small clay figurines are found in Mexico, freely modeled, and later made in molds. Even the most primitive, in which the eyes and mouth are merely indicated by slits, are often strikingly expressive. Ceramic art was highly developed in Peru; both beautifully painted earthenware and vases in sculptural form, often made in molds, have been found there. The latter had a handle-shaped spout, typical of the northern coastal region. In both Mexico and Peru, bone, wood, and shells were carved, wooden objects having been preserved mainly in the dry semidesert coastal regions of Peru. The Indians were true masters of the making of mosaics. In Peru, chiefly ornaments were decorated in this way; in Mexico, shields and masks. The masks presented to Cortes by Montezuma, king of the Aztecs, upon his arrival in Mexico are famous. Cortes sent them, with many other precious objects, to Charles V. The masks are now in museums in London, Copenhagen, and Rome. Palace walls were also decorated sometimes with a kind of mosaic in stone, as at Mitla (Mexico), where geometric motifs adorn the wall surfaces.

From both Mexico and Peru, and from the regions between, Columbia, Costa Rica, and Panama, fantastic reports of wealth in gold reached Europe in the sixteenth century. Many of these treasures, unfortunately, found their way to the melting pot, but still, over the centuries, masks and many kinds of ornaments from graves came to light, so that we can get a good idea of the metalwork in those countries. The most simple processes, which appeared almost everywhere, were hammering, chasing and engraving. These people also possessed the art of casting, even the lost-wax process, as well as gilding, coating with gold leaf, inlaying, alloying, soldering, and welding. Among the tools used were stone hammers and anvils, earthenware furnaces and crucibles, and blowpipes to make the flame hotter. This art, in the Western Hemisphere, seems to have originated in South America.

More perishable materials, such as the wood already mentioned and in particular cloth, have come down to us primarily from the dry semidesert coastal regions of Peru, where climate and soil contributed to conservation. The diversity of textile techniques and design is astonishing, as well as the richness of the colors. In Meso-America, all this has been destroyed by humidity; only the stone reliefs can give us some idea of the rich materials in which the mighty were clad.

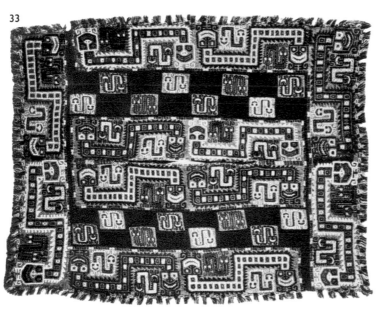

33

34

33. Serape, two joined portions with an opening for the head; beautifully worked colored textile, with repeated motif of two-headed snake. Southern coastal strip, probably Paracas. 34. Poncho with feather mosaic. Light yellow, light blue, and black motifs on a red background. Vicinity of Lima. Height about 41 inches. 35. Detail of woolen cloth, with catlike animals. Nazca. 36. Apron decorated with bone fishes; bone bobbins as fringe. 37. Gold plaques and bells from golden sacrificial chain, the Cenote Sagrada. Chichén Itzá, Yucatan, Mexico. 38. Gold cup, from Ica, southern coastal strip, Peru. Height about 3 inches.

35

36

37   38

NEGRO ART OF AFRICA

INTRODUCTION About two hundred million people inhabit Africa, differing widely in race, language, and culture. On the basis of skin color, we can distinguish the leucoderms, north of the Sahara, and the melanoderms, south of it. Ethnically, historically, and culturally, the white-skinned peoples belong to the Eurasiatic complex and not to the specifically African world, and accordingly they have not been discussed in this chapter. Of the dark-skinned peoples, the Negroids are most prominent. Although their artistic production includes more than the purely visual arts, it is these latter that merit most attention, especially their highly developed sculpture.

The arts of painting and architecture are much less developed than sculpture. The Negroids have no "easel painting" (apart from modern productions under direct European influence); some tribes, like the Dogon in Mali, have simple rock paintings (less strong than those of the Bushmen of the Kalahari Desert). Painting has mainly taken the form of rudimentary frescoes on the walls of some huts or other buildings, or decorations on useful objects like shields, etc. As for architecture, the impermanent materials used in building and the simple structures made of them do not, in the vast majority of cases, merit the name of an art of building. Exceptions are certain palaces and other public buildings of clay or wood to be found in West African cities, and some courts of local rulers in the Cameroons and the Congo. It is also true that in Rhodesia and other regions we find imposing stone ruins of large, structurally intricate buildings, such as Simbabwe, but the question arises as to how far these are expressions of an indigenous Negro culture.

As has been said, the situation is quite different in sculpture. Here we have not only an unusually vital art form, both independent and applied, but an art form with a sure sense of artistic quality, whose inherent power of communication speaks to non-Africans as well. Although European interest in African sculpture arose early—actually it dates from many years prior to its so-called discovery by the French Cubists—it has only been systematically studied for a relatively short time. Lack of data concerning the origins and cultural context of this art, as well as the absence of an accepted method of approach, certainly had much to to with delaying this study. Even today, deeper research is hindered by the largely perishable material with which African sculptors have worked and by the absence of written documentation. In recent years, largely due to systematic excavations, many objects have come to light, mostly in terracotta and bronze, from such old cultures as Nok, Ife, Jebba, Tada, and Sao, which may make easier a historical study of the sculpture.

GEOGRAPHICAL RANGE We must bear in mind, to begin with, that not all the so-called Negro peoples have produced works of plastic art. As a matter of fact, such production has been confined to a broad band bounded on the north by an imaginary line running from central Senegal through the outermost bend of the Niger River to Lake Chad, and then in a broad arc descending to Lake Albert Nyanza; in the east by the three great lakes; in the south by a line taking in Angola and a part of Rhodesia; in the west by the Atlantic Ocean. Few ethnic groups inside this region produce no sculpture; equally few are the groups outside it (such as the Makonde in southeast Tanganyika) that do produce it.

From the point of view of climate and vegetation, the area in question belongs to the region of equatorial rain forests (Guinea and Congo), with subequatorial savannas and park savannas on either side. Two great rivers flow through it: the Niger-Benue in the northwest and the Congo in the center.

Historical and cultural factors, and material conditions, may to a great extent be regarded as the causes of the regional limits of sculpture in Africa. One such historical factor is the early influence exerted by Islam, which led great regions to observe the prohibition of images that the Koran prescribes. Cultural factors include the nomadic way of life of the pastoral peoples of East Africa (originally

1

1. Wooden mask of the Pangwe, Gabon, with finely stylized features.
2. Wooden crown mask made by the Afo, a small tribe of southern Nigeria, of which little sculpture is yet known. The piece is crowned by a handsomely worked animal figure at the top. About 11½ inches high.

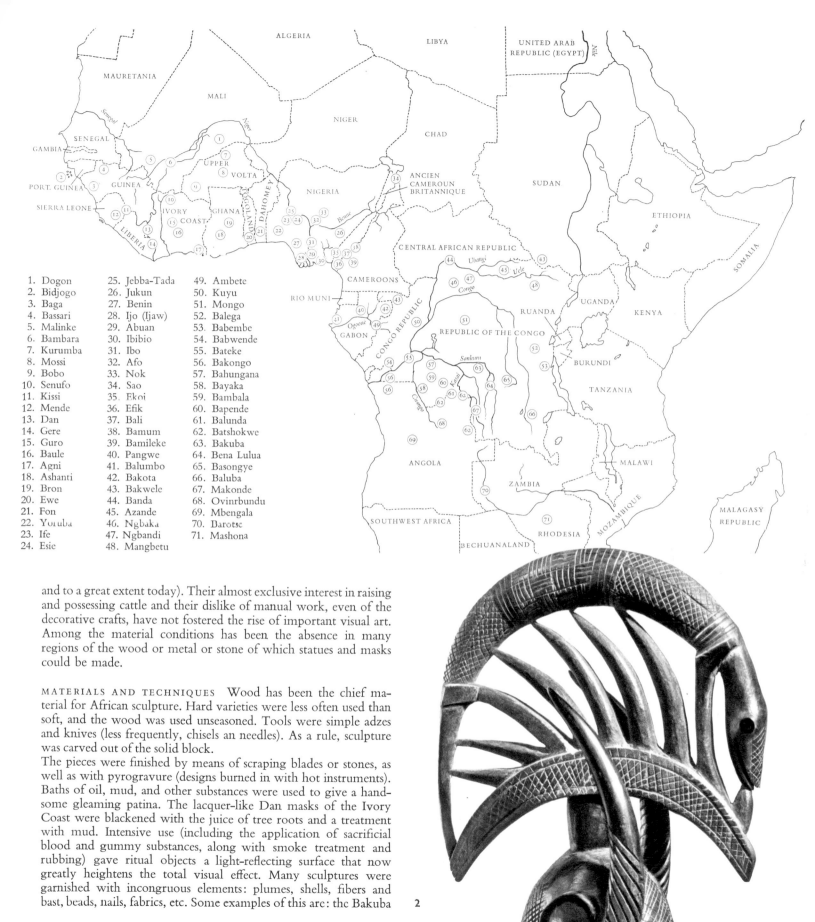

ALGERIA
LIBYA
UNITED ARAB REPUBLIC (EGYPT)
Nile
MAURETANIA
MALI
NIGER
CHAD
SUDAN
SENEGAL
Senegal
GAMBIA
PORT. GUINEA
SIERRA LEONE
GUINEA
LIBERIA
IVORY COAST
GHANA
Niger
UPPER VOLTA
DAHOMEY
NIGERIA
Benue
ANCIEN CAMEROUN BRITANNIQUE
ETHIOPIA
SOMALIA
CENTRAL AFRICAN REPUBLIC
CAMEROONS
RIO MUNI
Ubangi
Uele
GABON
Ogooue
CONGO REPUBLIC
Congo
REPUBLIC OF THE CONGO
RUANDA
BURUNDI
UGANDA
KENYA
TANZANIA
Sankuru
Kasai
Cuango
ANGOLA
MALAWI
ZAMBIA
MOZAMBIQUE
SOUTHWEST AFRICA
RHODESIA
BECHUANALAND
MALAGASY REPUBLIC

1. Dogon
2. Bidjogo
3. Baga
4. Bassari
5. Malinke
6. Bambara
7. Kurumba
8. Mossi
9. Bobo
10. Senufo
11. Kissi
12. Mende
13. Dan
14. Gere
15. Guro
16. Baule
17. Agni
18. Ashanti
19. Bron
20. Ewe
21. Fon
22. Yoruba
23. Ife
24. Esie

25. Jebba-Tada
26. Jukun
27. Benin
28. Ijo (Ijaw)
29. Abuan
30. Ibibio
31. Ibo
32. Afo
33. Nok
34. Sao
35. Ekoi
36. Efik
37. Bali
38. Bamum
39. Bamileke
40. Pangwe
41. Balumbo
42. Bakota
43. Bakwele
44. Banda
45. Azande
46. Ngbaka
47. Ngbandi
48. Mangbetu

49. Ambete
50. Kuyu
51. Mongo
52. Balega
53. Babembe
54. Babwende
55. Bateke
56. Bakongo
57. Bahungana
58. Bayaka
59. Bambala
60. Bapende
61. Balunda
62. Batshokwe
63. Bakuba
64. Bena Lulua
65. Basongye
66. Baluba
67. Makonde
68. Ovinrbundu
69. Mbengala
70. Barotse
71. Mashona

and to a great extent today). Their almost exclusive interest in raising and possessing cattle and their dislike of manual work, even of the decorative crafts, have not fostered the rise of important visual art. Among the material conditions has been the absence in many regions of the wood or metal or stone of which statues and masks could be made.

MATERIALS AND TECHNIQUES Wood has been the chief material for African sculpture. Hard varieties were less often used than soft, and the wood was used unseasoned. Tools were simple adzes and knives (less frequently, chisels an needles). As a rule, sculpture was carved out of the solid block.

The pieces were finished by means of scraping blades or stones, as well as with pyrogravure (designs burned in with hot instruments). Baths of oil, mud, and other substances were used to give a handsome gleaming patina. The lacquer-like Dan masks of the Ivory Coast were blackened with the juice of tree roots and a treatment with mud. Intensive use (including the application of sacrificial blood and gummy substances, along with smoke treatment and rubbing) gave ritual objects a light-reflecting surface that now greatly heightens the total visual effect. Many sculptures were garnished with incongruous elements: plumes, shells, fibers and bast, beads, nails, fabrics, etc. Some examples of this are: the Bakuba

2

3

4

5

3. *Wooden mask with expressively modeled face, presumably made by the Balega, Congo, and used within the Bwame sect. Partially polychromed in white, and decorated at the bottom with a beard of monkey hair. About 10 inches high. 4. Wooden mask of the Ibibio, Nigeria, with movable jaw and a palm-leaf fiber beard. About 19$^{1}/_{2}$ inches high. 5. Wooden mask of the Guro, Ivory Coast. It has the form of a stylized antelope head and is worn by the Guro during the assembling dance. About 15$^{3}/_{4}$ inches high.*

and Bambara masks with cowrie shells; the statues of the Ossyeba-Bakota and Fon, covered with strings or leaves of copper or brass; the skin-covered heads made by the Efik and Ekoi; and the statues and utensils of the Bamileke and Bamum in the Cameroons, decorated with colorful glass beads.

Most of the statues were left monochrome; the masks of many tribes were painted with mineral, vegetable, or animal colors. Other vegetable materials are the various fibers used in the manufacture of certain masks and associated garments. Basketry masks can seldom be included as sculpture, but still occur in various regions to supplement or to take the place of the wooden masks. Statues of such material are seldom or never encountered.

Another material for sculpture is the ivory of elephants' tusks, and those of hippopotami and wart hogs, together with various kinds of

bone. This material is less common than wood, and has been used chiefly in the regions where it occurs: the Congo (e.g., by the Bapende, Balega, Azande, and Mangbetu) and Nigeria, as in Benin, where huge carved elephant tusks are found in the palace of the *Oba* or local ruler. Although the material has its limitations (such as the mere factor of size), able workers in ivory have achieved good results with it. By immersion in boiling oil (as among the Mangbetu), the material is given a certain pliability; nonetheless, the original form of tusk or tooth is often preserved in the finished sculptures (as in the bent-over figurines that the Baluba make out of hippopotamus teeth). The masks carved of elephant ivory (such as those from the Balega) are naturally rather small in size.

Along with the carving of statues in Africa, cast metalwork is also common, at least in West Africa, as on the Ivory Coast (among the

6

7

6. Wooden mask of the Batshokwe, Congo. It is a Mwana-pwo mask representing a young woman, and is used by the Batshokwe for recreational dances. About 8³/₄ inches high. 7. Top piece, in the form of a woman's head, attached to a wooden mask of the Ekoi, Nigeria. Realistic images of this kind are used within the secret ekpo society of the Ekoi. About 13 inches high.

Baule and their neighbors), in Ghana (among the Ashanti and the Agni), and in Nigeria (at Benin and Ife). The technique employed was almost exclusively the lost-wax method. The metal used is brass or copper, rarely gold or silver. The complex nature of the technique has led to the assumption that it must be of foreign origin, possibly via the navigators who were in contact with West Africa from the thirteenth century. It is likely, however, that the casting of statues, based on the lost-wax technique, appeared in Ife as early as the eleventh century, so that direct European influence can be excluded. The question whether it is a locally invented process has not yet been satisfactorily answered. It is not impossible that the technique came from India and reached West Africa by roundabout routes.

Another metalwork technique is that of forging, only seldom used for statuary. Well known in this connection are: an imposing iron figure of the Fon, now in the Musée de l'Homme in Paris; the human figures of the Bakuba; and the forged work of the Basongye. Various peoples have used clay and mud as materials for modeling. Terracotta statues and heads remain from the old Sao civilization on Lake Chad and from those of Ife, Nok, and Jebba in Nigeria. The Bassari, the Kissi, the Agni, and some Dogon clans also have sculpture of this sort. Mention should be made of the often handsome anthropomorphic pottery of such tribes as the Akan, Ibo, Mangbetu, and Bakongo. Clay figures, sometimes life-size, in various attitudes are found among several tribes, for example in Dahomey, Mali, the Ivory Coast, Ghana, and northern Congo.

Sculpture in stone in Africa is chiefly limited to three great regions: Guinea–Sierra Leone, Nigeria, and lower Congo–northern Angola. In the first region we find the Mende and the Kissi; in the latter,

8. Wooden mask of the Makonde, Tanganyika. Face mask, used in girls' initiation rites. About 9¹/₂ inches high.
9. Ancestor mask of the southern Dan, Ivory Coast. According to them, the features represent a malicious youth. Outstanding example of evenly balanced, frontal composition. About 8³/₄ inches high.

8

9

10. *Wooden male figure (of an ancestor?) of the Senufo, Ivory Coast. A surprising plastic result is obtained with sober means. About 15 inches high. 11. Monkey-headed figure of the Baule, Ivory Coast. Represents Gbekre, a divinity ruling as judge of the dead. About 20³/₄ inches high. 12. Female figure of the Ambete, Gabon. A box in the back contains the remains of a dead person. About 27¹/₂ inches high.*

13. *Stylized human figure, made of wood with copper and brass mountings, Bakota, Gabon. Statues of this kind are used to surmount baskets in which the remains of the deceased are kept. About 27³/₄ inches high. 14. Wooden female figure of the Malinke, Mali.*

Fertility statue, carried by girls in certain dances. About 15 inches high. 15. Wooden female figure of the Ashanti, Ghana, an Akua'ba figure used for female fertility. Originally, these statues are said to have represented the moon goddess Nyame.

certain Bakongo clans. The material used is mostly steatite, a soft, greasy stone that lends itself easily to being worked with adze and knife. The result is that, as among the Bakongo, the final product bears a strong resemblance to work in wood. Soft sandstone, too, is easily worked, as for example in Guinea–Sierra Leone. The present inhabitants of Nigeria do stone sculpture only sporadically; in old cultures, on the other hand, such as that of Esie, stone was a traditional material.

Other materials and techniques were used only rarely for sculpture. The use of wax for modeling so-called puppets occurs in the Cameroons and Mali, and elsewhere.

IMAGES The plastic art of negroid Africa presents, basically, three kinds of images: anthropomorphic, zoomorphic, and "hybrid." Free-standing leaf-shaped representations are also encountered, but there are few of them, as of purely geometrical motifs. The human image predominates everywhere, either as statue or as mask. Most of the human statues in the round are full-length, single figures. Torsos, busts, and heads as such appear much less frequently, and the grouping of various figures happens only seldom. Very fine specimens of heads are found in the ancient court art of Nigeria, in particular from Ife, as well as from Benin, and by the Agni of Krinjabo. In other cultures which flourished earlier, as in those of Lake Chad and Esie, we likewise come across the head as an independent motif. The head is used more extensively in applied art. For example, we find it used in the cephalomorphic Bakuba cups, in many baked-clay pipes from the Cameroons, in the pitchers of the Mangbetu, and in the pottery of the Chad cultures.

Men and women, and sometimes children, are represented in various postures. Although a certain mobility is not lacking, especially in West Africa, the static aspect of the representation is characteristic of this sculpture as a whole, regardless of whether the figure is standing, squatting, sitting, or kneeling. The vertical posture is by far the most common; sitting or kneeling statues occur chiefly in the Congo (e.g., among the Bakongo and the Bakuba) and in Nigeria (Yoruba, etc.). Squatting figures are rarer; they are typical of the Bena-Lulua in the Congo.

Relatively complete representations of groups of several persons in the round are less common, as has been said. They appear for the most part in West Africa, particularly in Dahomey and Nigeria: in Dahomey, in the folk art in brass and the colorful clay reliefs of the palaces of the nobles and former rulers; in Nigeria, on the bronze reliefs of the royal residence at Benin, and in other places. The work in bronze of the Bini also has groups of figures in the round, although not very many. It is typical that when several personages are represented, there is seldom any connection among them; the figures lead separate existences. This is even the case in sculptures showing a mother with her child (in Nigeria and especially in the lower Congo). The child is in the arms or on the lap, as though the mother were quite unaware of its presence. The same applies for the double figures, side by side or back to back, that are carved in the Congo and in Mali, and elsewhere.

The result is that narrative scenes are more the exception than the rule. In the regions where they are more frequent, as in Dahomey, they are most likely due to European influence. Such emotional scenes as we find there are very rare in traditional African art, certainly in the case of autonomous sculptures. There are more narrative subjects in applied sculpture, as in certain divination pots of the Yoruba, some openwork chairs of the Yoruba and the Batokwe, and similarly carved elephant tusks from Nigeria and the Congo. We also see them on some large West African masks, surmounted by picturesque figures. Here, too, European influence cannot be excluded.

Other groups (in a sense) are the figures of riders, which occur rather frequently among the Yoruba and the Senufo. The grouping of men and animals is rather uncommon, except for masks. In the great majority of cases the various anthropomorphic mask types (face, hood, and helmet masks) are conceived singly. Double masks (paired Janus heads) are still made fairly freely among Nigerian groups, such as the Ijaw and the Yoruba, and among the Ekoi. Some masks are decorated at the top with a human figure in the round; e.g., those of the Ibibio and the Bamum. Other masks are crowned with a zoomorphic figure, as are various examples from the Dogon, Guro, and Bayaka. Animal figures often appear in other connections, sometimes separately, and the fauna represented vary greatly: all sorts of quadrupeds, as well as birds, fishes, reptiles, and insects. Animal motifs are very frequent on the little metal weights for weighing gold dust (Ghana and the Ivory Coast). Examples in wood, chiefly quadrupeds, are well represented in the art of various Congolese tribes, such as the Bakongo, Bayaka, Bakuba, and Batshokwe-Balunda.

Masks in the form of an animal head are widespread. They represent antelopes, elephants, buffaloes, wart hogs, leopards, monkeys, rams, and other animals. Especially noteworthy are the elegantly designed masks (*chiwara*) of the Bambara; for the most part they represent highly stylized antelopes, whose long horns and slender limbs set off a refined play of line. Animals are used as frequently in applied sculpture. There are few species that are not employed as motifs. For example, the slotted drums from the Central African Republic and northern Congo, with geometrically treated buffaloes and antelopes, are beautifully proportioned.

Hybrid images appear less frequently in statues than in masks. Often, the masks are just human faces in which one or more features (such as the nose or the ears) have been replaced by animal traits (e.g., trunk, beak, muzzle, tusks), or elements from the animal world have been added (e.g. horns). In this way a fantastic being is created, grotesque, dramatic, or comical in expression. Some peoples, such as the Gere, Wobe, and Mano in Liberia and the Ivory Coast, show a definite preference for hybrid images of this sort. Often, however, what is involved is rather a far-reaching stylization of an anthropomorphic or zoomorphic motif (with some organs greatly exaggerated) rather than "genuine" fantastic beings.

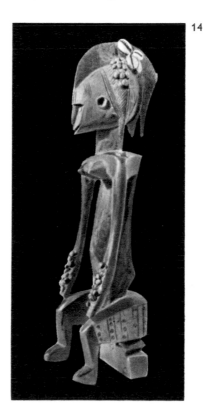

14

15

16   17

18   19

20

16. *Ivory female figurine of the Balega, used within the Bwame sect as a badge of high rank. About 5 inches high.*
17. *Richly tattooed wooden figure of a warrior of the Bena-Lulua, Congo. About 17½ inches high.* 18. *Wooden figure of Bope Kena, the 119th ruler of the Bakuba (Congo). About 21¾ inches high.*

19. *Wooden figure of a seated Ba-bembe warrior, Congo. About 14 inches high.* 20. *Wooden figure of a mother and child, an expressionistically executed sculpture of the Baluba, Congo. About 5½ inches high.*
21. *Bronze bas relief of a warrior; old court art of Benin, Nigeria. About 20¾ x 15 inches.*

As has been said, motifs from the plant world and purely geometrical subjects are far less frequent and widespread, at least as independent works of art done in the round. They are most frequent among the so-called "gold weights" of West Africa. Even in other areas, however, they occur frequently as decorative elements on autonomous sculptures or in applied carving. This applies especially to the geometrical patterns. Handsome instances of this ornamentation are to be found on all sorts of useful objects, for example those of the Bakuba.

ART AND SOCIAL CONDITIONS Since ancient times the plastic art of Africa has been a social art: it does not exist for its own sake, but exclusively as a function of the system of life in which it appears. It is completely rooted in its society and forms a part of it; without its society it loses its reason for being.

Integration of art into the life of the tribe, clan, or village appears in both the religious and secular domains. We hasten to add that some sculptures are ambivalant in character, while others seem to be only religious or only secular.

It is generally assumed that African sculpture is primarily a religious art. Actually, most of the pieces are not so much ritual in function as possessed of a symbolic content so clear that they cannot be regarded as profane. There is not the least doubt of this in the case of many statues and masks, but there are some carved objects that give a thoroughly secular impression at first sight and yet have in fact an equally sacred character.

Many anthropomorphic statues represent ancestors and have a function in the rites devoted to them. Since the weal or woe of the community is regarded as dependent upon the deceased, it is understandable that ancestors should play a large part in religious-social life and that they should be the object of a considerable ritual activity. When ancestors are represented in sculptured form, their likenesses are as a rule done with great care. It is striking to see how many statues of ancestors rank among the most beautiful of artistic productions.

Anthropomorphic images of deities are limited to West Africa, especially to such tribes as the Baule and the Yoruba, who possess a pantheon of gods. On the other hand, statues of spirits are particularly widespread in Central Africa. It should be noted that certain spirits are depicted as well-defined personalities, while others are much less clearly defined and represent impersonal forces. This last category includes most of the "fetishes" (a rather vague term for a complex concept), which are common in such tribes as the Bakongo, Bateke, Basongye, and others in the lower and southern Congo. Fetishes are not only in human or animal shape, and many other "non-representational" objects may likewise be fetishes. The Higher Being may also be identified with certain natural objects having no anthropomorphic connotation.

Other statues of a ritual nature are the *ibeji* figurines used in the twins cult of the Yoruba, the *aku-iba* fertility dolls of the Ashanti, the mythological figures of the Senufo, the divination sculptures of the Lobi, and so forth. Also comprised under religious sculpture in the broad sense are the figurative *itombwa* and *katatora* oracles of the Bakuba and the Baluba, respectively, and the anthropomorphic mouse or other oracles of the Baule, Yoruba, and other West African peoples. Similar wooden pots used by the Dogon priests, and such objects as the rams' heads of the Yoruba (for the yam-root rites), as well as the ivory initiation badges of the Bahungana in the Congo, all unquestionably have a sacral content. Equally ritualistic, despite their "unconsecrated" appearance, are the beautifully worked royal thrones and seats from Ghana, the Ivory Coast, and Dahomey. They are believed to embody spirits, and as such are the objects of an intensive cult. Other investiture symboles, such as smaller seats or stools, sometimes carved as caryatids, possessed by local rulers, also count as consecrated objects. This is the case, too, with the ceremonial chairs of the Baluba, Batshokwe, and other Central African

tribes. The role of the scepter is filled, among groups like the Baule, Agni, and Abron, by skillfully worked fly-whisks. Among the Dogon, certain doors carved in high relief are endowed with mystical powers. In Sierra Leone we find carved spatulas, likewise embodying spirits, used in the Sandé women's ceremonies. Among the Dan, spoons in human form have a similar sacramental character, being used for the partaking of ritual foods at certain functions.

The numerous sects and initiation societies, often secret, give rise to quite different sacral sculptures. This applies especially to masks, which in most ethnic groups are pre-eminently ritual objects.

The religious (and social) significance of masks extends in various directions. In West Africa they are, among other things, the "spokesmen" of the spiritual and political leaders in powerful closed societies, such as those of the Poro. They represent fertility-giving "spirits" among the Baga, water demons among the Abuan and Ijaw, mythical beings among the Senufo, male and female deities among the Baule; they are essential in performing the agricultural rites of such tribes as the Kurumba, Dogon, Bambara, Bobo, and Mossi; they represent ancestors among the Dan and Gere, and among the Fon and the Holli. They are employed at birth, initiation, and death, at all kinds of rites and festivals, and fulfill many functions, sometimes several at once. In the most diverse circumstances of life they are the great agents of the catharsis indispensable for the community and the individual. In such tribes as the Baga, Nalu, Dogon, Dan,

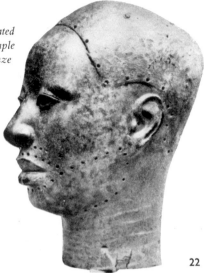

22. Handsome bronze head, excavated in the old city of Ife, Nigeria. Example of idealized realistic form. 23. Bronze head, representing a Benin king, probably made between 1575 and 1691. About 21 inches high.

22

The antipode of realism, which is abstraction carried to its extreme, is present in more than one region. Instances of far-reaching schematization are found in Nigeria among the Yukun, in the Congo Republic (some Bateke masks), and in the northern Congo (as in certain Azande statues). The *chiwara* mask-crowns of Bambara are another case.

The various conceptions of style, including those at the opposite poles, are often found alongside each other, and even intermingled, in relatively small areas. For example, such adjoining tribes as the Pangwe and the Bakota have completely different styles. The Pangwe produce sculptures of a realistic tendency, basically diverse from the highly schematic Bakota sculpture. Other neighbors, such as the Dan and the Gere, present some parallels, it is true, but the usually serene masks of the Dan are in strong contrast to the expressionistic, sometimes fantastically baroque forms of the Gere pieces. The

Page 295. Bronze relief from Benin.

Gere, and Guro masks are so widespread and their influence goes so deep that they have completely taken the place that elsewhere is reserved for statues.

It would lead us too far afield to enter more deeply into the religious character of African sculpture. That it is not exclusively ritualistic is proved by the hundreds of objects of secular sculpture, especially those in applied art. They take the form of handsomely worked weaving pulleys, cups, spoons, mortars, drums, doors, locks, chairs, boxes, pipes, combs, neckrests, quivers, and many other objects.

SPIRIT AND STYLE By means of the formal aspects of the work, the sculpture of Africa can be classified under several clearly demarcated styles. Although the concepts of "style" and "tribe" do not completely coincide, the fact emerges that there are not many autonomous sculpture-producing peoples without a style of their own. The number of sculptural styles is remarkably high. The presumption cannot be excluded that this could partly result from the feeling of belonging together that is so strong in primitive communities, and from the related need to differentiate, on the artistic level as well, among the potentially hostile others. But whatever the source of the great differences in style, the many styles so far recognized run through all gradations: from a rather idealized realism through a distorted expressionism to an extreme "abstract" design, with many ramifications along the way. Thoroughgoing naturalistic vision is rather rare in African sculpture. We find instances of it in the well-known bronze and terracotta heads of ancient Ife (and in the wooden images of the dead of the present-day Yoruba), as well as among the Ekoi and Bekom. Realistic tendencies were present in the former Nok and Esie cultures and, in part, in the court art of Benin; and also among such tribes as the Fon, Baule, Bakongo, Mangbetu, etc. In other cases fidelity to nature is confined to the representation of the head, with the natural proportions of the entire figure no longer adhered to, or realism is concentrated on some typical details relating to physiological or other specific qualities of the ethnic group.

23

aggressive Basongye fetishes are quite different from the Baluba figures, which are sunk in meditation. Earlier attempts at classification on the basis of physical environment—contrasting a barer sculpture, based on ideas, of the savanna tribes of the Sudan with a heavier sculpture, based on nature, of the inhabitants of West and Central Africa—are far from describing an actual situation. The sculpture of the various ethnic groups of Mali is not always strict and ascetic, nor is the work of the rain-forest dwellers always fleshy and exuberant in design. In both regions the exceptions are legion.

Some observers at the outset of this century, on being suddenly confronted with African sculpture, thought that the "Negro sculptor" rejoiced in complete plastic freedom. This opinion did not last long. Far from enjoying any such liberty, the sculptor is bound by a number of prescriptions enforced on him by the group within which he lives, thinks, and works.

The mental and material worlds of the artist, as well as the materials used and the technique applied, entail consequences that together determine the form and content of African sculpture. We have pointed out that it is an art linked to the tribe and based mainly on religion. Both facts go hand in hand with a tendency toward a clearly visible conservatism. Primitive societies are notoriously averse to innovation, and cultural objects in particular are very little subject to change. The fact that the sculptor is bound to the conventional stylistic pattern of his group does not at all signify that individual vision, based on skill of hand, expressive power, and feeling, is wanting completely. Within the framework of the imposed requirements, there is always room for the creative impulses of the artist to move freely. In fact, the personality of the sculptor can be so strongly expressed that his work can be readily distinguished from other sculpture of the same kind.

25   27

Agni of Krinjabo, Ivory Coast. Fragment of a full figure representing a deceased person. About 8 inches high. 27. Terracotta head, belonging to the Nok culture of Nigeria, which probably flourished from about 400 B.C.

to A.D. 200. 28. Baked pottery head, found in Ife. Another example of realism. Like the bronze heads, the terracotta statues were produced between the 12th and 14th centuries.

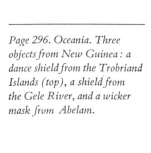

24

24. Brass figure of a horseman, an Ashanti "gold weight," Ivory Coast. Representation of the proverb: "Once the axe has struck off the head of the condemned man, he has nothing more to fear." 25. Detail of a half figure, carved in sandstone, from Sierra Leone. About 7¹/₂ inches high. 26. Black earthenware head, found among the

Page 296. Oceania. Three objects from New Guinea: a dance shield from the Trobriand Islands (top), a shield from the Gele River, and a wicker mask from Abelam.

26

28

We have said that the materials and technique influence the formal aspect of the sculpture. For example, in making a wooden figure the artist starts with a cylindrical block. As a rule, the head is carved first (being in every respect the most important part of the image), and only thereafter is the rest of the body freed from the wooden cylinder. A characteristic disproportion in the parts of the body (head too large and limbs too small) is a frequent result. Since the sculpture is intended primarily to maintain and conserve a system of life, with the instrinsic value of a figure dependent on completely separate factors, this absence of natural proportions does not present any difficulties either for the sculptor or for the viewer or the person giving the commission. Equally conspicuous is the fact that the statues and masks are virtually always conceived quite frontally, both halves being worked out identically: hence the strikingly static, hieratic, and monumental aspect of so many pieces of sculpture. The characteristic aesthetic value of African sculpture is based not least on a purged, essentially adynamic formal language.

With simple plastic means, supported only by thorough mastery of materials and technique, the African artist is often able to create a subtle play of volumes, surfaces, and lines, which speaks strongly to the European observer precisely because it usually remains sober. Although the concept of "beauty" is certainly not strange to the African, it is evident that the work he has produced is much more, in his eyes, a utilitarian object. This does not preclude many artists from striving toward a final result whose artistic significance as such is immediately obvious.

29. Wood panel with three female figures in high relief. Collected among the Dogon, Mali. About 15 inches high.

30. Wooden housing for weaving pulley of the Senufo, Ivory Coast, with a sensitively stylized head in the form of a toucan bird. About 9½ inches high.

31. Pipe bowl of baked clay, from the so-called Grassland of the Cameroons, possibly made by the Bamun. 32. So-called mouse oracle of the Baule, Ivory Coast, with a seated figure whose proportions, except for the head, are reproduced quite naturally. Wood, about 23½ inches high. 33. Wooden cup in the form of a human head, by the Bakuba, Congo. One of the many specimens of applied art carved by this tribe.

OCEANIA

Melanesia

Melanesia is an extremely interesting region for its primitive art. The numerous objects of art and their enormous diversity are overwhelming. Many were made especially for religious and ceremonial purposes, and gave the artists full opportunity to show their creative power. Objects for daily use were usually given attractive forms, enhanced by the application of ornament, often very fine.

NEW GUINEA In western New Guinea, in the Maccluer Gulf region, rock paintings of various kinds have been found. Indonesian traits can be perceived in the wooden sculpture, especially in the statues of Waigeo Island.

In northwestern New Guinea, the Geelvink Bay region is the domain of the *korwar*, the soul image that also plays a dominant role in decorative art. Along with the *korwar* and often in combination with it, a second characteristic of Geelvink Bay carvings are the arabesques that are reminiscent of Indonesia. These characteristics no longer apply to the east of Cape D'Urville. Wood sculpture in northern New Guinea has its own forms and traits, both along the coast and in the area around Lake Sentani. Monumental houseposts, statues of ancestors, roof decorations, etc., are examples. Men, fish, and animals are used as decorative motifs, as well as the important spiral motif. This is attested by many decorated wooden objects, as well as by paintings on pieces of tapa (cloth made of beaten tree bast).

In Northeast New Guinea the art of the Sepik River region has attracted attention by its incredible wealth of forms, the great size of some wood sculptures, and its strong sense of the dramatic. The secret societies, the great huts for the men (centers of religious life), and the belief in supernatural beings have been very important in the development of this art. Among the best-known works of art are statues of ancestors, ceremonial "stools," suspension hooks, masks, wooden stops of sacred flutes, wooden ridge and gable figures, large and smaller drums, canoe prows, pottery, what are called portrait skulls, and many ornaments and amulets.

The art of the Abelam is based on the cult and culture of the yam. The sacred village house is the center of religious life, in which the statues of the ancestors of the clan and the family are displayed and other sacral objects are kept. Along with the many interesting wood sculptures, the spirit masks and yam masks woven of rattan, and the painted sago-leaf sheaths, are important.

As in the Sepik Basin, secret societies have stimulated art in the Tami region. The Tami style is marked by its angular forms and taut decorative lines, while the human figures are shown with heads sunk between the shoulders. The art of the Massim region in eastern New Guinea lacks the emotional traits of the Sepik art; it is an art of lines, with lines and forms harmonizing remarkably. The prow ornaments, dance shields, clubs, and lime spatulas are familiar.

In southeast New Guinea the magic shields have first place among the woodcarving of the tribes on the Gulf of Papua. The traditional type of face on these shields is also found on the bull roarers, as on the masks of bark cloth which play an important part in periodic dramatic performances. Drums and shields of the Marind-Anim are the best-known woodcarvings of south New Guinea. Products of the art of the many islands in the Torres Straits have long since disappeared. Many woodcarvings have been found in southwest New Guinea. The carved wooden pole for the ceremony of piercing the nose, from the Mimika region, the remarkable spirit canoes and the often very handsomely carved Bis-pale figures from the Asmat district, along with the ancestor statues and carved snakes from the region of the Casuarin Coast, are among the most impressive art products of southwestern New Guinea. To these may be added the fine canoe carvings, the long oars, the shields, drums, dance accessories, and other ceremonial carvings, including bowls. Despite a certain relationship, there are marked differences in style among the carving of the Mimika, Asmat, and Casuarina regions.

1. *Korwar of the Schouten Islands, Geelvink Bay, northwestern New Guinea. A quite recent example.*

1

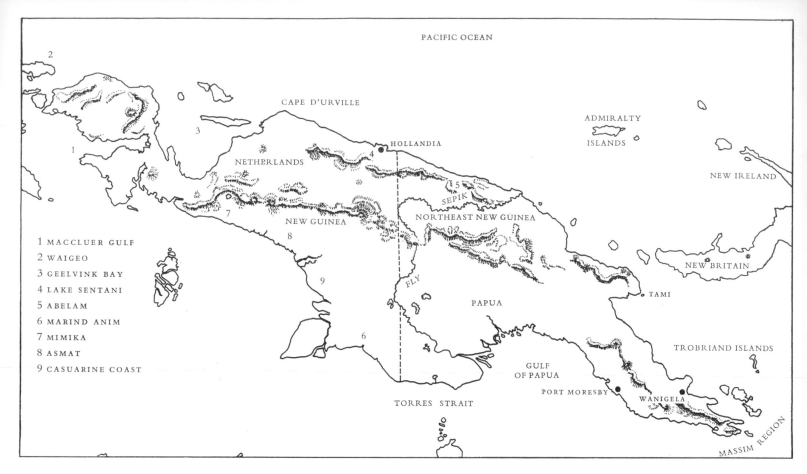

PACIFIC OCEAN

CAPE D'URVILLE

ADMIRALTY
ISLANDS

NEW IRELAND

HOLLANDIA

NETHERLANDS

NEW GUINEA

SEPIK

NORTHEAST NEW GUINEA

NEW BRITAIN

TAMI

FLY

PAPUA

TROBRIAND ISLANDS

GULF
OF PAPUA

PORT MORESBY

WANIGELA

TORRES STRAIT

MASSIM REGION

1 MACCLUER GULF
2 WAIGEO
3 GEELVINK BAY
4 LAKE SENTANI
5 ABELAM
6 MARIND ANIM
7 MIMIKA
8 ASMAT
9 CASUARINE COAST

NEW BRITAIN Masks are among the main works of art in New Britain. Two types of ceremonial masks are known from the mountain people of the Baining, each consisting of a bamboo frame covered with painted bark cloth. The *mendas* type represents a mythical being in the form of a great head with protruding mouth. The *miaus* type is almost cylindrical in form, varying greatly in size. Among the Sulka on the south coast, the development of the masks has been due to the existence of secret societies. The mask frames are covered with joined strips of leaves or brightly colored strips of pith. Of an entirely different type are the so-called skull masks of the Gazelle Peninsula. Wooden masks, completely different from the types mentioned above, have also been found.

3

2. Fragment of a doorpost with a crocodile, from a demolished bachelor house on the island of Djamna, northern New Guinea. As a rule,

2

the crocodile head points downward. 3. Tapa painted in the style of the Humboldt Bay–Sentani region, northern New Guinea.

ADMIRALTY ISLANDS Among the many objects carved out of wood on the Admiralty Islands, the bowls have become famous as works of art. In addition to the type cut out of a single piece (usually in the form of a stylized bird), there is the most famous type of all, with spiral handles carved separately and attached later. Human beings or heads, dogs, and crocodiles are important motifs in decorative art. In addition to wood, the artists have used other materials such as shell, tortoise shell, calabash, and the paste of finely crushed parinarium nuts.

The beautiful wooden spears of the St. Matthias Islands, each forming a unit with a piece of bamboo attached at the rear, have a place of their own among the artistic works of Melanesia.

NEW IRELAND Northern New Ireland has been an important woodcarving center. The *malagan* festivals in honor of the dead have had a stimulating effect. This carved work is fascinating because of the fantastic forms of panels, statues, dance accessories, and various masks. Of the latter, the *tatanua* mask for the fertility dances has become well known. Other notable woodcarvings are the *alut nut*, a remarkable friction instrument, and the imposing *uli* (ancestor statue). The chalk statues from the south, though simple, are impressive. The fine shell armlets (principally from the Namatanai chain of islands off the east coast of New Ireland) and handsome *kapkap* ornaments of sea shells and tortoise shell are famous.

SOLOMON ISLANDS The Solomon Islands, which extend in a double row for nine hundred miles, present many differences in culture and art. The importance of the initiation rites in the northwest has led, among other things, to the making of large wooden statues representing supernatural beings. A characteristic technique was the relief work using the motif of the *kokorra*; this image of a male figure with drawn-up knees has been carved in varying aspects on many objects. In the central island group the war canoes and black-tinted carvings were dramatically ornamented with inlaid bits of mother-of-pearl.

One of the best-known types of wood sculpture is the *musumusu*, a small head fastened to the bow of a war canoe just above the waterline. Typical of San Cristobal in the southeast are the wooden bowls in the shape of a bird and the clubs with sickle-shaped blades. Shell ornaments were made in great numbers; the *kapkap* ornaments of the central group are very pretty.

As for the woodcarvings of Santa Cruz, mention should be made of the characteristic dance clubs, the painted neckrests, and the carefully worked arrowheads. The tortoise-shell motif of the *kapkap* ornament differs completely from that of the other Solomon Islands and New Ireland.

NEW HEBRIDES The New Hebrides have a rigidly stratified society, and the efforts of ambitious men to get into a higher class have had a stimulating effect on art. In addition to the large number of pigs required for social climbing, the prescribed initiation feast called for the presence of important ancestors in the form of ancestor statues, which were carved out of hard wood or tree fern. Enormous slit drums made for the feast were set up on the site. The use of various types of masks was furthered by the existence of secret societies.

4

5

4. Ancestor statue from the Sepik coastal region, Northeast New Guinea. Beginning of 20th century. 5. Suspension hook from the Middle Sepik region. Hooks of this sort are still found.

NEW CALEDONIA Ancestor worship was of fundamental importance for the art of New Caledonia. It was best expressed in the architectural woodcarvings, such as the heavy doorposts (*talé*) of the houses of important people. Spirits of deceased ancestors who wished to protect the inhabitants of the house found an abode in the *talé*; accordingly, the top portion of the *talé* consisted of a powerfully carved human head. To the same category belonged the carvings on the roofs of the round houses. On the other hand, ancestor statues have been found that are not architectonic. The typical wooden masks with their huge and usually sharply hooked nose, their long beard, and enormous head of hair are very impressive indeed in their full force and vitality. Although the art of New Caledonia was in the main a figurative art, other objects too, such as ceremonial axes and decorated bamboo tubes, are famed for their artistic merits.

FIJI ISLANDS The Fiji Islanders were outstanding woodworkers. The round wooden *kava* bowls have a certain dignity; the oil bowls, too, are beautiful. Eloquent forms of their own for wooden clubs were developed. Great originality was shown in pottery.

7   8

6

Micronesia

Micronesian art has not at all that wealth of forms so characteristic in Melanesian art. Simplicity of form is the main characteristic of the relatively few wooden sculptures. Micronesian art is chiefly decorative.

CAROLINE ISLANDS From time immemorial the inhabitants of the western and central Carolines have been skillful seafarers and boatbuilders, qualities that they shared with most Micronesian islanders. Simplicity was the mark not only of objects for daily use, of which the charming wooden bowls of Yap and Palau, sometimes inlaid with pieces of nautilus shell, are such excellent examples; the objects of ceremonial and religious nature had the same stamp. A striking instance of this is the *tino* of Nukuoro Island. The gable masks found on Lukunor are equally impressive in their simplicity; in the old Palau society, the gables of the communal houses were adorned with carvings and paintings.

Among the Micronesian wooden dishes, those of Wuvulu and Aua are outstanding for their special characteristic forms.

In the eastern Carolines weaving was most developed on Kusaie, but the products were limited to ornamented girdles for women. The carved dance paddles of Ponape are well known for their decorative incised pattern standing out against the dark-tinted blade.

MARSHALL ISLANDS, GILBERT ISLANDS The art of mat-weaving was well developed in the Marshall Islands. Decoration was confined to the application of borders with geometrical patterns.

Tattooing was highly developed. In the Gilbert Islands, basketry was on a high level. Decorative art was formerly principally practiced in the tattooing of men and women, but the custom was never general.

MARIANA ISLANDS Archaeological investigations on some islands of the Mariana group have shown that the inhabitants were once acquainted with the art of the potter.

Polynesia

Along with the many woodcarvings, the painting of tapa (beaten bark cloth) and tattooing were important aspects of Polynesian art. Naturally, local conceptions and traditions left their mark on the art of the various island groups. Virtually everywhere the human figure, in local traditional style, played a part in this art, which was decorative in nature to a great extent.

SAMOA Samoa, a group of islands in western Polynesia, has among its woodcarvings various types of clubs. Some have a unilaterally or bilaterally serrated upper portion, while in other types this has the form of a paddle or a flattened mushroom, decorated at the same time with small geometrical motifs. Other examples of woodcarvings are the finely shaped *kava* bowls and elegant neckrests. The pieces of tapa, often of great size, are decorated by hand or with the aid of a matrix. Reddish brown, purple, and dark brown are the principal colors.

TONGA ARCHIPELAGO The art of the Tonga Archipelago is mainly a decorative art. It is strongly reminiscent of that of Samoa. In contrast to the clubs of Samoa, which are often remarkable in form, those of Tonga are much simpler, but have a finely executed geometrical decoration in which anthropomorphic and zoomorphic figures frequently appear.

COOK ISLANDS A characteristic feature of the art of the Cook Islands was the extensive use of geometrical motifs in woodcarving, basketry, and decorative painting of various objects. The ceremonial paddles and axes are outstanding in the domain of carving. The strikingly handsome polished blades were fastened to characteristic wood shafts, which were completely decorated with deeply incised geometrical motifs. Some types are said to have symbolized the god Tane.

EASTER ISLAND Everyone knows the large statues, cut out of soft tuff (volcanic rock) and found on the crater slopes of Rano-raraku volcano and on the terraces of the dead (*ahu*) of the various clans. Scarcity of first-class material had great influence on the forms of the objects carved of wood, and the difficulties were resolved in an artistic manner. Among the splendidly executed human figures, the statues of males are notable for their protruding thoraxes, with clearly marked ribs and vertebrae. Also of note are the beautiful sickle-shaped pectorals and the dance paddles, whose blades suggest a strongly stylized human face. The petroglyphs or carvings on rock are fascinating, most of them representing a being that is half-human and half-bird.

9

10

6. Ceremonial "stool," from Awatib; typical product of the middle Sepik region, Northeast New Guinea, collected in the winter of 1909–10.
7. Mask with totem bird, Sepik region, probably collected at the beginning of this century; now completely disappeared.
8. Wooden stop of sacred flute. Carved in the style characteristic of the region of the Yuat River, Northeast New Guinea. Early 20th century.
9. Ritual figure, named Maira, with arms in the form of hornbill birds, from Abelam, Northeast New Guinea. Figures of this kind are still being produced.
10. Neckrest in characteristic Tami style, Northeast New Guinea.

31

30

33

32

31. Basalt pestle, head decorated with tiki motifs. Marquesas Islands, 19th century.

28. Ceremonial paddle from Easter Island, 19th century. 29. Neck ornament, plaited human hair, and ivory pendant. Hawaii.
30. Head of a heavy wooden club, with tiki heads and tiki motifs. Marquesas Islands.

32. Head of a Maori club, known as taiaha, New Zealand. Beginning of this century ; no longer found. 33. Shield from West Australia, beginning of this century.

28

29

BIBLIOGRAPHY

1 RENAISSANCE

Benesch, O., *The Art of the Renaissance in Northern Europe*, Cambridge, Mass., and Oxford, 1945

Burckhardt, J. C., *The Civilization of the Renaissance in Italy*, 3d rev. ed., London, 1950

Castiglione, B., *The Book of the Courtier*, London, 1902; New York, 1903

Cellini, B., *Autobiography*, London, 1960

Cennini, C., *Il Libro dell'Arte*, tr. and ed. by D. V. Thompson, Jr., New Haven and Oxford, 1932–33

Gelder, H. A. E. van, *The Two Reformations in the 16th Century: A Study of the Religious Aspects and Consequences of Renaissance and Humanism*, The Hague, 1961

Leonardo, *The Notebooks of Leonardo da Vinci*, 2 vols., New York and London, 1938

Lucas-Dubreton, J., *Daily Life in Florence in the Time of the Medici*, New York and London, 1961

Nugent, E. M., *The Thought and Culture of the English Renaissance*, Cambridge, 1956

Panofsky, E., *Renaissance and Renascences in Western Art*, Stockholm, 1960

—, *Studies in Iconology*, New York and Oxford, 1939

Pater, W., *The Renaissance*, New York (no date); London, 1912

Vasari, G., *The Lives of the Painters, Sculptors, and Architects*, 4 vols., New York and London, 1927

Wölfflin, H., *Classic Art*, 2d ed., London, 1953

Architecture
Ackerman, J. S., *The Architecture of Michelangelo*, 2 vols., New York and London, 1961

Alberti, L. B., *Ten Books on Architecture*, London, 1955

Busch, H., and B. Lohse (eds.), *Renaissance Europe*, London, 1961

Harvey, J. H., *Tudor Architecture*, London, 1957

Painting
Alberti, L. B., *On Painting*, New Haven and London, 1956

Antal, F., *Florentine Painting and Its Social Background*, London, 1948

Berenson, B., *Italian Painters of the Renaissance*, London, 1953

—, *Italian Pictures of the Renaissance*, 2 vols., London, 1957

Borsook, E., *The Mural Painters of Tuscany*, London, 1960

Clark, K., *Leonardo da Vinci*, New York and Cambridge, 1939

—, *Piero della Francesca*, London, 1951

Crowe, J. A., and G. B. Cavalcaselle, *A History of Painting in Italy*, 6 vols., London, 1903–14

—, *A History of Painting in North Italy*, 3 vols., New York and London, 1912

De Tolnay, C., *Michelangelo*, 5 vols., Princeton, N. J., and Oxford, 1945–60

Dewald, E. T., *Italian Painting*, 1200–1600, New York, 1961

Dimier, L., *French Painting in the 16th Century*, New York, 1911

Fischel, O., *Raphael*, 2 vols., London, 1948

Freedberg, S. J., *Painting of the High Renaissance in Rome and Florence*, 2 vols., Cambridge, Mass., and Oxford, 1961

Panofsky, E., *Albrecht Dürer*, 3d ed., 2 vols., Princeton, N. J., and Oxford, 1948

—, *Early Netherlandish Painting*, 2 vols., Cambridge, Mass., 1953

Pope-Hennessy, J., *Fra Angelico*, London, 1952

—, *The Complete Works of Paolo Uccello*, London, 1950

Richter, G. M., *Giorgio da Castelfranco (Giorgione)*, Chicago and Cambridge, England, 1937

Ring, G., *A Century of French Painting*, London, 1949

Tietze, H., *Tintoretto*, London, 1948

Tietze-Conrat, E., *Mantegna*, London, 1955

Wethey, H. E., *El Greco and His School*, Princeton, N. J., 1962

Sculpture
Janson, H. W., *The Sculpture of Donatello*, 2 vols., Princeton, N. J., 1957; Oxford, 1958

Krautheimer, R., and T. Krautheimer-Hess, *Lorenzo Ghiberti*, Princeton, N. J., 1956

Molesworth, H. D., *Sculpture in England. Renaissance to Early 19th Century*, New York and London, 1951

Pope-Hennessy, J., *Italian Renaissance Sculpture*, London, 1958

Prints
Friedländer, M. J., *Early Netherlandish Painting from Van Eyck to Breugel*, London, 1956

Hind, A. M., *History of Engraving and Etching*, 3d rev. ed., Boston, 1927

—, *An Introduction to a History of Woodcut*, Boston, 1935

Ivins, W. M., Jr., *How Prints Look*, New York, 1943

2 SEVENTEENTH CENTURY

Denis, V., G. Knuttel, and R. Meischke, "Flemish and Dutch Art" in *Encyclopedia of World Art*, Vol. V, New York, 1961

Gardner, A. H., *Outline of English Architecture*, London, 1947

Gerson, H., and E. H. ter Kuile, *Art and Architecture in Belgium, 1600–1800*, Harmondsworth and Baltimore, 1960

Whinney, M., and O. Millar, *English Art, 1625–1714*, Oxford, 1957

Willey, B., *The Seventeenth-Century Background*, London, 1934; New York, 1950

Architecture
Blunt, A., *Art and Architecture in France, 1500–1700*, Harmondsworth and Baltimore, 1953

Busch, H., and B. Lohse (eds.), *Baroque Europe*, New York and London, 1962

Brown, M., *American Painting from the Armory Show to the Depression*, Princeton, N. J., 1955; Oxford, 1956
Chamot, M., *Modern Painting in England*, London, 1937
Duthuit, G., *The Fauvist Painters*, New York, 1950
Goldwater, R., *Primitivism in Modern Painting*, New York, 1938
Gray, C., *Cubist Aesthetic Theories*, Baltimore, 1953; Oxford, 1954
Haftmann, W., *Painting in the Twentieth Century*, 2 vols., New York and London, 1961
Jaffé, H. L. C., *De Stijl, 1917–1931*, London, 1956
Janis, S., *Abstract and Surrealist Art in America*, New York, 1944
Kandinsky, V., *Concerning the Spiritual in Art*, New York, 1947
Moholy-Nagy, L., *The New Vision*, London, 1939
Mondrian, P. C., *Plastic Art and Pure Plastic Art*, New York, 1945
Motherwell, R., *The Dada Painters and Poets*, New York, 1951
Read, H. E., *Art Now*, London, 1948
—, *Surrealism*, London, 1936
Ritchie, A. C., *Abstract Painting and Sculpture in America*, New York, 1951
Rosenblum, R., *Cubism and Twentieth-Century Art*, New York and London, 1961
Soby, J. T., *After Picasso*, New York, 1935
—, *Modern Art and the New Past*, Norman, Okla., 1957
Sweeney, J. J., *Plastic Redirections in Twentieth-Century Painting*, Chicago and Cambridge, England, 1934
Wight, F. S., *Milestones of American Painting in Our Century*, New York and London, 1949

Sculpture
Broadbent, T., *Sculpture To-day in Great Britain*, London, 1947
Giedion-Welcker, C., *Modern Plastic Art*, Zurich, 1937; new rev. ed., *Contemporary Sculpture*, New York, 1961
Martin, J. L., B. Nicholson, and N. Gabo (eds.), *Circle*, London, 1937
Ramsden, E. H., *Sculpture - Theme and Variations*, London, 1953
Ritchie, A. C., *Sculpture of the Twentieth Century*, New York, 1952

Cinema
Davy, C. (ed.), *Footnotes to the Film*, New York, 1937

Photography
Eisenstein, S., *Film Form: Essays in Film Theory*, New York, 1949; London, 1951
Manvell, R., *Film*, rev. ed., Harmondsworth, 1946
Pollack, P., *The Picture History of Photography*, New York, 1958

Industrial Design
Dreyfuss, H., *Industrial Design: A Pictorial Accounting, 1929–57*, New York, 1956
Nelson, G., *Problems of Design*, New York, 1957
Nervi, P. L., *Structures*, New York, 1956

12 INDIAN ART

Coomaraswamy, A. K., *History of Indian and Indonesian Art*, New York and London, 1927
Goetz, H., *India*, London, 1959; New York, 1961
Ingholt, H., *Gandharan Art in Pakistan*, New York, 1957
Kempers, A. J. B., *Ancient Indonesian Art*, Oxford, 1960

Kramrisch, S., *The Art of India*, London, 1954
Kramrisch, S., *The Art of Nepal*, New York, 1964
Marshall, J. H., *Mohenjo-daro and the Indus Civilization*, London, 1931
Rowland, B., *The Art and Architecture of India: Buddhist, Hindu, Jain*, Harmondsworth, 1953
Smith, V., *A History of Fine Art in India and Ceylon*, 3d ed., Bombay, 1961
Welch, S., *The Art of Mughal India*, New York
Zimmer, H., *Myth and Symbols in Indian Art and Civilization*, New York, 1946
Zimmer, H., and J. Campbell, *Art of Indian Asia*, 2 vols., New York, 1955

Architecture
Brown, P., *Indian Architecture—Buddhist and Hindu Periods*, Bombay, 1943
Kramrisch, S., *The Hindu Temple*, Calcutta, 1946

Painting
Lee, S. E., *Rajput Painting*, New York

Sculpture
Bachhofer, L., *Early Indian Sculpture*, 2 vols., New York, 1929
Kar, C., *Classical Indian Sculpture, 300 B.C. to A.D. 500*, London, 1950
Lippe, A., *The Art of India: Stone Sculpture*, New York
Rowland, B., Jr., *The Evolution of the Buddha Image*, New York
Rowland, B., Jr., *Gandhara Sculpture from Pakistan Museums*, New York

13 CHINA

Bachhofer, L., *A Short History of Chinese Art*, London, 1946
Cahill, J., *The Art of Southern Sung China*, New York
Creel, H. G., *The Birth of China*, rev. ed., New York, 1954
Fontein, J., "Chinese Art," in *Encyclopedia of World Art*, Vol. III, New York, 1960
Fry, R., et al., *Chinese Art. An Introductory Handbook*, London, 1949
Jourdain, M., and S. Jenyns, *Chinese Export Art*, London, 1950
Lee, S. E., *A History of Far Eastern Art*, New York, 1964
Willetts, W., *Chinese Art*, 2 vols., Harmondsworth and Baltimore, 1958

Architecture
Sickman, L., and A. Soper, *The Art and Architecture of China*, Baltimore, 1956
Siren, O., *Gardens of China*, New York, 1949

Painting
Cohn, W., *A History of Chinese Painting*, London, 1951
Gray, B., and J. B. Vincent, *Buddhist Cave Painting at Tun Huang*, London, 1959
Kuo Hsi, *An Essay on Landscape Painting*, London, 1935
Lee, S., *Chinese Landscape Painting*, rev. ed., Cleveland and London, 1962
Sirén, O., *A History of Early Chinese Painting*, 2 vols., London, 1933
—, *A History of Later Chinese Painting*, 2 vols., London, 1938

Sculpture
Lion-Goldschmidt, D., and J.-C. Moreau-Gobard, *Chinese Arts: Bronze, Jade, Sculpture, Ceramics*, New York, 1960; London, 1961
Lodge, J. E., A. G. Wenley, and J. A. Pope, *A Descriptive and Illustrative Catalogue of Chinese Bronze*, Washington, D.C., 1946

Rudolph, R., *Han Tomb Art of West China*, Berkeley, Calif., and Cambridge, 1951

Sirén, O., *Chinese Sculpture form the Fifth to the Fourteenth Centuries*, 4 vols., London, 1925

Ceramics

Hobson, R. L., *Handbook of Pottery and Porcelain of the Far East*, London, 1948

Honey, W. B., *The Ceramic Art of China and Other Countries of the Far East*, London, 1945

Volker, T., *Porcelain and the Dutch East India Company*, Amsterdam, 1954

Minor Arts

Hansford, H., *Chinese Jade Carving*, London, 1950

Herberts, K., *Oriental Lacquer: Art and Technique*, New York and London, 1962

Jenyns, R. S., and W. Watson, *Chinese Arts: The Minor Arts*, New York, 1963

Loehr, M., *Chinese Bronze Age Weapons*, London, 1956

Salmony, A., *Archaic Chinese Jades*, Chicago, 1952

Simmons, P., *Chinese Patterned Silks*, New York, 1948

14 JAPAN

Asahi Shimbun, *Fine Arts of Kamakura*, Tokyo, 1958

Paine, R. T., and A. Soper, *The Art and Architecture of Japan*, Harmondsworth and Baltimore, 1955

Tani, S., "Japanese Art," in *Encyclopedia of World Art*, Vol. VIII, New York, 1963

Terry, C. S. (ed.), *Masterworks of Japanese Art*, Rutland, Vt., 1956

Tokyo National Museum, *Pageant of Japanese Art*, 6 vols., Tokyo, 1954

Warner, L., *The Enduring Art of Japan*, Cambridge, Mass., 1952

Yashiro, Y., *2000 Years of Japanese Art*, New York and London, 1958

Architecture

Drexler, A., *The Architecture of Japan*, New York, 1955

Newson, S., *A Thousand Years of Japanese Gardens*, Tokyo, 1953

Soper, A. C., *The Evolution of Buddhist Architecture in Japan*, Princeton, N. J., 1942

Sculpture

Kuno, T., *Ancient Sculpture in the Hōryū-ji*, Tokyo, 1958

Painting

Minamoto, H., *Screen Painting of the Momyama Period*, London, 1935

Muensterberg, H., *The Landscape Painting of China and Japan*, Tokyo, 1955

Tanaka, I., *The Art of Kōrin*, Tokyo, 1959

Toda, K., *Japanese Scroll Painting*, Chicago and Cambridge, England, 1935

Prints

Binyon, L., and J. J. O'B. Sexton, *Japanese Colour Prints*, rev. ed., London, 1960

Fujikake, S., *Japanese Woodblock Prints*, Tokyo, 1953

Gray, B., *Japanese Woodcuts*, London, 1957

Hillier, J., *Japanese Masters of the Colour Print*, London, 1954

—, *The Japanese Print*, London, 1960

Holloway, O. E., *Graphic Art of Japan*, London, 1956

Ishida, M., *Japanese Buddhist Prints*, New York

Iwamiya, T., and D. Richie, *Katachi: Japanese Pattern and Design in Wood, Paper, and Clay*, New York

Meinertzhagen, F., *The Art of the Netsuke Carver*, London, 1956

Ceramics

Koyama, F., *The Story of Old Chinese Ceramics*, New York, 1949

Koyama, F., and J. Figess, *2000 Years of Oriental Ceramics*, New York

Mitsuoka, T., *Ceramic Art of Japan*, Tokyo, 1954

Minor Arts

Feddersen, M., *Japanese Decorative Art*, New York and London, 1962

Lee, S. E., *Japanese Decorative Style*, Cleveland, Ohio, 1961

Malm, W. P., *Japanese Music and Musical Instruments*, Tokyo, 1959

Noma, S., *Masks*, Rutland, Vt., 1957

Ohara, H., *Everyone's Flower Arrangement*, Tokyo, 1957

15 PRE-COLUMBIAN ART

Kelemen, P., *Medieval American Art*, New York, 1956

Lothrop, S. K., W. E. Foshag, and J. Mahler, *Pre-Columbian Art*, London, 1957

The Andes

Bennett, W. E., *Ancient Arts of the Andes*, New York, 1954

Bennett, W. C., and J. B. Bird, *Andean Culture History*, New York, 1949

Bushnell, A. H. S., *Peru*, London, 1956

Imbelloni, J., "Andean Protohistory," in *Encyclopedia of World Art*, Vol. I, New York, 1959

Lehmann, W., and H. Doering, *The Art of Old Peru*, London, 1924

Middle America

Covarrubias, M., *Indian Art of Mexico and Central America*, New York, 1946

Lothrop, S. K., *Coclé, an Archaeological Study of Central Panama*, Cambridge, Mass., 1937

Medioni, G., and M. T. Pinto, *Art in Ancient Mexico*, New York and Oxford, 1941

Morley, S. G., *The Ancient Maya*, Palo Alto, Calif., 1946; Oxford, 1947

Proskouriakoff, T. A., *Study of Classic Maya Sculpture*, Washington, D.C., 1950

Spinden, H. J., *A Study of Maya Art*, Cambridge, Mass., 1924

Thompson, J. E. S., *The Rise and Fall of Maya Civilization*, Norman, Okla., 1954; London, 1956

Unesco, *Mexico: Pre-Hispanic Paintings*, New York, 1958

Wolf, E. R., *Sons of the Shaking Earth*, Chicago, 1959; Cambridge, 1960

16 NEGRO ART OF AFRICA

Herskovits, M. J., *The Background of African Art*, Denver, 1945

Kochnitzky, L., *Negro Art of the Belgian Congo*, New York, 1948

Maesen, A., "Bantu Cultures," in *Encyclopedia of World Art*, Vol. II, New York, 1960

Murdock, G. P., *Africa: Its Peoples and Their Culture History*, New York, 1959

Rattray, R. S., *Religion and Art in Ashanti*, Oxford, 1927

Schmalenbach, W., *African Art*, New York and London, 1954

Trowell, M. *African Design*, London, 1929

Sculpture

Bascom, W. R., and P. Gebauer, *Handbook of West African Art*, Milwaukee, 1953

Elisofon, E., and W. Fagg, *The Sculpture of Africa*, New York and London, 1958

Kjersmeier, C., *African Negro Sculptures*, London, 1948

Plass, M., *African Tribal Sculpture*, Philadelphia, 1956

Radin, P., and J. J. Sweeney, *African Folktales and Sculpture*, New York, 1953

Segy, L., *African Sculpture Speaks*, New York, 1952

Trowell, K. M., *Classical African Sculpture*, New York and London, 1954

Underwood, L., *Bronzes of West Africa*, London, 1949

—, *Figures in Wood of West Africa*, London, 1947

—, *Masks of West Africa*, London, 1948

Wingert, P. S., *The Sculpture of Negro Africa*, Oxford, 1951; New York, 1959

17 OCEANIA

Adam, L., *Primitive Art*, London, 1954

Guiart, J., *The Arts of the South Pacific*, New York and London, 1963

Linton, R., P. S. Wingert, and R. d'Harnoncourt, *Arts of the South Seas* New York, 1946

Wingert, P. S., *Art of the South Pacific Islands*, New York and London, 1953

Melanesia

Firth, R., *Art and Life in New Guinea*, London, 1936

Newton, D., *Art Styles of the Papuan Gulf*, New York, 1961

Micronesia

Linton, R., *Ethnology of Polynesia and Micronesia*, Chicago, 1926

Polynesia

Buck, P. H., *Arts and Crafts of Hawaii*, Honolulu, 1957

Greiner, R., *Polynesian Decorative Designs*, Honolulu, 1923

Mead, M., *The Maoris and Their Art*, New York, 1945

Australia

McCarthy, F. D., *Australian Aboriginal Decorative Art*, Sydney, 1952

Mountford, C. P., *Art, Myth and Symbolism*, Vol. I, Melbourne, 1956

Read, H. (ed.), *Australia; Aboriginal Paintings in Arnhemland*, Paris, 1954

INDEX

LOCATIONS OF ILLUSTRATED WORKS

1 RENAISSANCE 39 KMV; 41 Bargello, Florence; 42 L; 45 St. Waldetrudis, Bergen; 54 VAM; 58 Cathedral, Prato; 64 L; 67 Vatican; 69 L; 70 Pinacoteca, Parma; 71 Galleria Pitti, Florence; 72 Accademia, Venice; 75 Scuola di San Rocco, Venice; 76 MNN; 77 Accademia, Venice; 78 Musée d'Art et d'Histoire, Geneva; 79, 80 L; 81 BN; 82 L; 83 Long Ford Castle; 84 Museum, Parma; 86 Herzog Anton Ulrich Museum, Brunswick; 87 Escorial, Madrid; 92 KMV; 95 Germanisches Nationalmuseum, Nuremberg; 97 APM; 98 Boymans-Van Beuningen Museum, Rotterdam; 104, 106 L; 107 Sacksische Landesbibliothek, Dresden; 108 KMV; 112 Germanisches Nationalmuseum, Nuremberg; 114 Accademia, Venice; 116 Musée de Condé, Chantilly; 117 NGL; 120 Musée des Arts Décoratifs, Paris; 121 MAHB; 122 VAM.
Page 15 Bargello, Florence; page 16 KMV; page 27 L.

2 SEVENTEENTH CENTURY 28 Bibliothèque Mazarine, Paris; 31 Museo Provincial, Sevilla; 38, 41 L; 42 APM; 44 KMV; 45, 46 Prado, Madrid; 47 APM; 48 Frans Hals Museum, Haarlem; 49 Mauritshuis, The Hague; 50, 51 RA; 52 Mauritshuis, The Hague; 56, 57 Boymans-Van Beuningen Museum, Rotterdam; 58 Mauritshuis, The Hague; 63, 65 APM; 66 Galleria Pitti, Florence; 67 Windsor Castle (copyright H. M. the Queen); 68, 69 APM; 72 Musée Royal des Beaux-Arts, Antwerp; 75 Tretiakov Museum, Moscow; 77 Palais Royal, Paris; 83 L; 85 RA.
Page 53 Frans Hals Museum, Haarlem.

3 ITALIAN BAROQUE 34 Museum of the Villa Borghese, Rome; 36 Pinacoteca, Bologna; 37 Galleria Pizzi, Florence; 40 Galleria, Parma; 41 Palazzo Palavicini Rospigliosi, Rome; 42 Villa Ludovisi, Rome; 43 Pinacoteca, Vatican; 44 Galleria Pizzi, Florence; 45 Pinacoteca, Turin; 46 Uffizi, Florence; 47 Städelsches Kunstinstitut, Frankfurt a.M.; 50 Castel Vecchio, Verona; 51, 52 Gemäldegalerie, Dresden; 53 Museo Grico, Bassano; 54 Accademia Carrara, Bergamo; 55 Galleria Corsini, Rome; 56 KMV; 57 MMA, Kennedy Fund 1910; 58 MNN.
Page 67 San Luigi de Francesi, Rome; page 68 Exhibition Galerie Charpentier, 1947.

4 LOUIS XIV STYLE 1 L; 14 Collection Duchesse de Caylus; 15, 18 L; 19 Wallace Collection, London; 20 Musée Carnavalet, Paris; 21 L; 22 Musée Royal des Beaux-Arts, Brussels; 29 Musée des Arts Décoratifs, Paris; 30 L; 31 Bibliothèque Mazarine, Paris; 32-35 Musée des Arts Décoratifs, Paris; 36, 37 BN; 38 BN, Cabinet des Estampes.
Page 95 L; page 96 Musée du Château de Versailles.

5 EIGHTEENTH CENTURY 1 L; 16 Musée Fabre, Montpellier; 20, 21 Musée Royal des Beaux-Arts, Brussels; 22 Dulwich College Picture Gallery; 23 Cholmondeley Collection, Houghton; 26 Collection Veil-Piccard, Paris; 27 Collection Béhaque; 30 Municipal Museum, Bruges; 32 Prado, Madrid; 35 RA, Print Room; 38 L; 42 Biblioteca Nazionale Centrale, Rome; 47 VAM (Crown Copyright).
Page 105, top, NGL; bottom, L; page 106 Collection Veil-Piccard, Paris.

6 LOUIS XV STYLE 16 L; 18 Barokmuseum, Vienna; 19 L; 20 Banque de France, Paris; 21 Huis Doorn, Doorn; 23 National Museum, Stockholm; 24, 25 Wallace Collection, London; 30 Musée des Arts Décoratifs, Paris; 31 Musée des Beaux-Arts, Tours; 33 Musée des Arts Décoratifs, Paris; 34 Quirinal Rome; 35 RA; 36-38 Musée des Arts Décoratifs, Paris; 39 SM.

Page 123 L; page 124 Musée des Beaux-Arts, Angers.

7 ENGLAND IN THE EIGHTEENTH CENTURY 6 Royal Academy of Art, London; 9 Sir John Soane's Museum; 10, 11, Foundling Hospital, London, 12 NGL; 13 Devonshire Collection, Chatsworth; 14 Tate Gallery, London; 15 National Gallery of Art, Washington, D.C.; 17 National Galleries of Scotland Edinburgh; 18 Musée Cognacq-Jay, Paris; 19 National Museum of Wales, Cardiff; 20, 21 Tate Gallery, London; 22 Kensington Palace, London; 23 NGL; 24 Tate Gallery, London; 25-27 VAM; 28 RA; 29 T. Crowther & Son; 30 Mallet & Son Ltd., London.
Page 137 NGL.

8 LOUIS XVI STYLE 7 Musée Carnavalet, Paris; 8 Bibliothèque Ste-Geneviève, Paris; 9 Musée d'Histoire Naturelle, Paris; 10 Museum, Aix-en-Provence; 13, 14 L; 15 Petit Palais, Paris; 16 L; 17 Museum, St.-Omer; 19 Wallace Collection, London; 20 Musée du Château de Versailles; 21 L; 22 Musée du Château de Versailles; 23 KMV; 24 Museum, Montpellier; 25 Museum, Le Havre; 26 APM; 27 L; 28 Musée du Château de Versailles; 29 Petit Palais, Paris; 30 L; 31-34 BN; 35 Château de Fontainebleau; 36 L; 37 Wallace Collection, London (Crown Copyright); 38 VAM (Crown Copyright); 39 L; 40 Wallace Collection, London (Crown Copyright); 41 RA.

9 EMPIRE 10 Thorvaldsen's Museum, Copenhagen; 19, 20 L; 25 Collection MacIkhenny, Philadelphia; 29 Municipal Museum, Bruges; 33 Musée des Beaux-Arts, Liège; 35 Collection Prof. Dr. S. van Brakel, Utrecht.

10 NINETEENTH CENTURY 23 L; 28 Musée Rodin, Paris; 31, 36 L; 37 Petit Palais, Paris; 38, 39, 41, 42 L; 47, 48 Stedelijk Museum, Amsterdam; 49 Kröller-Müller State Museum, Otterlo; 52 L; 54 Collection Philippe Dotremont; 55 Stedelijk Museum, Amsterdam; 57 Folkwang Museum, Essen; 58 Kunstmuseum, Düsseldorf; 59 Öffentliche Kunstsammlung, Basel; 62 Tate Gallery, London; 64 NGL; 65 Tate Gallery, London; 68 Museum, Dordrecht; 69 Boymans-Van Beuningen Museum, Rotterdam; 71 Private collection, Solothurn; 72 Musée d'Art Moderne, Brussels; 73 Musée Wiertz, Brussels; 74 Museum, Antwerp; 75 Museum, Brussels; 76 Detroit Institute of Arts; 82 MFAB; 83 Tate Gallery, London; 91 Musée de Verre, Liège; 92, 93, 96 Musée des Arts Décoratifs, Paris; 102 Boymans-Van Beuningen Museum, Rotterdam.
Page 185, top, Staatsgalerie, Stuttgart; bottom, NGL; page 186, top, L; bottom, Stedelijk Museum, Amsterdam.

11 TWENTIETH CENTURY 2 GMH (courtesy R. N. Ketterer, Campione d'Italia); 4 Öffentliche Kunstsammlung, Basel; 5 Galerie Louise Leiris, Paris; 8 Museum of Modern Art, New York; 10 Kröller-Müller State Museum, Otterlo; 53 Museum of Modern Art, New York; 63 Stedelijk Museum, Amsterdam; 64 Middelheim Park, Antwerp; 65 Stedelijk Museum, Amsterdam; 68 Städtisches Museum, Wuppertal; 69 Boymans-Van Beuningen Museum, Rotterdam; 73 Collection Mr. and Mrs. Pierre Matisse, New York; 76 Peggy Guggenheim Collection, Venice; 81 Middelheim Park, Antwerp; 83 Museum of Modern Art, New York; 86 Oesterreichische Galerie, Vienna; 87, 90 Stedelijk Museum, Amsterdam; 91 Collection Dr. Max Lütze, Bad Homburg; 92 Boymans-Van Beuningen Museum, Rotterdam (courtesy R. N. Ketterer, Campione d'Italia); 93 Stedelijk Museum, Amsterdam; 97 Wadsworth Atheneum, Hartford (courtesy

Downtown Gallery); 101 Collection Frankland Dark, FRIBA; 102, 103 Stedelijk Museum, Amsterdam; 104 Collection Van Bakel, Waalre; 106 Stedelijk Museum, Amsterdam; 107 Courtesy R. N. Ketterer, Campione d'Italia; 109 Collection Dr. Sabourand, Paris; 110 Collection Dr. Alvar Carrillo Gil; 115, 116 Stedelijk Museum, Amsterdam; 117 GMH; 120 Private collection, Paris; 121 Collection John Lefebre; 123 Galerie Anne Abels, Cologne; 124 World House Galleries; 125 Collection D. Domnick, Stuttgart; 128 Stedelijk Museum, Amsterdam; 129 Museum of Modern Art, New York.
Page 199 Collection Regnault, Laren; page 200 Collection Hannema, Goor; page 215, top, Museum of Modern Art, New York; bottom, Museum of Modern Art New York (Mrs. John D. Rockefeller, Jr., Fund); page 216 Galerie Beyeler, Basel.

12 INDIAN ART 2 Ashmolean Museum, Oxford; 3 Indian Museum, Calcutta; 11 Museum, Madras; 12 Detroit Institute of Arts; 13 Archaeological Museum, Mathura; 15 Musée Guimet, Paris; 16 Indian Museum, Calcutta; 17 Musée Guimet, Paris; 19 Museum, Peshawar; 25 Museum, Djakarta; 26 RA; 28 Museum, Djakarta; 29 BM; 30 Museum, Djakarta; 31 RA.
Pages 239, 240 RA.

13 CHINA 1 NGKC; 2 MAHB; 10 GMH; 12 Collection Mrs. Féron Stoclet, Brussels; 14 Musée Guimet, Paris; 15 MFAB; 16 UMP; 17 MFAB; 18 Collection Mrs. Féron Stoclet, Brussels; 19 UMP; 20 BM; 21, 22 MAHB; 23 UMP; 24 RA; 26 BM; 27, 28 MFAB; 29 Chinese Government Exhibition; 31 MFAB; 32 National Museum, Tokyo; 33 NGKC; 34 MFAB; 35 Museum, Malmö; 36 Östasiastika Museet, Stockholm; 37 RA; 38 MAHB; 39 Formerly Collection P.C. Huang; 40 Minneapolis Institute of Arts, Pillsbury Bequest; 41-43 MAHB; 44 Museum of the School of Fine Arts, Tokyo; 46 RA; 47 VAM (Crown Copyright); 48, 49 MAHB; 50 GMH; 51 BM; 52 GMH; 53, 54 MAHB; 55 Kunstindustrie Museet, Copenhagen; 56 MAHB; 57 VAM (Crown Copyright); 58 Museum, Mariemont; 59 GMH; 60 VAM (Crown Copyright); 61 MAHB; 62 Formerly Collection Maj. Gen. Sir Neill Malcolm (courtesy Royal Academy, London).
Page 253 RA; page 254 RVL.

14 JAPAN 1, 2 NMT; 3 RVL; 4, 6 NMT; 14 Collection Todai-ji, Nara; 15 Collection Jobon-Rendai-ji, Nara; 19 NMT; 25 Formerly Collection Baron Masuda Takashi; 27 Private collection, Japan; 31 Collection Sekido, Tokyo; 34 NMT;

36 MFAB; 37 NMT; 39, 41, 42 RVL; 43 Nezu Museum, Tokyo; 47 Private collection, Amsterdam; 51 Collection Hayashi, Tokyo; 52 Collection Kawaguchi, Tokyo; 53 Collection Hosokawa.
Page 269 MLVR; page 270 RVL.

15 PRE-COLUMBIAN ART 1 BM; 3 Museum für Völkerkunde, Munich; 5 BM; 6, 9, 10 Museo Nacional, Mexico City; 11 Private collection, Netherlands; 15 Merida Museum, Yucatan; 18 Private collection, Netherlands; 25, 26 RVL, Heldring Collection; 27 Lippisches Landesmuseum, Detmold; 28 RVL; 29 Lippisches Landesmuseum, Detmold; 30 MLVR; 31 RVL, Heldring Collection; 35, 36 Lippisches Landesmuseum, Detmold; 38 Landesmuseum, Gretzer Collection, Hannover.
Page 283 BM.

16 NEGRO ART OF AFRICA 1, 2 Collection Dr. Jan Ollers, Stockholm; 3 SEMS; 4 Museum für Völkerkunde, Basel; 5 Collection Dr. Jan Ollers, Stockholm; 6 Royal Museum for Central Africa, Tervuren; 7 Skådespelaren Benkt-Åke Bektsson, Göteborg; 8 Lindenmuseum, Stuttgart; 9 Collection J. Vandenhoute, Oostakker; 10 SEMS; 11 RVL; 12 Collection Mr. and Mrs. Pierre Matisse, New York; 13 Svenska Missions Förbundels Samling; 14, 15 Collection C. Kjersmeier, Copenhagen; 16 Fathers Redemptorists, Antwerp; 17, 18 Royal Museum for Central Africa, Tervuren; 19 Svenska Missions Förbundels Samling; 20 Museum, Malmö; 22 Collection Oni van Ife; 23 SEMS; 24 RVL; 25 BM; 26 Private collection, New York; 27 Jos Museum, Nigeria; 28 Collection Oni van Ife; 29 Musée de l'Homme, Paris; 30 Ethnographic Museum, Antwerp; 31 SEMS; 32 Musée de l'Homme, Paris; 33 Collection Dr. Jan Ollers, Stockholm.
Page 284 MLVR; page 297 KITA.

17 OCEANIA 1 Collection C. J. Gremmee, The Hague; 2 MLVR; 3 Rijksmuseum voor Volkenkunde, Breda; 4 MLVR; 5 Educational Museum, The Hague; 6 MLVR; 7 KITA; 8 Educational Museum, The Hague; 9, 10 MLVR; 11 RVL; 12 KITA; 13, 14 MLVR; 15 BM; 16 KITA; 17 MLVR; 18 RVL; 19 KITA; 20 Musée de l'Homme, Paris; 21, 22 MLVR; 23 RVL; 24-26 MLVR; 27 KITA; 28 BM; 29 MLVR; 30 KITA; 31 Collection Edgar Beer, Brussels; 32 KITA; 33 MLVR.
Page 298 MLVR.

PHOTOGRAPHIC CREDITS

Volume I

1 OLD STONE AGE Archives Photographiques, Paris: 2, 5, 11, 17, 24; P. Graziosi: 9, 23, 29; Laborie, Bergerac: 28, 30-32; Emil Schulthess: 38; Service Communal Des Monuments Historiques, Paris: 10, 14.

2 NEW STONE AGE Elsevier Archives: 1-25.

3 EARLY GERMANIC ART Elsevier Archives: 1-29.

4 EGYPT Ashmolean Museum, Oxford: 61; Michel Audrain, Mission Samivel: 3; L. van Beurden, Amsterdam: 15; Hirmer Verlag, Munich: 6; A. Mekhitarian, Brussels: 55, 57, 59, 60; Van der Veen, Leiden: 49; A. Vigneau: 42; World Press Photo, Amsterdam: 54.

5 MESOPOTAMIA Archives Photographiques, Paris: 9, 10, 14-16, 18, 23; Oriental Institute, University of Chicago: 4; W. van der Randen, Amsterdam: 25.

6 CRETE AND MYCENAE Bildarchiv Foto Marburg: 52; Deutsches Archäologisches Institut, Athens: 42, 47, 49-51; A. van der Heyden, Amsterdam: 33, 34, 36, 39, 40; Hirmer Verlag, Munich: 43, 53, 54; V. & N. Tombazi, Athens: 35.

7 GREECE ACL, Brussels: 102; Archives Photographiques, Paris: 62, 67, 94, 95; Bildarchiv Foto Marburg: 38; British Museum, London: 88, 96-98, 101, 123; Elsevier Archives: 32, 39, 40; Gabriele Busch-Hauck: 49; M. Chuzeville, Paris:

109; Deutsches Archäologisches Institut, Athens: 19, 27, 45, 53, 81, 114; École Française d'Athène, Athens: 20; Fréquin, The Hague: 107; Gallerie e Musei Vaticani, Vatican City: 74; Walter Hege, Naumburg-Saale: 4; A. van der Heyden, Amsterdam: 7-9, 12, 13, 16, 18, 21, 26, 59; Hirmer Verlag, Munich: 89; Spyros Meletzis, Athens: 33, 43, 44; Museum of Fine Arts, Boston: 113; Nellys Studios, Athens: 1; Photograph Sales, New York: 106; Reproduktions-Anstalt Frz. Kaufmann, Munich: 60; Rijksmuseum van Oudheden, Leiden: 99, 120; Soprintendenza alle Antichità, Salerno: 110; Staatliche Antikensammlungen, Munich: 71; Staatliche Museen, Berlin: 91; Walters Art Gallery, Baltimore: 108.

8 ETRURIA AND ROME Archives Photographiques, Paris: 24, 61; Archivio Photografico, Rome: 74; Boissonnas, Geneva: 94; Elsevier Archives: 1, 17, 32, 76, 79, 87, 90; Enit, Rome: 28; Gallerie e Musei Vaticani, Vatican City: 43, 55; A. van der Heyden, Amsterdam: 11, 13, 21, 33, 34, 44, 45; Kunsthistorisches Museum, Vienna: 36, 89; Landesmuseum, Trier: 96, 97; Ministero della Pifesa, Maggiove: 23; Rijksmuseum van Oudheden, Leiden: 82, 83; H. Sibbelee, Nederhorst den Berg: 25; Staatliche Museen, Berlin: 22.

9 EARLY CHRISTIAN ART British Museum, London: 29; Elsevier Archives: 18; Giraudon, Paris: 42; A. van der Heyden, Amsterdam: 9; Koninklijke Bibliotheek, The Hague: 7.

10 BYZANTIUM Archiepiscopal Museum, Utrecht: 20; Archives Photographiques, Paris: 17, 48; Bildarchiv der Oesterreichischen Nationalbibliothek, Vienna: 23; Bildarchiv Foto Marburg: 6, 47; British Museum, London: 25; Giraudon, Paris: 19, 51; Landesmuseum, Trier: 52; Maria Perotti, Milan: 22; Sender, Istanbul: 1, 31; Victoria and Albert Museum, London: 46.

11 ANCIENT IRAN ACL, Brussels: 3, 4; Archives Photographiques, Paris: 13; M. Chuzeville, Paris: 1, 17.

12 ISLAM ABC Press Service, Amsterdam: 13; A. Dingjan, The Hague: 35, 36, 38, 41 42, 44, 45; Haus Rottmann, St. Gall: 2.

13 EARLY MEDIEVAL AND ROMANESQUE ART ACL, Brussels: 18, 91, 110; Archives Photographiques, Paris: 58, 64, 70, 73, 80, 87, 94, 96-98, 100-103, 107; Bildarchiv Foto Marburg: 48; Caisse National, Paris: 41; M. Coppens: 3, 83; Dumas Satigny, Paris: 17; Giraudon, Paris: 1, 7; W. F. van Heemskerck Düker, The Hague: 10; A. van der Heyden, Amsterdam: 53, 55; De Jongh, Lausanne: 12; Mas, Barcelona: 2, 13, 57; Hildegard Morscher, St. Gall: 8; Musées Royaux, Brussels: 49; National Buildings Record, London: 52; National Gallery of Art, Washington, D.C.: 118; Rheinisches Bildarchiv, Cologne: 111; B. Saltel, Toulouse: 79; Services Photographiques, Brussels: 20; H. Sibbelee, Nederhorst den Berg: 11, 14, 21, 81, 84, 108, 117; Th. van Velzen, Netherlands: 23, 85.

14 GOTHIC ART ACL, Brussels: 62, 64, 71, 79, 80, 83, 101, 105, 109, 113, 114; Archives Photographiques, Paris: 1, 2, 9-11, 31, 42-44, 48, 49, 55-58, 74, 94, 96, 97, 110; Otto Bayer, Vienna: 20; Bildarchiv Foto Marburg: 17, 19, 26, 52-54; Cleveland Museum of Art, Cleveland, Ohio: 115; M. Coppens: 65; A. Dingjan, The Hague: 104; Giraudon, Paris: 51; Aart Klein, Amsterdam: 22; KLM-Aerocarto, Amsterdam: 23, 41; Jonkheer J. G. van Lennep, Amsterdam: 84; Lichtbildwerkstätte "Alpenland": 60; Mas, Barcelona:63; Prado, Madrid: 81; National Buildings Record, London: 15, 30, 33; National Gallery of Art, Washington, D.C.: 50; Rheinisches Bildarchiv, Cologne: 18; H. Sibbelee, Nederhorst den Berg: 12; Piet Slagmolen, Utrecht: 24.

Volume II

1 RENAISSANCE ACL, Brussels: 22, 45, 49, 83, 103, 111, 121; Archives Photographiques, Paris: 20, 21, 25, 42-44, 64, 79, 80, 82, 101, 102, 104, 106; M. van Beek, Oosterbeek: 24; Bildarchiv der Oesterreichischen Nationalbibliothek, Vienna: 48; Bayerische Staatsgemäldesammlung, Munich: 97; A. Bernard, Chantilly: 116; A. C. Cooper, London: 59; Country Life, London: 30; Elsevier Archives: 2, 4, 7, 9, 11, 17-19, 27, 39, 68-71, 74, 77, 90, 92, 93, 96, 99, 100, 108, 110, 115, 118, 119; Giraudon, Paris: 120; Kunsthistorisches Museum, Vienna: 87, 88, 113; Lichtbeeldeninstituut, Amsterdam: 47, 98; Mas, Barcelona: 26, 53, 91, 109; Ministry of Works, London: 29; National Buildings Record, London: 28; National Gallery, London: 73, 94; From *Portraits en Médaille*, photo J. Roubier: 37; W. Scott, Bradford: 55; Stadtbildstelle, Augsburg: 50; Victoria and Albert Museum, London (Crown Copyright): 54, 105, 122; N. Zomer, Amsterdam: 51.
Page 15: Scala, Florence; page 16: Elsevier Archives; page 27: Giraudon, Paris; page 28: Tortoli, Florence.

2 SEVENTEENTH CENTURY ACL, Brussels: 14, 20, 21, 34-36, 70; J. G. van Agtmaal, Hilversum: 13; Bildarchiv Foto Marburg: 5-7, 30; Bildarchiv der Oesterreichischen Nationalbibliothek, Vienna: 9; H. Braggaar, Delft: 33; Bayerische Staatsgemäldesammlung, Munich: 64; Department of Public Works, Amsterdam: 16, 17; A. Dingjan, The Hague: 48, 49, 53, 58; Elsevier Archives: 1, 3, 4, 8, 42, 44, 46, 54, 56, 59, 60, 62, 65, 68, 69, 71, 78-80, 82, 84; Ewing Galloway, New York: 11; Giraudon, Paris: 29; F. Lahaye, Maastricht: 18; Mas, Barcelona: 10, 32; National Gallery, London: 43; Nederland-U.S.S.R., Amsterdam: 26; National Portrait Gallery, London: 73; Refot, Stockholm: 25; Monumentenzorg, The Hague: 15; H. Sibbelee, Nederhorst den Berg: 27; Statens Museum for Kunst, Copenhagen: 61, 74; Vincents Kunst Forlag, Copenhagen: 24.
Pages 53, 54: Elsevier Archives.

3 ITALIAN BAROQUE Deutsche Fotothek, Dresden: 51; Elsevier Archives: 1-46, 48, 49, 52-55, 58, 59.
Pages 67, 68: Conzett und Huber, Zurich.

4 LOUIS XIV STYLE ACL, Brussels: 22; Archives Photographiques, Paris: 2, 3, 5, 7, 8, 10, 11, 13, 16, 20, 21, 23-27; *Connaissance des Arts*, Paris: 28; Elsevier Archives: 9; Giraudon, Paris: 15, 18, 29, 30; Hachette, Paris: 17, 38; KLM-Aerocarto, Amsterdam: 12; Larousse, Paris: 36; H. Sibbelee, Nederhorst den Berg: 4, 6; From Weigert, *Le Style Louis XIV* (Larousse, Paris): 29-31, 36.
Pages 95, 96: Giraudon, Paris.

5 EIGHTEENTH CENTURY ACL, Brussels: 12, 13, 20, 21, 30; Archives Photographiques, Paris: 1, 3, 15, 17; Bildarchiv Foto Marburg: 7-9, 14; W. J. van

Borselen, Haarlem: 28; Bulloz, Paris: 26, 27; *Connaissance des Arts*, Paris: 37; Department of Fine Arts, The Hague: 29; Dulwich College Picture Gallery: 22; Elsevier Archives: 5, 32, 34, 35, 39; Gemeentemuseum, The Hague: 41; A. F. Kersting, London: 2; Monumentenzorg, The Hague: 10, 11, 19; National Buildings Record, London: 4; National Gallery, London: 23; National Museum, Stockholm: 31; Oesterreichische Galerie, Vienna: 18; *Radio Times* Hulton Picture Library: 25; *Topographical Atlas*, Municipal Archives, Amsterdam: 45.
Page 105, top: Elsevier Archives; bottom: Giraudon, Paris; page 106: Conzett und Huber, Zurich.

6 LOUIS XV STYLE Archives Photographiques, Paris: 16, 17, 26, 27; Bildarchiv Foto Marburg: 6, 7, 29; Bulloz, Paris: 15; Deutsche Fotothek, Dresden: 10; Elsevier Archives: 2, 4, 5, 8, 18, 20-22, 32, 34, 35, 40, 41; Landesbildstelle Württemberg: 9; Mas, Barcelona: 13, 14; Rheinmuseum, Cologne: 12; H. Sibbelee, Nederhorst den Berg: 3.
Page 123: Giraudon, Paris; page 124: Conzett und Huber, Zurich.

7 ENGLAND IN THE EIGHTEENTH CENTURY Annan, Glasgow: 17; Bulloz, Paris: 18; A. C. Cooper Ltd., London: 16; Country Life, London: 15; Elsevier Archives: 8; London County Council, Architects Department: 7; National Buildings Record, London: 1-4.
Page 137: Elsevier Archives.

8 LOUIS XVI STYLE Archives Photographiques, Paris: 1, 5, 9, 11, 12, 14, 16, 21, 24, 25, 27, 28, 35, 36, 39; Bulloz, Paris: 7, 8; Elsevier Archives: 29, 30, 41; Giraudon, Paris: 3, 13, 15, 17, 20, 22; From *La Peinture Française*, Vol. I: 18; H. Sibbelee, Nederhorst den Berg: 2.
Page 138: Giraudon, Paris.

9 EMPIRE ACL, Brussels: 5, 11, 29, 31; Archives Photographiques, Paris: 1-3, 8, 9, 14, 15, 19, 37, 38; Bulloz, Paris: 13: Country Life, London: 42; Direction Générale du Tourisme, Paris: 7; Elsevier Archives: 6, 10, 21, 23, 27, 28, 33, 35, 36, 39-41, 44; Ewing Galloway, New York: 4; Giraudon, Paris: 16-18, 20, 22, 24, 30, 32, 34.

10 NINETEENTH CENTURY ABC Press Service, Amsterdam: 17; ACL, Brussels: 19-21, 24, 29, 72-75, 91; Hélène Adant: 96; Aerofilms, London: 8, 10; *Architectural Review*, London: 9; Archives Photographiques, Paris: 2, 3, 5, 23, 26, 31, 33-36, 41, 42, 47, 51; Bernès, Maronteau & Cie: 28; Bildarchiv Foto Marburg: 12, 13, 15, 16; Bildarchiv Foto Marburg und DVA, Stuttgart: 57; Bulloz, Paris: 39; Centocelle: 22; Elsevier Archives: 4, 14, 25, 30, 37, 43-45, 48, 69, 70, 80, 86, 102; Gemeentemuseum, The Hague: 40, 46, 90; Giraudon, Paris: 52; Giraudon-N.D., Paris: 38; W. Klein: 57; L. J. Kruger, The Hague: 67; Kunsthalle, Hamburg: 56; Larousse, Paris: 95; Lichtbeeldeninstituut, Amsterdam: 68, 71; National Buildings Record, London: 6; National Gallery, London: 63; Archives Roger-Violet, N.D.: 1; Warburg Institute: 7.
Page 185, top: Conzett und Huber, Zurich; bottom: Elsevier Archives; page 186, top: Giraudon, Paris; bottom: Stedelijk Museum, Amsterdam.
© SABAM, Brussels, SPADEM, Paris: 27, 28, 30, 43-45, page 186, top.

11 TWENTIETH CENTURY Anefo, Amsterdam: 38; Maria Austria, Particam, Amsterdam: 26; Bildarchiv Foto Marburg: 43; A. Buffinga: 39, 44, 55, 56, 69; Paul Bijtebier, Brussels: 6, 71, 80, 96, 104, 110, 114, 120, 122, 127, 130; Department of Fine Arts, The Hague: 105; DuMont Schauberg Bildarchiv, Cologne: 123, 131; Elsevier Archives: 9, 57, 68, 72, 77, 92, 98-100, 107, 108, 111, 129; *Elseviers Weekblad*, Amsterdam: 126; From *50 Jahre Moderne Kunst* (DuMont Schauberg, Cologne): 75, 85, 91, 95, 97, 118; P. Facchetti, Paris: 121; Studio Hartland, Amsterdam: 29; International Photopress, Rotterdam: 70; H. Jonker, Particam, Amsterdam: 74; KLM-Aerocarto, Amsterdam: 62; Kunstmuseum, Bern, 112; London County Council, Architects Department: 47; Lumina Film, Amsterdam: 54; Maeght, Paris: 124; Irene Markiewicz, Krakow: 58; Nederlands Filmmuseum, Amsterdam: 18-24; J. and M. d'Oliveira: 10; Ab Orrefors Glasburk, Sweden: 28; Philippi, Antwerp: 60; Poelli und Mertens, Zurich: 27; Sala Dino, Milan: 50; Sergysels en Dieters, Brussels: 46; A. Studer, Thun: 132; S. Sunami: 8; TWA: 59; Ullstein Bilderdienst, Berlin-Tempelhof: 11, 35; USIS: 49, 51, 52; L. van der Veen, Amsterdam: 82; Vrijthof: 61; H. van Wadenayer, Cheltenham: 83; Weverling, Arnhem: 63, 67.
Pages 199, 200: Elsevier Archives; page 215, top: Giraudon, Paris; bottom: Conzett und Huber, Zurich; page 216: Conzett und Huber, Zurich.

12 INDIAN ART Archaeological Survey of India: 1, 3-6, 9, 16, 20, 23, 24, 27, 37-39, 41, 47; Photo Collection Prof. Dr. A. J. Bernet Kempers: 8, 10, 14, 32; Photo Prof. Dr. A. J. Bernet Kempers: 21, 28, 43; Department of Archaeology, Pakistan: 19; Elsevier Archives: 48; T. van Erp: 18, 33; Dr. A. Hustinx, Roermond: 22; Archaeological Department Netherlands East Indies/Indonesia: 7, 30, 34-36, 40, 42, 44-46.
Pages 239, 240: Elsevier Archives.

13 CHINA ACL, Brussels: 2, 21, 22, 38, 39, 42, 43, 48, 49, 53, 54, 56, 61; Chavannes: 14; A. Dingjan, The Hague: 50; Elsevier Archives: 52; Ewing Galloway, New York: 5; M. Sakamoto: 32, 44; H. Sibbelee, Nederhorst den Berg: 7-9, 25.
Pages 253, 254: Elsevier Archives.

14 JAPAN Elsevier Archives: 22; Museum voor Land en Volkenkunde, Rotterdam: 44-50; M. Sakamoto: 1, 2, 4, 8, 9, 12-20, 23. 29-34, 37, 38, 43, 51-54; From C. S. Terry, *Masterworks of Japanese Art* (Ch. E. Tuttle Cy., Tokyo): 10. Pages 269, 270: Elsevier Archives.

15 PRE-COLUMBIAN ART Centraal Museum, Utrecht: 27-30, 38; Esso: 33; Hans Mann: 19, 23, 32; Paul Popper, London: 12, 13, 24; Van der Steen: 2; World Press Photo, Amsterdam: 4.
Page 283; Elsevier Archives.

16 NEGRO ART OF AFRICA From E. Elisofon and W. Fagg, *The Sculpture of Africa*: 12, 14, 27; Ethnographic Museum, Antwerp: 4, 6, 8; From Warner Muensterberger, *Sculpture of Primitive Man*: 11, 26, 29; Rijksmuseum voor Volkenkunde, Leiden: 24; C. Kjersmeier, Copenhagen: 15; Staatens Etnografisk Museum, Stockholm: 1-3, 5, 7, 10, 13, 19-21, 23, 31, 33; From Sweeny-Radin, *African Folk Tales and Sculpture:* 22, 28; Prof. Dr. P. J. Vandenhoute, Oostakker: 9, 30; R. Vanroelen, Bruges: 16.
Pages 284, 297: Elsevier Archives.

17 OCEANIA Photo Collection Dr. J. Victor Jansen: 1-33.
Page 298: Elsevier Archives.